A Companion to
Ancrene Wisse

A Companion to
Ancrene Wisse

Edited by Yoko Wada

D. S. BREWER

First published 2003
D. S. Brewer, Cambridge

ISBN 0 85991 762 2

D. S. Brewer is an imprint of Boydell & Brewer Ltd
PO Box 9, Woodbridge, Suffolk IP12 3DF, UK
and of Boydell & Brewer Inc.
PO Box 41026, Rochester, NY 14604–4126, USA
website: www.boydell.co.uk

A catalogue record for this book is available
from the British Library

Library of Congress Cataloging-in-Publication Data
A companion to Ancrene wisse / edited by Yoko Wada.
    p. cm.
Includes bibliographical references (p.) and index.
  ISBN 0–85991–762–2 (Hardback : alk. paper)
1. Ancren riwle. 2. Monasticism and religious orders for
women – England – History – Middle Ages, 600–1500. 3. Monastic and
religious life of women – England – History – Middle Ages, 600–1500.
4. Christian literature, English (Middle) – History and criticism.
5. Christianity and literature – England – History – To 1500. 6. Women
and literature – England – History – To 1500. 7. Recluses in literature.
8. Solitude in literature. I. Wada, Yoko.
PR1810.C657 2003
255′.901 – dc21   2002155074

This publication is printed on acid-free paper
Printed and bound in Great Britain by
The Cromwell Press, Trowbridge, Wiltshire.

Contents

This book is dedicated to
the memory of
E. J. DOBSON
whose scholarship continues to
stimulate studies of *Ancrene Wisse*

Acknowledgments

My thanks are first of all due to the contributors for their co-operation. I should also like to thank Professor Derek Brewer for his warm encouragement and generous support of the publication; David Dumville for his useful and constructive comments; and Ms Caroline Palmer and the staff of Boydell & Brewer.

The book was produced with the financial assistance of a Grant-in-Aid for Scientific Research (C)(2)(14510555) from the Japanese Ministry of Education, Culture, Sports, Science and Technology; I am grateful for their generosity.

Finally, I should like to acknowledge a colleague and great friend, Jennifer Miller of the University of California, Berkeley, who was to contribute a chapter on the English character of *Ancrene Wisse* to this volume, but through ill-health was unable to complete it. It is to be hoped that her research will be published elsewhere in due course.

Contributors

ROGER DAHOOD   Department of English, University of Arizona, U.S.A.

RICHARD DANCE   Department of Anglo-Saxon, Norse & Celtic, University of Cambridge, U.K.

A. S. G. EDWARDS   Department of English, University of Victoria, Canada

CATHERINE INNES-PARKER   Department of English, University of Prince Edward Island, Canada

BELLA MILLETT   Department of English, University of Southampton, U.K.

ELIZABETH ROBERTSON   Department of English, University of Colorado at Boulder, U.S.A.

ANNE SAVAGE   Department of English, McMaster University, Canada

D. A. TROTTER   Department of European Languages, University of Wales, Aberystwyth, U.K.

CHRISTINA VON NOLCKEN   Department of English, University of Chicago, U.S.A.

YOKO WADA   The Institute of Foreign Language Education and Research, Kansai University, Japan

NICHOLAS WATSON   Department of English, Harvard University, U.S.A.

Preface

The *Ancrene Wisse*, a thirteenth-century practical guide for female recluses, offers a glimpse of the real life which women led in England in the Middle Ages. It addresses three young sisters of gentle birth, who were admitted to a convent to live each in an individual cell, teaching them in considerable detail what truly good anchoresses should and should not do. In Part 3 of *Ancrene Wisse*, for example, we are told that noble people do not carry packs or travel strapped with bundles or purses, although female beggars wear bags on their backs and women in town carried purses; these are all worldly things and possessions, therefore anchoresses must not have them. In Part 8, the author forbids the female recluses to keep any animal, except for, we are happy to know, a cat!

One of the reasons why *Ancrene Wisse* has been considered such a very important work in the history of English literature is that it continues the Anglo-Saxon tradition of prose writing, as R. W. Chambers argued in *On the Continuity of English Prose from Alfred to More and his School* (London, 1932). Although we now know that Latin also had much influence on the style, we cannot deny that *Ancrene Wisse* owes much to Old English prose writing; after all, it was composed in the West Midlands where Old English writing conventions were retained and developed, even after the Norman conquest when English writing was on the decline. Worcester is the most notable place: Wulfstan the homilist (d. 1023) was bishop there and perhaps founded or extended an extensive English library. Throughout the eleventh century the scriptorium produced copies of a good number of English writings, particularly of the abbot and homilist Ælfric (*c.* 955 – *c.* 1020). Even into the twelfth century and beyond English was used as a written medium there. The literary style of *Ancrene Wisse* is known to have similarities in alliteration and rhythm to the works of Wulfstan and Ælfric.

As well as the issue of continuity of English prose, as I shall mention in Chapter 1 there are many other interesting questions to be answered, including the authorship, the original language, and so on. However, when compared with Chaucer's *Canterbury Tales* or *Sir Gawain and the Green Knight*, for instance, *Ancrene Wisse* appears neglected; it has always lacked attention from students of Middle English literature. The aim of this *Companion* is to introduce *Ancrene Wisse* to those who are interested in Middle English language and literature and to provide them with various approaches to the work. I hope this book will help the reader to find out what made *Ancrene Wisse* a best-seller of its day and that it will promote further study.

Yoko Wada
January, 2003

Abbreviations

AW	*Ancrene Wisse*
BL	British Library
CCCM	*Corpus Christianorum Continuatio Medieualis*
CUL	Cambridge University Library
EETS	Early English Text Society
n.s.	New Series
o.s.	Original Series
s.s.	Supplementary Series
KG	*Katherine Group*
ME	Middle English
MED	*Middle English Dictionary*
OED	*Oxford English Dictionary*
PL	*Patrologiæ Cursus Completus*, ed. J.-P. Migne, Series Latina, 221 vols (Paris, 1844–64)

1

What is *Ancrene Wisse*?

YOKO WADA

Ancrene Wisse is a beginner's guide for female recluses, which was probably written in or around the second quarter of the thirteenth century.[1] The guide is very likely to have been composed originally for three young sisters of a wealthy family.[2]

The word *ancrene* is a noun meaning 'anchorites' or 'recluses' (of either sex) in the genitive plural form, and *wisse*, 'a guide', which derives from the Old English verb *wissian*.[3] This title appears in the invocation on folio 1r of Cambridge, Corpus Christi College, MS 402, in the hand of the scribe who copied the text. No title is found in any other extant manuscript. *Ancrene Riwle*, 'a rule for anchoresses', which has been used as a title for almost the same work for many years, has no medieval authority, being just an editor's invention, and therefore is not at all appropriate, although the Early English Text Society has published all versions (including a few variorum editions) in eleven volumes under the title *Ancrene Riwle*.[4]

As far as we know, there are seventeen versions of the work, nine in English, four in French, and a further four in Latin.[5] The manuscripts date from the thirteenth to the sixteenth century,[6] and the texts seem to have

---

[1] See pp. 16–19, below.
[2] See p. 4, below.
[3] Cf. OE *wissian* 'to direct, instruct, guide'.
[4] As to how that title, *Ancrene Riwle*, came to establish squatter's rights, see Wada, *'Temptations'*, pp. xiii–xvii. A title-page given on the front cover of the edition of Cambridge, Corpus Christi College, MS 402, by the Early English Text Society, is 'Ancrene Wisse, MS Corpus Christi College 402', but the title reads 'The English Text of the Ancrene Riwle, Ancrene Wisse, Edited from MS Corpus Christi College Cambridge 402' (Tolkien, *The English Text*).
[5] Manuscripts of *Ancrene Wisse* in English are: Cambridge, Corpus Christi College, MS 402; Cambridge, Gonville and Caius College, MS 234/120; Cambridge, Magdalene College, MS Pepys 2498; London, British Library, MS Cotton Cleopatra C.vi; London, British Library, MS Cotton Nero A.xiv; London, British Library, MS Cotton Titus D.xviii; London, British Library, MS Royal 8.C.i; Oxford, Bodleian Library, MS Eng. poet. a.1 (*S.C.* 3938–3942); Oxford, Bodleian Library, MS Eng. th. c.70. French texts are in: Cambridge, Trinity College, MS R.14.7 (883); London, British Library, MS Cotton Vitellius F.vii; Oxford, Bodleian Library, MS Bodley 90 (*S.C.* 1887); Paris, Bibliothèque Nationale, MS français 8276. Manuscripts of *Ancrene Wisse* in Latin are: London, British Library, MS Cotton Vitellius E.vii; London, British Library, MS Royal 7.C.x; Oxford, Magdalen College, MS Latin 67; Oxford, Merton College, MS C.I.5 (Coxe 44). As for editions, all the vernacular texts have been printed separately; the Latin version has been published in a variorum edition and the French in two editions including the variants; all of these are publications of the Early English Text Society. See the Select Bibliography at the end of this volume. A critical edition, based on all texts of *Ancrene Wisse*, is being made by Bella Millett and Richard Dance.
[6] Texts written in the thirteenth century are in: Cambridge, Corpus Christi College, MS 402;

been modified for various kinds of audience: some are for male recluses, others for men and women in general, lay or religious. The wide circulation and readership are indicated by the fact that we have French and Latin versions. In some versions the text is rearranged, augmented, or truncated.[7] What the original was like or who the author was is an extremely intriguing and most crucial problem to solve in studies of *Ancrene Wisse*. Many attempts have been made to answer the question, but no decisive conclusion has yet been drawn. In this first chapter I should like to show how much we have learnt about *Ancrene Wisse* so far, giving an outline of some important problems which *Ancrene Wisse* presents.

Ancrene Wisse consists of an introduction and eight 'distinctions' or parts.[8] In the introduction the author explains that in this guide he will tell the reader about two rules in particular: the 'inner' rule which governs the heart and the 'outer' the body, in other words, how to behave or what to do in everyday life. He declares that the outer rule is completely subservient to the inner. Such is his religious principle that the author tells the sisters that if asked of which order they are, they should answer that they belong to the Order of St James, which did not exist: obviously the author wants to say that their faith matters much more than which order they belong to. He even says that '. . . this rule may change variously in accordance with each one's condition and nature. For one is strong, another weak and may very well be excused and please God with less.'[9] What is more, the author prohibits the audience to take vows of obligation except obedience, chastity, and fixity of place. 'If she does not vow it,' he says, 'she may still do it and leave off whenever she wishes – for example, with food, with drink, forgoing flesh or fish – all other such things; with clothing, with sleeping, with the hours, with other prayers – saying so many or in such a way.'[10] Thus it is

Cambridge, Gonville and Caius College, MS 234/120; London, British Library, MS Cotton Cleopatra C.vi; London, British Library, MS Cotton Nero A.xiv; and London, British Library, MS Cotton Titus D.xviii. Those written in the late thirteenth or early fourteenth century are in: Cambridge, Trinity College, MS R.14.7 (883); Oxford, Bodleian Library, MS Bodley 90 (*S.C.* 1887); and London, British Library, MS Cotton Vitellius E.vii. Fourteenth-century texts are in: Cambridge, Magdalene College, MS Pepys 2498; Oxford, Bodleian Library, MS Eng. poet. a.1 (*S.C.* 3938–3942); Oxford, Bodleian Library, MS Eng. th. c.70; London, British Library, MS Cotton Vitellius F.vii; Paris, Bibliothèque Nationale, MS français 8276; and Oxford, Merton College, MS C.I.5 (Coxe 44). Fifteenth-century texts are in London, British Library, MS Royal 8.C.i; and Oxford, Magdalen College, MS Latin 67. The only text written in the sixteenth century is: London, British Library, MS Royal 7.C.x. For more about each manuscript see Wada, *'Temptations'*, xlvi–lxiv.

[7] The Gonville and Caius text, for instance, is an abridgement and rearrangement of *Ancrene Wisse*. Cambridge, Trinity College, MS R.14.7 contains a French text of *Ancrene Wisse* which was rearranged and rewritten into five compilations; the manuscript also includes *Chronicon Anglie*, an abridgement and conflation of Geoffrey of Monmouth's *Historia* and several later sources.

[8] The author stated in the introduction that just as one can speak of what is right in grammar or geometry, and each of these studies has its own rules, he was going to deal with what is theologically right in the book. Then he mentioned two rules, the inner and the outer. Geoffrey Shepherd remarked, 'In this reduction of the spiritual life to a regular art the author must have deliberately recalled a type of treatment in vogue at Paris in the 1190s' and noted that the word *distinctiones* was a University word (Shepherd, *Ancrene Wisse*, pp. xxxvii–xxxviii).

[9] White, *Ancrene Wisse*, 3.

[10] White, *Ancrene Wisse*, 3.

noticeable that the author's attitude towards his recluses is not strict but rather thoughtful and practical.

Next is the first part on devotions, which provides practical instructions about religious service. The second part teaches how to keep five senses under control – sight, speech, hearing, smell, and touch. Part 3 is on how a true anchoress should behave and why. The fourth deals with the Seven Deadly Sins, bodily and spiritual temptations, and their remedies. Part 5, then, discusses the virtue of confession and how to make confession properly. Part 6, on penance, explains that earthly suffering in life is penitential and should be accepted gladly. The seventh on love and a pure heart tells how dearly Christ loves us with his supreme love and that we should love and desire Him only. Part 8 teaches the outer rule, everyday matters such as diet, clothes, possessions, occupations, blood-letting, hair-cutting, and employment of servants.

The text ends with the author's advice and request to the effect that the recluses should read some pages of this book every day whenever they have time to do so. 'Otherwise,' the author says, 'I have wasted the long time I spent on it. I would rather, God knows, start off for Rome than begin to do it again.'[11]

Ancrene Wisse is full of various interesting similes, metaphors, and everyday examples familiar to everyone, which enable any reader easily to understand the teaching in this guide. For example, the seven deadly sins are described in turn as the lion of pride, the serpent of venomous envy, the unicorn of wrath, the bear of heavy sloth, the fox of covetousness, the swine of greediness, the scorpion with the tail of stinking lechery or lustfulness. At another place the author likens God to a mother who plays with her young child: she runs away from him, hides herself and lets him sit alone; then the child looks anxiously around and call 'Mummy, mummy!' and weeps a while until the mother shows up laughing with her outspread arms, embraces and kisses him. In this way God sometimes behaves as if He has abandoned us, but we should keep in mind that He loves us very much. Another example using a child is that if a little boy stumbles against something or huts himself, people beat the thing which harms him, and then the child is very pleased, forgets all the pain, and stops his tears. In this way God will take vengeance for us on the Day of Judgment.

Interestingly enough, although *Ancrene Wisse* seems to have been composed for young girls to become recluses, a verbal picture of a married couple is drawn in Part 4: when a man has newly brought a wife home, if he finds some fault in her manners, he smiles at her cheerfully and tries his best to make her love him affectionately. However, once he is well assured that her love is truly fixed on him, he feels free to make critical comments to her about the things which he once bore with without any complaints. Then the husband becomes extremely stern and looks very severe in order to test her love towards him. When the wife stands the test, he shows her that he loves her sweetly and does whatever she desires. Thus all that sorrow turns to

---

[11] White, *Ancrene Wisse*, 199.

great joy. The author explains that Jesus also may start to test you when He knows that you love Him, but after the trial the joy will come to you in the end. This kind of anecdote and the examples of a little child might interest young girls, but it might suggest that widows were also part of the audience. A parable which reminds us of a romance is also found in Part 7: there Christ is a king, a knight, a noble wooer, who engages in a tournament for His lady's love.

As has been generally accepted, it is very likely that the work was originally composed for three daughters of good family whom the author knew quite well: in many versions 'three sisters' are mentioned or the author's personal references, of one sort or another, to them are found. The most explicit case[12] is the text in London, British Library, MS Cotton Nero A.xiv, where the author remarks, '. . . I know no anchoress who has all that she needs, so easily available, without loss of dignity, as you three have; Our Lord be thanked for it. You need take no thought about food or clothing for yourselves or for your maid-servants. . . . There is much talk of you, how you are women of gentle birth, sisters, with the same father and the same mother, once much sought after on account of your goodness and beauty, having now, in the flower of your youth, renounced all the pleasures of the world and become anchoresses.'[13] One should treat this passage with caution because there is no evidence that all the references to these sisters in the Nero text were inherited from the original text which no longer exists. However, the sisters had led a secular, high life recently, since *Ancrene Wisse* includes many examples from worldly affairs, as we have just seen. Also here and there we find quite a few indications of such an audience: for instance, their maidservants,[14] a ring, a brooch, silk bandages, and a girdle with plates[15] are mentioned; the author forbids them to make over-elaborate trimmings;[16] and he says, 'There ought to be a great difference between an anchoress and the lady of a house'.[17]

The treatise seems to have been so popular and in demand[18] to such a degree that it soon started to be transcribed and revised for other audiences. It eventually had a relatively wide readership. A version, for instance, was made for a bigger community of twenty or more women religious, which is attested by the Corpus text.[19] Some other texts were adapted for use by the laity. The Titus version was apparently intended mainly for men, but also

---

[12] A long passage in the Nero text, which I quote here, cannot be found in other versions. Although the Corpus text seems to have been rewritten for a group of anchoresses, on f. 31v of the Corpus manuscript there is a passage, 'I would much rather see you, all three, my dear sisters, women dearest to me, hang on a gibbet, in order to avoid sin' (Tolkien, *The English Text*, 62). The equivalent passage is also found on f. 47r of the Cleopatra text (whose audience was anchoresses), in the Titus text, which was a version revised for men and for women, and in the Nero text (Mack and Zettersten, *The English Text*, 30; Day, *The English Text*, 50).

[13] Salu, *Ancrene Wisse*, 84.

[14] White, *Ancrene Wisse*, 37, for example.

[15] White, *Ancrene Wisse*, 194.

[16] White, *Ancrene Wisse*, 195.

[17] White, *Ancrene Wisse*, 37.

[18] See pp. 12–13, below.

[19] The Corpus text alone has a passage, 'You are the anchoresses of England, so many together – twenty now or more' (White, *Ancrene Wisse*, 119).

for women; the readers were presumably very devout laypeople.[20] The Pepys text is a Lollard version compiled by seculars for devout laymen and laywomen.[21] As I have already mentioned,[22] we also have French and Latin versions of *Ancrene Wisse*, which suggests further readership in different circles. The French text of *Ancrene Wisse* in Cambridge, Trinity College, MS R.14.7, for example, does not include Parts 1 and 8,[23] or the addresses to sisters; and not only does the manuscript have ornamental capitals in red and blue but the borders are decorated beautifully, with many amusing pictures of people and animals; the whole is on very fine parchment.[24] From these versions we can deduce that the volume seems to have been designed for wider use, not for reading only within a religious house. Manuscripts of *Ancrene Wisse* in small format, in smallish untidy script on coarse parchment, were used by the secular clergy, as manuals of confession, especially since after 1215 confession had become compulsory.[25] Since then too, and until the Reformation, penitentials seem to have been much needed.[26] The Caius manuscript could have been used by a parish-priest because it contains a suitably abridged and rearranged version of *Ancrene Wisse*, and a scribbled memorandum on page 76 about payment for a parish in a hand from the fourteenth or fifteenth century seems to confirm this.[27] The English-language version in British Library MS Royal 8.C.i was an adaptation made by a preacher for a general public.[28]

Ancrene Wisse gained such great popularity that later authors often made use of the work. As the date of the Royal Latin manuscript indicates,[29] we know that it was still being incorporated into new work at the beginning of the sixteenth century. The treatise was even used by authors who wrote in languages other than English. A French work composed in the fourteenth or fifteenth century derives in part from *Ancrene Wisse*. Although that French text is now lost, its English translation, *The Tretyse of Loue*, was printed with 'The Chastising of God's Children' by Wynkyn de Worde in 1493.[30] The latter work is considered to have taken its title and theme from

---

[20] Many alterations seem to have been made in this text to make the treatise usable for both men and women: in Part 1, for example, we have a Latin prayer, '*Saluam fac famulam tuam, Deus meus, sperantem in te*' ('Save your [female] servant, my God, who hopes in you') in the Corpus text (f. 8v), whereas '*Saluos fac seruos tuos & ancillas tuas deus meus sperantes in te*' ('Save, O Lord, Your male servants and Your handmaids who hope in You') (f. 14rb). Also, the reviser often used 'friend' instead of 'sister' to address the reader.

[21] Colledge, '*The Recluse*'.

[22] See pp. 1–2, above.

[23] The work begins with a rearranged text of *Ancrene Wisse* on the seven deadly sins, and the following treatise about penance occupied almost half of the entire text.

[24] James, *Western Manuscripts*, II:289–91.

[25] At the Fourth Lateran Council, held in 1215, annual confession for all Christian people was prescribed (Cross and Livingstone, *Dictionary*, 802).

[26] Concerning the friars and penitential literature, see Fleming, 'The Friars', 355–9.

[27] Wilson, *The English Text*, p. xiii.

[28] Baugh, *The English Text*, p. xi.

[29] The manuscript was written at the beginning of the sixteenth century (D'Evelyn, *The Latin Text*, p. xv).

[30] Fisher, *The Tretyse*; Allen, 'Wynkyn de Worde'; Allen, 'Some Fourteenth Century Borrowings'; Fisher, 'Continental Associations'.

Part 4 of *Ancrene Wisse*.[31] *Regula reclusorum Dubliniensis* ('the Dublin Rule
of the Recluses'), written for both men and women in the early fourteenth
century by an Austin friar, is drawn from *Ancrene Wisse*.[32] Julian of
Norwich, a female recluse at Norwich, who was born about 1342 and
was still alive in 1416, possibly used *Ancrene Wisse* for her writing.[33] English
passages from *Ancrene Wisse* were found in the Northern compilation
Gracia Dei, an English version of Guillaume de Guilleville's *Pelerinage*.[34] It
is possible that William Lichfield (d. 1448), a famous preacher and a writer
of sermons, altered and adapted for a general public Parts 2 and 3 of
Ancrene Wisse and made from them his 'Treatise of the Five Senses'.[35] 'The
Life of Adam and Eve' in the Vernon text also shows much influence from
Ancrene Wisse.[36]

   The popularity of *Ancrene Wisse* during the Reformation-period is also
attested by the fact that the manuscripts were studied and collected
fervently. When great efforts were made by a few to collect important old
books from religious houses,[37] manuscripts of *Ancrene Wisse* received the
same treatment as those written in Old English. They were studied by
scholars in the circle of Archbishop Matthew Parker (1504–75), who tried
to justify the establishment of the Church of England by reference to
historical evidence.[38] It was the Latin Vitellius manuscript of *Ancrene Wisse*
which King Henry VIII wanted to have in his own library, and the King's
wish was obtained.[39] The treatise seems to have continued to provoke the
historical and religious mind from the mid-sixteenth to around the middle
of the seventeenth century when many manuscripts began to be transferred
into public libraries: Robert Talbot (d. 1558), prebendary of Norwich, had
one French manuscript;[40] Thomas Allen (1540?–1632), antiquary, might
have had one English copy;[41] Sir Robert Cotton (1571–1632), great collector
of manuscripts and printed books, possessed one French, one Latin, and
three English manuscripts;[42] George Willmer (d. 1626), Justice of the Peace

---

[31] Allen, 'Some Fourteenth Century Borrowings', 1. There is a reference to 'The Chastising of
   God's Children' in a penitential in Oxford, Bodleian Library, MS. Bodley 923 (*s.c.* 27701), of the
   fourteenth century, which belonged to Barking Abbey. It could originally have been written for
   the nuns of Barking Abbey (Deanesly, *Lollard Bible*, 337–9).
[32] Doyle, 'Survey', I:233.
[33] Reynolds, 'Some Literary Influences'; H., 'English Spiritual Writers', 706.
[34] Allen, 'Some Fourteenth Century Borrowings', 5.
[35] The text survives on ff. 122r–143v of London, British Library, MS Royal 8.C.i.
[36] Crawford, 'The Influence'. For a text see Blake, *Middle English Religious Prose*, 103–18.
[37] Wright, 'The Dispersal of the Libraries'; Wright, 'The Dispersal of the Monastic Libraries'.
[38] Graham, *The Recovery*, where Stuart Lee deals with studies of *Ancrene Wisse* in his 'Oxford,
   Bodleian Library, MS Laud Misc. 381.
[39] When John Leland (1503?–52), antiquary, travelled to note books in religious houses in
   Lincolnshire in the early 1540s, he listed six books in the old abbey of Bardney, Lincolnshire.
   From these, five were selected for Westminster and one of the five was the present book (Carley,
   'John Leland', 337).
[40] Cambridge, Trinity College, MS R.14.7 (883).
[41] London, British Library, MS Cotton Titus D.xviii.
[42] London, British Library, MS Cotton Vitellius F.vii; London, British Library, MS Cotton
   Vitellius E.vii; London, British Library, MS Cotton Cleopatra C.vi; London, British Library,
   MS Cotton Nero A.xiv; and London, British Library, MS Cotton Titus D.xviii.

for Middlesex, had one French manuscript;[43] John Theyer (1597–1673), antiquary and Catholic convert, had one English manuscript; William Moore, who matriculated at Gonville and Caius College, Cambridge, in 1606 and was teacher of Greek and Hebrew at Cambridge, bequeathed the Caius English manuscript to the college; Samuel Pepys (1633–1703), naval officer, famous diary-writer, and great lover of literature, had an English manuscript.[44]

It is generally held that *Ancrene Wisse* was originally composed in English, but conclusive evidence has yet to be found. In the seventeenth century some scholars thought that the original had been written in Latin.[45] Then in the middle of the nineteenth century James Morton and Frederic Madden favoured English as the original language.[46] In 1949 Charlotte D'Evelyn declared that Latin had not been the original language,[47] and four years later in 1953 M. L. Samuels tried to present evidence for the precedence of Middle English from alliteration, proverbs, word-play, and mistranslation.[48] Still, it is not easy to make one decisive deduction by comparing texts written in three languages. For example, if a text A includes alliterating passages and a text B written in another language has the equivalent passages which do not alliterate, we cannot necessarily say that the language of A is original. Here is another instance: although French influence found in the English text or English vocabulary found in the French text – *housewif*, for example[49] – has often been discussed in attempts to solve the question of the original language, it does not make good evidence, especially if, as is likely, the work had been composed by a bilingual author and translated – whether from English into French or vice versa – in a society where both languages were spoken and written;[50] whichever language might have been original, influence of each language on the other would have been inevitable. Although it is not impossible that *Ancrene Wisse* was originally composed in Latin,[51] English and /or French would fit better than Latin because it is very noticeable that the author consciously used many examples from everyday life, which suits the author's intimate tone of speech towards the young anchoresses.[52] Another

---

[43] Cambridge, Trinity College, MS R.14.7 (883).

[44] Cambridge, Magdalene College, MS Pepys 2498.

[45] Smith, *Catalogue*, 50–1, 97, 193; Wanley, *Librorum Veterum Septentrionalium Catalogus*, 228 and 248.

[46] Morton, *Ancren Riwle*, p. viii; Madden, 'Ancren Riwle', 5–6.

[47] D'Evelyn, 'Notes', 1164–79, at p. 1179.

[48] Samuels, '*Ancrene Riwle* studies', 1–9.

[49] Herbert, *The French Text*, 37; Macaulay, 'The "Ancren Riwle"', 69.

[50] See p. 14, below. The Latin version also includes a phrase, 'In Anglico "Eye therlle"' (D'Evelyn, *The Latin Text*, 15; D'Evelyn, 'Notes', 1178).

[51] It can be noted, for example, that Aelred's *De institutis inclusarum* and other works for anchoresses were written in Latin, and there are four surviving manuscripts of a Latin *Ancrene Wisse* – just the same number as of the French version.

[52] E. J. Dobson supposed that 'the work had been "published" by making a single fair copy' (Dobson, *Origins*, 287) but observed that the French Vitellius text, which he thought to be 'a translation of an English manuscript' was 'very closely allied to (and more correct than) the English Cleopatra text, which must have been the other copy made simultaneously from the same exemplar' (Dobson, *The English Text*, pp. x–xi).

possible argument as to the original language – which, as far as I know, has never been advanced – is that *Ancrene Wisse* was written bilingually, so that two versions originally existed. In fact the author gives a very suggestive instruction about saying prayers 'in your own language'[53] and 'reading of English or of French'.[54] However, we shall have no satisfactory solution to this problem until the textual history of the work has thoroughly examined and is comprehensively understood.[55]

In 1962 E. J. Dobson made the first and the most comprehensive attempt to construct a textual history of *Ancrene Wisse*.[56] He produced a stemma of the affiliations of the manuscripts based on his 'trial collations covering about two-fifths of the complete work',[57] giving an overview of the whole tradition and observing that the text in Cambridge, Corpus Christi College, MS 402 stood apart from the others.

The following two stemmata[58] are basically Dobson's but revised to take account of his discoveries or insights not included in the stemma which, after years of further research,[59] he revised and published in 1976.[60] Three alterations are made here. First, what is called the Lanhydrock fragment, that is, Oxford, Bodleian Library, MS Eng. th. c.70, which I shall call O, should be included in his stemma.[61] Secondly, according to Dobson a lost early copy, which I shall name ϕ, was behind the French version, F, in the Vitellius manuscript.[62] Lastly, Dobson found it necessary to hypothesise a lost copy which I shall call ω, a sister of A and a witness of some importance in the tradition in as much as it preserved, at a number of points in the text, readings preferable to those of A. The influence of ω was felt, and knowledge of its existence recovered, through its contaminatory impact on F, V, and the Latin version's English ancestor (whether μ or a descendant).[63]

Now I should like to explain how one version is related to another in stemma I. The original copy of *Ancrene Wisse*, X, which was written in the early thirteenth century,[64] does not survive. From it was made a fair copy, β, which can be defined as the source of the few identified errors common to all but one of the extant witnesses.[65] Two copies of β, that is, γ and δ, which are now lost, are more proximate ancestors of extant witnesses. γ was the source of the important early witness C,[66] and also of ϕ, the exemplar (textually very much more accurate than C)[67] from which the French

---

[53] Part 4: White, *Ancrene Wisse*, 135.
[54] Part 1: White, *Ancrene Wisse*, 24.
[55] The variorum edition and a stemma showing the relationship of all texts are being made at the moment (see p. 23, below).
[56] Dobson, 'Affiliations'.
[57] Dobson, 'Affiliations', 128 and n. 1.
[58] They are from Wada, *'Temptations'*, pp. lxxiv–lxxv.
[59] Dobson, 'Date', 181–208; Dobson, *The English Text*.
[60] Dobson, *Origins*, 287.
[61] Dobson, *Origins*, 297, n. 4; see further Dobson, [Review], 187–91.
[62] Dobson, *Origins*, 299–301.
[63] Dobson, *Origins*, 150–7; cf. p. 290, n. 3, for a further complication.
[64] Dobson, *Origins*, 163–6, 173.
[65] Dobson, *Origins*, 287–8.
[66] Dobson, *Origins*, 288.
[67] Dobson, *Origins*, 288 and 299–301; and Dobson, *The English Text*, p. x and p. xi, n. 1.

translation (now attested by the Vitellius text) was soon made – apparently before the middle of the thirteenth century.[68] Dobson regarded C as the most significant text because he thought that an early revision, C^b, made therein was authorial.[69] He stated firmly that in the Cleopatra manuscript 'Scribe B's orthography and linguistic forms, as shown in his revisions and additions, are unmistakably those of the "AB dialect" '.[70] This seems to have been one of the factors which encouraged him in his view of the authorial quality of scribe B's innovations. But later he found it necessary to modify this view to the extent of saying that 'the forms of his language, as displayed in his additions to the Cleopatra MS, are, when they differ from those of the two "AB" scribes, probably those 'of an older man, possibly less highly trained, and certainly less concerned to adhere strictly to the rule-book of the scribes" ',[71] in other words, 'a less developed stage of the orthography of the "AB dialect" '.[72]

The other derivative of β, that is δ, is the gateway to the rest of the tradition. Its closest extant descendant is G, a text written probably in the second half of the thirteenth century or possibly a little earlier.[73] G consists of rearranged long extracts by a scribe whose command of Middle English orthography was very imperfect and whose script suggests that he had been trained abroad.[74] The text is an adaptation for a male reader.[75] The other descendant of δ, namely ϵ, is the ancestor of the 'Nero-Titus group'; this ancestor gave rise to ζ and η. One of the copies derived from ζ, N, has been palaeographically dated to the second quarter of the thirteenth century;[76] two others are O, a text written probably in the first half of the fourteenth century,[77] and V, copied at the end of the fourteenth century.[78]

According to Dobson's account of the textual history (see stemma 1), in this branch of the tradition seven hypothesised texts, β, γ, ϕ, δ, ϵ, ζ, and η, were all authorial in the sense that they had been made either by the author or under his supervision.[79] If this is correct, there was certainly a substantial multiplication of copies within the first half-century of the text's life. As we further observe the rest of the history, this point becomes still more obvious.

From η, the ancestor of the Titus-group, descend P, a fourteenth-century witness,[80] and θ, from which T was produced. It is to be noted that, although it is low in the stemma, T is a copy still dated palaeographically to the second quarter of the thirteenth century.[81] λ, the other descendant of

---

[68] Dobson, *Origins*, 299–304.
[69] The case was set out at length by Dobson, *The English Text*, pp. ix–cxl.
[70] Dobson, *The English Text*, p. cxxxvi.
[71] Dobson, *Origins*, 317–18; cf. Dobson, *The English Text*, p. cxl, for the internal quotation.
[72] Dobson, *Origins*, 317–18.
[73] N. R. Ker, in Wilson, *The English Text*, p. ix.
[74] Dobson, *Origins*, 295; Ker, in Wilson, *The English Text*, pp. xi–xiii.
[75] Dobson, *Origins*, 296.
[76] Dobson, *Origins*, 288–9; Day, *The English Text*, p. xi.
[77] Mack and Zettersten, *The English Text*, 163.
[78] H. L. Spencer's introduction in Zettersten and Diensberg, *The English Text*, p. xii.
[79] Dobson, *Origins*, 286–9.
[80] Dobson, 'Affiliations', 135–6.
[81] Dobson, *Origins*, 288–9; Mack and Zettersten, *The English Text*, p. x.

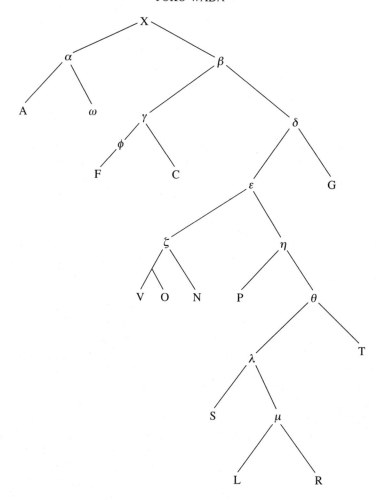

A Cambridge, Corpus Christi College, MS 402
F London, British Library, MS Cotton Vitellius F.vii
C London, British Library, MS Cotton Cleopatra C.vi
G Cambridge, Gonville and Caius College, MS 234/120
V Oxford, Bodleian Library, MS Eng. poet. a.1 (*S.C.* 3938–3942)
O Oxford, Bodleian Library, MS Eng. th. c.70
N London, British Library, MS Cotton Nero A.xiv
P Cambridge, Magdalene College, MS Pepys 2498
T London, British Library, MS Cotton Titus D.xviii
S Cambridge, Trinity College, MS R.14.7 (883)
L Oxford, Merton College, MS C.I.5 (Coxe 44) with Part 8 supplied in fragments from London,
   British Library, MS Cotton Vitellius E.vii (as edited by D'Evelyn in her EETS edition)
R London, British Library, MS Royal 8.C.i

1. E. J. Dobson's stemma of the versions of *Ancrene Wisse*

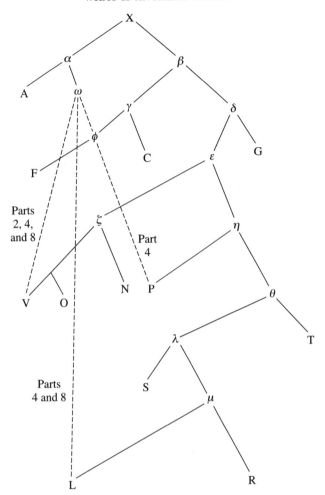

2. Stemma to illustrate E. J. Dobson's views of the influence of the revised text on the other versions of *Ancrene Wisse*

θ, gave rise to S, the other French text, which is a very extensive series of translated extracts rearranged and embodied in a vast compilation datable $1257 \times 1274(+)$.[82] μ is the other derivative of λ, from which descended R, a fifteenth-century copy, and the Latin translation, made for a community of women.[83] Thus, even at the extreme limit of the stemmatic descent of the text, barely a century had passed from the date of composition.

Although P and V, for example, are later manuscripts of *Ancrene Wisse*, they occupy a more elevated place in the tradition as derivatives of relatively good-quality and early texts. The text continued to be copied in the fourteenth and fifteenth centuries; however, the effective limit of significant corruption and innovation in the textual history had been reached by about 1300 in a century remarkable for its interest in reading *Ancrene Wisse* and manipulating it into new forms.

Lastly we need to deal with the other branch of the tradition. According to Dobson, the original text was revised by the author and several versions were created under authorial supervision.[84] He identified a second scribe of C as the author, who made an extensive series of changes to an unimpressive copy executed by a scribe from a different dialect-area.[85] These changes could in many cases be seen as first drafts of revisions which would later appear in more developed forms in subsequent witnesses.[86] The original (and now lost) text, X, was made the basis of a thorough revision of the work.[87] From X, α was produced and can be identified as the exemplar of an extant witness, A. Dobson thought that A had been written for a single person, not a community, about 1230 and that it had been given to Wigmore Abbey (Herefordshire) about 1300.[88] Many of the revisions which A embodies may be thought to have taken their origin in the alterations made in C by the second scribe of the Cleopatra manuscript.[89] However, A is not perfect and there is evidence for another and better copy, not α but a further derivative of it, here called ω, which is identified by its contaminatory influence on other parts of the tradition.

Stemma 2 shows in diagrammatic form Dobson's views on such influence:[90] ω was the source of new material from Part 4 in P, from Parts 4 and 8 in L, and from Parts 2, 4, and 8 in V.[91] This is the extent of the influence of the revised text represented by A. It is very strange that A does not have any derivatives – since *Ancrene Wisse* seems to have been read and

---

[82] Dobson, *Origins*, 296–7.
[83] The Latin translation was made perhaps by Simon of Ghent, bishop of Salisbury (1297–1315) (Dobson, *Origins*, 293–4 and 298, n. 2; cf. p. 65, n. 2, and p. 271).
[84] Dobson, *Origins*, 288–9, 195–6.
[85] Dobson, *Origins*, 259–64, 277–8, 285, 288, 300–1, 303, 345, 354; cf. Dobson, *The English Text*, pp. ix–cxl, and Dobson, 'Affiliations', 132.
[86] Dobson, 'Affiliations', 158–62; Dobson, *The English Text*, pp. cxvi–cxxv.
[87] Dobson, *Origins*, 289; cf. Dobson, 'Affiliations', 131, and Dobson, 'Date'.
[88] Dobson, *Origins*, 291.
[89] Dobson, 'Affiliations', 158–62; Dobson, *The English Text*, pp. cxvi–cxxv.
[90] For discussion, see Dobson, *Origins*, 289–92.
[91] Dobson, 'Affiliations', 150–7.

copied rather eagerly long after A was made – especially if, as Dobson maintained, this revision of *Ancrene Wisse* was authorial.[92]

Now I should like to explain how Dobson tried to seek to give a local and immediate context to most of the transmissional steps in the textual history. That context was defined by the circle of the religious of Wigmore Abbey, which was a house of regular Augustinian canons, and the Franciscan Friary at Hereford in the second quarter of the thirteenth century.[93] According to Dobson, as we have seen, the author kept extensive control of the transmission for approximately the first decade and the Hereford Franciscans did so in succession to him until about 1250. By then the ramifying tradition had almost run its course.

Dobson thought that *Ancrene Wisse* was originally written for three sisters, who are addressed in general at various points in the text and in particular in one long passage found in N.[94] Therefore, Dobson remarked, β, the great-grandparent of N, 'must have been the copy intended for presentation to the three sisters',[95] γ, in which the main reference to the three had been truncated, was made for Limebrook Prioty,[96] F was a French translation perhaps intended for Annora de Braose in 1227×1232,[97] and so on. The Hereford Franciscans were responsible for GNST and for revision of η.[98] Of the other group of revised derivatives of X, ω was for Limebrook Priory and A for an individual.[99] F was made while the revision to create α was in progress.[100] Since A, F, ζ, and η were all written about 1230,[101] copies higher in the stemma might be presumed to have been made before that date. N and T were written in the 1240s.[102] In short, Dobson left very little in the textual tradition lacking an immediate context of production. Variorum-texts are now being made by Bella Millett and Richard Dance, and a revised textual history of *Ancrene Wisse* is to be established based on the evidence from the whole texts of all versions. Dobson's view of origins of *Ancrene Wisse*, about which he drew conclusions largely from circumstantial evidence, will surely be challenged by their results.

It has generally been agreed that the language of the Corpus Christi College text (A) belongs to the West Midlands. Much the same spelling and

---

[92] Such a situation is not without parallel in text-histories. David Dumville has drawn my attention to an exact parallel in the textual history of *Historia Brittonum*, where the 'Sawley recension' of that text was created by a lengthy process of revision culminating in a fair copy made in the first decade of the thirteenth century. We have an 'authorially' annotated copy of a poor text, a clean copy of the revised text, and evidence for some contaminatory impact on the rest of the tradition, but no further new copies of the revision: Dumville, *Histories*, chapters VIII–XI.

[93] Dobson, *Origins*, 114–368; pp. 238–311 provide the core of the textually based arguments to this effect.

[94] Dobson, *Origins*, 253–60.

[95] Dobson, *Origins*, 288.

[96] Dobson, *Origins*, 288; cf. p. 260.

[97] Dobson, *Origins*, 299–310.

[98] Dobson, *Origins*, 297–9; cf. pp. 273, 285, 301, 304, 310.

[99] Dobson, *Origins*, 290–1.

[100] Dobson, *Origins*, 299–301.

[101] Dobson, *Origins*, 288–9.

[102] Dobson, *Origins*, 288–9.

language are found in the text of the 'Katherine group' in Oxford, Bodleian Library, MS Bodley 34. The former is called the 'A language' and the latter the 'B language'; because both texts show such a strong linguistic link, the shared features are called the 'AB language', which is considered to have been a literary form of the language of the West Midlands.[103] As for the vocabulary, the language of *Ancrene Wisse* contains five foreign elements, which may show the social milieu and geographical region in which the work was composed. They are French, Scandinavian, Welsh, Latin, and Flemish. Very often Middle English words of French origin are explained in the text by reference to their equivalents of Old English origin: an extreme case is an Old French word *triste* which is defined in full immediately after it is mentioned, 'A tryst is where they sit with the greyhounds to look out for the hare, or set the nets for it'.[104] Some words are used in what could be supposed to be natural speech; for example, a child looking for his mother cries, *'dame, dame'*, or when someone yields to a temptation of evil desire, the person cries out, *'Crauant, crauant'* ('I am vanquished, vanquished'), as she or he swoons weakly. Interjections such as *'deuleset'*, 'God knows' also appear. These strongly suggest a bilingual milieu to which the original anchoresses belonged.[105] Also indicative are the phrases *'o þin ahne ledene'*, that is, 'in your own language', about saying prayers and *'redunge of englisc oðer of frensch'*, 'reading of English or of French'.[106]

Many of the Scandinavian loanwords have something to do with every-day life.[107] From the nature of the vocabulary, it is very possible to imagine that the Scandinavian element was assimilated so well into Middle English that it was not felt foreign by contemporaries. This impression is supported by the fact that some Scandinavian loans in *Ancrene Wisse* display the same West Midland dialect-developments as do inherited Old English words.[108] Two words of Welsh origin appear in more than one thirteenth-century version of *Ancrene Wisse*: *cader*, 'cradle',[109] and *baban*, 'baby'.[110] In the works of the 'Katherine group', whose language is thought to be the same as that of *Ancrene Wisse*, we find *cader* again in *Hali meiðhad*, as well as two Welsh loanwords, *genow*, 'mouth' in *Seinte Margarete*, and *keis*, 'hench-men' in *Sawles Warde*.[111] This suggests that the treatise was originally composed somewhere near the border with Wales.

Most of the Latin loans were not adopted directly from Latin and are of

---

[103] For those characteristics of the AB language which indicate the West Midlands, see Zettersten, *Studies*, 284–5, and for the phonemic system, ibid., 269–74.
[104] White, *Ancrene Wisse*, 154.
[105] Clark, '"Wið scharpe sneateres"', 347.
[106] White, *Ancrene Wisse*, 135 and 24 respectively.
[107] For example, *cnif*, 'knife'; *deien*, 'die'; *feolahes*, 'companions'; *gris*, 'young pigs'; *lah*, 'low'; *lowse*, 'loose'; *takeð*, 'takes'; *wonteð*, 'is lacking' and so on.
[108] Zettersten, *Studies*, 285.
[109] Old English *cradel* also appears in the same text.
[110] Arne Zettersten has suggested that the word is an idiophone, but see Breeze, 'Welsh *baban*' and D'Ardenne, *þe Liflade*, 179, n. 1.
[111] Breeze, 'Welsh *genue*'. Until Breeze's work, there has been little discussion of borrowings into either French or English from Welsh, because the linguistic influences have usually been considered to run in the other direction only.

ecclesiastical interest. Many are used as Latin words in the text. It should be noted that there are also words of Dutch origin: for example, *bunkin*, 'beaten'; *dotie*, 'go out of mind'; *slubbri*, 'slippery'; *wigleð*, 'staggers'; *curre*, 'snapping dog; cowardly selfish fellow'.[112] The couple of Welsh loanwords in *Ancrene Wisse*, which have just been mentioned, are well known and have been very often talked about; on the other hand, the Dutch borrowings have never been given much consideration, although the text has as many as twelve words suspected to be of Dutch origin. Not only Welsh loans but also Dutch ones seem to be an important foreign element in determining the place of original composition, as we shall see below.

From the evidence of the language it is probable that *Ancrene Wisse* was originally composed somewhere in the West Midlands: the language of all five extant thirteenth-century English copies is based on a nucleus in the AB language.[113] Aspects of vocabulary, discussed above, obviously point to somewhere in and around the Welsh March. The foreign elements in the language of *Ancrene Wisse* reflect very well the linguistic situation in Marcher society in the twelfth and thirteenth centuries. To Wales the Anglo-Normans introduced French and English. About 1107–10 a major settlement of Flemings was despatched to Wales by King Henry I.[114] From the time when Henry I settled Flemings in Pembrokeshire (Dyfed) Dutch was spoken there, and it was still current in the late twelfth century.[115] The case of the author Gerald of Wales (1146–1223) reflects such multilingual situations in Wales very well. Although his mother-tongue was French, Gerald wrote in Latin, had a good command English, and understood Welsh too.[116] Gerald was so interested in languages that he noticed the similarities between some members of the Indo-European family: in one case, he listed the words for 'salt' in Greek, Latin, Welsh, Irish (in which he made a mistake), French, English, and Dutch, and gave a brief discussion of them.[117] In Gerald's *Speculum Duorum*, written in 1216, he reminded his nephew of 'what a knight from those pars [the area around Haverfordwest], a moderate and sensible man, called Ernaldus Rheting, once said in Flemish at Haverfordwest to your father.'[118] Gerald's brother, Philip, understood Dutch.[119]

Another example which tells us of the multilingual social circumstances is a charter, issued after 1174, of Raymond le Gros (d. 1188), constable of

---

[112] Arne Zettersten has thought only a few words to be Dutch (or Middle Low German, Middle Dutch or Middle Flemish – these three are almost always indistinguishable for this purpose) (Zettersten, *Studies*, 32, 80–1, 107–8, 119, 131, 137, 210, 225, and 237). He has had great doubts about many words considered to be Dutch by Bense, *Anglo-Dutch Relations*. Although Zettersten has often remarked that Bense allowed too much Flemish influence on *Ancrene Wisse*, there does not seem to be good reason to reject Bense's etymologies.

[113] Many dialectal features in the accidence of the Corpus, Caius, and Nero texts indicate the West Midland or Southern dialect-area (Zettersten, *Studies*, 269–74).

[114] Davies, *Conquest*, 99.

[115] Bartlett, *Gerald of Wales*, 13.

[116] Wada, 'Gerald on Gerald'.

[117] *Itinerarium Kambriae*, I.8, in Brewer *et al.*, *Giraldi*, VI:77–8; Thorpe, *Journey*, 135–6.

[118] Richter *et al.*, *Giraldus*, 36–7; Toorians, 'Wizo', 105.

[119] Philip's wife was a daughter of Richard fitz Tancred, castellan of Haverfordwest (Richter *et al.*, *Giraldus*, 38–9; Toorians, 'Wizo', 112; Davies, *Conquest*, 159).

Richard de Clare, 'Strongbow' (d. 1176), and Gerald's uncle, which was addressed to 'all present and to come, French, English, Flemish, Welsh and Irish'.[120] The Flemings were well mixed with other people(s) at every level. R. R. Davies has described how 'In many parts of lowland Wales – in the lordships of Chepstow, Abergavenny, Monmouth, Usk, Caeleon, Brecon, and lowland Glamorgan – colonists and natives lived in neighbouring vills, sometimes indeed cheek by jowl with each other in the same vill; rubbed shoulders with each other in the markets and fairs; exchanged land and intermarried'.[121] These colonists were mainly English people from the West-Midland area – western Herefordshire, for example.[122] Some Flemings even had their own castles and were related to ruling-class families.[123] In Herefordshire, a Flemish immigrant called 'Turstin the Fleming' *alias* 'Turstin of Wigmore' had already held Wigmore Castle for a time after 1066 before he was supplanted by the first Ralf de Mortimer.[124]

We know that Cambridge, Corpus Christi College, MS 402 was copied after 1224 when the Franciscans came to England,[125] because they are mentioned, as Friars Minor, in the text.[126] The date in question has long been considered crucial for the dating of *Ancrene Wisse*, but the Franciscans (and the Dominicans, who came in 1221) are referred to only in two surviving copies: the above-mentioned English text in Cambridge, Corpus Christi College, MS 402, and the French text in London, British Library, MS Cotton Vitellius F.vii.[127] The other copies – without mention of the Friars – are palaeographically datable to the same period, that is, either before or after the Franciscans' arrival in England.

The *terminus ante quem* for the composition of *Ancrene Wisse* lies in the first half of the thirteenth century, because the two oldest surviving manuscripts, Cambridge, Corpus Christi College, MS 402[128] and London, British Library, MS Cotton Cleopatra C.vi,[129] are datable to that period. Most other evidence points to the late twelfth century or the beginning of the thirteenth as the period of composition. E. J. Dobson concluded that the work had been originally written between 1215 and 1222.[130]

We can also deduce the date of composition from the sources of *Ancrene*

---

[120] Richard de Clare was earl of Pembroke and Strigoil (Chepstow). 1174 is the date when Raymond married Richard's sister and became constable: Brooks, 'Unpublished Charter'.

[121] Davies, *Conquest*, 160.

[122] Davies, *Conquest*, 99.

[123] For example, Gwladus, the aunt of Gerald of Wales and his brother Philip, had been married to Tancred, the first Flemish castellan of Haverfordwest; and one of their cousins, Odo of Carew, married a daughter of Richard fitz Tancred (Toorians, 'Wizo', 112, n. 70).

[124] Dobson, *Origins*, 204, n. 2.

[125] Cross and Livingstone, *Dictionary*, 532.

[126] Ff. 16v and 112v.

[127] The first mention is on f. 14r of the Vitellius manuscript but the second does not appear in this French text.

[128] First half of the thirteenth century: dating by Ker, in Tolkien, *The English Text*, p. xv.

[129] Dobson concluded on the date of the Cleopatra text, 'One could hardly be wrong to say that it was written between 1225 and 1230'; however he continued, 'This is of course a dating on textual, not on palaeographical grounds' (Dobson, *The English Text*, p. x).

[130] Dobson, 'Date'; Dobson, *Origins*, 238–9. Dobson's theories were often based on Talbot, 'Some Notes'.

Wisse. The treatise was influenced by many works of twelfth-century writers, especially those who lived towards the end of the century, and by the academic trend of that period.[131] The author of *Ancrene Wisse* knew, for example, *De institutis inclusarum* which an English Cistercian abbot, Aelred of Rievaulx (1110–67),[132] wrote for his sister; indeed the author knew it so well that he made some direct borrowings from it and even took thence the frame of the concept of the anchoritic life which he had in mind.[133] The Middle English translation of Aelred's text by 'Thomas N.'[134] is found in the Vernon manuscript which contains *Ancrene Wisse*.[135] Also, Dobson suggested that there might have been some influence from the Paris Sermons of Stephen Langton, archbishop of Canterbury 1207–1228.[136]

The treatment of Greek Fire in Part 7[137] of *Ancrene Wisse* is another criterion. This is a liquid incendiary which was used chiefly in siege-warfare by the defence.[138] It is recorded to have been used by the Greeks against the Arabs in the late seventh century,[139] but it was unknown in the West before the First Crusade (1099). It is referred to in Geoffrey of Monmouth's *Historia regum Britanniae* (before 1138):[140] 'when the enemy constructed a *testudo* and dug underneath their walls, they used Greek Fire and a deluge of boiling water to force them to retreat'.[141] In England, Greek Fire was used at the siege of Nottingham in 1194.[142]

As regards the hostility against Jews expressed in Part 7 of *Ancrene Wisse*, Geoffrey Shepherd remarked that hatred had become acute by the time of the fall of Jerusalem in 1099 and also during the preparations for the Third Crusade (1189–92).[143] Dobson also argued, with reference to Part 1 of *Ancrene Wisse*, that the description of Christians who suffered in prison or in servitude in pagan lands could indicate that *Ancrene Wisse* had been written in the knowledge that many Christian prisoners had been sold into slavery after Saladin's victory at Hattin in 1187.[144] Peter of Blois (*c.* 1135–

---

[131] Shepherd, *Ancrene Wisse*, pp. xxvi–xxix; Zettersten, *Studies*, 13–14.

[132] Stephen and Lee, *Dictionary of National Biography*, XVIII:33–5; Harvey, *St Aelred*; Squire, *Aelred*; Hallier, *Monastic Theology. De institutis* has been edited by C. H. Talbot ('"De institutis"', 167–217), and by A. Hoste and C. H. Talbot (*Aelredi Rievallensis Opera Omnia*). Cf. Constable, 'Aelred'; Barratt, '"De Institutione"'. 'St Aelred the Abbot' is mentioned in Part 6 (White, *Ancrene Wisse*, 169).

[133] Shepherd, *Ancrene Wisse*, pp. xxxvi–xxxvii.

[134] Horstmann, 'Informacio'; Ayto and Barratt, *De Institutione*.

[135] Doyle, 'Shaping', 3.

[136] However, as he himself admitted, 'the extent of which is still to be determined': Dobson, *Origins*, 144 and 315–16.

[137] White, *Ancrene Wisse*, 186.

[138] Partington, *History*; Tatlock, *Legendary History*, 322–3.

[139] Gibbon, *History*, chapter 52 (ed. Bury, VI:3, 9–12, 539–40).

[140] §11 (Book I, chapter vii): Wright, *Historia*, 5; Thorpe, *History*, 58. Geoffrey Shepherd mistakenly gave 'vi' as the chapter in question (*Ancrene Wisse*, 65). For the date of composition of the *Historia Regum Britanniae*, see Wright, *Historia*, I:xi.

[141] The use of 'scalding water' for defence appears in Part 4 of *Ancrene Wisse*, as also in the quoted part of *Historia Regum Britanniae*.

[142] Shepherd (*Ancrene Wisse*, 65) but without reference to the evidence. He also noted that 'it was encountered by the Western armies in the Third Crusade (1189–92)'. But see Tatlock, *Legendary History*, 322–3.

[143] Shepherd, *Ancrene Wisse*, 59–60.

[144] Dobson, *Origins*, 239, n. 2, and p. 249.

c. 1208) whose writing certainly influenced the author of *Ancrene Wisse* was among many authors of controversial literature directed against the Jews.[145]

Shepherd remarked that the author's somewhat relaxed attitude towards institutional religion[146] did not fit the ideology of the Fourth Lateran Council (1215) which insisted on stricter ecclesiastical control of unattached religious.[147] He thought, in consequence, that the date of composition might have been earlier than 1215.[148] However, as Dobson showed,[149] the treatment of confession in *Ancrene Wisse* is indeed influenced by the *acta* of the Fourth Lateran Council in 1215.[150] Since the decrees of this Council stressed that all the faithful must go to make confession, many manuals were written for confessors[151] and for the clergy at large to help them to teach the right method.[152]

Morton W. Bloomfield observed that on the basis of the elaborate treatment of the Seven Deadly Sins it was hard to date the work much before 1225.[153] As Bloomfield also noted, although sins had been from earliest times described in animal-form,[154] he noticed that the author's systematic attempt to portray sins as animals is outstanding and pointed out the novelty of that text as a harbinger of the Sins' subsequent treatment in English literature.[155] We know that *De animalibus* which consists of twenty-six books was written in 1256 by a zoologist, Albertus Magnus; the work's last four books classified animals with the interpretations often associated with the Seven Deadly Sins.[156] This indicates that the pseudo-science of animal-lore became popular in the thirteenth century. It is noteworthy that the unicorn, a symbol most commonly associated with chastity or fierceness, unusually symbolises wrath in *Ancrene Wisse*,

---

[145] Hunt, 'Disputation', 146–7.

[146] See pp. 2–3, above, for example. It should be noted here that Humbert of Romans (*c.* 1200–77), who was elected Master of the Dominican Order in 1254, at a General Chapter held in Budapest at the special invitation of Bela IV, king of Hungary, wrote in his commentary on the Prologue to the Dominican Constitutions, 'It is the general practice among approved religious orders which live by a common profession that they should display the highest degree of uniformity in external things, not only in their observances, but also in their habit, their buildings, and in various other things too. It is with a certain sadness that we must realize how far we differ from the rest on this point': Tugwell, *Early Dominicans*, 141.

[147] Shepherd, *Ancrene Wisse*, pp. xxiii–xxiv; cf. Dobson, *Origins*, 45, n. 3.

[148] Another thing which supports a date after 1215 is a scene of a love-tournament in Part 7 of *Ancrene Wisse*. Noel Denholm-Young pointed out that the earliest plausible record of a love-tourney in England was from 1215 at Kenilworth (Denholm-Young, 'Tournament', 265); Shepherd's note says 'at Staines' (*Ancrene Wisse*, 57); for the history of the tournament, see also Barber and Barker, *Tournaments*. Shepherd considered the scene of the love-tournament to be a reflexion of Geoffrey of Monmouth's *Historia Regum Britanniae* (Shepherd, *Ancrene Wisse*, 57; Wright, *Historia*, I:111–12, §157; Thorpe, *History*, 229), and this was also the view of Hope Emily Allen, 'The "Ancren Riwle"'. See also Dobson's argument ('Date', 180).

[149] Dobson, 'Date'.

[150] Dolan, 'Date'.

[151] Gerard Sitwell, 'Introduction', in Salu, *Ancrene Wisse*, pp. xii–xxii, at xix–xx. Cf. Martin, 'Middle English Manuals'.

[152] Cheney, *English Synodalia*, 40–2.

[153] Bloomfield, *Seven Deadly Sins*, 148.

[154] Bloomfield, *Seven Deadly Sins*, 28–9.

[155] Bloomfield, *Seven Deadly Sins*, 148, 150, 151, and 155.

[156] Bloomfield, *Seven Deadly Sins*, 150.

whereas the other animals in the description of the Seven Deadly Sins are treated more or less conventionally.[157]

Ancrene Wisse seems very likely to have been composed in an Anglo-French milieu, as I have already noted,[158] and Part 7 certainly suggests the author's acquaintance with French literature at large.[159] In the thirteenth century, France produced very famous works of literature dealing with the Seven Deadly Sins.[160] Among many using animal-symbolism, *Summa seu tractatus de uirtutibus et uitiis* (or simply the *Tractatus*), for example, written by Guillelmus Peraldus about 1236 or even earlier,[161] had great popularity. It illustrates some vices with animals and their stories.[162] Also a treatment almost as elaborate as in *Ancrene Wisse* can be observed in Anglo-French literature earlier than in English: *Besant Dieu* written by Guillaume le Clerc,[163] who is known to have been engaged on one section in 1210 or 1211 and who finished the whole work soon after 1226/7,[164] deals with the natures of the various beasts. His main source was Hugh of Saint-Victor (d. 1141),[165] whose work seems to have exercised much influence on the author of *Ancrene Wisse*.[166] Guillaume was possibly acquainted with 'The Bestiary', written after 1121 and probably before 1135[167] of Philippe de Thaon.[168] As an Anglo-Norman clerk very proud of his Norman birth and French allegiance, he wrote in French; but he lived in England, writing for English patrons.[169]

Taking into account all the points made so far, the date of composition of *Ancrene Wisse* can be estimated as between about 1215 (when the Fourth Lateran Council was held) and the end of the first half of the thirteenth century by which time the oldest manuscript had been copied. If the author was a Dominican[170] the date could have been narrowed down to sometime between 1221 when the Dominicans first arrived in England and about 1250.

Several persons have been suggested as the author – Simon of Ghent (1297–1315), bishop of Salisbury,[171] Richard Poore, bishop of Salisbury

---

[157] Bloomfield, *Seven Deadly Sins*, 151; Leach, *Standard Dictionary*, 1150.

[158] See pp. 7 and 14, below.

[159] Part 7 certainly suggests the author's acquaintance with French romance (Shepherd, *Ancrene Wisse*, p. xxix).

[160] Bloomfield, *Seven Deadly Sins*, 123.

[161] Petersen, *Sources*.

[162] Bloomfield, *Seven Deadly Sins*, 123–5.

[163] Balteau *et al.*, *Dictionnaire*, XVII, cols. 161–2; Reinsch, *Bestiaire*, and Druce, *Bestiary*.

[164] Legge, *Anglo-Norman Literature*, 207 and 228.

[165] Hugh came to Saint-Victor (Paris) from Lorraine or the Low Countries about 1118 and taught from about 1125 until his death in 1141: Smalley, *Study*, 85.

[166] Dobson, *Origins*, 142–4.

[167] Legge, *Anglo-Norman Literature*, 22; Crosland, *Medieval French Literature*, 245.

[168] Legge, *Anglo-Norman Literature*, 207.

[169] Legge, *Anglo-Norman Literature*, 207; leaving aside the question of the date of composition of each work, more investigation is needed to discover whether the author of *Ancrene Wisse* knew the work of Guillaume le Clerc or not. It is worth noting that Guillaume was considered by Legge (ibid.) to have lived in the diocese of Coventry and Lichfield, in the West Midlands.

[170] Bella Millett has convincingly shown the author's affiliation to the Dominican order (Millett, 'Origins').

[171] Oxford, Magdalen College, MS Latin 67, which contains a Latin version of *Ancrene Wisse*, bears

(1217–28),[172] Saint Gilbert of Sempringham (1089–1189)[173] – which were all more or less rapidly rejected by subsequent scholarship. In 1976 a long silence was broken by E. J. Dobson who drew the conclusion in his book *The Origins of Ancrene Wisse* that the author of *Ancrene Wisse* was very possibly a secular canon of Wigmore Abbey, called Brian of Lingen.[174] His argument is as follows in brief.

Dobson's starting point was Derek Brewer's discussion, published in 1956.[175] Dobson was convinced that the treatise had a strong connection with the Augustinians.[176] He then settled on Wigmore Abbey as a place where the work was originally written: according to Dobson, the monastery is the only religious house which fits the available profile of the author, including the dialectal area shown by the language of the work, the religious order indicated, the size of the community when *Ancrene Wisse* was originally composed (that is, '1215–22' on Dobson's dating),[177] and other internal evidence.[178] Between 1190 and 1225 there were at least two nunneries or groups of women religious in the neighbourhood of Wigmore Abbey. One was an Augustinian community founded by Ralph of Lingen (d. 1190) at Limebrook, about four miles south-west of the abbey. And in the Deerfold, situated approximately halfway between Limebrook Priory and Wigmore Abbey, lived sisters to whom Roger de Mortimer, lord of Wigmore 1181–1214, had granted the chapel of the Blessed Virgin and St Leonard.

Dobson observed that 'if "the author's own community" was Wigmore Abbey, then the groups of women must have lived within a short radius of Wigmore'.[179] From two considerations he deduced that *Ancrene Wisse* had been written for the sisters living in the Deerfold rather than those at Limebrook Priory. First, the Deerfold was closer, only two miles from Wigmore Abbey. Secondly, it was located only one mile from Wigmore Castle, the most important and the wealthiest centre in the district, and the seat, after 1214, of the son of Roger de Mortimer, which fits the situation described in the work: 'each of you has from one friend all that she requires, nor need the maiden seek either bread or food further than at his hall'.[180]

Following other examples of authorial anagram and cryptogram in

his name as the text's 'writer', 'Hic incipit prohemium uenerabilis patris magistri Simonis de Gandauo, episcopi Sarum, in librum de uita solitaria, quem scripsit sororibus suis anachoritis apud Tarente . . .' (f. 1r), but he cannot be the author of the original because earlier manuscripts of *Ancrene Wisse* exist. It is possible, however, that he was the translator of the Latin version, but there is no further evidence to support this.

[172] Morton, *Ancren Riwle*, p. xv.
[173] Hall, *Selections*, II:375–6.
[174] Dobson, *Origins*, 322–3. The book was reviewed by Arngart; Kristensson; Pearsall; and Wenzel. See also Millett, 'Origins'.
[175] Brewer, 'Two Notes'.
[176] Dobson, *Origins*, 1–54.
[177] Dobson, *Origins*, 239; cf. pp. 15–16.
[178] Dobson, *Origins*, 133–73.
[179] Dobson, *Origins*, 242.
[180] Dobson, *Origins*, 242.

medieval works,[181] Dobson found it possible to deduce that in an additional and final sentence in the Cleopatra manuscript, in the hand which Dobson thought to be the very author's, his signature was hidden: 'Inah meðful ich am, þe bidde se lutel', that is, 'inoh meðful' ('modest enough'), which could be decoded as Brian of Lingen.[182] This name is recorded as that of a secular canon of Wigmore Abbey, together with that of his father, Ralph of Lingen, the founder of Limebrook Priory, in a genealogy of the Lingen family written in a later sixteenth-century manuscript – London, British Library, MS Harley 1087.[183] This part of the list was probably compiled in 1522 × 1530, and Dobson remarked that it was very defective as a genealogy, in such a way that 'except for the direct male line (in which there are gaps), it is less interested in the men of the family than in the women'.[184] At an early stage Dobson's argument was defined by a conviction that 'the author must have been a member of the community of Wigmore Abbey, and yet a secular cleric or at least a man with pastoral interest, experience, and duties':[185] therefore Brian of Lingen could be one of those most likely to be the author of *Ancrene Wisse*.

It has been remarked that 'the problem of authorship . . . may be closer to a solution'[186] since 1976, but we are in fact nowhere near it. Although Dobson made elaborate historical investigations, he made a fatal mistake arising from one philological problem in deciphering the anagram – which was pointed out by Sally Thompson in 1991: he claimed that there had been a group of '*sororibus*' at La Derefaud, that is, the Deerfold, to whom Roger de Mortimer granted the chapel, showing in translation and in transcription (the latter in his footnote) the relevant part of the charter for Limebrook found in London, British Library, MS Harley 1240, f. 40r;[187] but in fact the charter says '*fratribus*' not *sororibus* and 'throughout the charter the reference is to brothers, not sisters, forming the community at La Derefaud'.[188] The Deerfold must therefore be removed from its place in Dobson's history of the origin of *Ancrene Wisse*. Furthermore, Dobson ruled out Limebrook as a place where the three sisters for whom the work was originally composed might have lived, because it is three miles in a direct line from Wigmore Castle, much farther than the distance between the Deerfold and Wigmore Castle;[189] but, as he himself wrote, the distance

---

[181] For other known examples, including the author of *Piers Plowman*, see Dobson, *Origins*, 327–43.

[182] As an anagram, the phrase can be unscrambled as *of Linðehum*, 'of Lingen'; the same phrase can also bring out a name, 'Brian', which derives from *bria*, 'moderation', in Latin. See Dobson, *Origins*, 312–68.

[183] This is 'An Hereldical book', containing *Genelogia illorum de Lingen*: Nares *et al.*, *Catalogue*, I:543–4; Dobson, *Origins*, 196–211.

[184] Dobson, *Origins*, 203.

[185] Dobson, *Origins*, 367.

[186] Dahood, '*Ancrene Wisse*', 11.

[187] Dobson, *Origins*, 218. MS Harley 1240, or *Liber Niger de Wigmore* ('The Black Book of Wigmore'), written during the reign of Richard II, contains deeds and evidence relating to the estate of the lords of the Mortimers (Nares *et al.*, *Catalogue*, I:619–20). See also Davis, *Medieval Cartularies*, 150, no. 1292.

[188] Thompson, *Women Religious*, 34, n. 126.

[189] Dobson, *Origins*, 242.

from Limebrook Priory to Lingen Castle is only three quarters of a mile, which is shorter than that from the Deerfold to Wigmore Castle, one mile.[190] If it is true that Lingen Castle was the residence until about 1235 of the son of the priory's 'first founder', that is, if Ralf of Lingen's elder son, John of Lingen I, lived in the castle, for which Dobson did not give evidence, then the relationship between Limebrook Priory, Lingen Castle, and Wigmore Abbey would naturally have been close. If the alleged author, Ralph of Lingen's younger son, was a secular canon, as the genealogy indicates, then he did not have to live inside the abbey: in other words, the distance between the priory and Wigmore Abbey does not need to be an issue in any discussion of why and how 'the author' knew the sisters very well; three miles are in any case not an unmanageably long distance.[191]

His confident deduction that the author was an Augustinian has been challenged by Alexandra Barratt, who has remarked that one cannot easily pinpoint the order to which the author belonged. She has shown that a few of the usages which Dobson thought to be Augustinian may not have been exclusively so, that the author, 'who was quite clearly not himself a Carthusian, should equally clearly have had access to the *Consuetudines*', and that he was not a Cistercian but made pervasive and profitable use of Aelred's treatise.[192] That diffirent orders and their rules influenced one another is, in itself, an uncontroversial proposition. If the author was not an Augustinian, Dobson's entire argument must be reconstructed. Dobson concluded that the author 'can hardly have been himself either a Friar Preacher or a Friar Minor' for two reasons: first, there is the warning to trust seculars little and religious still less; secondly, the author wrote, 'Our Friars Preachers and our Friars Minor are of such a discipline . . .', in other words, Dobson argued, if the author had been a friar of either order, he would have written 'any of us', or would not have written with such complete impartiality about both orders of Friars.[193]

Friars were religious, indeed, but as a group they had deserted monasteries long since and now lived in the secular world. The element of worldliness – examples from everyday life, and practical advice – in their sermons was one of the factors in their great success as preachers: they did not preach at people as from the pulpit but spoke to them in the secular world, as if on the corner of the street or in the market-place.[194] Then, 'Trust religious even less' does not seem irrelevant at all. There remains the question which order the author belonged to: was he a Friar Preacher or a Friar Minor?

---

[190] On the relationship between La Derefaud and the priory of Limebrook, see Dobson, *Origins*, 226.

[191] Dobson thought that the three sisters had 'lived near the author, who could visit them regularly: he was their director, and apparently their confessor; he knew their circumstances well and they were to tell him of everything each heard about the other' (Dobson, *Origins*, 241).

[192] Barratt, 'Anchoritic Aspects', 53.

[193] Dobson, *Origins*, 14–15. Cf. Millett, 'Origins', 218–19.

[194] They seem to have taken every opportunity to deliver sermons. A Dominican, Humbert of Romans (c. 1200–1283) (see p. 23, n. 196, below), for instance, wrote for his brethren, giving them practical advice about preaching: 'Provided you can get sufficient hearing, a sermon can be extremely useful at tournaments, because a lot of people attend them who are very much in need of instruction' (Tugwell, *Early Dominicans*, 336).

Dr Bella Millett has shown that it is highly likely that the author was a Dominican friar, on the evidence of practices described in *Ancrene Wisse*.[195] This is supported by the skilful rhetoric of the preaching style of the author of *Ancrene Wisse*, which has long been recognised[196] to have been composed by quite an experienced preacher. The Dominicans, who established a system of long and careful intellectual training and fostered close contact with university life,[197] abbreviated the daily office to allow more time for study.[198] This reminds us of the passage in *Ancrene Wisse*, '. . . you must pray less in order to read more. Reading is good prayer. Reading teaches how and what to pray, and prayer obtains it afterwards. During reading, when the heart is pleased, a devotion arises which is worth many prayers.'[199]

Points made so far seem to suggest strongly that the author was a very learned Dominican who composed *Ancrene Wisse* for three sisters of a wealthy family in the West Midlands near the border of England and Wales in the thirteenth century, probably after 1215 when the Fourth Lateran Council was held, or possibly after 1221 when Dominicans first arrived in England, but certainly before the end of the first half of the thirteenth century, to which period the two oldest surviving manuscripts are datable.[200] A satisfactory solution to the fundamental question of authorship depends on our achieving a proper understanding of the development of the text. Scholars are looking forward to publication of the variorum-edition and the stemma of all texts produced from that, on which Bella Millett and Richard Dance are working. As a result of their work, much more will be revealed about the origin of *Ancrene Wisse*.

Works Cited

Allen, Hope Emily, 'Some Fourteenth Century Borrowings from "Ancren Riwle" ', *Modern Language Review* 18 (1923), pp. 1–8

——, 'Wynkyn de Worde and a Second French Compilation from the "Ancren Riwle" with a Description of the First (Trinity Coll. Camb. MS 883)', in *Essays and Studies in Honor of Carleton Brown*, ed. P. W. L[ong] (New York, 1940), pp. 182–219

Arngart, O., review of Dobson, *Origins*, in *English Studies* 59 (1978), 154–5

Ayto, John, and Alexandra Barratt, ed., *Aelred of Rievaulx's De Institutione Inclusarum*, EETS o.s. 287 (Oxford, 1984)

---

[195] Millett, 'Origins'.

[196] Humbert, *Verbal Repetition*. Rhetoric was a matter of great importance to the Mendicants (Lawrence, *Medieval Monasticism*, 208–9; Owst, *Literature and Pulpit*). Among a large body of didactic literature which they produced, there was 'The Instruction of Preachers' by the Dominican Master General Humbert de Romans (see p. 22, n. 194, above). The work includes very practical advice on how to deliver sermons. See his *De Eruditione*, in Berthier, *Humberti*; and Conlon, *Treatise*.

[197] 'Above all the Dominicans took their place in the Universities. From 1229 onwards they held a chair of theology in Paris; soon they had two' (Tugwell, *Early Dominicans*, 25).

[198] Dickinson, *Monastic Life*, 90.

[199] White, *Ancrene Wisse*, 133.

[200] See p. 16, above.

Balteau, J., *et al.*, *Dictionnaire de biographie française* (Paris, 1933)

Barber, Richard, and Juliet Barker, *Tournaments, Jousts, Chivalry and Pageants in the Middle Ages* (Woodbridge, 1989)

Barratt, Alexandra, 'Anchoritic Aspects of *Ancrene Wisse*', *Medium Aevum* 49 (1980), pp. 32–56

——, 'The "De Institutione" of Aelred of Rievaulx and the Carthusian Order', *Journal of Theological Studies* new series 28 (1977), pp. 528–36

Bartlett, Robert, *Gerald of Wales 1146–1223* (Oxford, 1982)

Baugh, A. C., ed., *The English Text of the Ancrene Riwle edited from British Museum MS Royal 8.C.I*, EETS o.s. 232 (London, 1956)

Bense, J. F., *Anglo-Dutch Relations from the Earliest Times to the Death of William the Third, being an Historical Introduction to a Dictionary of the Low-Dutch Element in the English Vocabulary* (London, 1925)

Berthier, J. J., ed., *Humberti de Romanis Opera* (Marietti, 1956)

Blake, N. F., ed., *Middle English Religious Prose* (London, 1972)

Bloomfield, Morton W., *The Seven Deadly Sins: an Introduction to the History of a Religious Concept, with Special Reference to Medieval English Literature* (East Lansing, MI, 1952)

Breeze, Andrew, 'Welsh *baban* "baby" and *Ancrene Wisse*', *Notes and Queries* 238 (1993), pp. 12–13

——, 'Welsh *genue* "mouth, jaws" and the Middle English *Seinte Margarete*', *Notes and Queries* 238 (1993), pp. 13–14

Brewer, Derek, 'Two Notes on the Augustinian and Possible West Midland Origin of the *Ancrene Riwle*', *Notes and Queries* 201 (1956), pp. 232–5

Brewer, J. S., *et al.*, ed. *Giraldi Cambrensis Opera*, 8 vols. (London, 1861–91)

Brooks, E. St J., 'An Unpublished Charter of Raymond le Gros', *Journal of the Royal Society of Antiquaries of Ireland* 7th series 9 (1939), pp. 167–9

Brooks, E. St J., 'An Unpublished Charter of Raymond le Gros', *Journal of the Royal Society of Antiquaries of Ireland* 7th series 9 (1939), pp. 167–9

Carley, James P., 'John Leland and the Contents of English Pre-Dissolution Libraries: Lincolnshire', *Transactions of the Cambridge Bibliographical Society* 9 (1986–90), pp. 330–57

Cheney, C. R., *English Synodalia of the Thirteenth Century* (London, 1941; rev. imp., 1968)

Clark, Cecily, '"Wið scharpe sneateres": Some Aspects of Colloquialism in "Ancrene Wisse"', *Neuphilologische Mitteilungen* 79 (1978), pp. 341–53

Colledge, Eric, '*The Recluse*: a Lollard Interpolated Version of the *Ancren Riwle*', *Review of English Studies* 15 (1939), pp. 1–15 and 129–45

Conlon, Walter M., trans., *Treatise on Preaching by Humbert of Romans, Fifth Master-General of the Order of Preachers* (London, 1955)

Constable, Giles, 'Aelred of Rievaulx and the Nun of Watton', in *Medieval Women*, ed. Derek Baker (Oxford, 1978), pp. 205–26

Crawford, S. J., 'The Influence of the "Ancren Riwle" in the Late Fourteenth Century', *Modern Language Review* 25 (1930), pp. 191–2

Crosland, Jessie, *Medieval French Literature* (Oxford, 1956)

Cross, F. L., and E. A. Livingstone, ed., *The Oxford Dictionary of the Christian Church* (Oxford, rev. edn 1983)

Dahood, Roger, '*Ancrene Wisse*, Katherine Group, *Wohunge* Group', in *Middle English Prose*, ed. A. S. G. Edwards (New Brunswick, NJ, 1984), pp. 1–33

D'Ardenne, S. R. T. O., ed., *þe Liflade and te Passiun of Seinte Iuliene*, EETS o.s. 248 (London, 1961)

Davies, R. R., *Conquest, Coexistence, and Change: Wales 1063–1415* (Oxford, 1987)

Davis, G. R. C., *Medieval Cartularies of Great Britain: a Short Catalogue* (London, 1958)

Day, Mabel, ed., *The English Text of the Ancrene Riwle edited from Cotton Nero A.XIV*, EETS o.s. 225 (London, 1952)

Deanesly, Margaret, *The Lollard Bible and Other Medieval Biblical Versions* (London, 1920)

Denholm-Young, Noel, 'The Tournament in the Thirteenth Century', in *Studies in Medieval History presented to Frederick Maurice Powicke*, ed. R. W. Hunt *et al.* (Oxford, 1948), pp. 240–68

D'Evelyn, Charlotte, ed., *The Latin Text of the Ancrene Riwle edited from Merton College MS 44 and British Museum MS Cotton Vitellius E vii*, EETS o.s. 216 (London, 1944)

——, 'Notes on Some Interrelations between the Latin and English Texts of the *Ancrene Riwle*', *PMLA* 64 (1949), pp. 1164–79

Dickinson, J. C., *Monastic Life in Medieval England* (London, 1961)

Dobson, E. J., 'The Affiliations of the Manuscripts of *Ancrene Wisse*', in *English and Medieval Studies presented to J. R. R. Tolkien on the Occasion of his Seventieth Birthday*, ed. Norman Davis and C. L. Wrenn (London, 1962), pp. 128–63

——, 'The Date and Composition of *Ancrene Wisse*', *Proceedings of the British Academy* 52 (1966), pp. 181–208

——, ed., *The English Text of Ancrene Riwle edited from B.M. Cotton MS. Cleopatra C.VI*, EETS o.s. 267 (London, 1972)

——, *The Origins of* Ancrene Wisse (Oxford, 1976)

——, review of Mack and Zettersten, *The English Text*, in *Medium Aevum* 36 (1976), pp. 187–91

Dolan, T. P., 'The Date of *Ancrene Wisse*: a Corroborative Note', *Notes and Queries* 219 (1974), pp. 322–3

Doyle, A. I., 'The Shaping of the Vernon Manuscript', in *Studies in the Vernon Manuscript*, ed. Derek Pearsall (Cambridge, 1990), pp. 1–13

——, 'A Survey of the Origins and Circulation of Theological Writings in English in the 14th, 15th, and Early 16th Centuries with Special Consideration of the Part of the Clergy therein', 2 vols. (unpublished Ph.D. dissertation, University of Cambridge, 1953)

Druce, George Claridge, trans., *The Bestiary of Guillaume le Clerc originally written in 1210–11* (Ashford, Kent, 1936)

Dumville, David N., *Histories and Pseudo-Histories of the Insular Middle Ages* (Aldershot, 1990)

Fisher, John H., 'Continental Associations for the *Ancrene Riwle*', *PMLA* 64 (1949), pp. 1180–9

——, ed., *The Tretyse of Loue*, EETS o.s. 223 (London 1951)

Fleming, John V., 'The Friars and Medieval English Literature', in *The Cambridge History of Medieval English Literature*, ed. David Wallace (Cambridge, 1999), pp. 349–75

Gibbon, Edward, *The History of the Decline and Fall of the Roman Empire*, ed. J. B. Bury, 7 vols. (London, 1896–1900)

Graham, Timothy, ed., *The Recovery of Old English: Anglo-Saxon Studies in the Sixteenth and Seventeenth Centuries* (Kalamazoo, MI, 2000)

H. D. S., 'English Spiritual Writers, XII: Dame Julian of Norwich', *Clergy Review* new series 44 (1959), pp. 705–20

Hall, Joseph, ed., *Selections from Early Middle English 1130–1250*, 2 vols. (Oxford, 1920)

Hallier, Amédée, *The Monastic Theology of Aelred of Rievaulx: an Experiential Theology* (Spencer, MA, 1969)

Harvey, T. E., *St Aelred of Rievaulx* (London, 1932)

Herbert, J. A., ed., *The French Text of the Ancrene Riwle edited from British Museum MS Cotton Vitellius F vii*, EETS o.s. 219 (London, 1944)

Horstmann C., ed., 'Informacio Alredi abbatis monasterij de Rieualle ad sororem suam inclusam: translata de Latino in Anglicum per Thomam N.', *Englische Studien* 7 (1883/4), pp. 304–44

Hoste, A., and C. H. Talbot, *Aelredi Rievallensis Opera Omnia*, I, *Opera Ascetica*, Corpus Christianorum, Continuatio Mediaevalis 1 (Turnhout, 1971)

Humbert, Agnes Margaret, *Verbal Repetition in the* Ancren Riwle (Washington, DC, 1944)

Hunt, R. W., 'The Disputation of Peter of Cornwall against Symon the Jew', in *Studies in Medieval History presented to Frederick Maurice Powicke*, ed. R. W. Hunt *et al.* (Oxford, 1948), pp. 143–54

James, Montague Rhodes, *The Western Manuscripts in the Library of Trinity College, Cambridge: a Descriptive Catalogue*, 4 vols. (Cambridge, 1900–4)

Kristensson, Gillis, review of Dobson, *Origins*, in *Studia Neophilologica* 53 (1981), 371–6

Lawrence, C. H., *Medieval Monasticism: Forms of Religious Life in Western Europe in the Middle Ages* (London, 1984)

Leach, Maria, *Standard Dictionary of Folklore, Mythology and Legend* (London, 1972)

Lee, Stuart, 'Oxford, Bodleian Library, MS Laud Misc. 381: William L'Isle, Ælfric, and the *Ancrene Wisse*', in *The Recovery of Old English: Anglo-Saxon Studies in the Sixteenth and Seventeenth Centuries*, ed. Timothy Graham (Kalamazoo, MI, 2000), pp. 207–42

Legge, Dominica, *Anglo-Norman Literature and its Background* (Oxford, 1963)

Mack, Frances M., and A. Zettersten, ed., *The English Text of the Ancrene Riwle edited from Cotton MS Titus D.XVIII, together with the Lanhydrock Fragment, Bodleian MS Engl.th.c.70*, EETS o.s. 252 (London, 1963)

Macaulay, G. C., 'The "Ancren Riwle"', *Modern Language Review* 9 (1914), pp. 63–73, 145–60, 324–31, and 463–74

Madden, Frederic, 'The Ancren Riwle', *Notes and Queries* 9 (1854), pp. 1–8

Martin, C. A., 'Middle English Manuals of Religious Instruction', in *So Meny People Longages and Tonges: Philological Essays in Scots and Mediaeval English presented to Angus McIntosh*, ed. Michael Benskin and M. L. Samuels (Edinburgh, 1981), pp. 283–98

Millett, Bella, 'Origins of *Ancrene Wisse*: New Answers, New Questions', *Medium Aevum* 61 (1992), pp. 206–28

Morton, James, ed. and trans., *The Ancren Riwle: a Treatise of the Rules and Duties of Monastic Life* (London, 1853)

Nares, R., *et al.*, *A Catalogue of the Harleian Manuscripts in the British Museum*, 4 vols. (London, 1808–12)

Owst, G. R., *Literature and Pulpit in Medieval England* (Oxford, 1933; rev. edn 1961)

Partington, J. R., *A History of Greek Fire and Gunpowder* (Cambridge, 1960)

Pearsall, Derek, review of Dobson, *Origins*, in *Review of English Studies* new series 28 (1977), 316–18

Petersen, Kate O., *The Sources of the Parson's Tale* (Berkeley, CA, 1942)

Reinsch, Robert, ed., *Le Bestiaire. Das Thierbuch des normannischen Dichters Guillaume le Clerc* (Leipzig, 1890)

Reynolds, Anna Maria, 'Some Literary Influences in the *Revelations* of Julian of Norwich (c 1342–post-1416)', *Leeds Studies in English* 7/8 (1952), pp. 18–28

Richter, Michael, *et al.*, ed. and trans. *Giraldus Cambrensis, Speculum Duorum or A Mirror of Two Men, preserved in the Vatican Library in Rome, Cod. Reg. Lat. 470* (Cardiff, 1974)

Salu, M. B., trans., *Ancrene Riwle (The Corpus MS: Ancrene Wisse)* (London, 1955)

Samuels, M. L., '*Ancrene Riwle* Studies', *Medium Aevum* 22 (1953), pp. 1–9

Shepherd, Geoffrey, ed., *Ancrene Wisse. Parts Six and Seven*, rev. edn (Exeter, 1985)

Smalley, Beryl, *The Study of the Bible in the Middle Ages*, 3rd edn (Oxford, 1983)

Smith, Thomas, *Catalogue of the Manuscripts in the Cottonian Library 1696*, ed. C. G. C. Tite (Cambridge, 1984)

Squire, Aelred, *Aelred of Rievaulx: a Study*, 2nd edn (Kalamazoo, MI, 1981)

Stephen, Leslie, and Sidney Lee, ed., *The Dictionary of National Biography from the Earliest Times to 1900*, 63 vols (Oxford, 1885–1900)

Talbot, C. H., 'The "De institutis inclusarum" of Ailred of Rievaulx', *Analecta Sacri Ordinis Cisterciensis* 7 (1951), pp. 167–217

——, 'Some Notes on the Dating of the *Ancrene Riwle*', *Neophilologus* 40 (1956), pp. 38–50

Tatlock, J. S. P., *The Legendary History of Britain: Geoffrey of Monmouth's Historia Regum Britanniae and its Early Vernacular Versions* (Berkeley, CA, 1950)

Thompson, Sally, *Women Religious: the Founding of English Nunneries after the Norman Conquest* (Oxford, 1991)

Thorpe, Lewis, trans., *The History of the Kings of Britain, by Geoffrey of Monmouth* (Harmondsworth, 1966)

——, trans., *The Journey through Wales and the Description of Wales, by Gerald of Wales* (Harmondsworth, 1978)

Tolkien, J. R. R., ed., *The English Text of the Ancrene Riwle, Ancrene Wisse, edited from MS Corpus Christi College Cambridge 402*, EETS o.s. 249 (Oxford, 1962)

Toorians, Lauran, 'Wizo Flandrensis and the Flemish Settlement in Pembrokeshire', *Cambridge Medieval Celtic Studies* 20 (1990), pp. 99–118

Tugwell, Simon, ed. and trans., *Early Dominicans: Selected Writings* (New York, 1982)

Wada, Yoko, 'Gerald on Gerald: Self-Presentation by Giraldus Cambrensis', *Anglo-Norman Studies* 20 (1997), pp. 223–46

——, ed. and trans., *'Temptations' from* Ancrene Wisse, I (Osaka, 1994)

Wanley, Humfrey, *Librorum Vett. Septentrionalium, qui in Angliae bibliothecis extant, nec non multorum Vett. Codd. Septentrionalium alibi extantium Catalogus Historico-criticus* (Oxford, 1705)

Wenzel, Siegfried, review of Dobson, *Origins*, in *Speculum* 53 (1978), 354–6

White, Hugh, trans., *Ancrene Wisse, Guide for Anchoresses* (Harmondsworth, 1993)

Wilson, R. M., ed., *The English Text of the Ancrene Riwle edited from Gonville and Caius College MS 234/120*, EETS o.s. 229 (London, 1954)

Wright, C. E., 'The Dispersal of the Libraries in the Sixteenth Century', in *The English Library before 1700*, ed. Francis Wormald and C. E. Wright (London, 1958), pp. 148–75

Wright, C. E., 'The Dispersal of the Monastic Libraries and the Beginnings of
    Anglo-Saxon Studies', *Transactions of the Cambridge Bibliographical Society* 1
    (1949–53), pp. 208–37
Wright, Neil, ed., *The Historia Regum Britannie of Geoffrey of Monmouth*, I, *Bern,
    Burgerbibliothek, MS 568* (Cambridge, 1985)
Zettersten, Arne, *Studies in the Dialect and Vocabulary of the Ancrene Riwle* (Lund,
    1965)
——, and Bernhard Diensberg, ed., *The English Text of the Ancrene Riwle: the
    'Vernon' Text, edited from Oxford, Bodleian Library, MS Eng. poet. a.1*, EETS
    o.s. 310 (Oxford, 2000)

2

The Genre of *Ancrene Wisse*

BELLA MILLETT

Morton W. Bloomfield, assessing the state of *Ancrene Wisse* studies in a 1958 review, complained that 'the problem of genre has been almost universally ignored';[1] and not a great deal of attention has been paid to it since then. The most serious attempt to tackle it can be found in Mary Baldwin's unpublished 1974 thesis, which traced the influence on *Ancrene Wisse* of several different traditions of religious writing. Surveying earlier characterisations of its genre, she usefully summarized the problem:

> Scholars have seen different things in *Ancrene Wisse*; it resembles an ascetic treatise; it can be read, in large part, as devotional prose; it can be considered to be, as in Part 5, itself a contribution to penitential literature; in method and style it is undoubtedly related to the medieval sermon; it is, according to one of the author's stated purposes in writing it – to comfort anchoresses – related to consolation literature; and there is a sense in which, because of its unified structure, it can be considered to be a manual of the spiritual life. What is less clear is how, if it is all of these things, *Ancrene Wisse* is a rule.[2]

There is no doubt that *Ancrene Wisse* presents itself as a rule. Although its Middle English title is ambiguous (the noun *wisse*, which is not recorded elsewhere, is derived from a verb which in Old English could mean either 'guide' or 'rule'),[3] its author explicitly and repeatedly categorizes it as a rule. In the *Preface*, he tells us that he is writing it in response to the request of his 'dear sisters' for a rule (*riwle*), defines the term at some length (linking it with Latin *regula* and its cognates), and explains that his work is subdivided into the 'Outer Rule', which governs external observances (Parts 1 and 8), and the 'Inner Rule', which directs the heart (Parts 2–7); he also refers to it more than once in the body of the work as a *riwle*. Nevertheless, it is difficult to read those sections which make up the 'Inner Rule' as belonging to the rule as a genre, when they seem to have much more obvious links with other kinds of religious writing.

Baldwin approaches the problem by invoking the precedent of earlier

---

[1] Bloomfield, review, 129.
[2] Baldwin, '*Ancrene Wisse*', 333–4.
[3] See Dobson, *Origins*, 51–3. The title is found in a single manuscript, Cambridge, Corpus Christi College, MS 402; the alternative title *Ancren(e) Riwle* goes back only to the nineteenth century (see Magoun, '*Ancrene Wisse* vs. *Ancrene Riwle*', 112–13).

anchoritic rules, including Grimlaic of Metz's late ninth- or early tenth-century *Regula solitariorum*,[4] Peter Damian's eleventh-century *De Institutis eremitarum*,[5] and Aelred of Rievaulx's *De Institutione inclusarum* (c.1160–2).[6] She notes that they frequently include material of the kind found in the sections on the 'inner rule' in *Ancrene Wisse* as well as external regulations: 'Monastic rules were framed for the establishment and organization of institutions, and there was necessarily in them a good deal of detailed practical regulation . . . For solitaries, detailed legislation was less important than spiritual guidance in their individual spiritual progress' (p. 335). She concludes:

> What is *AW*? It is a rule in the broad sense that love of God is the rule of the Christian life, since it implies fulfilment of the commandments and the pursuit of virtue. It is also a rule in the narrower sense that it is a spiritual guide for women who, although perhaps beginners in the spiritual life, have undertaken to live according to the counsels of perfection, and further, have chosen the anchoritic life (p. 348).

This conclusion is, as far as it goes, a wholly accurate characterization of the work. Both of its points, however, involve stretching the definition of 'rule' to some extent. The first does not address the question of genre; and the second depends on an implicit equation of 'spiritual guide' with 'rule' which does not necessarily hold.

The relationship of *Ancrene Wisse* to earlier and contemporary traditions of legislative writing is complex and sometimes problematic. To make sense of it, it is necessary to look beyond rules written specifically for anchorites to the broader European tradition of monastic legislation, and to take into account not only the formal features of this legislation but its changing historical and institutional context.

Anchoritism in the early Middle Ages was characteristically an offshoot of monasticism (St Benedict in his *Regula monasteriorum* recommended that it should be undertaken only by those who had been prepared for its rigours by monastic life); and the anchoritic rules which Baldwin discusses are similarly connected with a broader tradition of monastic legislation. The differences in content and emphasis between anchoritic and monastic rules which Baldwin notes can be seen as a matter of degree rather than kind. Although works addressed to anchorites might be expected to be relatively personal in tone, discursive in style, and concerned with spiritual matters, these features do not distinguish them sharply from early medieval monastic rules. The latter may similarly claim, with conventional modesty, to have been reluctantly produced at the request of a friend, relation, superior, or fellow-religious;[7] and they may similarly include spiritual advice as well as

---

[4] *PL* 103:576–661.

[5] *Opusculum* 15, *De suae congregationis institutis, ad Stephanum monachum (De Institutis eremitarum)*, *PL* 145: 335–64.

[6] *CCCM* 1:635–82; translated in *Aelred of Rievaulx*, 45–102 (the translations here, however, are my own).

[7] See Curtius, *European Literature*, ch. 5, §3, pp. 83–5.

practical regulations. Cassian's *De Institutis coenobiorum* (c.420–4), which he tells us was produced at the request of the bishop of Apt (Provence) for his newly founded monastery, falls, like *Ancrene Wisse*, into two main sections, the first (Books 1–4) on monastic observances, the second and more substantial (Books 5–12) on the eight principal vices; and even the first, although it is primarily concerned with external observance (*exterioris hominis obseruantia*), includes some material on the inner life, anticipating the fuller and more advanced treatment of the spiritual life in his *Collationes*, which were more concerned with 'disciplinam interioris [hominis] ac perfectionem cordis et anachoretarum uitam atque doctrinam' ('the discipline of the inner [person] and perfection of heart and the life and teaching of solitaries').[8]

Such intermingling of the personal and the general, the practical and the spiritual, meant that the demarcation between the rule and other genres, such as the letter, was not always clearly marked. Perhaps the most obvious example of this is the *libellus* of practical and spiritual advice on the monastic life by Augustine of Hippo which was to become the central component of the 'Rule of St Augustine', widely adopted by regular canons and others from the eleventh century onwards. Although Augustine's injunctions (which survive in two versions, one addressed to men, one to women) were described as a *regula* from c.600, and were drawn on by a number of early medieval writers of monastic rules, they were also transmitted to the Middle Ages as part of his *Letter* 211 (§§5–16), where they are prefaced by a rebuke to a house of quarreling nuns (§§1–4); they are discursive in style, and Augustine does not use distinctively legislative vocabulary to describe them, introducing them instead with the verb *praecipio*, which can mean 'recommend' or 'advise' as well as 'command'.[9] A later parallel to this blurring of generic boundaries can be found in the early twelfth-century letter in which Abelard addresses the problems faced by Heloise's female community in following the Rule of St Benedict. The letter includes detailed practical prescriptions of the kind found in contemporary monastic legislation, and Abelard calls it 'aliquam . . . institutionem quasi quamdam propositi vestri regulam' ('a sort of organizational framework, a rule, as it were, for your way of life');[10] but much of it is general spiritual advice, similar in style and sometimes in content to the 'Inner Rule' of *Ancrene Wisse*.

From the late eleventh century onwards, however, new developments took place in monastic legislation, as new institutional structures appeared both within and alongside the traditional Western European form of communal religious life, Benedictine monasticism. These included new monastic orders (some, like the Cistercians, still following the Benedictine

---

[8] See Guy, *Jean Cassien*, Bk 2, ch. 9, pp. 72–5.

[9] 'Haec sunt quae ut observetis praecipimus . . .', *Ep.* 211, §5, *PL* 33: 960. For a useful survey of scholarship on the authorship, textual history, and relationship of male and female versions of this work, see Lawless, *Augustine of Hippo*, ch. 8.

[10] Edited (as *Ep.* 7) by McLaughlin, 'Abelard's Rule', 241–92 (p. 242); translated by Radice, *Letters*, 183–269.

Rule, some, like the Carthusians, adopting a semi-anchoritic way of life); new orders of regular canons (such as the Premonstratensians and the Victorines); and, in the early thirteenth century, the earliest mendicant orders (Dominicans and Franciscans). With the proliferation of different forms of the religious life, and the need felt by many religious communities for more detailed and specialized sets of regulations, monastic legislation became increasingly differentiated into a variety of sub-genres, each with its own conventions of content and form. The terminology used to describe the various genres is usefully surveyed by A. H. Thomas in his edition of the earliest Dominican constitutions. He begins with the rule proper (*regula*), which reflects the features of the early medieval rules or quasi-rules discussed above: 'The common life of monks was originally based on a rule, that is, a complex of spiritual directives and disciplinary prescriptions, which were usually drawn up or compiled by one person.'[11] The *Regula monasteriorum* of St Benedict (c.540) was the most generally observed monastic rule of the period; but the compilation known as the 'Rule of St Augustine' was increasingly widely adopted from the eleventh century onwards, and some of the new monastic orders of the eleventh and twelfth centuries produced new Rules of their own. The period from the eleventh century to the thirteenth was also marked by the rapid extension of an already-existing tendency for the basic 'Rules' to be supplemented by a set of written 'customs', *consuetudines* (or *usus*), which described (or, increasingly as time went on, prescribed) the detailed practices of a particular house or order. Liturgical observances might be recorded either in the customary itself or in a separate book, the *liber ordinarius*. The *consuetudines* could be further augmented or supplemented by administrative prescriptions (*statuta*) laid down by the ecclesiastical authorities, the general or provincial chapters of the order, or the individual house. Thomas also discusses the rather broader terms *institutio, institutiones*, and *instituta*:

> With regard to the monastic life, *institutio* means primarily the action of *instituere*, that is, the foundation or organization of a community, or the object or result of the action, that is, the whole of the legal regulations, customs and structures which rule the life of the community. The term *institutio*, in the singular, means the monastic state either in general, as an organized way of life with its own laws and institutions, or in particular, as realized in a particular abbey of the order. In many texts the plural *institutiones* is used as a collective noun for the different elements which belong to the framework of the monastic life, or for the written documents in which these norms are recorded . . . the term *instituta*, which has more or less the same range of meanings, can be seen as a synonym.[12]

[11] 'Het gemeenschapsleven van de kloosterlingen was aanvankelijk gebaseerd op een regel, d.w.z. een complex van geestelijke richtlijnen en disciplinaire voorschriften, die gewoonlijk door één persoon opgesteld of samengebracht waren.' Thomas, *De oudste Constituties*, 2.

[12] 'In verband met het kloosterleven betekent *institutio* vooral de handeling van *instituere*, dus het oprichten of inrichten van een gemeenschap of ook het object of resultaat van die handeling, namelijk het geheel van wettelijke bepalingen, gebruiken en organen die het gemeenschapsleven regelen. De term *institutio*, in het enkelvoud, bedoelt dan de kloosterstaat hetzij in het algemeen,

He also notes the use of *constitutiones* from the early thirteenth century onwards as a collective noun for legislative documents of this kind.

Ancrene Wisse is influenced by a number of works dating from different stages of this legislative development, and as a result shows a mixture of older and newer features; but both its treatment of its sources and its understanding of the implications of the term *riwle* reflect a distinctively thirteenth-century approach.

The legislative source on which the author draws most thoroughly and extensively is a product of reformed Benedictine monasticism, the guide to the anchoritic life by the Cistercian Aelred of Rievaulx, *De Institutione inclusarum* (c.1160–2). Aelred is clearly working within the early medieval legislative tradition discussed above, and his work shares many of its features. In the Prologue, he tells us that his sister had requested from him a set of instructions (*certam . . . formulam*) by which she could direct her conduct (*mores*) and the religious observances required of her (*necessaria . . . religioni . . . exercitia*). He agrees, with a conventionally modest show of reluctance, to do as she asks,

> et ex diuersis patrum institutis, aliquae quae tibi necessaria uidentur excerpens, ad componendum exterioris hominis statum, certam tibi regulam tradere curabo, pro loco et tempore quaedam adiciens, et spiritualia corporalibus, ubi utile uisum fuerit, interserens.[13]

> (and, selecting from various prescriptions of the Fathers a number which seem to suit your needs, to direct the conduct of the outer person, I shall do my best to give you a fixed rule (*regula*), adding some things appropriate for the place and time, and inserting spiritual matters among practical ones where it seems useful.)

Aelred makes here, like Cassian before him, a distinction between bodily or practical matters (*corporalia*) concerning the outer person (*exterior homo*) and spiritual matters (*spiritualia*), and reflects this distinction in the structure of his work. At the end of §13 he signals a transition from material 'on the outer way of life' (*de exterioris hominis conuersatione*) to the spiritual aims of the solitary life, and in the concluding section he gives a summary outline of the three different sections into which his work falls:

> Habes nunc sicut petisti corporales institutiones, quibus inclusa exterioris hominis mores componas; habes formam praescriptam qua interiorem hominem uel purges a uitiis, uel uirtutibus ornes; habes in triplici meditatione quomodo in te Dei dilectionem excites, nutrias et accendas.[14]

---

als een georganiseerde levenswijze met eigen wetten en instellingen, hetzij in het bijzonder, als verwezenlijkt in een bepaalde abdij of orde. In vele teksten wordt het meervoud *institutiones* gebruikt als een verzamelnaam voor de verschillende elementen die tot het kloosterlijke levenskader behoren of voor de geschreven documenten waarin deze normen werden vastgelegd . . . Als een synoniem kan de term *instituta* worden beschouwd, die ongeveer dezelfde nuances bezit.' Thomas, *De oudste Constituties*, 36–7.

[13] *De Institutione inclusarum*, §1, *CCCM* 1:637.

[14] *De Institutione inclusarum*, §33, *CCCM* 1:681–2.

(You have now, as you requested, practical regulations (*institutiones*), by which as an anchoress you may direct the conduct of the outer person; you have a prescribed form by which you may either purge your inner self of vices, or adorn it with virtues; you have in the triple meditation the means of arousing, nourishing, and kindling the love of God within you.)

But (again as in Cassian) the distinction between 'outer' and 'inner' matters is not a sharp one: the first part, on the outer life, mingles – as Aelred has promised – practical regulations with more general and discursive discussion of the principles which underlie them, and there is some overlap in content (in the treatment of almsgiving, for instance) with the second part. *Ancrene Wisse* draws extensively on the content of Aelred's work, and much of it is written in a similarly intimate and discursive style; it also follows him in the broad structural division between 'outer' and 'inner' observances. However, there are some structural features in *Ancrene Wisse* which are not explained by this model: in particular, the much sharper distinction in content and style between the 'Outer' and 'Inner Rule', and the separation of the material on prayer from that on other outward observances by the length of the 'Inner Rule'.

A second legislative source to which the author's debt has been noted is the Carthusian *Consuetudines* drawn up by Prior Guigo 1 c.1128.[15] The Carthusians, founded by St Bruno in 1084, and following a way of life which combined both monastic and anchoritic features, originally had no written rule of their own. Unlike most other eremitic groups who came to adopt a cenobitic way of life, they did not take over an existing Rule, and Guigo's *Consuetudines* are partly designed to fill that gap, not only describing the daily routine of the community but, particularly in the non-liturgical sections, expanding on its underlying spiritual rationale. In spite of its title, the work is rather more than a collection of 'customs'. In the words of their anonymous Carthusian editor, the *Consuetudines* 'are at the same time rule and customary, without being one or the other in any systematic way . . . the structure and the content of the *Carthusian Customs* link them much more with the old monastic rules than with the customaries contemporary with this work.'[16] Hope Emily Allen, in 1918, was the first to point out the use in *Ancrene Wisse* Part 3 of the final section of the *Consuetudines*, ch. 80, *De commendatione solitariae vitae*,[17] where Guigo, in a finale of untypical bravura, turns from the detailing of customs 'in quibus multa vilia sunt et minuta' ('many aspects of which are trivial and insignificant') to a lyrical celebration of the solitary life. Alexandra Barratt, in a 1980 article, suggested that the author of *Ancrene Wisse* might have gone beyond this chapter in his use of the *Consuetudines*.[18] But the

[15] *Coutumes de Chartreuse*.
[16] 'Elles sont à la fois règle et coutumier, sans être l'un ou l'autre de façon systématique . . . la structure et le contenu des *Coutumes de Chartreuse* les apparentent beaucoup plus aux règles monastiques anciennes qu'aux coutumiers contemporains de cet ouvrage', 'Introduction', *Coutumes de Chartreuse*, 19, 21.
[17] Allen, 'Origin', 488; see also du Moustier, 'Carthusian Inspiration?', 37–41.
[18] Barratt, 'Anchoritic Aspects', 32–56.

legislative parallels she draws (as she concedes) are not conclusive; the new orders of the twelfth and early thirteenth centuries drew to a large extent on a shared tradition of monastic legislation, and there are no parallels striking enough in content or wording to indicate a direct debt. There is a possible echo in *Ancrene Wisse* Part 8 of the brief excursus on Martha and Mary in ch. 20, 'De pauperibus et elemosinis';[19] but neither the structure of the *Consuetudines* nor its specifically legislative content seems to have had a significant influence on *Ancrene Wisse*.

To understand fully the links of *Ancrene Wisse* with the rule as a genre, we have to turn to yet another legislative tradition, Augustinian rather than Cistercian or Carthusian, and monastic rather than anchoritic. The term 'Augustinian' needs to be used with some care; the Augustinian tradition was a complex one, adopted by groups leading different kinds of religious life, and taking a variety of forms. At its heart was the 'Rule of St Augustine', a loosely defined compilation of Latin works whose two most significant elements were the *Ordo monasterii* (or *Regula secunda*), a short piece on monastic observances beginning 'Ante omnia, fratres carissimi, diligatur Deus . . .', and the *Praeceptum* (or *Regula tertia*), the male version of Augustine's *libellus* of injunctions on the monastic life.[20] Although there is some evidence that these two pieces had been linked together by the end of the patristic period, the 'Rule' was not widely used until the end of the eleventh century, when it began to be adopted by groups of regular canons; later it was adopted by the mendicants (apart from the Franciscans, who followed the Rule of St Francis), and by a variety of other religious and semireligious groups. However, its usefulness as a Rule was limited both by its brevity and by the inappropriateness of some of its regulations to the needs of its later-medieval users. In the early twelfth century, Pope Gelasius II dispensed the regular canons of Springiersbach from the requirements of the *Ordo monasterii*, and during this and the following century, there was an increasing tendency to drop all or most of the *Ordo* from the 'Rule'. Even more than in the Benedictine tradition (which had the advantage of the relatively full prescriptions in the Rule of St Benedict), customaries and statutes were needed to fill the legislative gap, incorporating fuller and more appropriate prescriptions.

For over a century, scholars have intermittently drawn attention to the influence of both the 'Rule of St Augustine' and the broader tradition of Augustinian legislation on *Ancrene Wisse*;[21] but the view that *Ancrene Wisse* was itself of Augustinian origin has only gained general acceptance over the

---

[19] ch. 20, §§2–3, *SC* 313: 206–8; at some points this is closer to *Ancrene Wisse*, Part 8 (ed. Tolkien, *Ancrene Wisse*, f. 112r/2–16) than the treatment of Martha and Mary in *De Institutione inclusarum*, chs. 28 and 31 (*CCCM* 1:660–1, 667) on which the author is also drawing (see Barratt, 'Anchoritic Aspects', 38–9 and 40–1).

[20] See p. 31 above. Critical edition by Verheijen, *La Règle*; Latin texts with translations in Lawless, *Augustine of Hippo*.

[21] Early examples were Dalgairns's 1870 connection of the addition on the 'lay brothers' hours' in Part 1 with Dominican practice, and the series of articles by the Dominican Vincent McNabb between 1907 and 1934 arguing for Augustinian, and specifically Dominican, origin for *Ancrene Wisse* as a whole; Allen in 1918 also argued for Augustinian (but not Dominican) origin. See Millett, *Ancrene Wisse*, 7–8, and the references given there.

last few decades, and the exact nature of that origin remains disputed. Derek Brewer in 1956 noted a number of parallels in the 'Outer Rule' to Augustinian observance, particularly that of the independent congregations of Augustinian canons (e.g. Premonstratensians, Victorines, Arrouaisians), who followed a relatively strict régime, and suggested the Victorine abbey at Wigmore in Herefordshire as a likely place of origin.[22] His arguments were followed up in much more detail by Eric Dobson in his influential 1976 study, *The Origins of* Ancrene Wisse. Dobson, like Brewer, argued for a link with Wigmore Abbey, which was sited in the right dialect area and connected with *Ancrene Wisse* by its ownership (though only from c.1300) of one of the best texts of the work (now Cambridge, Corpus Christi College, MS 402). However, his research into Victorine and other Augustinian legislation did not provide conclusive support for his theory. Although he was able to demonstrate influence on *Ancrene Wisse* from the 'Rule of St Augustine' itself, from commentaries on the Rule, and from other types of Augustinian legislation, the parallels which he identified in the Victorine customary of c.1200, the *Liber Ordinis*, were few and tenuous; he found much clearer evidence of influence from another branch of the tradition, the legislative codes developed by the Premonstratensian canons and later taken over by the Dominicans.

The earliest Premonstratensian customary had been produced in the 1130s, under the influence of Cistercian legislation, and during the twelfth and thirteenth centuries it underwent a series of revisions. The most important of these revisions for our purpose took place at some point between 1159 and 1174. It divided what was originally a continuous sequence of chapters into four major sections (*distinctiones*), covering daily observances, the functions of local officials, discipline, and the general organization of the Order; its editors Lefèvre and Grauwen suggest that it was influenced by the structure of Gratian's *Decretum* (c.1140).[23] A short Prologue was also added at this stage, emphasizing the need for uniformity of observance within the Order and explaining and justifying the revised structure. It was this version, with some minor updating, which provided the basis for the earliest Dominican *Constitutiones* of 1216. The early thirteenth-century preacher James of Vitry classified the Dominicans in one of his sermons not as a new kind of order, but as a seventh congregation of regular canons,[24] and there was some justification for this: Dominic, obliged by Canon 13 of the Fourth Lateran Council of 1215 to adopt the *institutiones* of an existing order,[25] chose to follow the 'Rule of St Augustine' (which he had previously followed in any case as a regular canon) and to use the Premonstratensian customary as the basis of his own regulations. Even in their earliest version, the Dominican regulations departed considerably from their model. The number of *distinctiones* was reduced from four to two (the first dealing with daily observances and discipline, the second with

---

[22] Brewer, 'Two Notes', 232–5.
[23] See Lefèvre and Grauwen, *Les Statuts*, vi.
[24] *Sermones vulgares*, no. 30, in Pitra, *Analecta novissima*, p. 387.
[25] See p. 41 below.

general and provincial chapters, study, and preaching), and the second Dominican *distinctio* shows hardly any trace of Premonstratensian influence. However, the *Prologue* (with some modifications) and the *distinctio* structure are maintained, and about a third of the first *distinctio* is taken over with little or no modification from the Premonstratensian customary.[26]

Both the overall structure and (to a lesser extent) the content of *Ancrene Wisse* were influenced by this particular tradition of legislation. The *Preface* of *Ancrene Wisse* takes up – though it also qualifies – the main theme of the Premonstratensian/Dominican *Prologue*, the need for uniformity of outward observance in the monastic life; and it concludes, like the *Prologue*, with an explanation of the structure of the remainder of the work, and a list of contents. *Ancrene Wisse* itself is divided into eight *distinctiones*, two of which, the first and last, deal with the 'customary' elements of its content, the anchoresses' outward observances. A further point of correspondence which been given less attention is the instructions for saying Matins at the beginning of the first *distinctio*; these are most closely linked in placing, content, style, and wording not just to the Premonstratensian/Dominican tradition but to the Dominican version of that tradition.[27]

What this suggests is that early medieval anchoritic and monastic rules were not the only legislative models which influenced *Ancrene Wisse*; the author also draws on a more recent tradition of monastic legislation, characterized by a relatively high degree of structural organization, and also by a sharper generic division between works dealing with the 'inner' and 'outer' aspects of the religious life. In his unfinished commentary on the Dominican Constitutions Humbert of Romans (d. 1277), distinguishing three different types of worship, of the heart, of the mouth, and of the body, commented,

> Ad cultum cordis pertinet fides, spes, charitas, et hujusmodi spiritualia, quibus animus erigitur in Deum; et de iis non agitur in constitutionibus humanis, cum ipsae versentur circa exteriora.[28]

> (The worship of the heart involves faith, hope, charity, and spiritual things of this kind, by which the soul is raised to God; and they are not dealt with in human constitutions, because these are concerned with exterior things (*exteriora*).)

To summarize the argument so far: *Ancrene Wisse* reflects the influence of a long and varied tradition of legislative writing, beginning with Augustine's late fourth-century *libellus* of precepts on the monastic life, and ending with a customary produced only a few years before it was written, the earliest Dominican Constitutions of 1216. Some of its features can be traced back a long way within this tradition: the presentation of the work as a response to personal request, the predominantly informal and discursive

---

[26] See the detailed source-study in Thomas, *De oudste Constituties*, ch. 3.
[27] See Dist. 1, ch. 1 of the earliest Dominican Constitutions in Thomas, *De oudste Constituties*, pp. 312–14, discussed in Millett, '*Ancrene Wisse* and the Book of Hours', 32–4.
[28] *Expositio in Constitutiones*, ch. 2, §52, in Berthier, *B. Humberti de Romanis*, 2:160.

style, the distinction between the 'inner' and 'outer' aspects of the religious
life, even the combination (found as early as Cassian's *Institutiones*) of
legislative advice with a discussion of the major sins. Others, however, show
the influence of new twelfth- and thirteenth-century developments in
monastic legislation, particularly the *distinctio* structure first introduced
in the later-twelfth-century revision of the Premonstratensian customary,
and the marked structural and stylistic separation of the 'customary'
elements of the first and last *distinctio* from the more discursive treatment
of the inner life in the intervening *distinctiones*.

This does not, however, entirely answer Baldwin's question about 'how . . .
[*Ancrene Wisse*] is a rule'. Although *Ancrene Wisse* presents itself as a
response to a request for a rule, and speaks of both the 'outer rule' and the
'inner rule', these descriptions are not necessarily to be taken literally; the
author throughout seems concerned to disclaim any legislative authority for
his work, and to deny it any official connection with the legislative tradition
on which it draws. In his *Preface*, he quotes from a passage in Bernard of
Clairvaux's *De praecepto et dispensatione* on the question of how far
monastic rules should be seen as binding. Bernard argues that those of
their precepts (such as charity and humility) which are ordained by God are
binding on everybody; otherwise a monastic regulation, 'quantum duntaxat
ad corporales observantias pertinet'[29] ('at least insofar as it concerns
physical observances') is binding only on those who have vowed it, and
may even so be dispensed by those with the authority to do so. In *Ancrene
Wisse*, the author widens the gap between the two kinds of precept further,
dismantling the framework of human legislation which which links them
together in Bernard's work.

In the first place, he denies any formal legislative authority to the 'Outer
Rule'. Historically, solitaries had been less strictly regulated than members
of monastic communities; according to the anonymous author of the
twelfth-century *Libellus de diversis ordinibus*,

> Caeterum non moueat quemquam si in hoc ordine quaedam diuersitas
> appareat, et aliter atque aliter unusquisque uitam suam instituat, ueluti
> est illud, ut quidam horum soli habitent, quidam uero adiunctis sibi
> duobus aut tribus aut pluribus, et illud quod alter altero leuius aut durius
> uiuit, cum et hanc diuersitatem in antiquis heremitis inueniamus, et
> unusquisque arbitrii sui potestate utatur, ut quantumlibet, et quantum
> uires suas pensat aggrediatur, nec a Domino inde dampnetur.

> (Let no one else be disturbed if a certain diversity should appear in this
> order [of hermits], and each arranges his life differently, with some living
> alone, some with two or three or more, living a life that is easier for some
> and harder for others, with a diversity such as we find among the hermits
> of old, and let each use the judgement and strength he has so that he may
> attempt as much as he wishes and as much as his powers allow, and not be
> condemned by the Lord for it.)[30]

---

[29] §3, Leclerq *et al.*, *Sancti Bernardi opera*, vol. 3, p. 256.
[30] Constable and Smith, *Libellus*, 14–17.

The author of *Ancrene Wisse* offers a similarly informal régime; in the *Preface*, he stresses that its prescriptions are are 'monnes fundles'[31] ('a human invention'), and advises the anchoresses to take only the basic religious vows of chastity, obedience, and stability of abode, not binding themselves by vow to any outward observance. They should observe the 'Outer Rule' only 'as þah ȝe hit hefden bihaten'[32] ('as if you had vowed it'), and its prescriptions may be modified by each anchoress's confessor at his discretion.[33] This advice is reiterated more emphatically at the beginning of Part 8, which deals with the anchoresses' outward observances in general:

> Biuoren on earst Ich seide þet ȝe ne schulden nawiht as i vu bihaten for te halden nan of þe uttre riwlen; þet ilke Ich segge ȝetten. Ne nane ne write Ich ham buten ow ane. Ich segge þis for-þi þet oþre ancren ne seggen nawt þet Ich þurh mi meistrie makie ham neowe Riwle. Ne bidde Ich nawt þet ha halden ham; ah ȝe ȝet moten changin, hwen-se ȝe eauer wulleð, þeose for betere. Aȝein þinges þet beoð biuoren, of ham is lutel strengðe.[34]

> (I said earlier, at the beginning, that you should not commit yourself to keeping any of the outer rules by a vow; I say the same now. And I am not writing them for anyone apart from you. I mention this so that other recluses may not claim that I, *þurh mi meistrie*, am making a new Rule for them. I do not ask that they should observe them, and even you may change them for better ones whenever you wish. Compared with the matters dealt with earlier, they are of little importance.)

The exact translation of *þurh mi meistrie* is disputed. The fourteenth-century Latin version of *Ancrene Wisse* renders it *per presum[ptionem]* 'through presumption'; Dobson (arguing that the author of *Ancrene Wisse* was also the anchoresses' spiritual director) translates 'by my authority'.[35] But in either case, the point is the same: the author stresses that he is not producing a 'new Rule', only an *ad hoc* set of recommendations which carry no legislative authority, even for their immediate audience. The point is reinforced yet again by an addition to the original version of Part 8 in one of the early MSS, London, British Library, Cotton Cleopatra C. vi, which is incorporated into the more fully revised version found in Corpus 402 and the Latin translation of *Ancrene Wisse*:

> Vnderstondeð eauer of alle þeose þinges þet nan nis heast ne forbod þet beoð of þe Uttre Riwle, þet is lute strengðe of, for-hwon þet te inre beo wel iwist, as Ich seide i þe frumðe. þeos mei beon ichanget hwer-se eani neod oðer eani skile hit easkeð, efter þet ha best mei þe leafdi Riwle seruin as hire eadmode þuften.[36]

---

[31] Tolkien, *The English Text, Preface*, f. 2r/5. All quotations from *Ancrene Wisse* are from this version, but the MS punctuation retained in Tolkien's edition has been modernized, and the text emended where necessary.

[32] Tolkien, *The English Text, Preface*, f. 2v/27.

[33] Tolkien, *The English Text, Preface*, f. 2r/15–20.

[34] Tolkien, *The English Text*, 8, f. 111r/11–20.

[35] Dobson, *Origins*, 48–9.

[36] Tolkien, *The English Text*, 8, f. 115r/15–20; see also Dobson, *The English Text*, 308–9, and d'Evelyn, *The Latin Text*, 174, lines 9–15. Another addition at the beginning of Part 8, in

(Where all these matters are concerned, you should always understand that nothing which comes under the Outer Rule is a command or a prohibition, since this rule matters little as long as the Inner Rule is observed, as I said at the beginning. The former may be changed wherever any need or any reason requires it, depending on how it may best serve the lady Rule as its humble maidservant.)

In the second place, the prescriptions of the 'Inner Rule' are attributed to divine rather than human authority. They are presented not as the requirements of a specific Rule, but as obligations binding on humanity in general; the anchoresses may be expected to observe them more strictly, but the author implies that this is a matter of degree rather than kind. In the *Preface*, he follows Bernard in distinguishing divine prescriptions from human ones:

Ah chearite – þet is, luue – ant eadmodnesse ant þolemodnesse, treoweschipe ant haldunge of [alle] þe ten heastes, schrift ant penitence, þeos ant þulliche oþre, þe beoð summe of þe alde lahe, summe of þe neowe, ne beoð nawt monnes fundles ne riwle þet mon stalde, ah beoð Godes heastes, ant forþi euch mon mot ham nede halden, ant ȝe ouer alle, for þeos riwl[i]ð þe heorte. Of hire riwlunge is al meast þet Ich write, bute i þe frumðe of þis boc ant i þe leaste ende.[37]

(But charity – that is, love – and humility and patience, faithfulness and keeping all the ten commandments, confession and penance, these and others like them, some of which belong to the old law, some to the new, are not human inventions or a rule established by man, but are God's commands, and therefore everyone is obliged to keep them, and you above all, because these rule the heart. Nearly everything that I write is about ruling the heart, except at the beginning of this book and at the very end.)

A marked difference between *Ancrene Wisse* and the early medieval rules and quasi-rules on which it draws is the almost complete separation – signalled in the last sentence above – between these two types of prescription. Unlike Aelred in *De Institutione Inclusarum*, 'spiritualia . . . corporalibus interserens' ('inserting spiritual matters among practical ones'), the author of *Ancrene Wisse* confines each almost entirely to its own part of the work. Only in Part 2, where he is dealing with the custody of the senses and so (inevitably) to some extent with the anchoresses' external conduct and routine, is there a significant overlap between the two. As a result, the 'Inner Rule' lacks almost entirely those features which would link it distinctively with the 'rule' as a genre.

Ancrene Wisse, then, is something of a paradox: a Rule which is not a Rule, drawing on existing legislative models but also reacting against them. The 'Outer Rule', although it draws extensively on earlier and contempor-

---

Cleopatra C.vi only, stresses that all its prescriptions are open to modification by the anchoresses' confessor or spiritual director (Dobson, *The English Text*, 301).

[37] Tolkien, *The English Text*, Preface, f. 2v/6–15.

ary anchoritic and monastic legislation, downplays the significance of its own prescriptions, offering them as recommendations rather than as rules; and the 'Inner Rule' is concerned with divine rather than human legislation, providing a series of treatises on 'God's commands' which by their scale and their central position in the work further emphasize the peripheral importance of the 'Outer Rule'.

Why should the author of *Ancrene Wisse* have been so anxious to disclaim the legislative authority of his own Rule? Aelred of Rievaulx, responding to a similar request in the previous century, seems to have felt no such anxiety. It is possible that the answer lies in the historical and institutional context of *Ancrene Wisse*. What exactly that context was has not yet been established beyond doubt; but the apparent influence from the earliest (1216) version of the Dominican Constitutions suggests that the work was composed not long after the Fourth Lateran Council of 1215, and that it may have been of Dominican origin.[38] Both of these factors could have helped to determine the author's approach.

The convenor of the Fourth Lateran Council, Pope Innocent III, was sympathetic to the development of new forms of the religious life; he was alert to their potential for containing as well as encouraging heresy, and had personally encouraged both the Franciscans and the Dominicans in the early stages of their development. The Council as a whole, however, did not share his attitude, and recorded its disapproval of the continuing proliferation of new orders in Canon 13, *De novis religionis prohibitis*:

> Ne nimia religionum diversitas gravem in ecclesia Dei confusionem inducat, firmiter prohibemus, ne quis de caetero novam religionem inveniat, sed quicumque voluerit ad religionem converti, unam de approbatis assumat. Similiter qui voluerit religiosam domum fundare de novo, regulam et institutionem accipiat de religionibus approbatis . . .[39]

> (So that too much diversity of religious orders should not introduce serious confusion in the Church of God, we strictly forbid anyone to establish a new order (*religio*) in the future; anyone who wishes to take up the religious life should adopt one of the approved forms instead. Similarly, anyone who wants to found a new religious house should accept a rule (*regula*) and organization (*institutio*) from the approved religious orders . . .)

This prohibition caused particular difficulties for women wishing to enter the religious life, since there was an increasing reluctance in this period among the established religious orders to take responsibility for houses of nuns. The Dominicans were not immune to this development; although Dominic himself had founded three women's houses, the responsibilities involved in supporting enclosed female communities soon came to be seen as incompatible with the preaching mission of the order, and the Dominican General Chapter of 1228 forbade 'cura vel custodia monialium vel quarumlibet aliarum mulierum' ('the care or custody of nuns or of any other

---

[38] See above, pp. 35–7.
[39] Alberigo *et al.*, *Conciliorum*, 242.

women'), a prohibition repeated in stronger terms in the mid-1230s.[40] Although the Dominicans maintained a strong commitment to the pastoral care of women, their connection with groups of religious or semi-religious women in this period was characteristically advisory rather than economic or organizational.[41]

In this context, a request by a group of anchoresses for a Rule became far more problematic than it would have been in Aelred's time. The original audience of *Ancrene Wisse* were lay-anchoresses, who had entered the anchor-house directly from the world rather than from a convent, and the evidence of the *Preface* suggests that they were troubled by their relatively marginal status as women religious – unattached to any religious order, lacking a distinctive habit, and not following an approved Rule. The author addresses all these issues, but he is clearly not in a position to resolve them institutionally; instead, he argues that institutional frameworks are only an outward sign of inner realities, and that the anchoresses' main concern should be with what they signify. He emphasizes that the prescriptions of the first and final distinctions, however indebted they may be to existing monastic legislation, are not binding on the anchoresses, and also that they do not constitute a *neowe riwle* which might be followed by others; as for the central part of his work, it is a 'Rule' only in the metaphorical sense, an extended exposition of divine rather than human precepts.

How far does this help us in addressing Baldwin's question, 'how . . . *Ancrene Wisse* is a rule'? Baldwin suggested that it could be defined as a rule partly 'in the broad sense that love of God is the rule of the Christian life', partly 'in the narrower sense that it is a spiritual guide for women who . . . have chosen the anchoritic life'. It could, however, be argued that these are precisely the senses in which *Ancrene Wisse* is not a rule. There is no doubt that the author drew both his overall structure and much of his content from a medieval tradition of anchoritic and monastic legislation; but these parallels in structure and content are not matched by a parallel in function. The prescriptions of the 'Outer Rule' are advisory, not mandatory, and the 'Inner Rule' has only divine, not human, authority. If we look at the question in terms of literary genre rather than function, it seems reasonable to assign the *Preface*, and the first and final *distinctiones*, to the genre of 'rule' – or more accurately, given the contemporary generic divisions of monastic legislation, to that of 'customary'. The 'Inner Rule', however, shares no distinctive features with the 'rule' as a genre, and could even be seen, to some extent, as defined in opposition to it; its main debt is to other genres of religious writing, and it is more usefully studied in this broader generic context.

---

[40] See Grundmann, *Religious Movements*, 96 and 105–6.
[41] See Grundmann, *Religious Movements*, ch. 5, §2, pp. 92–109.

Works Cited

Aelred of Rievaulx: Treatises, the Pastoral Prayer, Cistercian Fathers Series 2 (Kalamazoo, 1971)

Alberigo, Josepho, *et al.*, *Conciliorum Oecumenicorum Decreta* (Bologna, 1973)

Allen, Hope Emily, 'The Origin of the *Ancren Riwle*', *PMLA* 33 (1918)

Baldwin, Mary, '*Ancrene Wisse* and its Background in the Christian Tradition of Religious Instruction and Spirituality', Diss. (U of Toronto, 1974)

Barratt, Alexandra, 'Anchoritic Aspects of *Ancrene Wisse*', *Medium Aevum* 49 (1980)

Berthier, Joachim Joseph, ed., *B. Humberti de Romanis . . . Opera de Vita Regulari* (Rome, 1956)

Bloomfield, Morton W., review of M. B. Salu, trans., *The* Ancrene Riwle (*The Corpus MS*: Ancrene Wisse), *Speculum* 33 (1958)

Brewer, Derek S., 'Two Notes on the Augustinian and Possibly West Midland Origin of the *Ancren Riwle*', *Notes and Queries* n.s. 3 (1956)

CCCM

Constable G., and B. Smith, ed. and trans., *Libellus de diversis ordinibus et professionibus qui sunt in aecclesia*, Oxford Medieval Texts (Oxford, 1972)

Coutumes de Chartreuse: Guiges 1er, Prieur de Chartreuse: Coutumes de Chartreuse, ed. *par un Chartreux*, Sources Chrétiennes 313 (Paris, 1984)

Curtius, Ernst Robert, *European Literature and the Latin Middle Ages* [1948], trans. Willard R. Trask (London, 1953)

De Institutione inclusarum: Aelred of Rievaulx, *De Institutione inclusarum*

d'Evelyn, Charlotte, ed., *The Latin Text of the* Ancrene Riwle, *edited from Merton College MS 44 and British Museum MS Cotton Vitellius E.vii*, EETS 216 (London, 1944)

Dobson, E. J., ed., *The English Text of the* Ancrene Riwle, *edited from B.M. Cotton MS Cleopatra C.vi*, EETS 267 (London, 1972)

——, *The Origins of* Ancrene Wisse (Oxford, 1976)

du Moustier, Benoit, 'Carthusian Inspiration in the *Ancren Riwle*?', *Pax* 25, no. 163 (May 1935)

Grundmann, Herbert, *Religious Movements in the Middle Ages* [1935, 2nd edn 1961], trans. Steven Rowan (Notre Dame, 1995)

Guy, Jean-Claude, ed. and trans., *Jean Cassien: Institutions cénobitiques*, Sources Chrétiennes 109

Lawless, G., *Augustine of Hippo and his Monastic Rule* (Oxford, 1987)

Leclercq, Jean, Charles H. Talbot and Henri-Marie Rochais, eds., *Sancti Bernardi opera* (Rome, 1957–77)

Lefèvre, Pl. F., and W. M. Grauwen, eds., *Les Statuts de Prémontré au milieu du xiie siècle*, Bibliotheca Analectorum Praemonstratensium Fasc. 12 (Averbode, 1978)

McLaughlin, T. P., 'Abelard's Rule for Religious Women', *Mediaeval Studies* 18 (1956)

Magoun, Francis P., Jr, '*Ancrene Wisse* vs. *Ancrene Riwle*', *ELH* 4 (1937)

Millett, Bella, *Annotated Bibliographies of Old and Middle English Literature, vol. 2: Ancrene Wisse, the Katherine Group, and the Wooing Group* (Cambridge, 1996)

——, '*Ancrene Wisse* and the Book of Hours', in *Writing Religious Women*, ed. by Denis Renevey and Christiania Whitehead (Cardiff, 2000)

PL

Radice, Betty, *The Letters of Abelard and Heloise* (London, 1974)

Pitra, Joannes Baptista, ed., *Analecta novissima spicilegii Solesmensis, altera continuatio*, vol. 2: *Tusculana* (Typis Tusculanis, 1888; repr. Farnborough, 1967)

Thomas, A. H., *De oudste Constituties van de Dominicanen: voorgeschiedenis, tekst, bronnen, ontstaan en ontwikkeling (1215–1237) met uitgave van de tekst,* Bibliothèque de la Revue d'histoire ecclésiastique, fasc. 42 (Leuven, 1965)

Tolkien, J. R. R., ed., *The English Text of the* Ancrene Riwle*:* Ancrene Wisse*, edited from MS Corpus Christi College Cambridge 402*, EETS 249 (London, 1962)

Verheijen, Luc, *La Règle de saint Augustin*, 2 vols. (Paris, 1967)

3

The Communal Authorship of *Ancrene Wisse*

ANNE SAVAGE

Within the group comprised of *Ancrene Wisse, Holy Maidenhood, The Wooing of Our Lord, The Soul's Keeper*, and the passions of three virgin martyrs, *Katherine, Margaret*, and *Juliana*, the suggestion of a female author is only taken seriously in *The Wooing of Our Lord*, because it is in the female voice, wooing Jesus to become her lover. Otherwise, a single male author to several of them has been accepted for the rest;[1] very likely a Dominican, as Bella Millett has convincingly argued.[2] Millett and Wogan-Browne's *Medieval English Prose for Women* outlines the affiliations of *Ancrene Wisse* and anchoritic writing generally to many other kinds of writing 'ranging from the personal letter to full-scale treatises and from simple prescription to doctrinal and theological discussion';[3] I want to address the climate of composition itself from a different point of view. *Ancrene Wisse* and its associated texts reworked their sources, made their way out of their specialized community into the popular domain and find parallels within the romances and other genres; for example, Bella Millett's paper in this volume considers the relationship of the anchoritic Little Office of the Virgin with the growth of the immensely popular Book of Hours; anchoritic literature and practices moved well into, and strongly influenced, lay piety. Here I will consider the specific 'community of solitaries' which produced *Ancrene Wisse*, along with their role in its writing, as a starting-point for this succession of feminine influences on Middle English literature.

While these literary affiliations produced much of the actual text of *Ancrene Wisse*, I contend that the women who used it were, directly or indirectly, significantly responsible for the organization and recomposition of this material. Its serially-inherited nature, its succession of many male authors, and bureaucratic masculine-Christian attitudes to women, perhaps especially to women religious, have left many of us with a view of *Ancrene Wisse* as a masculine text with a few details designed by men to appeal to women – as though the imagery of housekeeping appeals to anybody, male or female. Elizabeth Robertson has argued that, while 'the dialectic between material circumstances and misogynistic views of women influences the style' of the English anchoritic corpus,

[1] See Millett, *Annotated Bibliographies*.
[2] Millett, 'Origins', 206–28.
[3] Millet and Wogan-Browne, *Medieval English Prose*, p. xxx.

> All six AB works exhibit a style (often associated in recent times with literature written *by* women rather than *for* women) that is pragmatic, nonteleological, and emotional . . . As a group, these works set forth, within the context of a specific environment, a masculine vision of a particularly feminine spirituality.[4]

The *inherited sources* replicated this masculine view, but I contend that there is little to support it as a defining principle in *Ancrene Wisse*. Such a view puts male authorship in control of the entire anchoritic project, subordinating any interests the female community might have to some purpose of his which excludes them. Given that the work was at their request, we have to be wary of a defining principle which allows them no agency *whatever*. What I will show here is a pattern of many elements pointing to a kind of agency which is 'authorial', even if no woman in the community was an 'author'.

We have been burdened by an inheritance from nineteenth-century notions of the individual writer as artist, and have done our best to find out who he was with respect to *Ancrene Wisse*, letting this direct our reading of the work; likewise the only alternative model for us has been the instructional manual, with the male writer as master and the anchoritic reader or listener as student. I think that both these ideas demand revising when we look at many medieval texts which grow out of communities: lyrical poetry and romances, for example, and writing for and within religious communities.

Although Robertson's view in the main is very different from the one presented here, her observations suggest it: 'Because critics have failed to take into account the influence of the audience on the production of these works, they have misunderstood the place of these works within the English tradition . . .'.[5] I will argue that *Ancrene Wisse* was not written as an instructional manual for the three sister-anchoresses who appear to have comprised its original audience/readership, and then the larger group of solitaries following their example; I propose that, while a wider range of sources provided its basis, it was written both *about* and *with* these anchoresses; that a very great part of its intention was to take the founding sisters and their lives as models for the others who had followed their example by the time of writing, and others who would in the future become anchoresses. By 'written with them' I do not mean that they necessarily sat at the writer's elbow dictating, but that they conveyed their needs, desires, and situation in a way that requires our attention in any question of authorship here – by any combination of written revisions, speech, and, most forcefully of all, by living the perilous anchoritic life successfully in the writer's eyes. In this reconsideration of the climate and development of *Ancrene Wisse*, I wish to qualify Benedicta Ward's statement in the *Preface* to *Anchoritic Spirituality*, that 'The content of these texts did not come from the solitaries themselves, but was offered for their use by those who knew

---

[4] Robertson, *Early English Devotional Prose*, 10–11.
[5] Robertson, *Early English Devotional Prose*, 11.

them well':[6] while the inherited materials fall into this category of 'content', its redesigning, the anchoritic sensibilities which are addressed, and much of the advice given derive from the 'beloved sisters' themselves.

While other professional religious women had reasons to write, the anchoress denied herself involvement with the world in this way, just as she died to her family and to secular concerns. Much of the *work* of the anchoress is *not* to have an outwardly-directed voice, except to God. Writing is like teaching, or talking except at great need through the window, both of which are extremely dangerous to her status, reputation and spiritual health:

> hwase is wis 7 seli wið þe schute wite hire. Wið þis wite hire echnen. For al þ uvel þerefter kimeð of þechne arewen. 7 nis ha muche chang oðer to fol hardi þe hald hire heued bradliche vt of þe opene carnel. hwil me wið quarreus vte wið assailleð þe castel.[7]

> [I]f she lingers at her window with an eye or a mouth, or ever receives a hand or a foolish word, she is all adorned and falsely tricked out in a spurious sanctity.[8]

> sum is swa wel ileared oðer swa wis iworded. þ ha walde he wiste hit þe sit 7 spekeð towart hire. 7 ʒeld him word aʒeinword. 7 forwurðeð meister þe schulde beon ancre. 7 leareþ him þ is icumen hire for to learen. walde bi hire tale wið þe wise sone beon icuð ðet 7 icnawen Icnawen ha is for ðurch þ ilke ha weneð to beon wis ihalden. he vnder stont þ ha is asot for ha huntet efter Pris 7 kech⟨e⟩t lastunge. for ed þe leste wenne he is ifaren he wule segge. þis ancre is of long tale.[9]

> ʒe ne schulen senden leattres. Ne underuon leattres. ne writen bute leaue[10]

Prohibitions like these, and there are many, against speaking learnedly, or even speaking at all to other people under most conditions, and against writing, forbid both implicitly and explicitly what we normally consider 'authorship'. Even writing to other anchoresses would break that isolation which is both her stronghold and her wilderness testing-ground, symbolic in its enclosure of her virginity. In the long, detailed interpretation of I Kings

---

[6] Benedicta Ward in Savage and Watson, *Anchoritic Spirituality*, 5.

[7] *Ancrene Wisse*, Part 2, quoted from Dobson, *The English Text*, 51: 'Whoever is wise and innocent should guard herself from the arrows, that is, guard her eyes; for all the evil that follows comes from the arrows of the eyes. And is she not most reckless and foolhardy, who holds her head out boldly over and exposed battlement, when someone is attacking the castle with bolts from outside?' *Anchoritic Spirituality*, *AW* Part 2, p. 70.

[8] *Anchoritic Spirituality*, *AW* Part 2, p. 71.

[9] Dobson, *The English Text*, 54: 'Someone, perhaps, is so learned or wise in speaking that she wants him who sits and speaks with her to know it, and pays him back word for word, And she who should be an anchoress becomes a teacher, and teaches him who has come to teach her. She wants to be recognized and known at once for her talk among the wise. Known she is – because on account of the very things for which she expects to be held wise, he understands that she is a fool, since she hunts for praise and catches blame; for at the very least, when he has gone away, he will say, "This anchoress talks a lot."' *Anchoritic Spirituality*, *AW* Part 2, pp. 72–73.

[10] Tolkien, *The English Text*, 17: 'You must not send letters, nor receive letters, nor write without leave.' *Anchoritic Spirituality*, *AW* Part 8, p. 204. Cleopatra omits 'ne writen'.

(236–46 in Part 3), the anchoress is likened to Shimei, who left a safe hiding-place and was captured, then executed.

> Vnderstondeð ȝeorne þi mine leoue sustren. Semey bitacneð þe utwarde ancre . . . ȝef ha entremeateð hire of þinges wið uten mare þen ha þurfte. 7 hire heorte be utewið . . . ha is iwende wið Semei ut of jerusalem alswa as he dude efter his þrealles. þeos þrealles beoð þe eðele fif wittes. þe schulden beon et hame 7 serven hare leafdi; hwen ha notieð ham wel in hare sawle neode. hwen þe ehe oþe boc. oþer o sum oðer god. þe eare to godes word. þe muð in hali bonen. ȝef ha wit ham uuele 7 let hem þurh ȝemeles etfleon hire scruise . 7 folhi ham utwart wið hire heorte . . . ha brekeð Salomen foreward wið þe unseli Semey; 7 is to deað idemet.[11]

Keeping her life and all thoughts about it within the anchorhold is, then, a matter of life and death. The anchoresses wrote out their own office-books, but there is no evidence that they wrote anything else (Evechan segge [.] hire vres as ha haueð Iwr⟨i⟩ten ham.[12]).

Julian of Norwich's *A Revelation of Love* breaks these prohibitions: Julian, however, eventually became an anchoress in order to understand her visionary revelations; once understood, they were written because Julian believed that, while the visions were hers, their meaning was for everyone. This necessitated not only understanding, but communicating. Julian's exception points, in its own way, to the prohibitions I have just mentioned: her extraordinary experience directs her to solitude, then understanding, and, then, only after many years, writing and revising.[13]

While the early *Ancrene Wisse* anchoresses clearly were not 'authors' in the same way that Julian was, nevertheless there is a connection between the writing of their respective books. Julian's long, long consideration of the meaning of her revelations, turning eventually to the solitude of the anchoritic life, involved an inward-looking, vigilant and rigorous adherence to that life. Her writing, in spite of its imperative to convey a universal message, was not the product of letting her heart go outside the anchorhold, but of keeping it in, for many years, until she had understood the message. In the same way, the anchoritic sisters who stand behind the *Ancrene Wisse* would not have violated any prohibition by meditating on the anchoritic life itself, or by sharing these with their spiritual director. In fact, the spiritual director's permission can be given the anchoress for many kinds of

[11] Tolkien, *The English Text*, 90: 'Understand this fully, my dear sisters. Shimei stands for the anchoress who is outward-looking . . . [I]f she meddles with outward things more than is needful, and her heart is turned outward, she has gone out of Jerusalem with Shimei, as he did after his servants. These servants are the five senses, which should be at home and serve their lady. They serve their lady the anchoress well when she uses them well for her soul's needs – when the eye is on a book or some other good thing, the ear turned to God's word, the mouth in holy prayers. If she guards them badly, carelessly lets them flee from her service, and follows them outward with her heart . . . she breaks Solomon's agreement with the unfortunate Shimei, and is condemned to death.' *Anchoritic Spirituality*, *AW* Part 3, p. 112.

[12] Dobson, *The English Text*, 19: 'Let each one say her Hours as she has written them out.' *Anchoritic Spirituality*, *AW* Part 1, p. 55.

[13] Watson, 'The Composition', 637–683, suggests that the short text was written up to fifteen years after the visions, and the long text ten or more years after that.

encounters and actions which are elsewhere rigidly prohibited, like letting men speak to her, or even rolling up her curtain so they can see her;[14] or inviting people in to eat with her.[15] Everywhere it is confirmed that

> þinre is eauer ilich. þe vtterre is mislich. For uh an schal halde þuttere efter þ heo beste mei. wið hire seruin þeo inner.[16]

The sisters are implicitly granted permission to do anything that does not violate the inner rule, 'Anonden Purte of heorte'.[17] They are also free, under certain circumstances, to refuse their director's advice to let a man look at them, for example, and to refuse the request of an ecclesiastical superior like a bishop who asks to see them.[18] So, in spite of the rigid framework of prohibitions and rules to keep, they are freer to make some kinds of decisions than nuns. This would include revealing and recounting intimately their anchoritic experience, at their own discretion, to their director; there is nothing to indicate that a rule of their own, written out by him, could not be shaped in some fashion by them, or could not include material they asked for or contributed.

While this is not 'authorship' in the way we generally think of it, nevertheless *Ancrene Wisse* is clearly implicated in feminine authorship of some kind. Firstly, the writer insists that he is not writing this book for its apparent audience. In the introduction, he speaks directly to the apparent objects of his effort, the 'sister' anchoresses, apologizing that *much of what he writes is not directed at them at all*, but other, less experienced women:[19]

> Ich write muche for oðere þ naut ne rinet to ou mine leoue sustren for nabbe ȝe naut to nome ne ne schulen habben þorche þe grace of gode of totinde ancren . . .[20]

> Nu ȝe habbeð an dale iherd mine leoue sustren. of þeo þe me cleopeð seoue moder sunnen 7 of hare teames. 7 of hwiche meosters swicher men serueð i þe feondescurt . . . ȝe beoð ful feor fram ham ure lauerd be iþonked . . .[21]

---

[14] *AW* Part 2, pp. 71–72.

[15] *AW* Part 8, p. 201.

[16] Dobson, *The English Text*, 2: 'The inner [rule] is always the same, the outer differs; for each should keep the outer according to the way she can best serve the inner.' *Anchoritic Spirituality*, *AW* Introduction, p. 48.

[17] Dobson, *The English Text*, 3: 'To do with purity of heart'. Ibid.

[18] St Martin is said to have commended an anchoress who refused to let him see her: Tolkien, *The English Text*, 34; *Anchoritic Spirituality*, *AW* Part 2, p. 72.

[19] Similarly, Aelred's sister was already very experienced when he wrote for her; he spells out the role of his rule in her life: 'Haec tibi, soror (gratias Deo), dicenda non fuerant: sed quia nec solum propter te, sed etiam propter adolescentiores, quae similem vitam tuo consilio arripere gestiunt . . .'. *PL* 32, col. 1454.

[20] Dobson, *The English Text*, 41: 'I write much for others that in no way touches you, my dear sisters. For you do not have a name – nor ever will have through the grace of God – for being peeping anchoresses . . .'. *Anchoritic Spirituality*, *AW* Part 2, p. 67. See also Dobson, *The English Text*, 55: 'is nis naut for ow iseid mine leoue sustren ne for oder swiche; "This is not said for your sakes, dear sisters, nor for others like you." ' *AW* Part 2, p. 74.

[21] Dobson, *The English Text*, 161: 'Now, my dear sisters, you have heard the first part, about those we call mother-sins and about their children, and of what offices these people who have married

AL þ ich habbe iseid of flesches Pinsunge. nis naut for ow mine leoue sustren. þe oðer hwiles þolieð mare þenn ic walde. Ach is for sum þe schal rede þis inoch raðe þe grapeð hire to softe.[22]

These comments stand in apparent contrast to the opening, in which he says,

þeo beoð [þe] richte. þe liueð efter riwle[.] mine l[e]oue sustren habbeð moni dei icraued [on] me efter riwle.[23]

The writer turns then to the distinction differentiating the inner rule, which is always the same, from the outer rule, which differs from circumstance to circumstance and person to person. This is contextualized: he has known the sisters for a long time ('You have for a long time begged me for a rule'[24]); even if he went to Aelred of Riveaulx's *Institutiones Inclusarum* as an authority, he could only find Aelred confirmed, or that he needed revision, through his experience with the anchoresses. Given his comments about their superiority; he is well-aware that their lives go beyond what he writes. It seems unlikely that the sisters themselves do *not* know already this basic difference between the inner and outer rule, given his reverence for their mastery of the profession. Certainly the humility topos has a high visibility among professional religious people, for many reasons. I bring to mind the enclosed nuns whom John Paul II released from their enclosure during his visit to the United States, so they could travel to see him. Their response to the high magnanimity was their 'special sacrifice' to Jesus: they returned a grateful message that they had decided *not to accept* this gift, and to stay enclosed. They showed a very deliberate solidarity, a choice of their profession over what in comparison was a worldly honour, like the anchoress in *Ancrene Wisse* who refused to show herself to St Martin when he asked to see her, and was commended by him for her holiness.[25] The anchoritic humility behind their petition for a written rule was most likely motivated by this kind of solidarity, rather than an obviously false protestation of their lack of expertise to a director who knew them.

From the anchoritic sisters, 'Begging their director for a rule for a long time' is clearly driven by something other than ignorance of how an anchoress should conduct her life – as with Aelred's sister's own request for something like this (see note 24). He does not say that they begged him for a rule for themselves, exactly, and I will keep that in mind here, even though having it would have helped them structure many existing practices,

with those seven hags fulfil at the devil's court . . . You are very far from them, our Lord be thanked.' *Anchoritic Spirituality*, *AW* Part 4, pp. 127–28.

[22] Dobson, *The English Text*, 278: 'All that I have said of the mortification of the flesh is not meant for you, my dear sisters, who sometimes suffer more than I would like; but it is for anyone who handles herself too gently who reads this willingly enough.' *Anchoritic Spirituality*, *AW* Part 6, p. 187.

[23] Dobson, *The English Text*, 1: 'They are righteous who live according to a rule; and you, my beloved sisters, have for a long time begged me for a rule.' *Anchoritic Spirituality*, *AW* Introduction, p. 47.

[24] *AW* Introduction, p. 47; see Aelred of Rievaulx, *De Institutione Inclusarum*, col. 1451.

[25] See note 19, above.

as well as introducing some new ones to serve their needs. It seems very likely that at least some of the original sisters and their immediate 'community of solitaries' knew Aelred's rule in some fashion, either by reading or having it read or translated to them. I suggest that they found it insufficient for a growing anchoritic community, even though it appears to have been written for one. Aelred Squire notes,

> Aelred's sister had, according to his own confession, waited a long time for him to write something for her, and was an anchoress of experience by the time she received a work she had requested not just for herself, but for other younger women, whom she had encouraged to embrace this form of life, and to whom she was having to give counsel.[26]

De Institutione lacks the *practical* dimensions of *Ancrene Wisse*; Aelred's sister, as an experienced anchoress, may well have provided this kind of advice herself, or may have been a model for others to follow; perhaps she had fewer women to advise. *Ancrene Wisse* is more methodical about presenting the distinctions between an inner and outer rule; it has more advice; it has more extended and highly-organized devotions and meditations.

As Ayto and Barratt point out, the two works exemplify quite different attitudes to the anchoritic experience:

> In general, the author of *Ancrene Wisse* follows Aelred closely but not slavishly, omitting passages from the Latin uncongenial to his own outlook and developing those aspects which appeal to him. His attitude towards mortification is throughout less extreme than Aelred's . . . As the passage [on chastity] develops, *Ancrene Wisse* introduces the idea of the glad and willing, almost gay and chivalrous, acceptance of suffering, an attitude quite alien to Aelred.[27]

While this 'gay and chivalrous' attitude may indeed have emanated from the male author, who was not suffering, is it not equally or more likely that his anchoritic models, the experienced sisters, exemplified it? They were the ones whose suffering was, after all, the focus of attention. That the sisters wanted a manual more in harmony with the order of their day is not surprising. Having the complete devotional sequence laid out at the beginning of *Ancrene Wisse* gives a flexible form which takes into consideration a wide range of anchoritic needs and demands. Aelred's devotions are spread out in the course of his text, ending with the extended meditations on the life of Christ together with the past, present and future at the end. While Aelred's meditations do contain concrete details like those to be focused on during the *Ave Maria* – she should go in her imagination with Mary to visit Elizabeth in the mountains and behold their greeting, prostrate herself at their feet and worship their lord and husband in Mary's womb[28] – the meditations are short. I suggest that the original anchoritic

---

[26] See Squire, *Aelred of Rievaulx*, 119.
[27] Ayto and Barratt, *Aelred of Rievaulx's De Institutione Inclusarum*, p. xxxix.
[28] Ayto and Barratt, *Aelred of Rievaulx's De Institutione Inclusarum*, 8.

community addressed in *Ancrene Wisse* thought that devotions and meditations should be longer, with sensory directions, if not for themselves then for newer members of the profession; that is, that the meditations themselves illustrate *how* to meditate in the first place, even if they invented their own when they had more experience.

While the basis and struggles of the anchoritic life are essentially the same across the centuries, Aelred gives no directions as to setting up this life in the varying circumstances treated in *Ancrene Wisse. De Institutione Inclusarum* gives no extended discussion of the outer rule as in *Ancrene Wisse*, which begins with the devotional shape of the day, an outline with built-in flexibility regarding time constraints, personal choice, and the recognition that all are not able to live in the same external circumstances. The goal of the *Wisse* is to enable the anchoresses to 'pull in one direction'. While it appears that Aelred did not have this as a concern, and neither did his sister, the notion of the outer life as servant to the inner taken is taken very seriously, in vastly greater detail in *Ancrene Wisse*, and has been specifically tailored to this brand of the anchoritic life, and this particular 'community of solitaries'.

The fact that the anchoresses ask for a rule has often, among other aspects of their relationship to the male writer, been interpreted as one of the signs that the sisters were spiritual beginners, an idea I have rejected elsewhere already.[29] I suggest instead that he modelled the rule on their own practice, adding to it where he thought useful, primarily for the benefit of the growing anchoritic population:

> Al þis is iseid mine leoue sustren. Þ ower leoue nebbes beon eauer iwent somet wið luueful semblant 7 wið swote chere. Þ ȝe beon aa wið annesse of heorte 7 of wil ilimet togederes . . . ge beoð þe ancren of englond swa feole togederes. twenti nuðe oðer ma . . . of anred lif efter a riwle. Swa þ alle teoð an. alle iturnet anesweis . . . for euch is wiðward oþer in an manere of liflade. as þah ȝe weren an cuuent . . . þis is nunan wide cuð. swa þet ower cuuent biginneð to spreaden toward englondes ende. ȝe beoð as þe moderhus þ heo beoð of istreonet. ȝe beoð ase wealle . . . A weila ȝef ȝe worið ne bide ich hit neauer.[30]

Here the writer addresses not only three original sisters, but a 'convent' of twenty or more who have tried to pull in the same direction as the original three. Without a written guide (which *Ancrene Wisse* is, rather than a rule), they and others joining this 'community of solitaries' would find this more

---

[29] Savage, 'The Solitary Heroine'.

[30] Tolkien, *The English Text*, 130: 'All this is said, my dear sisters, so that your dear faces may always be turned to one another with a loving expression . . . so that you are always cemented together in the oneness of a single heart . . . You are the anchoresses of England, very many together – twenty, now, or more . . . following a single rule, so that all pull one way, and all are turned in the same direction . . . for you are all turned toward one another in a single manner of living, as though you were a single convent . . . This is now widely known, so that your convent is beginning to spread toward the end of England. You are like the mother-house from which they have sprung; you are like the spring . . . [I]f you failed I could not bear it!' *Anchoritic Spirituality*, *AW* Part 4, pp. 140–41.

and more difficult, if not impossible, *without talking to each other*. If they were to do that, they would have to cease to be anchoresses, and become enclosed nuns, holding meetings to discuss practice. Their spiritual director has such a personal stake in the success of their lives as anchoresses that he has taken on the task of producing such a guide. If we take what he says seriously, that seems largely to have been recording the practices and revealing the difficulties they have already faced and overcome, along with adding material from other helpful sources.

While the basis and struggles of the anchoritic life are essentially the same across the centuries, Aelred gives no directions as to setting up this life in the varying circumstances treated in *Ancrene Wisse*. *De Institutione Inclusarum* gives no extended discussion of the outer rule as in *Ancrene Wisse*, which begins with the devotional shape of the day, an outline with built-in flexibility regarding time constraints, personal choice, and the recognition that all are not able to live in the same external circumstances. The goal of the *Wisse* is to enable the anchoresses to 'pull in one direction'. While it appears that Aelred did not have this as a concern, and neither did his sister, the notion of the outer life as servant to the inner is taken very seriously and in greater detail in *Ancrene Wisse*, and has been specifically tailored to this particular brand of the anchoritic life, and this particular 'community of solitaries'.

An apparently offhand comment in the introduction points directly to a particular kind of community participation in the composition of *Ancrene Wisse*:

> Nv mine leoue sustren þis boc ic[h] to deale on ahte destincciouns þ ȝe cleopeð dalen.[31]

The sisters could only call the divisions in his book 'parts' if they knew what he was writing, and already had some idea of its structure. The way the writer puts it, they already call such distinctions 'parts'; the comment is with respect to a request from them that these parts or distinctions be there. The very first part, or distinction, on 'Devotions,' illustrates one reason why even the original sisters might have asked him for a section like this. The prayers are many, time-consuming, accompanied by ritual gestures, and immensely variable. If they were formally structured by a spiritual director, it would ease the burden of *having to decide* which prayers to say when. There is a lot of leeway in what prayers may be said when, or how much of a long prayer can be dropped, and what can be decided by the anchoress when. But there is not too much; she does not have to spend much time or effort planning her prayer-day, and deciding which of several prayers she is going to say on every occasion. Experienced anchoresses, who knew hours of prayers by heart in English and sometimes Latin, might be relieved to have a written text to refer to on troubled days, in times of spiritual turmoil, or when ill; much less experienced members of

---

[31] Dobson, *The English Text*, 13: 'Now, my beloved sisters, I divide this book into eight distinctions, which you call parts.' *Anchoritic Spirituality*, *AW* Introduction, p. 51.

the profession would have something to learn from that had been proven by their own models.

The anchoresses the writer addresses are, it seems, fairly secure in the inner rule, with some qualms about the outer one, but probably not for themselves: they are well-established. *Ancrene Wisse*, particularly Part 8 on the Outer Rule, is largely for the benefit of newer members of the profession, and others whose circumstances were more uncertain. With so many anchoresses trying to live the life – twenty or more – and the perception that many more are likely to join them over the years, the most well-established of them would be well-aware that not all would be able to live in the same physical circumstances. Some, with very few resources, might even need to keep a cow for their nourishment.[32] What seems most likely behind the writing of *Ancrene Wisse* is not only the writer's personal stake in the success of those trying to live an anchoritic life, but the concerns of the community that its less experienced and poorly-endowed members avoid unnecessary difficulties; the outer rule needed to be adaptable to many different conditions of anchoritic life.

The profound knowledge of the anchoritic life the writer displays comes from a long experience with enclosed religious, most likely these very sisters he addresses. He is not one of them, but has been listening to their confessions for a long time; I suggest then that he has been in the process of writing *Ancrene Wisse* not just at their suggestion, but with their help. As a priest, he is preaching to the converted in just the way he has been informed that they need to be preached to, not as spiritual beginners; nevertheless he must write also for new anchoresses now and in the future. The text has to be both practical and useful over their ranges of experience; only with the conscious contribution to the project of the most experienced members of the profession could the writer produce such a text. I suggest that he provided the traditional source material, but compiled it into the basic form we now have it *with* a founding group of anchoresses, in a way we have been unable to consider because of our idea of the author as an inviolable unit, rather than a participant with others in a unified project – all 'cemented together in the oneness of a single heart and a single will'[33] – and book.

Works Cited

Aelred of Rievaulx, *De Institutione Inclusarum*, PL 32

Ayto, John, and Alexandra Barratt, eds., *Aelred of Rievaulx's De Institutione Inclusarum*, EETS o.s. 287 (Oxford, 1984)

Dobson, E. J., ed., *The English Text of the Ancrene Riwle edited from B. M. MS Cotton Cleopatra C. vi*, EETS o.s. 267 (London, 1972)

---

[32] *AW* Part 8, p. 201.
[33] *Anchoritic Spirituality*, *AW* Part 4, p. 140.

Millett, Bella, *Annotated Bibliographies of Old and Middle English Literature, Vol. 2: Ancrene Wisse, the Katherine Group and the Wooing Group* (Cambridge, 1996)

——, 'The Origins of *Ancrene Wisse*: New Answers, New Questions', *Medium Aevum* 61 (1992)

——, and Jocelyn Wogan-Browne, eds., *Medieval English Prose for Women: Selections from the Katherine Group and Ancrene Wisse* (Oxford, 1990)

Robertson, Elizabeth, *Early English Devotional Prose and the Female Audience* (Knoxville, 1990)

Savage, Anne, 'The Solitary Heroine: Aspects of Meditation and Mysticism in *Ancrene Wisse*, the Katherine Group, and the Wooing Group', in *Mysticism and Spirituality in Medieval England*, ed. Pollard and Boenig (Cambridge, 1997)

——, and Nicholas Watson, trans. and intro., *Anchoritic Spirituality: Ancrene Wisse and Associated Works*, with a preface by Benedicta Ward (Paulist Press, 1991)

Squire, Aelred, O.P., *Aelred of Riveaulx* (London, 1969)

Tolkien, J. R. R., ed., *The English Text of the* Ancrene Riwle, Ancrene Wisse, *edited from MS Corpus Christi College Cambridge 402*, EETS o.s. 249 (London, 1962)

Watson, Nicholas, 'The Composition of Julian of Norwich's "Revelation of Love"', *Speculum* 68 (1993)

4

The AB Language: the Recluse, the Gossip and the Language Historian[1]

RICHARD DANCE

I silence ꝣ in hope schal beon ower strengðe . . . for hwa se is muche stille. ꝣ halt silence longe; ha mei hopien sikerliche þ hwen ha spekeð toward godd; þ he hire ihere. ha mei ec hopien þ ha schal singen þurh hire silence sweteliche in heouene. (*Ancrene Wisse*, MS A, 20a 15–20 (ed. Tolkien))[2]

Me seið up on ancren þ euch meast haueð an ald cwene to feden hire earen. A meaðelilt þe meaðeleð hire alle þe talen of þe lond. a rikelot þe cakeleð al þ ha sið ꝣ hereð. swa þ me seið i bisahe. From mulne ꝣ from chepinge. from smiððe ꝣ from ancre hus me tidinge bringeð. Wat crist þis is a sari sahe þ ancre hus þ schulde beon anlukest stude of alle; schal beon ifeiet to þe ilke þreo studen; þ meast is in of chaffle. (*Ancrene Wisse*, MS A, 23a 14–22 (ed. Tolkien))[3]

For a linguistic medium used to express sentiments like these, and one so intimately associated with the origins and composition of the text in which they are found, the 'AB language' has always seemed to have a lot to say for itself. It is one of the most celebrated dialectal and textual varieties of medieval English, ranking with that belonging to Orrm in our characterization of the language at its 'early Middle' stage. It has accordingly been cited and dissected in scholarly writings no less for its own sake than for purposes of excerpting the texts through whose copying it has been transmitted. This well-founded fame is a sign above all of the extent to which the language of Cambridge, Corpus Christi College MS 402 and of Oxford, Bodleian Library MS Bodley 34 has captured the attention of its more recent readers.

The author of *Ancrene Wisse* remarks at one point that 'Me hefde iherde

---

[1] I am grateful to those who have read and commented upon earlier drafts of this paper or have otherwise rendered assistance, especially Merja Black, Margaret Laing, Katie Lowe, Jeremy Smith and Matthew Townend. The opinions expressed here nevertheless remain my own.

[2] 'Your strength must be in silence and in hope . . . for whoever is often still, and keeps silence for a long time, she can hope certainly that when she speaks to God, he will hear her. She can also hope that she will sing sweetly in heaven because of her silence.'

[3] 'People say about anchoresses that practically each has an old woman to feed her cats, a chatterer who chatters all the stories of the land to her; a gossip who cackles out all that she sees and hears, just as they say in the proverb, 'From mill and from market-place, from smithy and from anchoress's house people bring news. Christ knows, this is a sorry saying when an anchoress's house, which should be the most solitary place of all, is connected with the other three places, where there is the greatest nattering.'

oft þ deade speken wið cwike' (A 111b 23–4).[4] The recognition of 'voices from the past' in the writings of bygone ages is of course a sentimental commonplace, but nevertheless much of the attractiveness that scholars of medieval texts have found in the AB works may stem from a perception of the peculiar aptness of such a conceit where they are concerned. The two excerpts cited above might well proscribe the activities of the garrulous, that is, but the colour and vitality of their language do not appear to be restricted by such qualms: hence, alongside the measured idealism of the ascetic and pious in the exegetical note struck by the first passage, we meet with a rather different, more worldly-wise tone in the down-to-earth implications of the second, which effectively encapsulates the verbal characteristics of the local gossip in its plain-talking pithiness even as it chastises any anchoress who would behave in such a manner. These two complementary impressions of authorial 'voice' are, moreover, useful in the characterization of some of the different facets that belong to the AB language, and which govern our attitudes towards the most important aspects of its study. These facets are typically present in the following comment by J. R. R. Tolkien, made in an article which has attained essential status for those interested in AB. Tolkien writes of this dialect as

> an English older than Dan Michel's and richer, as regular in spelling as Orm's but less queer; one that has preserved something of its former cultivation. It is not a language long relegated to the 'uplands' struggling once more for expression in apologetic emulation of its betters or out of compassion for the lewd, but rather one that has never fallen back into 'lewdness', and has contrived in troublous times to maintain the air of a gentleman, if a country gentleman. It has traditions and some acquaintance with books and the pen, but it is also in close touch with a good living speech – a soil somewhere in England. (Tolkien, '*AW* and *Hali Meiðhad*', 106)

In comparing AB to two of the most important Middle English authorial dialects, the fourteenth-century Kentish of Dan Michel's *Ayenbite of Inwyt* and the late twelfth-century East Midland *Orrmulum*,[5] Tolkien marks it out as a linguistic medium of comparable value. The different elements in his rather fond personification, what is more, remain crucial to anybody concerned with the AB language, and with its history and significance in a medieval context: how and why is AB so regular in its spelling, and why should this be important? what are its origins, its links with the past and with the 'former cultivation' of the native vernacular? how far should we see it as rooted in local soil and as relevant to its own time and place, and to what extent do its relationship with 'books and the pen' matter? Questions such as these have taxed the collective language historian in diverse ways

---

[4] 'One has often heard that the dead speak with the living.' He is forbidding any more extensive contact between the 'dead within the world' (the anchoresses) and the 'living'.

[5] The *Ayenbite* is edited by Morris, with introduction and notes in Gradon. The *Orrmulum* is edited in Holt and White; on its spelling see especially Burchfield and the useful notes in Bennett and Smithers, pp. 360–4.

over the years, and numerous studies have seen in AB material relevant to a grasp of various aspects of these problems; it has accordingly been characterized as a prime source in the understanding of medieval language both written and spoken, both conventional and contemporary.

Textual History, or Getting from A to B

Although one could on occasions be forgiven for assuming otherwise, particularly given the degree to which its study has dominated thinking about the text from a linguistic perspective for such a long time, the 'AB language' is not the only language of *Ancrene Wisse* (or of the 'Katherine Group'). To begin with, *AW* exists in versions in both Latin and French as well as English. Even though early arguments as to which of these ought to be regarded as the tongue of composition are now usually regarded as settled in favour of the native vernacular (see e.g. Samuels and the summary in Millett, *Bibliography* 20–1), the particular dialect of medieval English towards which scholarly attention has mainly been turned has itself varied over the years. Choice is of course quite plentiful: even confining ourselves to thirteenth-century English copies of *AW*, there are some five different manuscripts, each diverging from the other in terms of linguistic features, in some cases in smaller ways, in others quite extremely. It was James Morton who first printed *AW* in 1853 as *The Ancren Riwle: a Treatise on the Rules and Duties of Monastic Life, Edited and Translated from a Semi-Saxon MS. of the Thirteenth Century*, and the 'Semi-Saxon MS.' in question is not the now better-known Corpus 402 ('A') but London, British Library Cotton MS Nero A. xiv ('N'). Morton's was to remain the standard available authority until the new editions of the Early English Text Society well into the next century, particularly Tolkien's text of A as late as 1962, and the vast majority of early linguistic studies of *AW* were thus based upon the version found in Morton's book. Morton's sub-title now sounds rather quaint, probably inescapably, even though the implied sense of the language of *AW* as stuck somewhere typologically inconvenient between Old and Middle English is one intuitively encountered by many students today (especially those more used to the apparent modernity of the Middle English of Chaucer or Gower); it is an implication, moreover, that hints at a certain level of continuity with pre-Conquest traditions, a subject that will be returned to below.

The English manuscripts of *AW* and the 'Katherine Group' other than A and B indeed contain a great deal of interest in their own right, and from a purely dialectological standpoint their linguistic features are of course no less important than those of AB itself; the dialects of most are, indeed, quite similar to AB, throw important light on the characteristics of their more famous fellow, and are often not much less internally consistent. Aside from N, with its busy redactor bent on transforming the text into a form more consistent with his own local idiom, they include codices of especial importance for the *AW* tradition like C (London, British Library MS

Cotton Cleopatra C. vi), whose marginal corrections are written in a hand identified by Dobson as that of the author, and T (Cotton Titus D. xviii), which appears to have been copied in a dialect to be located somewhat further north than those of the other early versions.[6] But, despite having so much to tell us about early thirteenth-century scribes and the dialects in which they wrote, it is fair to say that the language of these other versions of *AW* (apart from N) has only recently emerged from the shadow of AB and received any degree of proper attention of its own, this thanks largely to changing attitudes towards the value of certain sorts of dialectal evidence from the period. And even the early primacy of the language of N in terms of initial interest was rapidly overtaken after the efforts of Tolkien in 1929. The impact of these efforts, crucially, has as much to do with textual history and the perception of the written transmission of dialects as it does with linguistic history *per se*. The celebrity of AB is therefore also to be sought first amongst these fields.

With Tolkien's work, the dialect to be found in both MS A of *AW* and MS B of the 'Katherine Group'[7] became established not merely as a shared, homogeneous written medium of exceptional consistency, but was also cemented as the language probably lying behind all the other copies of these texts. This is an important reason for Tolkien's comparison of this language with those of the *Ayenbite* and *Orrmulum*, each of which is normally regarded as surviving in the hand of its author. Tolkien it was who coined the description 'Language (AB)' from a combination of the two (rather fortuitous, though long previously established) manuscript sigla, and he was evidently rather taken with his discovery.[8] His characterization of its nobility and robust patriotism has already been cited above. But if it is possible to overplay the role of the AB language as a latter-day native hero striving, like some linguistic Hereward the Wake, to uphold the pre-Conquest virtues of honest-to-goodness English culture, it can on the other hand hardly be denied that it stands at a crucial place in the development of vernacular writing and text production. Moreover, the impression that it makes at this juncture is an imposing one, and owes a great deal to its qualities as a written medium.

The word 'dialect' is, and was, the more conventional way to describe geographically and/or textually-bounded medieval language varieties on the

---

[6] The only other thirteenth-century English manuscript is Cambridge, Gonville and Caius College MS 234/120 (= 'G'), which contains a heavily rearranged text. On aspects of the language of N see e.g. Zettersten, *Studies*, Jack, 'Archaizing'; on C, esp. Dobson, 'Date' and *English Text*; on T, Laing and McIntosh; and on all these manuscripts, see further Millett, *Bibliography*, 50–53. Standard editions are Day for N; Dobson, *English Text*, for C; Mack, *English Text*, for T; and Wilson, *English Text*, for G.

[7] The standard editions of its texts, and those used here, are d'Ardenne and Dobson; Mack, *Marherete*; d'Ardenne; Millett, *Hali Meiðhad*; and Wilson, *Sawles Warde* (though reference to the text of *Sawles Warde* in Bennett and Smithers, 247–61, is also advisable).

[8] And aside from a throwaway remark in Hall (II:503–4) as to the similarity of A and B, the credit for this discovery is generally accepted to be Tolkien's. His parentheses in 'Language (AB)' are intended to indicate that it is the language of the two manuscripts (which he designated '(A)' and '(B)') rather than the manuscripts themselves ('A' and 'B') that is at issue; but subsequent writers have not by and large followed his notation, and most have chosen the more idiomatic word order 'AB Language', which according to recent convention is also that adopted here.

small scale. Consequently, Tolkien's use of the term 'language' with which to label 'AB', and the fact that this appellation has stuck, is itself telling in connection with its apparently most impressive aspects. The two separate manuscripts A and B, though copied by different scribes, evince an extremely consistent shared orthography. In this AB surpasses the (so far as we are aware) lone text to bear the hallmarks of Orrm's spelling system in the claims it makes as something of a consciously promulgated and controlled medium; it is, it would appear, a form of language cooked up to a high degree of perfection and that deliberately for the purpose of writing. As such it seems to give the lie to the commonly-held preconception that Middle English scribes, following upon the collapse of late Old English normative spelling practices, simply threw up their hands and 'wrote how they spoke'. Set next to an impression like this, one can certainly sense in AB something more akin to the way the modern age treats its written 'language' than to popular ideas about the disorder present in less refined and more rustic 'dialectal' forms. Equally important from Tolkien's point of view was the implication that, if such a carefully orchestrated medium were to survive transmission to at least these two scribes whose work is extant, then they themselves must also have belonged to much the same area as that in which it was devised, and have a good understanding of how to reproduce it; if not, then the vicissitudes inherent in the process of copying and re-copying of manuscripts in the Middle Ages would inevitably, it was assumed, have destroyed its consistency, since it was thought that scribes of this period were incapable of reproducing someone else's spellings without stamping onto them their own regionally-idiosyncratic habits. In the face of these arguments, it is not difficult to see why interest in the scribal dialects of the AB texts other than AB itself dwindled: since it was established as the head of the textual tradition and the dialect of the author(s) of *AW* and the 'Katherine Group', and since its purity theoretically made it a much more reliable witness to 'real' language than did the more or less bastardized dialects of more distant copies, AB became unassailably the first port of call for those concerned with *AW* and 'Katherine Group' matters.

Opinions such as these indeed long dominated AB scholarship, and it is not difficult to see their attractiveness. Few engaged now upon the study of medieval copying habits and textual transmission would be prepared to countenance them so unguardedly, however. Certainly, one cannot prove that A and B descend from originals with identical linguistic features by means such as those employed by Tolkien, most importantly because it has been copiously proven in the meantime that scribes could and in fact did 'translate' consistently between one written dialect and another, often leaving little or no residue from the forms of their exemplar that would tend to illustrate the fact.[9] And the notion, in some senses an alternative, that careful, shared usage might imply a sort of locally authoritative

---

[9] See especially Benskin and Laing (87–97, esp. p. 92), though d'Ardenne (xxxiv–xxxiv) already doubted Tolkien's certainty in the case of AB.

'standardization' (an attitude adopted by some following upon Tolkien's discussion,[10] and prevalent since) is equally open to criticism, since copyists could be just as capable of reproducing the forms in their exemplars 'literatim', i.e. changing little or nothing in the process (Benskin and Laing, 56), regardless of the dialectal variants that they themselves would ordinarily have employed. This latter, the literatim approach, is a feature of copying practice that has recently been used to characterize the earlier part of the Middle English period (and particularly moreover that prior to c.1250, see e.g. Smith, 'Innovation', 65). One could, accordingly, comfortably account for the exactness of the similarities between A and B by the simple expedient of supposing both to be precise copies of manuscripts originally produced by the same single scribe in a (perhaps then idiosyncratic) consistent written version of his own dialect. Since it has long been realized that the scribe of B appears to have had only a very shaky capacity to reproduce AB forms without the guidance of a good exemplar,[11] and has to correct his spellings on numerous other occasions, this theory has quite a lot to recommend it.[12] Despite their clear and important similarities, indeed, A and B have since Tolkien's time been discovered to differ in some relatively minor but intriguing ways, and this has potentially very great significance for our perceptions of the 'homogeneity' of the textual traditions that they contain.[13] Furthermore, and tending to cement the impression that the consistency we see between A and B themselves may be something of a fortuitous accident ascribable to their textual history, is the existence of other pieces of written dialect by yet other scribes that seem to be rather similar to 'AB' in terms of spelling practice and localizable features, but which merely lack the level of *precision* of their more illustrious counterparts. Most notable in this respect are the 'B' hand in MS C (identified by Dobson as that of the author of *AW*), which is very like the language in A and B but with minor variation,[14] and the 'C2' section of *The Owl and the Nightingale* in London, British Library MS Cotton Caligula A. ix.[15]

The status of AB as the sacred cow for those interested in the language of

---

[10] See e.g. Hulbert, Bliss.

[11] As witness the problems he encounters at the opening of *Seinte Marherete*, when he would appear to have run into difficulties of this kind; see Mack, *Marherete*, xiv–xv.

[12] And see especially: Black, 'AB' (also 'Studies', 259–63 and 272–4); Laing, 'Never the Twain', note 8; Smith, 'Standard Language'.

[13] These differences tend to be lexical and syntactic (see Dahood, 12; Jack, 'Pronouns'; Jack, 'Adverbs'; Wilson, 'Continuity', 492–3), but points of orthographic divergence have also been noted (e.g. Jack, 'Oþer').

[14] Thus for example it has the distinctively AB ⟨h⟩ standing for the voiced velar spirant and other typical features such as a tendency to separate orthographically oðer, 'or' from oþer, 'other' (Jack, 'Oþer', 435), but does not agree in all particulars with the A and B handling of ⟨e⟩ and ⟨ea⟩ (on which see below). It also goes out of its way on occasion to correct the main C scribe's spellings, including some of the features described above, where these are out of step with the AB type. See especially Dobson, 'Affiliations', 157–62, 'Date', and *English Text*, xciii–cxl (esp. cxxvi–cxxxv); for some doubts over his identification of this scribe with the author, see also Dahood, 3–4.

[15] i.e. the language of lines 901–60 and 1184–1794 of the poem in this manuscript, which differs from that of the other portions of the text; this difference has been presumed to descend from alternating scribal stints in an exemplar, since the version of *Owl* in Caligula A. ix is the work of a single copyist. See further Stanley, 6–18; Black, 'Studies', 289–91.

AW has therefore in recent years very rightly been moderated; in terms both linguistic and textual it can only be appreciated when put next to all the other written media of the contemporary South-West Midlands, from which we should be careful how far we distinguish it on purely ideological grounds, and its development must be viewed in common with them. Having said all this, though, there remain important reasons why the AB tradition should retain at least something of its conventional significance at the centre of our studies of linguistic phenomena relevant to *AW* itself. Even discarding Tolkien's beliefs based on the practices of scribes, it is still generally supposed that exemplars in something very like the AB language lie behind not only A and B themselves but also all the copies of the texts they contain (i.e. *AW* and the 'Katherine Group'), as well as the several others beside that make up the '*Wohunge* Group',[16] whether these are found in South-West Midland manuscripts (hence N, R, C, G, L) or in those from slightly further afield (T), and there are good reasons for this supposition.[17] If we take all the possibilities into account, of course, it must remain unknown whether AB was the original dialect of these texts, and in some cases in fact this cannot at all be taken for granted;[18] but it seems overwhelmingly likely for the majority that it was, and hence the crucial importance of AB as a very close counterpart to the language of the author of these works secures it an essential place, at any rate, in any study of the texts involved. The fact that it would appear to have belonged to a centre with such a tradition of composition, copying and dissemination also remains vital to our perceptions of it. This is the reason why it is still useful to refer to an 'AB Group' when describing these texts collectively, and why the extreme internal consistency of the surviving examples of the scribal dialect central to their existence must retain a special significance, even if the fact of A and B sharing a language is no longer accorded the same weight. Rightly or wrongly, AB itself persistently strikes one as a written language suited as the counterpart to the production of such an important series of texts and such a vital local copying tradition; and as the product of a centre, or perhaps even a single mind, as keen on the promotion of regular copying habits as it was on the regulated order explicitly defined in the text of *AW*.

Moreover, even if the scribe of B were not a 'native' user of this written language himself (and probably he was not), the forms contained in his production remain a part of that language; they give virtually as authoritative a witness to its lexemes and locutions, many of which of course fail to appear in A through the accidents of differences in subject matter or style,

---

[16] Found in MSS L, N, R and T and edited in Thompson and in Morris, *Homilies*. In addition to sigla defined already, R = London, British Library MS Royal 17 A. xxvii, and L = London, Lambeth Palace Library MS Lambeth, p. 487.

[17] On textual history see the standard editions and the remarks in Millett, *Bibliography*, 6.

[18] Thus the strong possibility that *þe Wohunge of ure Lauerd* in MS T derives from a version in a more northerly dialect is treated in the recent study of T by Laing and McIntosh. *On God Ureisun of Ure Lefdi* in N (edited in Morris, *Homilies*) would also from its rhyme evidence appear to descend from an original probably of the East Midlands, though this has been comparatively little noted (but see Hall II:535; Dobson 'Lengthening', 133–4).

as does A itself. 'AB' remains, in short, as handy a description of the language jointly attested in the two manuscripts as we are likely to find, and is the term retained below, in precisely this sense.

Spelling and Dialect: 'A soil somewhere in England'?

The conventions of spelling adopted in AB, and their consistency, are therefore of paramount importance in what they contribute to our perception of it. If these spellings seemed 'less queer' to Tolkien than those taken up by Orrm, then this is not surprising, for they own in important ways a greater connection than does the system of *The Orrmulum* to others with which the modern scholar is familiar. When Orrm devised new spelling conventions of his own, suited to the needs of portraying his local dialect and with particular stress placed on the elimination of ambiguity, he undertook a rather more noticeable break from past traditions of writing and produced something distinctly different in important details from what we see in Old English.[19] But while the AB system is in many ways as careful, and keen to avoid the confusion of certain potential homographs, it is by no means as iconoclastic in its outlook. Like the other (and closely comparable) orthographies of the South-West Midlands in the thirteenth century, it maintains strong links with the spelling of older, pre-Conquest traditions. Indeed, with the overlay of some more recent habits demonstrating the influence of originally French conventions, it can be viewed as taking its lead directly from these earlier traditions. This element of continuity consists not only in the maintenance of distinctively 'Old English'-looking graphical combinations (e.g. the digraphs ⟨eo, ea⟩, though now with somewhat different phonetic implications), but can extend even to the use of some letters in purely diacritic functions, just as they were employed in Old English.[20]

This continuity with the Anglo-Saxon past is hardly unexpected in the South-West Midlands, since it was here if anywhere in England that the traditions of pre-Conquest copying and reading were held most dear for longest. Worcester is especially significant in this connexion: it had been an important centre of manuscript culture for many generations, and was moreover the only see to retain an Anglo-Saxon bishop, St Wulfstan, after the Norman reforms. Old English texts, especially homilies by luminaries like Ælfric and Wulfstan, but also a great variety of other things, continued to be read and copied there well into the twelfth century and beyond, as collections such as that in the Oxford, Bodleian Library MS Bodley 343

---

[19] Orrm's use of doubled consonants to imply a short preceding vowel in a closed syllable (viz. his spelling of ⟨onn⟩, 'on') is one of his most innovative and characteristic features; but his reforms go further, extending even to the creation of a new version of ⟨g⟩ (see e.g. Burchfield; Scragg, 29–31).

[20] Hence ⟨eo⟩ can stand for a back vowel after ⟨sch⟩, as in *scheome*; compare the OE spelling *sceamu* (= *scamu*). This tradition is maintained even though the ambiguity that the ⟨e⟩ was inserted to resolve in OE (i.e. the quality of the preceding consonant group) has been removed by the ME differentiation of ⟨sc, sk⟩ and ⟨sch⟩; see further below, and moreover d'Ardenne, 175.

bear witness (see especially Irvine). These have their counterpart in repeatedly updated and transmitted pieces like those that we now know as the 'Lambeth Homilies' (London, Lambeth Palace Library MS Lambeth 487, also from the South-West Midlands). Textually and linguistically these are a fascinating mish-mash of the old and the more recent, and illustrate how hard it is to separate in such circumstances the traditions of the eleventh, twelfth and later centuries into discrete units.[21] The considerable efforts made by the owner of the famous 'Tremulous Hand' of Worcester to gloss and to understand Old English manuscripts as late as the thirteenth century (see Franzen) are another indication, if any were needed, that the traditions they contained did not simply fall at the hurdle of the Norman Conquest: especially in the West Midlands, they underlie the entire sustenance and development of native vernacular literacy in an age when the production of *new* works was, it seems, only rarely envisaged. But if programmes like those of the Tremulous Hand imply that interest in the older books in English persisted in his day, they point equally clearly to the difficulties inherent in the exercising of that interest at a period so far removed from the time at which the Anglo-Saxon tradition had flourished, and moreover in a place linguistically different in important ways from its focal point (i.e. what was western Mercia as opposed to Wessex). By this stage, if new works were to be produced in the English language, even though their homiletic bent and alliterative stylistic bias demonstrate their debt to the vitality of the earlier tradition,[22] then the need was manifest for the appearance of more thoroughly *modern* spelling practices with relevance to the language of their time. The orthography of AB and its development must be viewed against this backdrop: it is a system eminently traditional in its pedigree, but one with an applicability to the language not only of the time but also of the region to which its texts belong, and is in these ways both thoroughly conventional and refreshingly at home and up-to-date. Given the necessarily heightened awareness of the written medium possessed by those who would wish to produce texts in the native vernacular at this period, as well as the very local loyalties and allegiances of their efforts at a time when any sort of national or even provincial standard could scarcely be imagined, we should expect little else.[23]

[21] On the textual history of the Lambeth Homilies see especially Sisam; they are edited in Morris, *Homilies*.

[22] The continuity of prose style from the later OE period into the AB texts and beyond has of course been the subject of much comment in the past; see e.g. Wilson, 'Continuity'; Millett, 'Continuity'; and also Millett, *Bibliography*, 21–3 for a summary.

[23] See further on this topic Smith, 'Standard Language', who remarks upon 'a shift from the restricted literacy of the Anglo-Saxon period, focused on a few provincial and monastic centres, to a parish-based literacy associated with the rise of characteristic twelfth-century institutions, such as grammar schools'. It can be questioned how far, as part of this shift, the conventions of West Saxon OE spelling have been mingled with those of a tradition of copying in a written dialect more proper to the West itself, since this is unclear. Certainly, South-West Midland texts survive from older periods in a West Mercian guise (cf. especially the glosses to the Vespasian Psalter, ed. Kuhn), and the existence of the similarly local *Life of St Chad* in a twelfth-century manuscript also has a bearing on the matter (ed. Vleeskruyer). But given the extent to which the surviving eleventh- and twelfth-century codices look to the West Saxon-dominated written OE culture for their contents, it would be very unwise to rule out this latter tradition as the primary

Hence, the language in the A and B manuscripts, along with the similar systems to be found in associated codices like R, N and C (and also other pieces in manuscripts from the South-West Midlands like Laȝamon's *Brut* and *The Owl and the Nightingale*), are of fundamental importance in establishing the development of the new spelling traditions of 'Middle English' as they emerge from a knotty period of transition leading back ultimately to the written language of the Anglo-Saxons. Because of their relatively confined usage and dialectal loyalties, moreover, these written forms also reflect features of the underlying spoken language that may help us to determine local provenance; certainly, they offer various challenges to those interested in understanding thirteenth-century English phonology and dialectology. For these reasons, amongst numerous others, the detailed study of every aspect of the AB language has blossomed considerably since Tolkien's early exhortations. One of the first analyses of the dialect in traditional philological terms was by Tolkien' s student d'Ardenne (*Iuliene*), and her work remains the best guide to the details of AB, particularly its orthography and grammar. Other attempts on the various sub-systems of the dialect particularly worthy of mention are the full-scale studies of Zettersten (*Studies*; vocabulary, phonology), Diensberg (*Morphologische*; verbal morphology), and de Caluwé-Dor (verbs), alongside a multitude of more specific analyses, culminating in the recent applications of modem dialectological criteria by Smith ('Innovation', 'Typology') and Black ('Studies'). These and other studies are recommended to the reader interested in the detailed characterization of the AB language.[24]

Aside from its characteristic consistency, the choices made by the spelling system of AB are in most respects very like those made by others of the early Middle English period, especially in the South-West Midlands, with which it has a great deal in common. Whilst AB spellings express a clear continuity with Old English orthography, the general tendency is towards making distinctions where possible based on the graphic forms now available, and this has in several cases resulted in the tidying up of ambiguities in the pre-Conquest system. Many conventional written features of Middle English, ultimately derived from French practice, have therefore by now firmly taken hold: the digraph ⟨ch⟩ replaces OE ⟨c⟩ when standing for the affricate /tʃ/ (e.g. AB *child*, 'child'),[25] ⟨c⟩ is retained for plosive /k/ but only before back vowels (*cald*, 'cold'), and the essentially novel ⟨k⟩ appears before front vowels (*kene*, 'keen'); a parallel development disambiguates ⟨sc, sk⟩ (= /sk/, as in *sculle*, 'skull' and *skile*, 'skill') from ⟨sch⟩

---

source of South-West Midland early ME spelling habits. The fact that AB resembles VP in important ways is hardly surprising given that both reflect spoken dialects of a very similar area (and see further Black, 'Studies', 259–71). Some scholars (e.g. d'Ardenne, 178) have however viewed the correspondence in vowel symbols between e.g. AB *fearen* and VP *fearan*, 'to go', as likely to indicate something more significant than this (d'Ardenne romantically describes it as 'a thread of connection with the ancient West').

[24] For a fuller summary of linguistic accounts of AB see especially Jack in Millett, *Bibliography*, 17–18.

[25] Examples are taken from either A or B, though preference is given to common forms that occur in both.

(= /ʃ/, as in *schip*, 'ship').[26] As elsewhere in Middle English, the carolingian ⟨g⟩ has similarly been brought in to separate the plosive /g/, which it represents, from the semi-vowel /j/, for which insular ⟨ȝ⟩ is maintained in initial position (compare *godd*, 'God' with *ȝe*, 'you'). This reorganization is therefore primarily of help in determining pronunciation, at least in broad terms. It should not be assumed that the trend towards nicer distinction was always that followed: in the case of the vowel symbol ⟨u⟩, for instance, the weight placed on French-based spelling norms has in fact *created* ambiguity, since ⟨u⟩ in South-West Midland early Middle English now stands not only for the high back rounded vowels /u(:)/ as it did in Old English (e.g. AB *ut*, 'out'), but also for its front rounded counterparts /y(:)/, as in French (hence AB *lut*, 'little'; cf. French *tu*), whereas Old English had a separate symbol ⟨y⟩ for these latter.

Nevertheless, the move towards clarity in the representation of the sounds belonging to the contemporary language seems the dominant ambition. This ambition is moreover expressed particularly strongly by the AB system in some orthographic developments largely peculiar to itself. These include the careful working out of spellings for individual words. Hence, for instance, *godd*, 'God' and *god*, 'good' are very consistently (if not always, especially in B) distinguished, even though doubling of the ⟨d⟩ in the former can have no phonetic significance. Something analogous has happened to differentiate *oþer*, 'other'[27] from *oðer*, 'or', although this openly contradicts the otherwise tightly-maintained rationalization of the Old English system that results elsewhere in AB ⟨þ⟩ only initially, and ⟨ð⟩ only word-medially and finally. And this drive for clarity extends also to the use of particular letters in ways virtually unique to AB. The best example is to be found in one of the functions of ⟨h⟩, and it is worth going into detail in describing it.

Unlike in most other systems, that is, the symbol ⟨h⟩ has been extended in AB to replace OE ⟨ȝ⟩ in representing the voiced velar fricative [ɣ]; this is the sound found in forms like OE ⟨boȝa⟩, 'bow', ⟨daȝas⟩, 'days' (nom. and acc. pl.), which develops into later Middle and Modern English [w] (compare e.g. the modern *bow* and the old-fashioned or dialectal *early daws* = 'early days'). Elsewhere in early South-West Midland Middle English, this sound is usually spelt ⟨ȝ⟩ when it is retained (so compare AB *dahes* with C *daȝes*).[28] This development in spelling is more difficult to explain than it is to cite as a good example of AB taking its own clearly worked-out path in things orthographic. The availability of ⟨h⟩ as a representation of both voiced and voiceless velar fricatives ([ɣ] and [χ]) is not in itself hard to understand: it turns probably on the fact that, after the devoicing of final [ɣ] in later Old

---

[26] The sounds [f] and [v], both spelt ⟨f⟩ in Old English, are now also differentiated as ⟨f⟩ and ⟨u⟩ (AB *feader*, 'father', *heouene*, 'heaven'; OE *fæder*, *heofon*), though this also represents a change in the English phonological system, with the phonemicization of [v], an allophone of /f/ in OE.

[27] By the AB stage most regularly in the plural and in A; see Jack, 'Oþer'.

[28] The AB usage is shared with the spelling of R, which in other matters shows very great similarity to AB (see especially Jack, 'Language'), and is also found (though not consistently) in the otherwise quite AB-like 'C2' section of *The Owl and the Nightingale* in Caligula A. ix (see note 15 above, and Stanley, 9).

English (as in e.g. *burh*, 'stronghold'), [ɣ] and [χ] were put in contrastive distribution, and could be regarded as members of the same phoneme; they could accordingly be spelt with the same graph ⟨h⟩, just as the Old English system itself allows ⟨f⟩ as the graphic sign for both [f] and [v], likewise allophones of the one phoneme at this period.[29] This is the usual explanation offered for the use in AB of ⟨h⟩ for both sounds (see e.g. d'Ardenne 173). While it may stand as a phonological rationale for the *availability* of ⟨h⟩ to depict [ɣ], however, this idea fails to account for this option being exercised by the users of the AB system, since it is far from obvious or traditional: such uses of ⟨h⟩ are at best rare in Old English as a whole, and do not feature conspicuously in the late West Saxon literary norm whose orthographic practices (found in the homilies in the Ælfric and Wulfstan tradition so frequently copied during this period) were probably those with which post-Conquest scribes were most familiar;[30] the absence of the feature from most other early Middle English orthographies, and moreover the loss of the [f], [v] parallel (the two sounds are now kept apart graphically), also seems to require that we offer some motivation for AB's very obvious divergence. A case can accordingly be made for the use of ⟨h⟩ for [ɣ] in a slightly earlier stage of AB as a deliberate orthographic strategy, with the aim of helping to eliminate another ambiguity in the more conventional spelling system. Hence in the C MS ⟨ȝ⟩ is still used to represent [ɣ], and also for [j] between vowels. The occasional confusion in signification that this could create between the sounds in different words like C *deiȝen*, 'to die' (with [j], AB *deien*) and *seȝe*, pret. pl. of 'to see' (with [ɣ] AB *sehen*) may have been felt to be a problem, particularly given the efforts that had already been made to distinguish between the other potentially ambiguous uses of ⟨ȝ⟩ that had come down from Old English spelling and which were noticed above (i.e. ⟨ȝ⟩ for both [g] and [j]).[31] Probably more to the point, there were individual words which could themselves demonstrate varying pronunciations in early Middle English; OE *wrēgan*, 'to accuse' (cf. C *wreȝen*, AB *wreien*) is one of these, and can be found with either a palatal or a guttural medial consonant in medieval texts. The desire to clarify which sound was meant in such cases may well lie behind Orrm's clear distinction of the two, which he makes in his own inimitable way – compare his spellings *wreȝenn* and *wreȝ*[h]*enn* of the respective variants (and see e.g. Burchfield). The same will also hold for the system as found in the 'B' correcting hand in the C MS, which has adopted ⟨h⟩ for the guttural spirant (e.g. *wahes*, 'walls') and retains the ⟨ȝ⟩ for medial [j] (cf. 'B'*ifeȝet*, AB *iueiet*, 'joined'); there is now no chance of confusing these sounds, and the grounds for the original importation of ⟨h⟩ are still clear. This 'B' is in many other ways very like the full AB system, but nevertheless as here appears slightly

---

[29] See note 26 above.

[30] Campbell (§§446–7) and Hogg (§7.64) cite forms like *dahum*, 'days', as most frequent in the OE Boethius.

[31] The ambiguous signification of ⟨ȝ⟩ inter-vocalically was to a great extent the result of the merger of the OE unstressed vowels in a sound spelt ⟨e⟩, since now the quality (frontness or backness) of the vowels surrounding ⟨ȝ⟩ could not be taken as a sign of its own characteristics as they could ordinarily be in OE.

more primitive in some of its preferences (Dobson, *English Text*, cxxx–cxxxviii), something that would chime with the notion that it is the hand of the author of *A W*.[32] AB as we find it in A and B themselves has, on the other hand, abandoned the usage of ⟨ȝ⟩ for intervocalic [j], preferring ⟨i⟩ in such positions, probably owing both to the continued influence of French-derived orthography and the sense that medial [j] had by this time become vocalized and formed part of a diphthong in the first syllable of words like *wreien*. There is hence no living reason to maintain ⟨h⟩ for [ɣ] any more, and its appearance thus in AB must have become purely traditional; it remains as the relic of an orthographic reorganization that was originally well-motivated, but which belongs to a stage of the AB language already somewhat in the past by the time of the A and B manuscripts. Nevertheless, the existence of such a studied reorganization of the graphic tools available to it fits well with what else we know of the AB system in this regard; many of its distinctions seem to be based on a very high awareness of its role as a *written* language, whose potential ambiguities would have to be resolved in the visual medium. And the importance of these features lies not merely in their regularity, since the majority of the comparable thirteenth-century spelling systems of the *A W* Group also perform with some measure of economy and consistency; if AB stands out, and in important characteristics it continues to do so, it is in the particular care and intelligence with which its spellings function in relation to one another, as a *system*.

Specific features of AB spelling like these, together with the implications for phonological development they bear, of course carry considerable value for investigations into the development of English sounds in this part of the country. They also go some way towards pinpointing when the system was solidified. The acceptance of significant aspects of French-derived orthographic practices, next to the continuation of so many originally pre-Conquest habits, help us with the general period. More importantly, furthermore, the degree to which the precise nature of the symbols used still seems to concur fairly well, if not absolutely perfectly, with the language of the extant manuscripts tends to demonstrate no great gap of years between the organization of the orthography and their copying.[33] Dobson (*Origins*, 122–6) puts the working-out of the distinctive features of the AB spelling system, perhaps as a sort of 'house style', in the last quarter of the twelfth century on precisely these grounds.

As regards the more precise localization of the dialect behind 'AB', there are probably limits to the degree of accuracy we can obtain on linguistic grounds alone, especially during a period when the geographical coverage provided by comparable texts is not at all dense. There are nevertheless

---

[32] The main hand of C does itself vary between ⟨ȝ⟩ and the idiosyncratic ⟨chȝ⟩ for [ɣ], perhaps demonstrating an earlier or peculiar attempt at solving the same problem; compared to the AB ⟨h⟩, however, C's practice is clumsy, and is applied far from consistently.

[33] That there was *some* gap is indicated by those features already noted as betraying development since their inception: i.e. the use of ⟨h⟩ and ⟨ȝ⟩/⟨i⟩; and the spellings *oþer*, *oðer* (see Jack, 'Oþer'). There was also probably some breakdown in the precise distinction between the AB values of ⟨e⟩ and ⟨ea⟩, on which see below (and Jack, 'Second Fronting').

many features of dialectal phonology that can be noted as implied in the spellings.[34] Characteristic of the west in general are, for instance, the ⟨u⟩ in words like AB *lut*, 'little' (compare East Midland *lite*) and the ⟨eo⟩ in *beon*, 'to be' (East Midland *ben*), both of which indicate the South-West Midland retention of front rounded sounds that were unrounded further east; ⟨o⟩ in *mon*, 'man' (East Midland *man*) also points to a rounded sound, and is typical of West Mercia already in the Anglo-Saxon period.[35] The digraph ⟨ea⟩ in AB *wealle*, 'well' is more restricted, and therefore more specifically indicative of locality;[36] other spellings that reflect idiosyncrasies of this particular part of the South-West Midlands include ⟨o⟩ rather than more general ⟨a⟩ in words like AB *marhen*, 'morning', and consistent ⟨t⟩ for ⟨d⟩ finally in positions of low stress (especially in the weak past participial ending *-et*).[37] An important western feature is in addition the sound change known as 'second fronting'. The details of this change are too complex to go into here, and the interpretation of the spellings that relate to its products has often been controversial; nevertheless, these spellings include the distinctive ⟨e⟩ rather than ⟨a⟩ in words like AB *hwet*, 'what', *dei*, 'day' (cf. East Midland *hwat*, *dai*), alongside AB ⟨ea⟩ in e.g. *fearen*, 'to go' (East Midland *faren*).[38] This latter digraph, when indicating a short sound, is indeed peculiar to the AB tradition itself. It appears to represent a sound like that spelt ⟨æ⟩ (i.e. /æ/) in Old English,[39] in the retention of which AB is

---

[34] There are useful summaries also in Zettersten, *Studies*, 284–5, and Bennett and Smithers, 399–401; and on the phonology in general see d'Ardenne, Language §§1–57.

[35] See further Jordan/Crook, respectively §§39–42, 65 and 84, 30. The ⟨eo⟩ stands for the descendants of OE /e(:)o/, but phonetic changes have by the stage of AB probably resulted in the monophthongization of the earlier sounds to give the front rounded /ø(:)/ (as witness the use of the same digraph for French-derived /ø(:)/, e.g. in *preoue*, 'proof'). Other sounds typical of Anglian OE also feature strongly in AB: thus e.g. West Saxon /æ:/ as the descendant of PGmc. */æ:/ corresponds to close /e:/ in Angl. (e.g. AB *weren*, 'were' (WS. *wæron*)); OE /æ/ before /l/ plus consonant is retracted to /ɑ/ (or perhaps was never fronted) in Anglian (AB *ald*, 'old'; cf. OE West Saxon *eald*); the *i*-mutation product of OE /æ:ɑ/ is /e:/ in Anglian dialects (thus AB *afleiet*; cf. West Saxon *afliegan*, *aflygan*); and the sound change known as 'Anglian smoothing' means that West Saxon /æ(:)ɑ/ and /e(:)o/ correspond to close monophthongs in Anglian ME before certain palatal consonants (e.g. AB *hehe*, 'high', *feht*, 'fight'). See e.g. Hogg, respectively §§3.22–5, 5.15, 5.82 and 5.93.

[36] It represents the *i*-mutation product of earlier OE /ɑ/ before /l/ plus consonant, probably /æ/ (see Hogg §5.79(2); d'Ardenne, Language §1).

[37] i.e. respectively the unrounding of OE /o/ to /ɑ/ between a liquid and a labial, and the devoicing of final /d/ to /t/ in unemphatic circumstances (see d'Ardenne, Language §§12 and 33).

[38] A good summary and discussion of previous work can be found in Jack, 'Second Fronting'; see also the grammars (e.g. Campbell, §130; Hogg §§5.87–92). A distinctive, recent view of the causation of the change is in Black, 'Studies', 366–75. Phonetically, it seems to involve a raising of earlier OE /æ/ (fronted PGmc. */ɑ/) in most environments to a sound spelt ⟨e⟩, just as earlier OE /ɑ/ (unfronted PGmc. */ɑ/) appears to have been fronted to a sound spelt ⟨æ⟩ (presumably /æ/), which could then undergo back mutation in susceptible environments (cf. AB *fearen*, VP *fearan*, 'to go'). It has been argued that the raising of earlier /æ/ was to /e/, resulting in a merger with earlier OE /e/ (see d'Ardenne, §§1–5; Dobson, *English Text*, lxxiii note 1); but recent theories prefer a different, more open phoneme (more like /ɛ/, see Kristensson, and Zettersten, *Studies*, 66–71). It is further debatable as to whether this sound was itself falling together with /æ/ by the time of AB, as some spellings seem to imply it was. It is however the opinion of Jack ('Second Fronting') that such was not the case at the time the AB system was itself worked out, judging by the extent to which AB ⟨ea⟩ and ⟨e⟩ from these sources are kept separate in the orthographic system.

[39] Though historically it represents the merger of short /æɑ/ (from back mutation and breaking, e.g.

unique amongst its contemporary South-West Midland orthographies. In the other traditions, this sound has continued to develop and appears either as ⟨a⟩, as elsewhere in the country (= /a/, thus R, C, G, etc.), or as ⟨e⟩ (hence N, probably = /e/); compare R *harde*, N *herde*, with AB *hearde*, 'hard'. The ordinarily consistent manner in which AB contrasts its short vowels is accordingly of great interest to those scholars concerned with the development of the English phonological system.

Morphological features also firmly support a western localization, though space does not allow a detailed examination here.[40] Especially diagnostic in general terms is the relative conservatism of the accidence. Though much analogical levelling has taken place in the nominal and adjectival inflexions, no inroads from the largely Scandinavian-influenced North-East Midland paradigms have been made at all as yet (thus in the third person plural we find AB *ha, hare, ham* rather than the precursors of MnE *they, their* and *them*). In the area of verbal morphology AB is, in particular, virtually intact when put next to Old English. And especially striking are the weak verbs of class two, whose shapes represent another of the most systematically-applied preferences of AB, in that they demonstrate a refinement of the Old English system: verbs with 'light' stem syllables take *-ien* in the infinitive (and have corresponding endings elsewhere in the paradigm), those with 'heavy' stems take *-in* (compare AB *lokin*, 'to look' (OE *lōcian*) with *luuien*, 'to love' (OE *lufian*)).[41]

From considerations like these, and moreover comparison of AB with the other written dialects of the period, there can be no doubting the validity of assigning it to the South-West Midlands, and more particularly the accepted wisdom of a home in the Herefordshire/Shropshire area. Beyond this, matters become more problematic, and the issue is inevitably tied up with non-linguistic verdicts about the origins of the AB texts, especially *AW*, which have a long and complex history of their own. The best-known of such localizations of recent years, Dobson's famous (and often ingenious) association of *AW* with Wigmore (*Origins*), in particular now looks dubious on certain fronts (and see especially Millett, 'New Answers');[42] confidence to the point of identifying single institutions, let alone individual authors, perhaps may now more sensibly be put aside. Nevertheless it has to be admitted that we still have to deal with strong circumstantial grounds that link the A MS with Wigmore, just as B also has firm associations with the same area.[43] The evidence of later texts, belonging

---

fearan, 'go', *hearde*, 'hard') and simple /æ/ (e.g. *wealle*, 'well'), presumably in a late OE /æ/. OE long /æːɑ/ (⟨ea⟩) and /æː/ (⟨æ⟩) also appear to have met in the long open /ɛː/, distinguished from close /eː/, which is still spelt ⟨e⟩ (cf. AB *dead*, 'dead' and *leafdi*, 'lady' with AB *kepen*, 'keep'). See d'Ardenne, Language §§1, 20–21.

[40] D'Ardenne's is still the major discussion (Language §§58–129); for a useful summary of the features germane to dialect, see also Bennett and Smithers, 401–2.

[41] Discussed first of all by Tolkien, '*AW* and *Hali Meiðhad*', 117–26, and see also d'Ardenne, Language §§114–15.

[42] And for an excellent summary of the monuments in the debate over the origins of *AW*, see Millett, *Bibliography*, 7–13.

[43] i.e. A was given to Wigmore by one John Purcel c.1300; B contains later (sixteenth-century at

to an age very different in scribal outlook and encompassing intervening years that may have seen significant shifts in dialectal characteristics, is only to be applied carefully. Nevertheless the considerable weight of recent investigations bringing the techniques and data of the *Linguistic Atlas of Late Mediaeval English* (McIntosh *et al.*) to bear upon the problem, especially the excellent study by Black ('Studies'), also strongly suggest the same small area of northern Herefordshire and southern Shropshire as overwhelmingly the most likely district to be the home of the AB language.[44]

Based on the linguistic evidence alone, however, it has to be said that a transparent capacity for exact localization is not the most striking of AB's legacies. When one comes to describe the features that mark out this written dialect, especially as against its often very similar contemporaries, one returns to its particular qualities *as* a written language, which have manifested themselves repeatedly in the discussion above. Perhaps, as Tolkien expressed it, it is its consistency and systematic awareness that lend AB what can be regarded as 'the air of a gentleman', something which he, and numerous amongst those writing since, seem to have valued more highly than they did its exact geographical placement. In short, that the idiosyncrasies and uniquely worked-out features of AB belong somewhere and perhaps even to someone in particular is not to be doubted, and they lead us quite a long way in the right direction, but it is this very fact itself rather than that particular place that may ultimately be the more fruitful pursuit, certainly in terms of medieval English textual culture. The firm basis of the AB language in a real local variety of English is manifest, but the impression it has made on us thus far associates it most clearly with the ascetic and the studious; its acquaintance with 'the pen' is one of its most defining characteristics.

Vocabulary: the Parochial and the Eclectic

The use to which the AB language is put in the texts we have is moreover not merely a *written* one. It belongs not only to *literate* but to *literary* culture, and this distinction has important ramifications when one comes to look at aspects of the written works that survive in the AB guise beyond their orthography, phonology and morphology, and especially at their vocabulary. It should be pointed out of course that aspects such as this,

least) scribblings by several people who belong to the Herefordshire locality. For doubts about the relevance of this information, however (note for instance that Purcel belonged to a South Shropshire family), see Millett, *Bibliography*, 11.

[44] Black ('Studies', 271) describes the area in question as that 'around Ludlow, Wigmore and Leinthall the medieval Mortimer lordship in the borderlands of Herefordshire and Shropshire'. She notes the similarity in particular to AB of the later London, British Library MS Harley 2253; Oxford, St John's College MS 6; and Longleat, Marquess of Bath's MS 5, all of which can be localized to within this precise region. Much the same conclusions as to area had clearly been reached earlier by e.g. Smith (cited in Millett, *Bibliography* 11 n. 7) and Samuels (cited in Zettersten, *Studies*, 287 n. 1). And note that the other most important early South-West Midland manuscripts of *AW*, C and N, are usually now localized respectively to northern and southern Worcestershire (see Smith, 'Tradition', 62).

more consciously willed and controlled by the individual author, pertain more readily to the stage of composition of the texts than to the scribal forms in which we find them, and by which their close relationship can rather more safely be defined; since we have already noted the possibility that *AW* and the 'Katherine Group' began life in some different form, whether considerably or only slightly different from what we have, one should add the caveat that the lexis to be found in the AB texts cannot be said necessarily to belong to the 'AB dialect' purely and simply. But the vocabulary of the works in question nevertheless presents us, by and large, with a sense of cohesion and similarity and, given the prevalent assumption that these works were first written down in a dialect not too alien from that in which posterity preserves them, one can still venture a few observations about 'the AB lexis'.[45]

It may be said to begin with that, at least in certain features, the vocabulary of the AB texts is as parochial and locally-distinctive as its orthography: even though their lexis may not help us place the language any more precisely, that is, it clearly has properties belonging to a particular area and time and characteristic elements all its own. Hence there are numerous words that either entirely escape record in any other English tradition, Old or Middle, than that descending into the manuscripts of the 'AB Group' (e.g. *heascin* 'to persecute', *edene* 'threshing floor', *keis* 'henchmen', *cang* 'stupid', *nurð* 'noise', *riuen* 'to sew up loosely'), or which are but rarely found anywhere else, and which testify to an idiosyncratic local word-hoard with its own favourite lexical ploys.[46] Many of these items apparently have connotations suited to an inclusive, pragmatic social function: they are local words aimed at local speakers, and one wonders how far some of them would have been understood further afield; the number of changes made to the vocabulary in other manuscript copies (especially N) in fact indicates that several were not felt acceptable elsewhere.[47] This type of vocabulary may indeed have its counterpart in the mode of address that surfaces frequently in the AB texts, especially the more

---

[45] The agreements between A and B in terms of vocabulary far outweigh their dissimilarities, many of which may depend upon stylistic differences between *AW* and the Katherine Group texts as much as upon any historical or dialectal divergence. Hence the somewhat more old-fashioned flavour of some of the Katherine Group lexis, whilst possibly ascribable to an earlier date than *AW* (and see below on the number of French-derived words), can equally be viewed as dependent upon the more traditional, formulaic character of the style of these texts, something which facilitates the *passé* more readily than it does the novel. A good example is the fact that the Katherine Group texts contain the last recorded instance of the native word for 'unicorn' (*anihurnde*, gen. pl., *Seinte Marherete*; cf. B 16/13), whereas *AW* contains the first appearance of its replacement, *unicorne* itself (cf. A, 32b 27). But *anihurnde* in *Seinte Marherete* is found tellingly in the alliterative phrase 'anihurnde hornes', 'the horns of unicorns', whose etymological pun would also collapse with the substitution of the Latinate term.

[46] From the standpoint of later Middle English, especially those varieties that came under the influence of the East Midland dialects, the AB vocabulary will inevitably appear still more idiosyncratic; see especially Diensberg ('Lexical Change'), who notes that words typical of the earlier copies of *AW* (e.g. *eadi*, 'blessed', *þolien*, 'suffer', as well as the 'gossip' words *meaðelen* and *chaffle*) are frequently replaced in later ones. This sort of reduction in lexical variety, especially as regards words that may have been felt more provincial or archaic, is a feature of the later ME period (with the notable exception of most alliterative poetry).

[47] See e.g. Zettersten, 'Studies', 294, and Jacobsson, 187–8.

instructive *AW* and *Hali Meiðhad*, whose apparent aura of homespun commonsense, often characteristically direct or earthy, is manifested through their stylistic features as much as their subject matter. It is of course very difficult for the modern reader to claim a definitely 'colloquial' or 'conversational' tone for a passage of Middle English, and we should be aware of the perceptual distance involved when we attempt to make such identifications.[48] Nevertheless, the variety of stylistic modes encompassed by the AB texts has long been recognized, and an informal note certainly seems to be struck, if anywhere, in the passage from *AW* A 23a 14–22 quoted at the head of this paper; consider especially its cautionary proverb about anchoresses and gossips, its parenthetically irked exclamation 'wat crist . . .', and its demotically expressive accumulation of descriptive epithets, none of which is at all flattering to its referent ('ald cwene . . . meaðelilt . . . rikelot').[49]

It is this at times cosy, and not necessarily subtle, familiarity with their audience, still obvious enough to the modern reader, that is one of the most attractive aspects about the language of these texts. We can still gather much from the tone of the author of *AW* when he admonishes the anchoresses about the wicked ways of the world, and recognize the feelings motivating the writer of *Hali Meiðhad* (whether or not they are one and the same) when he warns of the frustrations peculiar to domestic discord. Our perception of these pragmatic authorial 'voices' can however have its pitfalls, especially if it lulls us into the impression on occasion that there is no study or skill about the expressive potential of AB, that we have access to a particular, very local blend of words that can lead us directly, if we know how to dissect it properly, into a precise idea about where and when it must belong. This impression should be rejected not only as unhelpful in scholarly terms, but also as rather unflattering to the considerable artistic skills of the authors of the AB texts.[50]

Even without gossipy old women spreading titillating tidings from parish to parish, and even somewhere as apparently off the beaten track as the backwoods of northern Herefordshire, the reality of communication in twelfth and thirteenth-century England could be a much more complicated affair than we might sometimes give it credit. The choice of language itself was of course by no means cut and dried, especially in a learned and written context. We can very often presume competence for contemporary writers in French and Latin as well as in English; the latter, indeed, must still have been something of a poor relation, despite the noble tradition of English letters that survived in the West Midlands, and these things render cross-influence in lexical choice no less crucial than in literary-stylistic features. The complexity of the situation at this time and the inter-connectedness of these three tongues in the products of literate culture are indeed exemplified well by *AW* itself,

[48] For some comments on methodology, see e.g. Rygiel.
[49] On the colloquial in *AW*, see further especially Clark, '*Scharpe*'.
[50] At any rate von Lindheim, in contrasting pre- and post-Conquest prose styles more generally, certainly overplays this sense of colloquialism when he writes of 'the drastic outspokenness and slangy character of early ME speech' (24 n. 1).

which is not only a text composed in English and subsequently translated into each of the other languages belonging to its learned climate, but moreover contains as part of its own input in its turn a significant number of words themselves derived originally from Latin and French. The AB texts of course contain, historically-speaking, foreign words of a variety of other origins; especially interesting are those derived from Old Norse, and there is also a small number of loans from Welsh. But in terms of the perception of users contemporary with the composition of the AB works, it is much more difficult to separate words of these other origins from the native vocabulary, and we cannot necessarily claim for them any overtones peculiar to them as groups, since their descent (especially in the case of the Scandinavian borrowings) must ordinarily have been far less transparent than those from French or Latin.[51] Some of these latter, particularly the Latin-based, are longstanding elements within English, of course, going back to Old English and even beyond (viz. *abbat* ('abbot'), *win* ('wine'), etc.); and the newer set of Latinisms in AB does not in fact amount to a very large number.[52] The words in AB originally borrowed from the Romance languages are nonetheless crucial. The majority descend from French, perhaps another sign that the anchoresses were familiar with this language (see *AW*, MS A, 11a 22–3); most are relatively recent interlopers whose status as fully assimilated into English can at times be questioned (see Dor). Certainly they very often represent novelties, and it is fair to say that the proportion of the lexis in the AB texts that is French-derived (i.e. the number of different lexical items of this origin), and especially that of *AW* at approximately ten per cent (c. 570 words), is higher than it had been in any prior stage of English, even if this figure falls far short of the more than fifty per cent Romance derivations reckoned for Chaucer (Zettersten, 'French'). Some discussion has taken place amongst students of AB as to the significance of these words, and of their somewhat different proportions in the different AB texts. Some have cautiously proposed (Clark, 'Divergence';

---

[51] As regards the Norse-derived vocabulary, I have reckoned elsewhere (Dance) that it extends to more than 150 separate items in A, and about 120 in B. These cover conceptual fields as wide-ranging as the legal (*lahe*, 'law', *grið*, 'peace', *utlahe*, 'outlaw'), the militaristic (*genge*, 'troop', *brunie*, 'corselet'), and the natural world (*gris*, 'piglets', *wengen*, *rote*, *skiwes*), as well as extending to very numerous more general means of describing action, emotion and impression (*deien*, *keasten*, *semen*, *taken*, *skile*, *meoke*, *derf*, *hap*, *callen*, *greiðe*, *gein*, etc.). None need necessarily be regarded as a direct borrowing from ON into the South-West Midlands, and hence their evidence for 'local' AB usage of a restricted kind is at best dubious, despite Dobson's attempt to use them to localize AB (*Origins*, 115–16 and 118–21). Even the rare Welsh-derived element in the AB texts (*genow* (*Seinte Marherete*); see Breeze, 'Geneu', *cader* (*AW*, *Hali Meiðhad*), *keis* (*Sawles Warde*), perhaps *baban* (*AW*; see Breeze, 'Baban' (though also Zettersten, *Studies*, 27)), although it points to the western parts of England, does not have to mean we should put AB in the westernmost parts of Herefordshire or Shropshire themselves, since Welsh speech cannot have been unusual much more widely across the South-West Midlands even after the Norman Conquest (see especially Gelling, 70). The word *cader*, 'cradle', is indeed recorded for modern dialects in Wright (1898) in counties as far afield as Yorks., Lancs., Cheshire and Staffs. (Zettersten, *Studies*, 285).

[52] See especially Zettersten, *Studies*, 281–2, where Latin-derived items are numbered at only about twenty (presumably discounting those already found in OE). Most predictably belong to the language of religious observance (e.g. *apocalipse*, *cherubines*, *testament*, *pater noster*) and its preoccupations (*ypocrisis*, *torpor*), though others intrude from fields like that of natural history (*pellican*, *strucoin* ('ostrich'), etc.).

Dobson, *Origins*, 157) that a case can be made for their demonstrating the order in which the texts were composed, hence the more words of French origin, the later the text;[53] this is now, however, usually regarded as something of a naive proposition (see especially Bately, 67–77), given the differences in subject matter and style amongst the AB works. Nonetheless, that the numbers of French-derived lexemes finding their way into English texts is so relatively high may well be significant in what it tells us about the developing acquisition of French vocabulary at this period, and more especially about the words regarded as suitable and necessary for written works in English. There are many amongst the originally Romance elements that own no especially learned or stylistically charged connotations, nor belong to any particular subject with overtones of Norman culture; so note words like *manere, itachet* ('fastened'), *ioie, estoires* ('stories') and especially the basic conjunction *me*, 'but', which are perhaps more relevant to an appreciation of the everyday vocabulary of the intended audience of the AB texts.[54] Nevertheless, many of the French-derived items do possess flavours of a more particular sort, notably amongst fields like theology and religious practice (e.g. *abstinence, blasphemie, temptatiun, freres, riwle* and *religiun* itself), fashion and the courtly life (*broche, curteisie, peintunge, urnamenz*), social order and relationships (*noble, gentil, poure, seruin*), and more martial concerns (*banere, baret* ('fighting'), *peis, turneiment, weorre*), and these are a tiny sample.[55] That they are comfortable in a language which equally clearly favours at other turns the pragmatic and distinctly ungenteel is as manifest a reminder of the multitude of tastes and flavours which AB is capable of expressing as are its stylistic strategies: it has long been recognized that its authors are as capable in their use of techniques borrowed from Latinate rhetorical composition (giving a studied and deceptively simple turn to the clarity of its arguments) as in those representing more homespun alliterative and rhythmical collocation.[56]

Lexical choice is of course intimately tied up with style. It is this most especially that means that an impression of available vocabulary based simply on the words that occur, without giving any consideration to the reasons (in a literary-artistic sense) *why* they occur, is doomed to misrepresent the facts. There is indeed a considerable variety of different words in the AB texts, far more so than in some contemporary works.[57] Many of these words lexicalize the same or very similar concepts, and there can be no doubt

[53] *AW* has the highest number (about 10.5 per cent in Parts 6 and 7), *Seinte Marherete* the lowest (2.5 per cent); see Clark, 'Divergence'.

[54] Words relating to culinary expertise may also belong to a more 'homely' sphere (e.g. *beast, seim* ('fat, grease'), *potage*).

[55] For a full list see Zettersten, 'French'.

[56] On Latinate devices, see especially Dolan, Clark ('Seint Austin') and further Millett ('Continuity' and *Hali Meiðhad*, lii–lvi), Shepherd, lix–lxxiii, and Samuels, esp. pp. 7–8; and on the alliterative structure of the saints' lives and style generally in the Katherine Group, Millett, 'Continuity', 'Saints' Lives'. Millett, *Bibliography*, 21–3, has summary discussion and further references.

[57] Laȝamon's *Brut* (ed. Brook and Leslie), for example, with its sober, formulaic chronicler's style, has a far smaller proportion of different words than the AB texts, and its narrative technique accordingly appears less impassioned or eclectic than comparable examples of storytelling in AB (notably the Katherine Group saints' lives).

that a large number are simply superfluous if looked upon from this point of view alone. But any application of semantic theory must highlight the fact that nature abhors plain synonymy,[58] and that there must be other reasons for such an apparently high level of redundancy in the lexical stock; these reasons are to be sought in the variety of stylistic modes expressed in the AB texts, and the wealth of vocabulary required to fill out their more expansive moments. In addition to the proverbial and earthy, and the learned and often French-based, that is, there are plenty of occasions in the A and B manuscripts when their language simply takes off in the narrative mode. It sustains remarkable stretches of purple prose that owe much of their impact to the expressiveness of their vocabulary, something in which the sequences of variation and repetition inherent especially in passages invoking the native alliterative tradition are so steeped. Such effects are most noticeable in the consistently alliterative saints' lives of the 'Katherine Group' (though not without parallel by any means in the enumerating rhetoric of *AW* and *Hali Meiðhad*).[59] As an example, note the following, which occurs in *Seinte Marherete*. The heroine is here being menaced by a terrifying dragon:

He strahte him ⁊ sturede toward tis meoke meiden, ⁊ geapede wið his genow up-on hire ungeinliche, ant begon to crahien ⁊ crenge wið swire, as þe þe hire walde forswolhe mid alle. (ed. Mack, 20/34–22/3).[60]

There is not much in this passage that could be described as 'necessary' in purely practical terms; all we need to know in order to further the narrative is that the dragon approaches Margaret, and perhaps that it does not look particularly friendly.[61] But the emotive impact of the extended phrasing that is used, in line with the emphatic repetition, goes far beyond the requirements of the bare narrative, and much of this impact is achieved through the use of some very unusual and highly charged words. Thus the pair 'crahien ⁊ crenge' are decidedly rare and not a little sound-symbolic; the [g] alliteration in the second clause is achieved through the use of two ultimately Norse-derived items (*geapede*, *ungeinliche*), the first a rarity at this period[62] and the second a hefty and perhaps nonce product of the native word-formation process; and this sequence is topped off with a *hapax legomenon*, the only occurrence in written English anywhere of the Welsh-derived *genow*, 'jaws'. We cannot, of course, tell how common each of these

---

[58] For a useful recent description of lexical systems and their role in language change, see Smith, *Study*, 112–26.

[59] Closely comparable to the passage from *Seinte Marherete* cited below is indeed a sequence of patterned clauses given by Dolan (210) from *AW* (A, 53a 15–17), which also incorporates the collocation 'crenge wið swire'.

[60] 'He twisted and moved towards this meek maiden, and gaped with his jaw threateningly upon her, and began to stretch and arch his neck, as one who intended to swallow her up completely.'

[61] The passage in the Latin original is of course also necessarily dramatic, but the English redactor is translating as ever very freely and expands it significantly. There is nothing in the Latin text as printed by Mack corresponding to the dragon's actions described in the lines from B cited above, excepting perhaps that the monster 'erexit se in medio car[ceris], et fortiter sibillauit', 'stood erect in the middle of the cell and shrieked loudly' (Mack, *Marherete*, 133 (11, pp. 26–7)).

[62] It is the only thirteenth-century South-West Midland occurrence of *gape*, and the R MS replaces it with the native ȝeonede, 'yawned' (R 21/35).

words might have been in the spoken language of the AB writers, or what specific associations they might have had otherwise.[63] But it is their rarity in literary texts, and most especially the stylistic density created by their combination here, that makes their choice on the part of the author of *Seinte Marherete* interesting and effective. He is clearly prepared to go to creative lexical lengths not only, one feels, to fill alliterative gaps, but for the sheer showiness that is implicit in the alliterative tradition.[64] There are many words that one senses are recorded in the AB texts by virtue of their potential usefulness in moments of literary expressiveness like this; and therefore that the circumstances of their occurrence are perhaps just as, if not more, significant than that they were known and used in the South-West Midlands at this period. At any rate, we should be very careful how far we see this broad and resourceful vocabulary as a key simply to the 'everyday words' current in the spoken dialect behind the AB language.

The author of *AW* may then well have heard 'þ deade speken wið cwike'. But we should not allow the understandable, comfortable impression of authorial voice that permeates the AB texts to divert us from the plain fact that they are *written* documents. Local dialect features are crucial to their existence, and supply a very great deal of the flavour of the AB language, but they are handled by writers (perhaps a single writer) who express their learning and erudition on the written page through a language that controls its colourfully disparate traditions in vocabulary and style as adeptly as its scribes do the orthographic system in which it is couched. If at times it seems eloquent to the point of garrulousness, then this cannot be regarded as a fault for the very reason that it *is* written down, and a proper, edifying thing to read or to hear read: it is not idle gossip or untamed loquaciousness of the sort dismissed by the author of *AW*, but a controlled, authoritative language that only flatters to deceive us otherwise.

The interest to be found in the lexis of the AB works is then another, and often-neglected reason, for studying the language behind them. Its words and their combination can be manifestly literary, and draw their members ultimately from diverse foreign models as well as from the homespun cosiness of local tradition, just as the stylistic devices which they are used to fill can be characterized according to a variety of different aims and flavours, and just as their orthography can be described as both uniquely local and classically durable in its particular engagement with the needs of written culture. The tension between the written and the spoken, the literary and learned next to the commonplace and parochial, plays a central role in our perception of 'Language AB'. It is hardly surprising that, despite being saddled with a rather pedestrian modern name, it continues to fascinate those who read it.

[63] In an analysis of this same passage, in fact, Clark ('Stylistics', 368) chooses to see *crahien* and *genow* as belonging to 'familiar speech' and therefore contributing an effect of immediacy.

[64] For the same reasons, some of the diction and effects otherwise typical of later alliterative poetry are also recognizable in the AB texts; amongst collocations featuring Norse-derived vocabulary, for example, conspicuous are combinations such as *ro* and *reste*, *gold* and *gersum*, *king* and *keiser*, *wa* and *wontreaðe* (and see the relevant entries in the *Middle English Dictionary*).

Works Cited

Bately, Janet, 'On Some Aspects of the Vocabulary of the West Midlands in the Early Middle Ages: the Language of the Katherine-Group', in *Medieval English Studies presented to George Kane*, ed. E. D. Kennedy, R. Waldron and J. S. Wittig (Cambridge, 1988), 55–77

Bennett, J. A. W., and G. V. Smithers, eds., *Early Middle English Verse and Prose*, with a glossary by Norman Davis, 2nd edn (Oxford, 1968)

Benskin, Michael, and Margaret Laing, 'Translations and *Mischsprachen* in Middle English Manuscripts', in *So Meny People, Longages and Tonges: Philological Essays in Scots and Mediaeval English presented to Angus McIntosh*, ed. Michael Benskin and M. L. Samuels (Edinburgh, 1981), 55–106

Black, Merja Riitta, 'AB or Simply A? Reconsidering the Case for a Standard', *Neuphilologische Mitteilungen* 100 (1999), 155–74

——, 'Studies in the Dialect Materials of Medieval Herefordshire', 2 vols., Diss. (Glasgow U, 1997)

Bliss, A. J., 'A Note on "Language AB"', *English and Germanic Studies* 5 (1952–3), 1–6

Breeze, Andrew, 'Welsh *Baban* "Baby" and *Ancrene Wisse*', *Notes and Queries* n.s. 40 (1993), 12–13

——, 'Welsh *Geneu* "Mouth, Jaws" and the Middle English *Seinte Marherete*', *Notes and Queries* n.s. 40 (1993), 13–14

Brook, G. L., and R. F. Leslie, eds., *Laȝamon: Brut*, 2 vols., EETS o.s. 250 and 277 (Oxford, 1963–78)

Burchfield, R. W., 'The Language and Orthography of the Ormulum MS', *Transactions of the Philological Society* (1956), 56–87

Campbell, A., *Old English Grammar* (Oxford, 1959)

Clark, Cecily, '*Ancrene Wisse* and *Katherine Group*: A Lexical Divergence', *Neophilologus* 50 (1966), 117–24

——, 'As Seint Austin Seith . . .', *Medium Aevum* 46 (1977), 212–18

——, 'Early Middle English Prose: Three Essays in Stylistics', *Essays in Criticism* 18 (1968), 361–82

——, '"Wið Scharpe Sneateres": Some Aspects of Colloquialism in *Ancrene Wisse*', *Neuphilologische Mitteilungen* 79 (1978), 341–53

Dahood, Roger, '*Ancrene Wisse*, the Katherine Group, and the *Wohunge Group*', in *Middle English Prose: a Critical Guide to Major Authors and Genres*, ed. A. S. G. Edwards (New Brunswick, 1984), 1–33

Dance, Richard William, *Words Derived from Old Norse in Early Middle English: Studies in the Vocabulary of the South-West Midland Texts* (Tempe, forthcoming)

d'Ardenne, S. R. T. O., ed., *þe Liflade ant te Passiun of Seinte Iuliene*, 1936, Bibliothèque de la Faculté de Philosophie et Lettres de l'Université de Liège 64, reprinted with corrections as EETS o.s. 248 (Oxford, 1961)

d'Ardenne, S. R. T. O., and E. J. Dobson, eds., *Seinte Katerine, Re-Edited from MS Bodley 34 and the Other Manuscripts*, EETS s.s. 7 (Oxford, 1981)

Davis, Norman, and C. L. Wrenn, eds., *English and Medieval Studies presented to J. R. R. Tolkien on the Occasion of his Seventieth Birthday* (London, 1962)

Day, Mabel, ed., *The English Text of the Ancrene Riwle, edited from Cotton MS Nero A. xiv, on the basis of a transcript by J. A. Herbert*, EETS o.s. 225 (London, 1952 (for 1946))

de Caluwé-Dor, Juliette [= Dor], *Forms and Meanings of the Verbs Contained in MS*

Bodley 34, Publications de l'association des médiévistes anglicistes de l'enseignement supérieur 7 (Paris, 1982)

Diensberg, Bernhard, 'Lexical Change in the "Ancrene Riwle", with Special Consideration of the Romance and Scandinavian Loanwords', in *Symposium on Lexicography V: Proceedings of the Fifth International Symposium on Lexicography, May 3–5, 1990 at the University of Copenhagen*, ed. Karl Hyldgaard-Jensen and Arne Zettersten, Lexicographica, series maior 43 (Tübingen, 1992), 295–313

——, *Morphologische Untersuchungen zur Ancrene Riwle. Die Verbalflexion nach den MSS. Corpus Christi College Cambridge 402, B. M. Cotton Cleopatra C vi, B. M. Cotton Nero A xiv* (Bonn, 1975)

Dobson, E. J., 'The Affiliations of the Manuscripts of *Ancrene Wisse*', in Davis and Wrenn, 128–63

——, 'The Date and Composition of *Ancrene Wisse*', Sir Israel Gollancz Mermorial Lecture 1966, *Proceedings of the British Academy* 52 (1966), 181–208

——, ed., *The English Text of the Ancrene Riwle, edited from B. M. Cotton MS Cleopatra C. vi*, EETS. o.s. 267 (Oxford, 1972)

——, 'Middle English Lengthening in Open Syllables', *Transactions of the Philological Society* (1962), 124–48

——, *The Origins of Ancrene Wisse* (Oxford, 1976)

Dolan, T. P., 'The Rhetoric of *Ancrene Wisse*', in *Langland, the Mystics, and the Medieval English Religious Tradition: Essays in Honour of S. S. Hussey*, ed. Helen Phillips (Cambridge, 1990), 203–13

Dor, Juliette, 'Post-dating Romance Loan-words in Middle English: Are the French Words of the *Katherine Group* English?', in *History of Englishes: New Methods and Interpretations in Historical Linguistics*, ed. Matti Rissanen, Ossi Ihalainen, Terttu Nevalainen, and Inna Taavitsainen, Topics in English Linguistics 10 (Berlin and New York, 1992), 483–505

Franzen, Christine, *The Tremulous Hand of Worcester: a Study of Old English in the Thirteenth Century* (Oxford, 1991)

Gelling, Margaret, *The West Midlands in the Early Middle Ages* (Leicester, 1992)

Gradon, Pamela, ed., *The Ayenbite of Inwyt, Volume II: Introduction, Notes and Glossary*, EETS o.s. 278 (Oxford, 1979)

Hall, Joseph, *Selections from Early Middle English, 1130–1250*, 2 vols. (Oxford, 1920)

Hogg, Richard M., *A Grammar of Old English, Volume One: Phonology* (Oxford, 1992)

Holt, Robert, and R. M. White, eds., *The Ormulum*, 2 vols. (Oxford, 1878)

Hulbert, James R., 'A Thirteenth-Century English Literary Standard', *Journal of English and Germanic Philology* 45 (1946), 411–14

Irvine, Susan, ed., *Old English Homilies from MS Bodley 343*, EETS o.s. 302 (Oxford, 1993)

Ives, D. V., 'The Proverbs in the "Ancren Riwle"', *Modern Language Review* 29 (1934), 257–66

Jack, G. B., 'Archaizing in the Nero version of *Ancrene Wisse*', *Neuphilologische Mitteilungen* 80 (1979), 325–6

——, 'The Language of MS Royal 17 A. xxvii', *Studia Neophilologica* 63 (1991), 129–42

——, 'Negative Adverbs in Early Middle English', *English Studies* 59 (1978), 295–309

——, '*Oþer* in the "AB Language"', *Anglia* 96 (1976), 431–5

——, 'The Reflexes of Second Fronting in the AB Language', *English Studies* 71 (1990), 289–306

——, 'Relative Pronouns in Language AB', *English Studies* 56 (1975), 100–7

Jacobsson, Ulf, Review of Zettersten [*Studies*], *Studia Neophilologica* 38 (1966), 181–94

Jordan, Richard, *Handbook of Middle English Grammar: Phonology*, trans. and rev. Eugene Joseph Crook, Janua Linguarum, Series Practica 218 (The Hague and Paris, 1974)

Ker, N. R., ed., *Facsimile of MS Bodley 34*, EETS o.s. 247 (London, 1960)

Kristensson, Gillis, 'Old English "Second Fronting" Revisited', *NOWELE* 1 (1983), 61–76

Kuhn, Sherman M., ed., *The Vespasian Psalter* (Ann Arbor, 1965)

Laing, Margaret, ' "Never the Twain shall meet": Early Middle English – the East–West Divide', in *Placing Middle English in Context*, ed. Irma Taavitsainen, Terttu Nevalainen, Päivi Pahta and Matti Rissanen, Topics in English Linguistics 35 (Berlin and New York, 2000), 97–124

——, and Angus McIntosh, 'The Language of *Ancrene Riwle*, the Katherine Group Texts and *þe Wohunge of ure Lauerd* in BL Cotton Titus D. xviii', *Neuphilologische Mitteilungen* 96 (1995), 235–63

Logan, H. M., *The Dialect of the Life of Saint Katherine: a Linguistic Study of the Phonology and Inflections*, Janua Linguarum, Series Practica 130 (The Hague and Paris, 1973)

Mack, Frances M., ed., *The English Text of the Ancrene Riwle, edited from Cotton MS Titus D. xviii (together with The Lanhydrock fragment, Bodleian MS Eng. th. c.70, edited by A. Zettersten)*, EETS o.s. 252 (Oxford, 1963)

——, ed., *Seinte Marherete, þe Meiden ant Martyr*, EETS o.s. 193 (London, 1934)

McIntosh, Angus, Michael Benskin and M. L. Samuels, eds., with the assistance of Margaret Laing and Keith Williamson, *A Linguistic Atlas of Late Mediaeval English* (Aberdeen, 1986)

Middle English Dictionary, ed. Hans Kurath, Sherman M. Kuhn and Robert E. Lewis (Ann Arbor; London, 1956)

Millett, Bella, with the assistance of George B. Jack and Yoko Wada, *Annotated Bibliographies of Old and Middle English Literature Volume 2: Ancrene Wisse, the Katherine Group and the Wooing Group* (Cambridge, 1996)

——, ed., *Hali Meiðhad*, EETS o.s. 284 (London, 1982)

——, ' "Hali Meiðhad", "Sawles Warde", and the Continuity of English Prose', in *Five Hundred Years of Words and Sounds: a Festschrift for Eric Dobson*, ed. E. G. Stanley and Douglas Gray (Cambridge, 1983), 100–8

——, 'The Origins of *Ancrene Wisse*: New Answers, New Questions', *Medium Aevum* 61 (1992), 206–28

——, 'The Saints' Lives of the Katherine Group and the Alliterative Tradition', *Journal of English and Germanic Philology* 87 (1988), 16–34

Morris, Richard, ed., *Dan Michel: Ayenbite of Inwyt*, rev. Pamela Gradon, EETS o.s. 23 (London, 1866; rev. edn 1965)

Morris, Richard, ed., *Old English Homilies of the Twelfth and Thirteenth Centuries*, EETS o.s. 29 and 34 (London, 1868)

Morton, James, ed., *The Ancren Riwle: a Treatise on the Rules and Duties of Monastic Life, edited and translated from a Semi-Saxon MS of the Thirteenth Century* (London, 1853)

Rissanen, Matti, Ossi Ihalainen, Terttu Nevalainen, and Irma Taavitsainen, eds., *History of Englishes: New Methods and Interpretations in Historical Linguistics*, Topcs in English Linguistics 10 (Berlin and New York, 1992)

Rygiel, Dennis, '*Ancrene Wisse* and "Colloquial" Style: a Caveat', *Neophilologus* 65 (1981), 137–43

Samuels, M. L., 'Ancrene Riwle Studies', Medium Aevum 22 (1953), 1–9

Scragg, D. G., A History of English Spelling, Mont Follick Series 3 (Manchester and New York, 1974)

Shepherd, Geoffrey, ed., Ancrene Wisse, Parts Six and Seven (London and Edinburgh, 1959)

Sisam, Celia, 'The Scribal Tradition of the Lambeth Homilies', RES n.s. 2 (1951), 105–13

Smith, Jeremy J., An Historical Study of English: Function, Form and Change (London and New York, 1996)

——, 'A Linguistic Atlas of Early Middle English: Tradition and Typology', in History of Englishes: New Methods and Interpretations in Historical Linguistics, ed. Matti Risannen, Ossi Ihalainen, Terttu Nevalainen, and Irma Taavitsainen, Topics in English Linguistics 10 (Berlin and New York, 1992), 582–91

——, 'Standard Language in Early Middle English?', in Placing Middle English in Context, ed. Irma Taavitsainen, Terttu Nevalainen, Päivi Pahta, and Matti Rissanen, Topics in English Linguistics 35 (Berlin and New York, 2000), 125–39

——, 'Tradition and Innovation in South-West Midland Middle English', in Regionalism in Late Medieval Manuscripts and Texts: Essays Celebrating the Publication of 'A Linguistic Atlas of Late Medieval English', ed. Felicity Riddy (Cambridge, 1991), 53–65

Stanley, Eric Gerald, ed., The Owl and the Nightingale (1960); 2nd edn, Old and Middle English Texts (Manchester, 1972)

Thompson, W. Meredith, ed., þe Wohunge of Ure Lauerd, EETS o.s. 241 (London, 1958)

Tolkien, J. R. R., 'Ancrene Wisse and Hali Meiðhad', Essays and Studies 14 (1929), 104–26

——, ed., Ancrene Wisse: the English Text of the Ancrene Riwle edited from MS Corpus Christi College, Cambridge 402, EETS o.s. 249 (London, 1962)

Vleeskruyer, R., ed., The Life of St Chad: an Old English Homily (Amsterdam, 1953)

von Lindheim, Bogislav, 'Traces of Colloquial Speech in OE', Anglia 70 (1951–2), 22–42

Wilson, R. M., ed., The English Text of the Ancrene Riwle, edited from Gonville and Caius College MS 234/120, EETS o.s. 229 (London, 1954)

——, 'On the Continuity of English Prose', Mélanges de linguistique et de philologie, Fernand Mossé in Memoriam, Ouvrage publié par le concours du Centre National de la Recherche Scientifique (Paris, 1959), 486–94

——, ed., Sawles Warde: an Early Middle English Homily edited from the Bodley, Royal and Cotton MSS, Leeds School of English Language, Texts and Monographs 3 (Kendal, 1938)

Wright, Joseph, ed., The English Dialect Dictionary, being the complete vocabulary of all dialect words still in use, or known to have been in use during the last two hundred years, 6 vols. (London, 1898)

Zettersten, Arne, 'French Loan-words in the Ancrene Riwle and their Frequency', Mélanges de philologie offerts à Alf Lombard à l'occasion de son soixante-cinquième anniversaire par ses collègues et ses amis, Études Romanes de Lund 18 (Lund, 1969), 227–50

——, Studies in the Dialect and Vocabulary of the Ancrene Riwle, Lund Studies in English 34 (Lund, 1965)

5

The Anglo-French Lexis of *Ancrene Wisse*: a Re-evaluation

D. A. TROTTER

Introduction

The aim of this chapter is to review the evidence for Anglo-French influence on the Middle English *Ancrene Wisse*. By this I mean not necessarily that there was an Anglo-French original. On balance the case for a direct Anglo-French exemplar for the existing ME versions seems hard to make (Samuels; Wada, xxiv). What is indisputable, though, is that there evidently was, behind the text, a linguistic context where Anglo-French was important. In itself this is not a new idea. Where I hope nonetheless to be able to add to the discussion is in emphasizing that it is *Anglo*-French which is involved. This is an important point which goes beyond the issue of the language or languages involved in the composition of *Ancrene Wisse*, touching as it does on a question of major significance for the history of the lexis of English as a whole. It is clearly crucial to determine where this massive influx of 'loanwords' came from; whether it is correct to think of them as loanwords at all; and whether the chronology normally assumed for the process is accurate. In the vast majority of studies of 'French loanwords' in Middle English texts, it is assumed that 'French' was all of a piece, whether its literary manifestations were generated in England or France; that it was irremediably 'foreign', so that loanwords from it may be discussed in the same way as borrowings from Latin, Scandinavian, or Dutch; that, if a distinction needs to be made between 'French' and 'Anglo-French', then it can de drawn by fitting the surviving loanwords into the matrix of morphological and phonetic criteria formulated by Neo-Grammarian scholarship of the nineteenth century and adopted by converts of the twentieth; and that all 'French loanwords' are of the 'cultural' type, and may thus be regarded as deliberate and isolated acquisitions rather than as part of an everyday process of exchange characteristic of all more or less bilingual communities. I shall take a rather different approach. Firstly, it will be regarded as axiomatic that in late-medieval England, English and Anglo-French co-existed in close proximity, influenced one another incessantly, and ultimately merged in the hybrid which is modern English. That Anglo-French was no longer a vernacular is irrelevant. For the scribal class, which is what we are concerned with, it was at the very least an ever-present language of record (Jefferson and Rothwell, 280–281; Rothwell, 'Arrivals',

159, 165). Secondly, the shortcomings of the documentary evidence available mean that we have to accept that it will not resolve everything.
   I shall reconsider three issues:

1. The status and function of 'French loanwords' in *Ancrene Wisse*, against
   a background of endemic multilingualism, and in the light of modern
   studies of code-switching and of the lexis of Anglo-French;
2. A number of loanwords allegedly derived from hypothetical French or
   Anglo-French etyma (Zettersten, *Studies*; 'French loan-words');
3. Hybrid loanwords or 'loanblends' in *Ancrene Wisse*.

Language Contact and Metalinguistic Knowledge

The general, and erroneous, supposition has been that words of Romance
origin in Middle English texts are 'French' (cf. Rothwell, 'Arrivals', 144);
French was, after Latin, *the* prestige language across much of western
Europe. The 'loanwords' are 'borrowings' in the normal sense of the term,
that is, isolated lexical items appropriated in order to fill gaps in the host
language's lexicon, or to adorn or enhance a vernacular which had
aspirations to literary grandeur. Loanwords of this (traditional) type are
typically assumed to be borrowed and used consciously, with a clear
awareness on the part of the writer that an essentially 'foreign' element
has been incorporated into his language. But a basic problem is that neither
the historical nor the sociolinguistic evidence suggests that Anglo-French
may be treated as though it was a 'foreign' element in medieval England.
This elementary fact seems not always to have been noticed. The distinguished English medievalist Derek Brewer writes that 'Chaucer learned
Continental French, the "French of Paris", and any influence from Anglo-
French was indirect and general' (Brewer, 8). There is copious evidence in
print to gainsay such a statement (Rothwell, 'Chaucer', 'Trilingual England'), even if it were not inherently implausible as a statement of how
language contact functions in a demonstrably multilingual society like
medieval England (Short; Trotter, 'Language Contact'). Later Anglo-
French of course has not fared well at the hands of its own specialists,
and no doubt the neglect of it by Anglicists is in part attributable to the
harsh verdicts passed on it by the founding fathers (and mothers) of Anglo-
Norman studies (Rothwell, 'Faus franceis'). Part of the explanation for
such misunderstandings may also be that scholars whose main interest is
ME literature have unwittingly adopted an inappropriate model which,
stressing as it does the emergence of ME balanced against the decline of
Anglo-French, constructs a false binary opposition within the field of
literary production (cf. Calin; Trotter, review of Calin), which is then
unconsciously carried over into discussion of the two languages concerned.
The implicit argument is that these co-exist, perhaps occupying different
positions in a situation of diglossia, but that they are, fundamentally,
apprehended by their users as separate entities. Yet a disturbing amount

of evidence from medieval England in respect not only of Middle English and Anglo-French, but also of medieval Latin, suggests that this convenient separation of languages may owe more to modern ideologies of linguistic development than to contemporary perceptions of linguistic reality. Users plainly drew (as all multilinguals do) on each and every language at their disposal, and it seems, moreover, that they did not understand the distinctions between different vernaculars (or between vernaculars and Latin) in such a clear-cut way as we now wish to (Rothwell, 'Anglo-French Lexical Contacts'; 'Lexical Borrowing'; 'Trilingual England'). The voluminous material published by Tony Hunt on glossaries reveals, on virtually every page, a measure of confusion concerning metalinguistic labelling which it would be presumptuous to dismiss as simple ignorance. Time and time again, words are marked 'gallice' when they are not French but English; conversely, the indication 'anglice' is still more frequently applied to words which are transparently French (Rothwell, 'From Latin'; Trotter, 'Language Contact'). The mixed-language texts edited and studied by (amongst others) Laura Wright and Herbert Schendl are further evidence of a form of linguistic coalescence which goes far beyond what is normally envisaged by those who used the somewhat derogatory terms 'contamination' or 'interference'. The *Dictionary of Medieval Latin from British Sources* (DMLBS) provides ample evidence that the users of medieval Latin exploited the vernacular languages at their disposal with a frequency which implies not only familiarity, but scant respect for any idea that these were somehow languages which it would be inappropriate to use. Forms in DMLBS such as **abatare** < *abatre*, **bacinus** < *bacin*, and **bachelarius** < *bacheler* indicate, too, that the traditional expectation that Latin > (Anglo-)French has to be revised for form as well as semantic content.

Multilingualism, 'Loanwords', and Code-Switching

This state of affairs alone calls into question the whole notion of the 'loanword' in such a context. This discussion, even with regard to literary texts, makes little sense without reference to multilingualism, and to its concomitant (and indeed constituent process), code-switching. In a study of the *York Memorandum Book*, William Rothwell has shown conclusively not only that traditional concepts of separate and separable languages must be revised in this type of document, but also that, together with language-mixing of various types, there is an abundance of hybrid forms (Rothwell, 'Aspects'; cf. Rothwell, 'Arrivals'). Thus, for example, there are forms with ME suffixes such as *-man* or *-werk*, preceded by an Anglo-French stem *tasche*. We are dealing here with what has been called, in another context, a 'loanblend' (Romaine, 56). Rothwell, and Laura Wright in a series of important studies of business language of the Middle Ages, are predominantly concerned with particular registers, or text-types. Wright's work is explicitly focused on business language, one of whose defining characteristics is that it is *sui generis*, and involves complex although rule-governed conventions of code-switching, facilitated by the use of suspension marks at the end of word-stems which permit the lexeme to be interpreted as belonging to one of three languages (e.g. *carpentar'*, which could be Latin, ME or Anglo-French); a text-type which, in her estimation (Wright, 6), produces a class of documents whose macaronic language is more common than are monolingual documents in the Public Record Office. Rothwell's studies of the *York Memorandum Book* or of the records of the Grocers' Company are likewise concerned with specific text-types. But Herbert Schendl has observed that 'C[ode] S[witching] in written texts was clearly not an exception but a widespread specific *mode of discourse* over much of the attested history of English. *It occurs across domains, genres and text types – business, religious, legal and scientific texts, as well as literary ones.*' (my emphasis in the second sentence). What have been conveniently deemed the eccentricities of specific text-types, Wright's 'business language' or Rothwell's administrative texts, are far more widespread than has habitually been assumed – and, as we shall see, they occur far earlier. Schendl quotes, indeed, *Ancrene Wisse*. It is two hundred years older than the texts normally associated with the process, and it is a 'literary' text. The mechanisms concerned cannot be relegated to the domain of oddities unworthy of serious interest: they are implicated in the production of literary ME, and are part of the history, therefore, of literary English.

Another major area of linguistic investigation, of much more general import and based on a much wider range of data, needs to be incorporated into the 'loanword' discussion, and even in respect of seemingly straightforward literary texts. This is the substantial body of work which is now available on code-switching, both in terms of specific studies of particular languages, and, perhaps more importantly, at a more general and theoretical level. The models proposed are undoubtedly of relevance to the issue of 'loanwords' in ME. Thus, for example, a recent book on code-switching includes a thought-provoking chapter on 'Relating Lexical Borrowing and Codeswitching' (Myers-Scotton, *Duelling Languages*, 163–207); the now standard study on bilingualism, by Suzanne Romaine, devotes twenty pages to 'Distinguishing Borrowing from Code-Switching' (Romaine, 142–161). The basic argument of both scholars is that borrowing and code-switching must be considered together. The morphosyntactic and psycholinguistic processes are more similar than different, albeit with significant discrepancies in the ways in which the lexemes concerned function in terms of the 'mental lexicon' of the user. The important point for our purposes is, however, the fact that borrowing and code-switching involve very similar *morphosyntactic* processes. In essence, the parallels drawn between loanwords and single-lexeme code-switching underscore Schendl's point discussed earlier: code-switching, irrespective of the mechanisms which are held to govern it (and opinions vary on this) is not only widespread amongst bilinguals, but is the *norm* for such individuals. It has been plausibly argued in the context of both Strasbourg (Gardner-Chloros, 164) and East Africa (Myers-Scotton, *Duelling Languages*, 174; 'Codeswitching and Borrowing') that all loans start life as single-lexeme switches. This seems to be true in particular of the seemingly 'gratuitous' (that is, strictly unnecessary) 'core' borrowings (Myers-Scotton, *Duelling Languages*, 169). These are defined as words for which the host language already has equivalents, and where no perceived gap can be postulated as a motive for the borrowing. The literature on code-switching suggests that so-called 'cultural' borrowings (where prestige, elitism and so on play a major part) retain a separate status and enter the host language as a result of a deliberate choice by speakers rather than as part of the routine process of code-switching. This suggests that whereas we may be right to regard (say) the use of a word like *deboneirte* in *Ancrene Wisse* as a 'true' borrowing (that is, a 'cultural' borrowing), we should not so consider (for example) *spuse*, since ME clearly has a perfectly acceptable word for this already, and indeed it has never been supplanted in the vernacular by the Anglo-French alternative. *Spuse* is thus not 'necessary' to English. Needless to say, not all the conclusions reached in respect of spoken language use will transfer without further ado to the purely written evidence from the Middle Ages. The whole issue of the 'mental lexicon' of a dead language, and of psycholinguistic explanations, is far more difficult to evaluate than would be the case when dealing with a corpus of modern spoken data. One of the criteria enabling Myers-Scotton to differentiate between borrowings (particularly of the 'cultural' type) from code-switched lexemes is that of frequency of use: and in this respect too, the written data (patently incomplete) is far less revealing than can be a properly constituted corpus of speech data. It would nonetheless be perverse to disregard the information which modern linguistic studies can yield, and the divergence between the types of data is smaller than might at first be expected.

The ME *Ancrene Wisse* is explicitly a text which is in literary terms macaronic, and which in linguistic terms deploys code-switching. Thus, a short Latin phrase is followed by an English gloss, explanation, and amplification. This is a perfectly normal pattern within medieval didactic writing, and it is present, for example, within Anglo-French in Nicholas Bozon's *Contes* (Toulmin Smith and Meyer). This, in itself, should perhaps alert us to the likelihood that, within a text where code-switching is not only an integral but a structural element, manifestations of the same pattern of language use can be expected at the level of the individual lexeme as well as at that of sentences and clauses. What we in fact have in *Ancrene Wisse* is the 'literary' equivalent of a perfectly normal record of code-switching, which, quite predictably, functions with different-sized units. That it is a written text does not in itself mean that we cannot expect the normal mechanisms associated with this linguistic phenomenon to recur. Tony Hunt's analysis of 'Code-switching in medical texts' demonstrates clearly that the application of this type of analysis is perfectly valid in the case of a written document. There can be little doubt that, given what is known about the sociolinguistic situation in medieval England, it is a far more fruitful approach to the whole question of 'loanwords' than that which has traditionally been adopted.

'French' or 'Anglo-French'?

The second major issue is whether the 'loanwords' in *Ancrene Wisse*, and in Middle English more generally, are indeed 'French' at all. A sensible *a priori* hypothesis would be that until they are proven to be 'French', i.e. imports from the Continent, we should assume that Romance words in Middle English are more likely to be local acquisitions, i.e. Anglo-French. This is a matter of common sense. It seems likely that the inhabitants of Kent will stop bothering to shuttle over to the Calais Mammouth to buy their croissants when the French hypermarket chain opens a branch in Sidcup. Yet in literary scholarship the converse is normally assumed: the first source is thought to be French, and the local variety is forgotten, or its role downplayed. How the categories of French and Anglo-French are in any case to be distinguished is also a vexed question. It is usually imagined that it is legitimate to identify borrowings as 'French' or 'Anglo-French' on the basis of formal criteria. A series of morphological, phonological, and ultimately orthographic criteria has been established, on the basis of which the provenance of a given word can allegedly be determined. Thus, for example, an unpalatalized initial /k/ is meant to produce (before /a/) *ch-* in French, and *c-* in the insular dialect (*chastel ~ castel*). Key Anglo-French orthographic (and possible phonetic) features such as the velarization of /a/ before nasal (giving characteristic 'Anglo-French' spellings such as *-aun-*) are also held to be infallible guides to whether a borrowing is French or not. There are very serious problems associated with this approach. Firstly, an increasing body of evidence suggests that these distinctions are not grounded in documentary reality. Anglo-French displays regrettably little regard for the theories of the late nineteenth-century: the *ch- ~ c-* opposition, for example, just does not work as a means of differentiating Continental from Insular French (Rothwell, 'Arrivals', 154–55). Although 'form' is ostensibly the product of a complex and well-regulated process of historical development, very often, and especially in prose texts, it is simply a matter of the vagaries of scribal orthography. A striking illustration is offered by the entries for **affre** and **aver**[1], which will be substantially more complex in AND2 (*Anglo-Norman Dictionary*, second edition) but already exemplify the point in AND1. Etymologically the words are distinct: OE *eafor*, and Latin *habere* used substantivally. Insofar as at this remove it is possible to organize the material as it presents itself *synchronically*, however (i.e. within the *état de la langue* of Anglo-French), it can *only* be done on semantic lines: a distribution by form is impossible. Whilst **aver**[1] ('property, possessions', etc.) always seems to have the form *av-*, **affre** ('draught-horse, plough animal, pack-horse', etc.) clearly has a range of forms in *av-* too (*aver, avere, havere, avoir*). If form were followed, the pattern (which is not all that clear in any case, cf. Möhren, 'Agn. *afre*'; *Untersuchungen*, 75–76, 91) would be irretrievably lost. Another commonsense assumption about language is borne out: meaning really *does* matter more than form.

Lexicographical Sources

Probably the authoritative, and certainly the most convenient, starting-point for any study of loanwords in *Ancrene Wisse* is the work of Arne Zettersten, and particularly his 'French loan-words in the *Ancrene Riwle*', which contains a complete list of all such lexical items in three *Ancrene Wisse* manuscripts. The lexicography of Anglo-French has advanced substantially in the last thirty years, and it is now possible to revise Zettersten's conclusions regarding the etymology of the problem words identified in 1969. Not only the completed AND (1977–1992, second edition under way) needs now to be brought into the equation. In addition to Godefroy and Tobler-Lommatzsch, with which ME specialists will be familiar (though the latter has received scandalously little attention from reviewers in British-based journals: Trotter, 'Néologismes'), a number of other and more recent dictionaries can add very substantially to the information available on Anglo-French. Not all ME (or for that matter Anglo-French) specialists make as much use of the *Französisches Etymologisches Wörterbuch* (FEW) as they should. This is in practice not only a massive (if at times frustrating) etymological dictionary of French but also a record of medieval French and all its forms (Baldinger). All too often it is overlooked or ignored or simply avoided (Trotter, 'Néologismes'). The *Dictionary of Medieval Latin from British Sources* (DMLBS, 1975–), the successor to Latham's *Revised Medieval Latin Word-List* (1965), contains on virtually every page either genuine Anglo-French words, or medieval Latin words which are thinly-disguised latinizations of Anglo-French. The ground-breaking *Dictionnaire Etymologique de l'Ancien Français* (DEAF) in Heidelberg (1971–) contains, in its richly-detailed discussions of etymology, usage and semantics, far and away the most comprehensive treatment of the lexis of medieval French which has yet been attempted. It is gratifying to note that Anglo-French is fully integrated into this most impressive dictionary. Finally, the *Dictionnaire du Moyen Français* (DMF) being prepared in Nancy under the direction of Robert Martin, whilst it does not claim to cover Anglo-French, will almost inevitably trespass into insular texts and equally inevitably, will shed light on a chronological area which is of considerable importance to Anglo-French and thus to ME.

Ancrene Wisse and 'Loanwords'

The treatise known variously as *Ancrene Wisse*, *Ancrene Riwle* or (less grammatically) *Ancren Riwle* was originally written for three noble female recluses, probably in the first third of the thirteenth century. The consensus is that it was first composed in English, being subsequently translated twice into Anglo-Norman, once faithfully, once rather more imaginatively. Dobson (*Origins*, 43) describes the earlier French version (the Vitellius MS) as 'a close translation of a good text of the original Rule'; the later (Trinity) text is 'a collection of very extensive translated extracts from the

Rule, [. . .], embodied in a vast Anglo-Norman "Compilation" [. . .] of which *Ancrene Wisse* was only one of the sources' (ibid., 296–7). A further difference is that, whilst the Vitellius text seems to have been intended (like the original Rule) for a female audience, the Trinity version is addressed more generally to men and women alike (Dobson, *Origins*, 303; Dobson, 'Date', 192–4; cf. Riehle, 13). These Anglo-Norman versions have received remarkably little attention since they were edited in 1944 and 1958 (Herbert; Trethewey). If we accept that the original Rule (not preserved in any of the extant manuscripts) was indeed written in English, there remains the curiosity that the Middle English texts contain an unusually high percentage of 'French' loanwords, including many first attestations of particular borrowings. That there might have been a French (rather, Anglo-French) original is no longer regarded as a serious possibility, although one study in 1974 (to which I return below) attempted with some success to revive the idea. A number of significant articles have been devoted to this aspect of the text, often, although not invariably, linking it to the use of 'French' loanwords in the dialectally similar *Katherine Group* (Clark, 'Lexical Divergence'; 'Early Middle English Prose'; Caluwé-Dor; Diensberg; Lee). It is frequently observed that Parts VI and VI of *Ancrene Wisse*, featuring much recourse to 'fashionable fiction' (Clark, 'Early Middle English Prose'), are especially rich in loanwords of a literary type (Dobson, *Origins*, 157). In part of course this is simply because such fiction was wont to be in French, or more precisely, in a type of Anglo-French much influenced by the literary French of France: it should be noted, for example, that the traditional *topos* of the besieged castle (Woolf) also occurs in the solidly Anglo-French *Livre de Seyntz Medicines* by Henry, Duke of Lancaster (Arnould, *Seyntz Medicines*, 64–84; Arnould, *Etude*, lxxv–lxxvi, xcviii–ci; Shepherd, xlviii–li). Berta Grattan Lee cites this same passage, with its use of 'French' words such as *pris, gentil, saluz, dame, deboneirté*, as possible evidence for a pre-existing French form from which the ME versions derive (Lee, 23). At the same time, it has also been observed that the 'intimate penetration of this text by French words and forms' (Clark, 'Lexical Divergence', 120) is shown by the use not only of loanwords of a learned and cultivated register, but also by the prevalence of everyday words, of (Anglo-)French origin, for everyday objects. There is a degree of inconsistency in the analysis which should alert us to the questionable nature of the underlying hypothesis, namely that this is borrowing as that process is normally understood. On the one hand, 'French', more correctly Anglo-French, has supplied numerous 'literary' terms: nothing surprising in that, in an obviously literary passage. These are genuine loanwords, from the worlds, typically, of courtly romance, literature, and religion, in this last category often lightly-gallicized Latinisms, or more precisely, Latinisms which have been passed through Anglo-French. These are the words which are well-known from the manuals of the history of English and from the pages of Walter Scott and his successors; they fall into the category of 'cultural borrowings' (Myers-Scotton, *Duelling Languages*, 169). How far they have contributed to the world outside *belles-lettres* is debatable. The second category, 'everyday' words, involves Anglo-French words which have been incorporated into English, assimilated morphologically and phonologically, sometimes hybridized and in general, incorporated into the 'mental lexicon' of users. These may be characterized as 'core borrowings' (Myers-Scotton, *Duelling Languages*, 169). We have here in miniature the basic problem of the nature of the Anglo-French 'loanword' in ME, and of the need to distinguish between different types thereof. In general, the fact that Anglo-French contributed to English in registers outside the elevated and literary has been neglected, even though the evidence of modern English itself suggests incontrovertibly that it did make a significant impact: in colloquial and in dialectal forms of English far removed from London, Anglo-French words are regularly encountered even at the end of the twentieth century (Rothwell, 'Adding Insult to Injury'; 'Anglo-French Element'; 'Arrivals', 157 n. 28). Reference has already been made above to the study by Berta Grattan Lee, in which the linguistic evidence for the priority of the French text of *Ancrene Wisse* is reassessed. The author adduces, from the Corpus manuscript, items of vocabulary, negative constructions, aspects of morphology, and a number of proper names, which display 'French' tendencies or features to such an extent that (in comparison with the Vitellius manuscript) these appear to indicate that the Corpus ME text is itself a reworking of an Anglo-French original. There is little doubt (Lee, 21–29) that, as far as lexical items and their use within the text are concerned, Vitellius and Corpus are strikingly similar. But where Lee's approach is inadequate is that it considers only the issue of *textual* transmission: it omits any consideration of the bilingualism of the putative author or authors, of the consequences of language contact, or indeed, more generally, of strictly *linguistic* matters as opposed to textual ones. It is certainly possible to interpret the interesting data assembled by Lee in a somewhat different manner. Leaving aside the issue of the relationship between the two manuscripts which she considers, and the evident complexities and lacunae in the manuscript transmission (Dobson, *Origins*, 287), we might consider that if the Corpus manuscript was composed by an author or scribe operating within a substantially bilingual environment, then it would be entirely normal that his text should contain the high percentage of 'French loanwords' noted by all scholars. If Vitellius is a transposition of a ME original closely related to, and perhaps the ancestor of, Corpus then it is equally to be expected that we should find, in an Anglo-French 'translation' of a ME text itself larded with Anglo-French loanwords, that those same words should simply be carried over into a version in the language from which they originally came.

Some Hypothetical Etyma: Cases Dismissed

The 'standard' list of 'French loanwords' in *Ancrene Wisse* (Zettersten, 'French Loan-words', 234–49) is the basis of what follows. My investigation does not extend to the other *Ancrene Wisse* texts, of which the most interesting is the Cleopatra manuscript – not least because of Dobson's important introduction, rare in the detail of its linguistic analysis (Dobson, *English Text*). Scribe D, in particular, writing in 1284–1299 (ibid., cxlvii), offers early attestations of a number of Anglo-French borrowings into ME, in additions and modifications to a base text dating from the late 1220s. There is no doubt that this text would repay further lexical study. Zettersten's list (based on the Corpus Christi Cambridge, Nero, and Gonville and Caius manuscripts) contains seven interesting cases where a hypothetical OF or AF etymon is adduced. All of these may be dismissed as unnecessary if we turn to the evidence now available (and in some cases, available in 1969) in respect of Anglo-French. They are: *diggin* < AFr **diguer*; *gridil* < OFr **gredil*; *pinchen* < ONFr **pinchier* 'to pluck'; *spieden* < AFr **aspier*; *trochiờ* < OFr **trochier*; *vampez* < AFr **vampé*; and *wencheờ* < AFr **wenchier*.

diggin is problematic: Zettersten suggests an Anglo-French origin (unattested **diguer*), AND2 labels its **digger** (with only one supporting quotation) a ME loan. AND's quotation is late, from the *Merchant Taylors' Accounts* from 3 Henry IV (= 1402): 'Item pur iiij laborers [. . .] a deboter les velx maisons, ripper tiles, *digger* vowtes pur privés'. Chronology is apparently on the side of ME as the source language, although the picture is unclear. The first MED attestation (4.1082b) is *Ancrene Wisse*'s 'diggin. & deluen deoppre & deoppre' (has the use of *diggin* been triggered by alliteration?); there is then nothing for over a century. OED 4.646a attaches no hypothetical asterisk to the etymon *diguer*, does not quote *Ancrene Wisse*, and has no attestation before 1320. All authorities agree on an ultimate Germanic etymon: OED calls it 'Teutonic', FEW 15.ii.60b suggests Middle Dutch *dijc*, attested in a French source (from Flanders) as OF *diic* in 1303; the verb *dikier* 'munir d'une digue' is found from 1285 (again, in Flanders). Clearly the documents are not giving us the full picture.

gridil is attested in AF in Alexander Neckam's *De Utensilibus* of c.1200 (DEAF G1134 sub **graïlle**); although its provenance is not immediately apparent to the uninitiated, the form is cited in Gdf 9.725b from 'GARL' = John of Garland, and in FEW 2.1287a, from Gdf and labelled 'agn'. TL 4.514 quotes Neckham. Forms in all sources are Anglo-French; DEAF also quotes RMLWL 212a sub **girdalium** and see now DMLBS 1077a s.v. Conversely, it is not certain that the form ever existed outside Anglo-French (i.e. in 'OFr').

pinchen does not need to be taken back to a hypothetical 'Old Northern French' form **pinchier* (OED 11.854b) since this is attested in Anglo-French p. p. as a. *pinché* (AND1, s.v.) from Neckham (c. 1200: DEAF). MED adduces 'OF [sic] *pincier, pincer, pincher*' (12.942a sub **pinchen**). TL and Gdf have nothing to add. ME *pinchen* is otherwise unattested before the fourteenth century (MED 12.942a, OED 11.854b) except, interestingly, in proper names, which look remarkably as if they started life as nicknames, where it surfaces from 1130 onwards. This is a phenomenon already noted by Rothwell ('Arrivals', 160–61).

spieden is a perfectly normal ME rendition of the attested aphetic *spier* (AND1). Zettersten's etymon *aspier, moreover, although no longer necessary to the discussion, is also attested. The commonest form of the verb is of course *espier* (cf. GdfC 9.544c, TL 3.1205); but Anglo-French prefixes (and the absence or presence of them) are notoriously and indeed *systematically* unstable in Anglo-French. It is possible that outside the more literary registers of Old French itself, they are too.

trochiŏ may plausibly be linked to two Anglo-French forms in AND1, namely the problematic and rare adj. (or probably p. p.) **troche** meaning second-hand (AND1 **troche**[1]) and the expression **a le truck** (sub **truck**), 'by barter' (cf. modern French *troc, troquer*), from the *Rotuli Parliamentorum* for 1400/01 (iii 468b), antedated by an Anglo-French document quoted in OED sub **truck** sb. (18.602a) but omitted from AND1 (whose gloss sub **truck** it confirms). TL (10.687) supplies the earliest Old French use of *troquier* from the *Clef d'Amors* (1280); FEW (13.ii.317a) suggests derivation from Germanic *trokk-*, also quotes the *Clef d'Amors* and like TL, has nothing thereafter for some time. A possible derivation of the Old French verb from the semantically similar Old Spanish *trocar* (cf. FEW 2.124b) is now rejected sub **trokk-** (13.ii.317b) on phonetic grounds and because *trocar* is attested only from 1330 onwards. FEW also notes medieval Latin *trocare* (1257, Anjou, from Du Cange). TLF (16.16.677a) essentially reiterates the FEW data, mentioning however ME *trukie* (*Ancrene Wisse*), and noting sub **troc** (the related substantive) the 1364 first attestation from OED (18.602a); FEW does not mention the English and Anglo-Latin evidence. There seems to be clear evidence of a complex relationship within French of a whole series of morphosemantically related words such as *troquer/truquer/trucher* (Old French), and *tricher*, some or all of which may also have some bearing on the English reflexes of these items (Guiraud, 1962). In *Ancrene Wisse*, then, we have a ME reflex of an Anglo-French word, and it is substantially earlier than the attestations in French, Anglo-French, or Latin (British or Continental). Once more, this calls into question the quality (and quantity) of the evidence now at our disposal for this period.

vampez is straightforward: *vampé* is amply attested and is a standard Anglo-French aphetic form: cf. AND1 sub **vampe** and a number of comparable forms for **(a)vant-**, ibid., and sub **avant-** in AND2 (forthcoming). The English *vampe* is phonetically problematic since it would appear that the final [e] of -*pé* = *pié* has been lost, presumably via a transitional stage where it survived orthographically as -*pe*. The word is discussed by W. Rothwell in a forthcoming paper where he notes the existence of additional forms not cited in AND1 (Hunt, *Teaching and Learning Latin*), where the final [e] = *é* is more satisfactorily indicated by forms like *vampié, wampeys* (Rothwell, 'Aspects'). Chronology remains problematic since the attestations in Hunt are all later than that in *Ancrene Wisse*: they come either from a Glasgow Glossary of c.1250 (Hunt,

Teaching and Learning Latin, 1:416) or from John of Garland's *Dictionarius* (of c.1220: ibid., 2:191), from manuscripts from the thirteenth and fourteenth centuries (ibid., 2:129, 149, 170).

wencheð is visibly an AF form of *guenchi(e)r* (cf. AND 345a sub **guenchier**): 'ONFr' (even if so precise a variety could be identified at the date required) does not need to be invoked: see DEAF G1547, citing Adgar (c. 1200) and earlier ChGuill's *venchir*, which it is proposed to correct to *wenchir*; FEW 17.55a has only Walloon forms in *w-*.

The first and most obvious (and most encouraging) point to be made here is that lexicography has indeed advanced: hypothetical forms have now been replaced by real ones. A second observation, consonant with the general observations made above, is that it is indeed the case that the derivation is not from Continental French but from the Insular variety. Against this reassuring news must be set the considerable chronological and documentary problems which these few examples reveal. It is clear that *Ancrene Wisse* preserves a number of what must be ME reflexes of Anglo-French words, but at a date considerably earlier than the date of the first attestation in Anglo-French itself (**diggin, trochið, vampez, pinchen**). Commentators have remarked on both the number of loanwords from 'French' (Anglo-French), and the fact that many such words in *Ancrene Wisse* are first attestations, but not on this point, which seems of considerable significance in sociolinguistic terms and in the context of language contact between Anglo-French and ME. It also suggests that Anglo-French and for that matter French lexicographers would be well advised to consider ME texts as possible sources for information on words which may not be attested in the parent language.

Hybrid Forms and Integration

A second and perhaps more important area of investigation is that of what might be called hybrid forms or loanblends in either the ME or French *Ancrene Wisse* texts. What is striking is how many of these there are. Yoko Wada's judicious discussion of *Ancrene Wisse* vocabulary (Wada, xxx–xxvii) considers, as examples of the phenomenon, fifteen French loanwords: four are in some way hybrids, that is, they combine Anglo-French and ME forms: *prinschipe* (i.e. *privschipe*), *pinchunge, acemunge, coverschipe*. To these we might add further examples from Zettersten ('French Loanwords', 234–49): *acemin, amendin, bibarret, departunge, overfeble, frotunge, unheite* (cf. Zettersten, *Studies*, 87), *hurtunge, peintunge, forpreiseð, preisungen, overpreisunge, priveiliche, propreliche, rivunges* (pl.), *unstable, turpelnesse* (Zettersten, *Studies*, 278), *trichunge, bitruileð, bitrufleð, untrusset, verseilunge*. Of this list, several are seemingly hapax legomena (*privschipe, acemunge, bibarret*) and others antedate quite substantially the other attestations in MED and OED (*pinchunge, unheite, overfeble, priveiliche*). These words, I would suggest, are of far greater historical and linguistic

significance than the standard courtly terms (French or Anglo-French) like
dame, deboneire, danger, and so on, of which we might accurately say that
they have been 'borrowed'. What the hybrids show is a process of much
greater consequence for the history of English. These words have been
naturalized; their implantation in ME is such that they been accommodated
to ME verb morphology (*acem-in, amend-in, forpreis-eð*), attached to bound
ME morphemes (*depart-unge, frot-unge*), or to adjectival and adverbial
affixes (*un-heité, un-stable, privei-liche, bi-barret, over-feble*), and thus consist in fact of two elements, one of ME origin, one of Anglo-French
provenance. The process of insertion of a Romance word into a Germanic
language may be illustrated by the existence of the variant forms *coverschipe, kulvert-schipe, culward-schipe* (Zettersten, *Studies*, 276), each of
which displays to differing degrees the process of phonological assimilation
to the host language. At the microeconomic level, this is the process of
merger which leads in due course at a more general, macroeconomic level to
the development of a hybrid Germano-Romance language, modern English
(Rothwell, 'Arrivals', 163–64). There can be no question of these words
being traced back to 'French', since they cannot have come from 'French'
sources: this is locally-grown produce, grafted onto ME elements. That the
individual content morphemes of these compounds (themselves from
Anglo-French) are attested within the same manuscript of the same text,
suggests strongly that the process of 'borrowing' had been completed at an
earlier date even than that of the already very early *Ancrene Wisse*, with the
option of subsequent compounding (integration at morphosyntactic level)
thereby becoming available for the author(s)/scribe(s) of that work by the
beginning of the thirteenth century. This is especially important when we
bear in mind that several of the words are not otherwise attested in ME
until much later than *Ancrene Wisse*, in any form (compounded or not). The
implication is a deep and possibly near-bilingual knowledge of the
languages concerned, a capacity successfully to manipulate the morphemes
and morphological structures of two languages, an acquired (rather than
instinctive) skill in taking words apart and putting them back together.
Whether this is a matter of the individual author's own (as it were) idiolectal
bilingualism, or a reflection of societal bilingualism within the scribal class
at the time, is an open question.

Not the least of the questions raised by this pattern of hybridization is
that of determining what language these words are. If there are difficulties
in deciding how contemporaries classified the seemingly monolingual
individual items in Latin-vernacular glossaries, and the technical terms in
medical texts (Hunt, 'Codeswitching'), then the dilemma is still more
insoluble when the word-form itself indicates a hybrid. Moreover, Anglo-
French texts also contain such forms: *crossearke*, for example ('crossbow'),
in a collection of trade documents (Smit, 563.913), or an example of exactly
the same type as those found in *Ancrene Wisse*, *asselyng/selyng*, 'sealing', in
the records of the Grocers (Rothwell, 'French Vocabulary', 29; cf. also
pavynge). In the case of the former an Anglo-French noun, *arke* (a variant
orthography of *arc*) is qualified by a preposed ME adjective 'cross'; in the

case of the latter, a ME suffix, the bound morpheme –*ing*, is appended to an Anglo-French verb stem *assel-* from *asseler*. The productivity of both these processes (Anglo-French noun + ME noun, or Anglo-French stem + ME suffix) is apparent not only from the Grocers' Accounts but also from those of the Merchant Taylors' Company (Jefferson and Rothwell, 297) and the Goldsmiths' Company (Jefferson), where further examples abound. Juxtaposed noun compounds are also characteristic of later Anglo-French documents of this type. To take just three alphabetically adjacent words

almesdich 'alms dish': les mazers et le grant almesdych d'argent quex j'ay en ma garderobe a Loundres *Test Ebor* i 114.
almeshous 'almshouse': Espenses faitz sur le novelle overage appellé Almeshous *Mch Tayl Accs* 3 Hen V
almoshomme, almose- 'almsman': Item paié pur prestres et almoshommez (*ms.* almos hommez) le seconde quarter jour – xvj li. [. . .] Item paié pur la beryeng de Hastenges almosehomme (*ms.* almose homme) – iij s. x d. *Mch Tayl Accs* 8 Hen V.

In all three cases, a ME qualifier (*almes-*) is attached to a noun: *dich*, *hous*, *homme*. About the status of this second element there is no doubt: ME in the first two cases, Anglo-French in the third. The form *almes-* itself is apparently unambiguously ME (though compare the forms of **aumoner** or **aumonerie** (AND) in Anglo-French, which feature for example **ammosenerie** or **aumosn(i)er**). In the case of *almesdich*, there is an apparent ME borrowing (or a code-switch?) in the midst of a list of items bequeathed. This is not unusual. *Almeshous* is a proper noun and thus inconclusive as evidence. *Almoshomme* appears, though, in two syntactically similar phrases, in the same text. In the first it is coupled with an Anglo-French noun (*prestres*), but in the second it is used in a context where ME is already present (*pur la beryeng de Hastenges*). In code-switching terms, it could be argued that this is the trigger for the use of the ME word *almosehomme*. What we have here is a ME element (*almes-*) which can quite readily be combined with elements from either ME or Anglo-French, within a host language (what Myers-Scotton would call a 'matrix language') which is Anglo-French. In short, *almes-* functions as an autonomous content morpheme in Anglo-French: it has been fully integrated into the mental lexicon of these users. I would conjecture that it is only a matter of time before it will be found, on its own (i.e. uncompounded) in an Anglo-French text.

Now this is exactly the same pattern that we encounter, albeit in the matrix language of ME, and thus with imported Anglo-French morphemes, within the hybrid forms in *Ancrene Wisse*. In other words, whether or not the matrix language is ME or Anglo-French, the same process operates, in different directions, and a good deal earlier than is usually suggested. In *Ancrene Wisse*, many of the hybrids or loanblends discussed above are paralleled by simplex forms, uncompounded Anglo-French morphemes. The words of which this is not true need further attention (below). But in most cases, either the simplex forms are found, in the same text, or at the very least there is a hybrid involving (again) an Anglo-French stem and a bound morpheme: either another Anglo-French element (e.g. an adverbial suffix) or a ME verb morpheme:

coverschipe cf. *cover*;
overfeble cf. *feble, febli, feblesce, feblete*;
hurtunge cf. *hurten* (Anglo-French stem, ME verb ending);
peintunge cf. *peinture, depeint*;
forpreiseð, preisungen, overpreisunge cf. *preisin* (Anglo-French stem, ME verb ending);
priveiliche cf. *prive, privement, privite*;
propreliche cf. *proprement*;
rivunges (pl.) cf. *riveð* (Anglo-French stem, ME verb ending);
turpelnesse cf. *torplin* (Anglo-French stem, ME verb ending);
trichunge cf. *triccherie*; *bitruileð* cf. *truilles* (variant *bitrufleð* in MS N, cf. *trufles* in N);
untrusset cf. *trussen* (sbst.), *trussews, trussin* (Anglo-French stem, ME verb ending);
verseilunge cf. *verset, verseilin* (Anglo-French stem, ME verb ending).

There is, in other words, internal evidence within *Ancrene Wisse* that the relevant Anglo-French content morphemes had been integrated into the mental lexicon of the author/scribe of *Ancrene Wisse*. This perhaps puts into perspective his coining of new (not previously attested) hybrids. In other cases the text preserves a straightforward hybrid, an Anglo-French stem and a ME verb ending: *acemin, amendin*, a relatively basic form of loan-blending.

The hybrids of which this is not true are *privschipe, pinchunge, bibarret, departunge, frotunge, unheite, unstable*: They raise a number of important problems, some of which have already surfaced in the discussion of the no longer hypothetical etyma, above.

(prinschipe), privschipe: The relevant (later) volume of the MED indicates that this should read *privschipe* (see MED 12.1344b sub **privshipe**) so that the search for an etymon must be redirected towards (as MED indicates) forms in **priv-** (no semantically plausible etymon for **prin* exists in French or Anglo-French). Yet even here there are problems, themselves symptomatic of several other difficulties. MED states that *privschipe* (the headword form **privshipe** is not supported by a quotation) derives from *priven*; but there are no attestations of the ME verb which are less than 150 years later than *Ancrene Wisse*'s hybrid *privschipe*. Moreover, if *priven* derives from 'OF' *priver*, as both MED and OED assert, we are also faced with a conundrum: *priver* is itself not attested before 1307 (Gdf C 10.421b; OED 12.521; FEW 9.396a). Anglo-French evidence (AND1 sub **priver**) does not appear to permit an antedating. It is inconceivable that ME should have constructed the compound (and hybrid) *priv-schipe* a century and a half before the simplex form had been transferred into

ME, and also a century or so before the existence (in French or Anglo-French) of the verb from which the ME verb came. The only conclusion is that the documentary evidence available to lexicographers is incomplete.

pinchunge: All the examples of *pinchunge* sub **pinching(e** in MED 12.943a, except that in *Ancrene Wisse*, are substantially later. This once more raises the question of the nature of the linguistic evidence available to us. (See also **pinchen**, above.)

bibarret: attested (in MED) only in *Ancrene Wisse* (sub **bibarren**, 2.794a). It patently derives from the OE prefix *bi-* and *barren* ⟨ Anglo-French *barrer* (ibid., 2.657b). Again MED and OED have no use of *barren* before 1300; it is found earlier in Anglo-French, and Anglo-French also creates a reflex in Anglo-Latin in the transparent form of *barrare* (DMLBS s.v., 1.184a), attested in the sense in which the ME is used, from 1218 onwards.

departunge: MED **departing(e** (4.977b) is attested from *Ancrene Wisse*, and then from 1300 in the same sense, with no other sense recorded before 1300. The earliest use of the simplex *departen* (4.973b) is c.1250 (from a c.1300 manuscript); the verb is found in French from the *Vie de saint Alexis* onwards (cf. FEW 7.684b). The medieval Latin reflex of the Anglo-French verb (DMLBS sub **departire**, 3.615a) is found from William of Malmesbury on. (For *departure*, cf. Rothwell, 'Arrivals' 146.)

frotunge: derived from the Anglo-French *froter* (found in French 'seit 12.jh.', FEW 3.786a), whether or not via the intermediary of ME *froten* (MED 6.918a), itself only attested from 1330 onwards, is again found only in *Ancrene Wisse*, and thereafter not until 1398 (MED 6.9178 sub **frotinge**). DMLBS has **frotare** from 1291 (4.1015b).

unheite: An obvious compound of the ME negative prefix *un-* and *hait* < Anglo-French *heité/haité*; but the simplex *hait* is only attested in ME from c.1325 (as an adjective), with the noun *hait* found from 1280 (MED sub *hait*, 8.436b). In French, *hait*, of ultimately Germanic provenance, exists from 1100 onwards (DEAF H76–92) and generates a large number of compounds.

Certain common factors emerge from the examination of the hybrid forms in *Ancrene Wisse*. Firstly, it is striking that *Ancrene Wisse* should consistently offer such early attestations, typically a century, and often the better part of two centuries, earlier than those found in any other source known to MED or OED. Secondly, the hybridization process is quite obviously in operation long before the late medieval texts with which it has normally been associated. This is of considerable relevance to the history of English. It does tend to suggest that we are here dealing with an author with (at the very least) a high level of exposure to Anglo-French. Thirdly, it is only too apparent that the written evidence is seriously defective in both ME and Anglo-French. There are many missing links in the transmission process. The ME *Ancrene Wisse* is a valuable source of information about this form of advanced language contact, and evidence of the coexistence of the two languages long before most other documentary evidence reveals the degree of intimacy of the relationship between them.

Conclusions

From an Anglo-French perspective, and still more from a perspective of Anglo-French contact with ME, the ME *Ancrene Wisse* texts are important and fascinating documents. They attest, at an early date, to processes of merger both in the incorporation into ME of discrete Anglo-French word-units, and at the level of morphemes which are combined to form new hybrids, the Anglo-French components of which seem often to be attested for the first time in the ME coining. *Ancrene Wisse* thus permits not only the ME specialist, but his Anglo-French counterpart, to glimpse the reality of language contact within a subsection of contemporary society, the functionally bi- or trilingual scribal class of medieval England at the beginning of the thirteenth century. To understand this aspect of the history of English, a knowledge of Anglo-French is as indispensable now as it was to the scribes of medieval England eight hundred years ago; and French etymologists, too, need to remember that ME may sometimes preserve records of the existence of Anglo-French words long before they find their way into sources in that language.

Works Cited

Arnould, E. J., ed., *Le Livre de Seyntz Medicines*, Anglo-Norman Texts Society 2 (Oxford, 1940)
——, *Etude sur le Livre des Saintes Médecines du duc Henri de Lancastre* (Paris, 1948)
Baldinger, Kurt, 'Le FEW de Walther von Wartburg: Introduction', *Bulletin des Jeunes Romanistes* [Strasbourg] 18–19 (1973), 11–47
Brewer, Derek, *A New Introduction to Chaucer*, 2nd edn (London, 1998)
Calin, William, *The French Tradition and the Literature of Medieval England* (Toronto, 1995)
Caluwé-Dor, Juliette de, 'Divergence lexicale entre le *Katherine Group* et l'*Ancrene Riwle*: valeur stylistique des premières attestations de mots d'origine française en anglais', *Etudes anglaises* 30 (1977), 463–72
Clark, Cecily, '*Ancrene Wisse* and the *Katherine Group*: a Lexical Divergence', *Neophilologus* 50 (1966), 117–23
——, 'Early Middle English Prose: Three Essays in Stylistics', *Essays in Criticism* 18 (1968), 361–82
Diensberg, Bernhard, '*Ancrene Wisse/Riwle surquide, caue, creauant/creaunt, trusse, bereget* and *babanliche*', *Archiv für das Studium der neueren Sprachen und Literaturen* 215 (1978), 79–82
Dobson, E. J., 'The Date and Composition of *Ancrene Wisse*', *Proceedings of the British Academy* 52 (1966), 181–208

Dobson, E. J., ed., *The English Text of the Ancrene Riwle edited from B.M. Cotton MS Cleopatra C.VI*, EETS o.s. 267 (London, 1972)

——, *The Origins of 'Ancrene Wisse'* (Oxford, 1976)

Gardner-Chloros, P., *Language Selection and Switching in Strasbourg* (Oxford, 1991)

Guiraud, P., '*Tric, trac, troc, truc*, etc. Etude du champ morpho-sémantique de la racine T.K.', *Bulletin de la Société de Linguistique de Paris* 57 (1962), 103–125

Herbert, J. A, ed., *The French Text of the Ancren Riwle*, EETS o.s. 219 (London, 1944)

Hunt, Tony, 'Code-switching in Medical Texts', in *Multilingualism*, ed. Trotter.

——, *Teaching and Learning Latin in Thirteenth-Century England* (Cambridge, 1991)

Jefferson, Lisa, 'The Anglo-French Vocabulary of the Goldsmiths' Company Archives', in *Multilingualism*, ed. Trotter

——, and W. Rothwell, 'Society and Lexis: the Language of the Records of the Merchant Taylors' Company', *Zeitschrift für französische Sprache und Literatur* 107 (1997), 273–301

Lee, Berta Grattan, *Linguistic Evidence for the Priority of the French Text of the 'Ancrene Wisse'*, Janua Linguarum, Series Practica 242 (The Hague, 1974)

Möhren, Frankwalt, '*Agn. afre/aver*: Eine wortgeschichtliche und wissenschafts-geschichtliche Untersuchung', *Archiv für das Studium der neueren Sprachen und Literaturen* 218 (1981), 129–136

——, *Wort- und sachgeschichtliche Untersuchungen an französischen landwirtschaft-lichen Texten, 13. bis 18. Jahrhundert (Seneschaucie, Ménagier, Encyclopédie)*, Beihefte zur Zeitschrift für romanische Philologie 197 (Tübingen, 1986)

Myers-Scotton, C., 'Comparing Codeswitching and Borrowing', in *Codeswitching*, ed. Carol M. Eastman (Clevedon, 1992), 19–39

——, *Duelling Languages: Grammatical Structure in Codeswitching* (Oxford, 1993)

Riehle, Wolfgang, *The Middle English Mystics* (London, 1981)

Romaine, Suzanne, *Bilingualism*, 2nd edn (Oxford, 1995)

Rothwell, W., 'Adding Insult to Injury: the English who Curse in Borrowed French', in *The Origins and Development of Emigrant Languages: Proceedings from the Second Rasmus Rask Colloquium, Odense University, November 1994*, ed. Hans-Frede Nielsen and Lene Schøsler (Odense, 1996), 41–54

——, 'The Anglo-French Element in the Vulgar Register of Late Middle English', *Neuphilologische Mitteilungen* 97 (1996), 423–36

——, 'Anglo-French Lexical Contacts, Old and New', *Modern Language Review* 74 (1979), 287–96

——, 'Arrivals and Departures: the Adoption of French Terminology into Middle English', *English Studies* 79 (1998), 144–165

——, 'Aspects of Lexical and Morphosyntactical Mixing in the Languages of Medieval England', in *Multilingualism*, ed. Trotter

——, 'Chaucer and Stratford atte Bowe', *Bulletin of the John Rylands University Library of Manchester* 74 (1992), 3–28

——, 'The "Faus franceis d'Angleterre": Later Anglo-Norman', in *Anglo-Norman Anniversary Essays*, ed. Ian Short (London, 1993), 309–326

——, 'French Vocabulary in the Archive of the London Grocers' Company', *Zeitschrift für französische Sprache und Literatur* 102 (1992), 23–41

——, 'From Latin to Anglo-French and Middle English: the Role of the Multi-lingual Gloss', *Modern Language Review* 88 (1993), 581–99

——, 'The Legacy of Anglo-French: *faux amis* in French and English', *Zeitschrift für romanische Philologie* 109 (1993), 16–46

——, 'Lexical Borrowing in a Medieval Context', *Bulletin of the John Rylands University Library of Manchester* 63 (1980–81), 118–43

——, 'The Missing Link in English Etymology: Anglo-French', *Medium Aevum* 60 (1991), pp. 173–96

——, 'The Trilingual England of Geoffrey Chaucer', *Studies in the Age of Chaucer* 16 (1994), pp. 45–67

Samuels, M. L., '*Ancrene Riwle* studies', *Medium Aevum* 22 (1953), 1–9

Schendl, Herbert, 'Linguistic Aspects of Code-switching in Medieval English Texts', in *Multilingualism*, ed. Trotter

Shepherd, G., ed., *Ancrene Wisse, Parts Six and Seven* (London, 1959)

Short, Ian, 'Patrons and Polyglots: French Literature in Twelfth-Century England', *Anglo-Norman Studies, 14: Proceedings of the Battle Conference 1991*, ed. Marjorie Chibnall (Woodbridge, Suffolk, 1992), 229–49

Smit, H. J., *Bronnen tot de Geschiedenis van den Handel met Engeland, Schotland en Ierland 1, 1150–1485* ('s Gravenhage, 1928)

Toulmin Smith, L., and P. Meyer, eds., *Les Contes moralisés de Nicole Bozon* (Paris, 1889)

Trethewey, W. A, ed., *The French Text of the Ancren Riwle*, EETS o.s. 240 (London, 1958)

Trotter, D. A., 'Language Contact and Lexicography: the Case of Anglo-Norman', in *The Origins and Development of Emigrant Languages: Proceedings from the Second Rasmus Rask Colloquium, Odense University, November 1994*, ed. Hans-Frede Nielsen and Lene Schøsler (Odense, 1996), 21–39

——, ed., *Multilingualism in Later Medieval Britain: Proceedings of the 1997 Aberystwyth Colloquium* (Cambridge, 2000)

——, 'Les néologismes de l'anglo-français et le *FEW*', in *Néologie et création verbale: Actes du VIIIe Colloque international sur le moyen français, McGill University, Montréal, octobre 1996*, ed. Giuseppe di Stefano (Montreal, 1998)

——, review of Calin, *Zeitschrift für romanische Philologie* 113 (1997), 139–40

Wada, Yoko, '*Temptations' from 'Ancrene Wisse' Volume 1* (Osaka, 1994)

Woolf, Rosemary, 'The Theme of Christ the Lover-Knight in Medieval English Literature', *Review of English Studies* n.s. 13 (1962), 1–16

Wright, Laura, *Sources of London English: Medieval Thames Vocabulary* (Oxford, 1996)

Zettersten, Arne, *Studies in the Dialect and Vocabulary of the 'Ancrene Riwle'*, Lund Studies in English 34 (Lund, 1965)

——, 'French Loan-words in the *Ancrene Riwle*', in *Mélanges de philologie offerts à Alf Lombard à l'occasion de son soixante-cinquième anniversaire par ses collègues et ses amis* (Lund, 1969), 227–250

6

The Middle English Manuscripts and Early Readers of *Ancrene Wisse*

A. S. G. EDWARDS

Ancrene Wisse possibly circulated for a longer period than any other Middle English prose work. It was copied, in whole or in part, from the mid-thirteenth to the early seventeenth centuries and addressed to a range of audiences far more diverse than that for which it was initially intended. It is the manuscripts and the different forms of the text that they contain that provide that bases for our understanding of these processes of transmission. In what follows I will briefly discuss the distinctive features of each of the manuscripts which contains *Ancrene Wisse* and examine the more obvious early evidence of its reception.

There are nine surviving Middle English versions of the *Ancrene Wisse*.[1] They are as follows:[2]

A Cambridge, Corpus Christi College 402, ff. 1–117v; ed. J. R. R. Tolkien, *The English Text of the Ancrene Riwle: Ancrene Wisse, edited from MS Corpus Christi College Cambridge 402*, with an Introduction by N. R. Ker, EETS o.s. 249 (1962)

G Cambridge, Gonville and Caius College 234/120, pp. 1–185; ed. R. M. Wilson, *The English Text of the Ancrene Riwle, edited from Gonville and Caius College MS 234/120*, with an Introduction by N. R. Ker, EETS o.s. 229 (1954)

P Cambridge, Magdalene College Pepys 2498, pp. 371–449; ed. A. Zettersten, *The English Text of the Ancrene Riwle, edited from Magdalene College Cambridge MS 2498*, EETS 274 (1976)

C London, BL Cotton Cleopatra C. vi, ff. 4–199; ed. E. J. Dobson, *The English Text of the Ancrene Riwle, edited from B. M. MS Cottlon Cleopatra C. vi*, EETS 267 (1972)

N London, BL Cotton Nero A. xiv, ff. 1–120v; ed. Mabel Day, *The English Text of the Ancrene Riwle: Cotton Nero A. xiv, on the basis of a transcript by J. A. Herbert*, EETS o.s. 225 (1952)

---

[1] This account does not discuss the French or Latin manuscripts of the *Ancrene Wisse* of which there are four each: in French, BL Cotton Vitellius F. vii, Trinity College, Cambridge R. 14. 7, Oxford, Bodley 90 and Paris BN Fr. 6276; in Latin: BL Cotton Vitellius E. vii, BL Royal 7. C. x, Oxford, Magdalen College Lat. 67 and Oxford, Merton College 44.

[2] The sigla used here are those employed in Dobson, 'Affiliations', 128, to which the siglum **E** has been added.

T   London, BL Cotton Titus D. xviii, ff. 14–105; ed. F. M. Mack, *The English Text of the Ancrene Riwle, edited from B. M. MS Cotton Titus D. xviii, together with the Llanhydrock Fragment, Bodleian MS Eng. th. c.70*, EETS o.s. 252 (1963)

R   London, BL Royal 8 C. i, ff. 122v–143v; ed. A. C. Baugh, *The English Text of the Ancrene Riwle, edited from British Museum MS Royal 8 C. i*, EETS o.s. 232 (1956)

V   Oxford, Bodleian Library Eng. poet. a 1, ff. 371v–392r; ed. Arne Zettersten and Bernhard Diensberg, *The English Text of the Ancrene Riwle, edited from Oxford, Bodleian Library, MS Engl. poet. a. I*, EETS 310 (2000)

E   Oxford, Bodleian Library Eng. th. c.70, f. 61r–v; see **T** above, pp. 163–173

The main manuscripts (i.e. leaving aside **E**[3]) range in date from the mid-thirteenth to the fifteenth centuries. The earliest seem to be **C** and **A**. These manuscripts both seem to date on textual and palaeographical grounds from around the middle of the first half of the thirteenth century (**C** has revisions by other scribes in hands from towards the end of the century). **N** and **T** are probably from the second quarter of the thirteenth century.[4] **T** seems to be very slightly the later.[5] The copy in **G** has been authoritatively dated on palaeographical grounds to the second half of the thirteenth century.[6] **P** dates from the second half of the fourteenth century. **V** clearly was copied at the very end of that century. The latest of the manuscripts is **R**, which seems to date from the middle of the fifteenth century.

Such marked variations in date have predictable parallels in place of origin. **A** is from the West Midlands; its dialect suggests north Herefordshire or south Cheshire.[7] A similar origin must be assumed on dialectal grounds for **C** from which **A** derives.[8] Both are written in the AB dialect associated with other texts composed in this region in the early part of the thirteenth century.[9] These include some of those in **T** which seems, however, for *Ancrene Wisse* to 'display more northerly characteristics' but still seems to be south Cheshire.[10] **N** seems to be further south in either Worcestershire or Gloucestershire.[11] The other manuscripts are all much later and reflect wider processes of transmission. **V** is from Worcestershire. The farthest afield on dialectal grounds are **P**, written in an Essex dialect and **R**, in a Nottinghamshire one. But, as is usually the case with dialectal evidence, it is

---

[3] **E** has been largely excluded from this discussion since it is a fragment.
[4] N: ix.
[5] See Dobson, *The Origins*, 81–2, n. 3. Earlier, he suggests that this manuscript 'is likely to have been written fairly well into the second quarter of the century' (65, n. 3).
[6] G: ix.
[7] See Dobson, 'Date', 181.
[8] Although Dobson locates the scribes' dialects as (for scribe A) 'on the periphery . . . of the district in which the "AB language" itself was spoken' (xciii) and (for scribe B) 'a less developed stage in the orthography of the "AB dialect"' (cxl).
[9] On this dialect see seminally Tolkien, '*Ancrene Wisse* and *Hali Meiðhad*', 104–26.
[10] See Laing, *Catalogue*, 82.
[11] Laing, *Catalogue*, 78.

the scribe's ideolect, not necessarily the location in which he was copying that is revealed.[12]

All the manuscripts are written on parchment, but vary in size, decoration and other contents. The earliest, **A**, is a quite large volume (215 × 148 mm) containing only *Ancrene Wisse*. **C** is also quite large (194 × 140 mm) but includes a number brief additional items, as we have seen. These are the manuscripts which can be most directly associated with the anchoritic and female religious audiences for which the *Ancrene Wisse* was originally created. Like all the other manuscripts they do not have any illustration; and like most of them the overall level of decoration is modest.[13] Both contain simple blue or red initials with some paraph marks in these colours and some rubrication. **C** occasionally has simple, abstract patterns in blue and red ink, extending down and/or across, inner or outer margins. The issues of size and modest decoration have some bearing on the purposes for which these manuscripts were produced. Were they intended for private reading within religious communities, or to be read aloud – or both? It is difficult to draw clear-cut conclusions; quite probably they were employed in both functions given the doubtless modest size of the houses. Certainly such of the early history of **A** as can be recovered, places it in a house of Augustinian canons at Wigmore, in Herefordshire, not very far from the putative origins of the *Ancrene Wisse*.[14]

G, the other manuscript which contains only *Ancrene Wisse*, is smaller: 100 × 67 mm. This manuscript, too, is not very elaborate in terms of its production, with only minimal rubrication and few simply coloured initials. Here the correlation of modest size and limited decoration may suggest rather more compellingly that it was intended primarily for private reading.[15]

Some other manuscripts are also modest in size but differ from these by linking *Ancrene Wisse*, sometimes quite deliberately, with related works. **T** (155 × 120 mm) is the earliest collection to include the *Ancrene Wisse*; it also contains *Sawles Warde* (ff. 105v–112v) as well as the major works of the 'Katherine Group', *Hali Meiðhad* (ff. 112v–127), þe *Wohunge of Ure Lauerd* (ff. 127–33) and *St Katherine* (ff. 133v–147v). It is written in a version of the AB dialect of **A** and **C**. A number of these texts (*Sawles Warde, St Katherine*, and *Hali Meiðhad*) also appear together in BL Royal 17. A. xxvii, but not, of course, with *Ancrene Wisse*, but again written in a dialect related to the AB language.

N (144 × 107 mm) and **R** (145 × 220 mm) are also fairly small books. The primary content of **N** is *Ancrene Wisse*, but it also contains a number of

---

[12] Information on the dialects of these manuscripts is taken from McIntosh *et al.*, *Linguistic Atlas*, 1, 64, 113 and 148.

[13] For discussion of some aspects of the decoration and layout of the *Ancrene Riwle* manuscripts see Dahood, 'Coloured Initials', 79–98.

[14] Ker, *Medieval Libraries*, 198.

[15] Although **G** is now bound up with other material it was clearly originally conceived as a separate work; see Ker in Wilson, *The English Text*, ix.

short devotional and instructional texts in prose (ff. 123v–131v).[16] *Ancrene Wisse* also forms the principal content of **R**, but it is preceded by various Latin works of John Waldeby, the Augustinian friar, and followed by a Middle English tract on the Seven Deadly Sins.[17] **R**'s contents invite the assumption that the manuscript was constructed for some monastic or clerical audience, but no clear indication of early ownership is to be found. The change in the forms of address from female to male (see below) provides some support for such a view.

Other manuscripts are larger and, in some instances, join the *Ancrene Wisse* to a wider range of Middle English religious works. **V**, the so-called Vernon manuscript, forms the largest surviving collection of such materials in both verse and prose. It is also physically by far the biggest; it measures 544 × 393 mm, and originally probably contained nearly four hundred leaves. As it is, in its surviving state it weighs over forty-eight pounds. Its verse contents include *The South English Legendary*, *The Northern Homily Cycle*, and *The Prick of Conscience*. The *Ancrene Wisse* is among the longest of its prose works (ff. 371v–392r) which also include the *Stimulus Amoris*, *The Abbey* and *The Charter of the Holy Ghost* and works by Rolle and Hilton.[18] Its massive size and weight confirm that its 'display and reading must have been as [a] coucher or ledger book, on a lectern or desk'.[19] But the nature of the audience and forms it which it might be used remain unclear. The assemblage of vernacular texts might suggest an audience of female religious or pious lay women; but it is not impossible that it may have been conceived for some male religious house.[20]

V is also the most elaborately decorated of the surviving manuscripts. Although it does not contain any illustrations it does a large number of elaborate initials and is also unusual in marking some of the various divisions of the text into books usually by elaborate demi-vinets.[21] It has been linked circumstantially to Bordesley Abbey in Warwickshire.[22]

P is the next most substantial collection of works including the *Ancrene Wisse*. Although not as big as **V**, it is also large, measuring 340 × 240 mm. Its other prose contents include *The Harmony of the Gospels*, the *Mirror*, a version of the Apocalypse, the prose psalter and *The Gospel of Nicodemus*. Like **V** it was very probably constructed for some form of institutional use rather than for private reading.

As will be apparent, there is no significant correlation between manuscripts which links *Ancrene Wisse* and other prose texts. The most recurrent correlation is a six-line Middle English verse passage incorporated into the work in **A**, **C**, **N**, **D**, **V** and **T**.[23] This does appear elsewhere in a single manuscript that does not contain *Ancrene Wisse*, BL Arundel 507, but it

---

[16] Thompson, *Wohunge*, 5–18.
[17] For a full description see Warner and Gilson, *Catalogue*, I:228.
[18] For the fullest recent description of the prose works in **V** see Hanna, *Index*, 4–8.
[19] See Doyle, *Vernon Manuscript*, 1.
[20] For discussion of these issues see Doyle, *Vernon Manuscript*, 14–15.
[21] For discussion of the decoration of **V** see Scott, *Later Gothic Manuscripts*, II:19–24.
[22] See Doyle, *Vernon Manuscript*, 14–15.
[23] This is number 3568 in Brown and Robbins, *Index*, and in Robbins and Cutler, *Supplement*.

seems more likely that it was excerpted there from some version of *Ancrene Wisse* rather than that *Ancrene Wisse* incorporated a separately circulating lyric.

Nor do the manuscripts generally offer any specific indications of authorship. Only one manuscript gives an attribution specifically to a named individual. This is **R** in which a fifteenth-century contents list describes *Ancrene Wisse* as 'optimus tractus [*sic*] de v sensibus secundum lichef[last part torn away]' (f. 1v). The person thus named is generally identified with William Lichfield, the apparent author of a long Middle English poem, *The Complaint of God*. There is no authority for this attribution and it is of interest primarily because it shows how distanced any understanding of the work's authorship, and hence its origins, had become during the two hundred year period since its initial composition.

It is not possible to provide a wider context for the production of most of these manuscripts, beyond their language and early provenance. In a few cases the scribes have been identified in other surviving manuscripts. In **C**, the hand of Scribe D, the more extensive corrector of the text is also the copyist of a number of Middle English items in verse and prose in this manuscript.[24] A number of these items recur in another manuscript this scribe copied, Trinity College, Cambridge MS B. 1. 45, in which this scribe is again the main corrector. As Dobson has argued, both manuscripts were probably made for an Augustinian house, Canonsleigh in Devon.[25]

V is copied largely by a scribe who also copied British Library Add. 22283, the so-called Simeon manuscript. This is a sister manuscript to **V**, with which it shares a significant number of contents, although the full extent of their correspondence is obscured by the loss of a large number of leaves in Simeon. It has been estimated that it would have taken this scribe nearly four years to copy both manuscripts.[26] The copying of *Ancrene Wisse* in **V** must be seen, therefore, as part of a much wider commitment to the regional circulation of vernacular devotional texts with which this scribe can be closely identified.

The scribe of **P**, another very large collection, is known to have copied two other manuscripts: BL Harley 874 and Bodleian Laud misc. 622. The Harley manuscript is a copy of Wycliffe on the Apocalypse. The Laud manuscript contains various Middle English texts, primarily in verse.[27] These include various religious works, notably the *South English Legendary* and the *Life of St Alexis*; but it also contains a number of romances, *King Alexander* and *Titus* and *Vespasian*. The interest of the scribe in secular writings lacks any parallel among the *Ancrene Wisse* scribes. The copying of a work by Wycliffe in the Harley manuscript is also suggestive of a range of interest, whether on the part of the scribe or its commissioners, that is untypically heterodox for these scribes. The point is of importance to the text of *Ancrene Wisse* in **P**. This has generally

---

[24] Enumerated in Dobson, *The English Text*, cxlii–iii.
[25] See Ker, *Medieval Libraries*, 29.
[26] See Doyle, *Vernon Manuscript*, 6, where this scribe is designated Scribe B.
[27] Mainly edited by Furnivall.

characterized as a 'Lollard version' reflecting the preoccupations of Wycliffe's reformist followers.[28]

Unsurprisingly, given their transmission over such an extended period, some of these manuscripts vary extensively in length and content. The text as originally constituted comprised eight parts, a form that is reflected most fully in the two earliest manuscripts, **C** and **A** and is also preserved in the fourteenth century **P** and **N**.[29]

However, several comprise only selections or extracts from the larger work. Thus **R** comprises parts of Parts II–III only, while **G** contains a series of extracts in non-sequential order. Such variations and adaptations testify to the extent to which the *Ancrene Wisse* remained a living work capable of being modified to new contexts and circumstances.

Indeed, even among the complete manuscripts, where there are broad correlations in section divisions, there is usually extensive variation between witnesses. In part this the consequence of the re-adaptation of the work as its audience changed and widened. The circulation of these versions is obviously linked to their accommodation to a variety of different audiences from the initial female, anchoritic one for which the *Ancrene Wisse* was originally written. One obvious, but significant indication of this change in audience is the changing forms of pronouns in the different manuscripts. The earliest ones, **A** and **C** specify a female, enclosed readership ('ȝe ancren' C 2/5). This is also the case in **N**. But other manuscripts widen their sense of audience. **G** is gender neutral ('Herknent mine leue frend' 4/15–16; cf. 86/32). **P** specifies gender inclusiveness: 'Now to onelich men & wymmen & to alle oþer þat desiren forto seruen god what þat is ȝoure reule ȝe schulleþ riȝth wel witen' (2/10–12). And Baugh has noted that, in the latest version, in **R**, that 'nothing is more certain than that the adaptation of the *Ancrene Wisse* in the Royal manuscript was not intended for hermits or anchoresses' (x). He draws attention to a passage in **N**: 'þe uoxes þet beoð ðe valse ancren as vox is best falsest' (56/12–13). In **R** this reads: 'By Foxes may wele be vnderstonden fals men' (24/3–4). But the passage goes on to imply the applicability of the work to a comprehensive range of religious of both genders: 'And ȝit many prestes. many monkys Chanons. Freres. ankyrs. and ankeresses Nunnys & heremytes are. more worldly. lifen more lustily. are more delauy in curiose talkyng of þe world an luken more after worldly reuerense & honour þen þay shold haue' (24/15–20). There is no parallel passage in the earlier versions.

Such variations demonstrate the continuity of engagement by scribes and readers with the work during the Middle Ages. There is further testimony to this engagement in the various selections incorporated into devotional compendia.

Some sections seem to have achieved a distinct identity of their own. Two manuscripts preserve a Latin version of a passage from the beginning of the

---

[28] For discussion of this version see College, '*The Recluse*', 1–15 and 129–45; his views are modified in Hudson, *Premature Reformation*, 27–8.

[29] It should be noted that the manuscripts do not usually reflect these divisions in their presentation of the text.

Ancrene Wisse that survives in Middle English as part of a fourteenth-century devotional treatise, *The Chastising of God's Children*.[30] The same section is also included in an early printed edition of Rolle's *Emendatio Vitae*.[31] Another fourteenth-century religious compilation, the extremely popular *Pore Caitif*, includes extracts from Book VII,[32] as did the collection known as 'þe holy boke Gratia Dei'.[33] Such selections or extracts indicate the ways in which *Ancrene Wisse* had become assimilated into wider vernacular devotional traditions by this period.

Such traditions continued into early print culture. A number of early printed editions of *The Chastising of God's Children* are bound up with Wynkyn de Worde's 1496 edition of the *Tretyse of Love* (no manuscript of this work survives).[34] The compilation is made up of ten distinct devotional tracts in English of which the first three are borrowed largely from *Ancrene Wisse*,[35] mainly from Part VII. It seems most likely that these borrowings are a re-translation back into English from a French version.[36] In the form that they now survive these the latest major borrowings from the work during the Middle Ages. There was to be no further edition of any part of *Ancrene Wisse* until the nineteenth century.

But evidence of the reception of *Ancrene Wisse* is not confined to these borrowings and adaptations. For some insight into the ways it was perceived by early post-medieval readers it is necessary to return to the manuscripts of the work itself.

Several of the manuscripts engaged the interest of such readers in various ways. Some manuscripts found their way into important clerical circles. **A** was evidently 'read again carefully in the sixteenth century.'[37] One of its most important readers was Matthew Parker (1504–1575), Elizabeth I's first Archbishop of Canterbury, whose characteristic red chalk marks are found at several points. A member of the circle of this great collector, Stephen Batman (d. 1584), owned **P** in the mid-sixteenth century. Batman was one of the first collectors of Middle English manuscripts,[38] and seems to have had a particular interest in devotional literature.[39] Batman added a number of comments in both verse and prose to the manuscripts he owned. His notes on *Ancrene Wisse*, however, are disappointingly meagre, being largely confined to the opening pages. Batman seems to have had primarily doctrinal and historical concerns. He notes at the top of the first page: 'The Canticle vpon the Masse, worth the keping, to answer their wilfull blindnes. & svmwhat strainge' (p. 1), and on an early page 'An olde

---

[30] See further Allen, 'Fourteenth-Century Borrowings', 1–4.
[31] Allen, 'Further Borrowings', 1–15 (at 13).
[32] See further Allen, 'Fourteenth-Century Borrowings', 3–4, and Brady, '*Pore Caitif*', 529–48. Over fifty manuscripts of this work survive; see Jolliffe, *Check-List*, 65–67, to which may be added Durham, University Library Add. 754.
[33] On this work see Keiser, 'Gratia Dei', 289–317.
[34] The standard edition is Fisher, *Tretyse*.
[35] For details see Fisher, *Tretyse*, xiii–xvi, xix–xxii.
[36] See Allen, 'Wynkyn de Worde', 182–220.
[37] Tolkien, *The English Text*, xviii.
[38] On Batman's collections see Parkes, 'Batman's Manuscripts', 125–156.
[39] On some aspects of that interest see Edwards 'Batman', 267–78.

supersticius rule which requireth wisely too be readd of the Masse. & purgatorie' (p. 6). It is striking that circles most closely involved with the reformed church found themselves prompted to careful and energetic responses to *Ancrene Wisse*.

Others seem to have been interested in the work as part of a wider bibliographical or historical curiosity. **C**, for example, was owned in the mid-sixteenth century by a noted antiquarian and book-collector, Robert Talbot (1505?–1558), a cleric and Fellow of New College, Oxford, who possessed a number of other early English manuscripts.[40] It also contains a brief note by Richard James, librarian to Robert Cotton in the early seventeenth century, in whose great collection of medieval manuscripts both **C** and **N** were. James also annotated **N**,[41] but rather more extensively, partly in Latin and partly in English. His notes at times point to matters, of social or religious usage: 'Noblemen weare no purses', 'The sacrament not receiued to often, Monachi et presbyteri proprijs nominibus non appellandi.' They also a degree of interest in the practises of nuns. James notes at the beginning that the author of the *Ancrene Wisse* 'scribit praecipue ad fœminas anchoritas' and he makes specific points in relation to this gendered audience: 'nonnes must not foule their Holliday clothes'; 'He would have Nunnes keepe no beaste but a chat'; 'Nuns let blood to preserve chastitie.' Such post-Reformation comments reflect James's antiquarian and historical concerns, concerns far removed from the spiritual ones of the work itself.

Such antiquarian sympathies are also demonstrated in the last evidence of engagement with *Ancrene Wisse* which occurs in Bodleian Library MS Laud 201. This is a series of early seventeenth century notes from the *Ancrene Wisse* made from **A** by the Anglo-Saxon scholar, Edward Lye (1694–1767).[42] The motives for Lye's transcriptions are presumably linked to his interest in Anglo-Saxon philology. It is an undertaking that removes the work from any contact with living devotional traditions or with Middle English literature at all. Study of *Ancrene Wisse* effectively ceases henceforward until Morton's 1843 edition for the Camden Society which marks the beginnings of modern interest in the manuscript forms of this work.

Works Cited

Allen, H. E., 'Some Fourteenth-Century Borrowings from "Ancren Riwle"', *Modern Language Review* 18 (1923)

——, 'Further Borrowings from "Ancren Riwle"', *Modern Language Review* 24 (1929)

——, 'Wynkyn de Worde and a Second French Version Compilation from the

---

[40] On Talbot's collections see Ker, *Catalogue* i.
[41] His annotations are printed in Day, *The English Text*, xx–xxii.
[42] Printed by Heuser, 'Ancrene Riwle', 103–22, and discussed by Napier, 'Ancrene Riwle', 433–6.

"Ancren Riwle" with a Description of the First (Trinity Coll. Camb. MS 883)', in *Essays and Studies in Honor of Carleton Brown* (New York, 1940)

Baugh, A. C., ed., *The English Text of the Ancrene Riwle, edited from British Museum MS Royal 8 C. i*, EETS o.s. 232 (1956)

Brady, M. T., '*The Pore Caitif*: an Introductory Study', *Traditio* 10 (1954)

Brown, Carleton, and Rossell Hope Robbins, *The Index of Middle English Verse* (New York, 1943)

Colledge, E., '*The Recluse*: a Lollard Interpolated Version of the Ancren Riwle', *Review of English Studies* 15 (1939)

Dahood, R., 'The Use of Coloured Initials and Other Division Markers in Early Versions of the *Ancrene Riwle*', in *Medieval English Studies presented to George Kane*, ed. Edward Donald Kennedy, Ronald Waldron and Joseph S. Wittig (Cambridge, 1988)

Day, Mabel, ed., *The English Text of the Ancrene Riwle: Cotton Nero A. xiv, on the basis of a transcript by J. A. Herbert*, EETS o.s. 225 (1952)

Dobson, E. J., 'The Affiliations of Manuscripts of the *Ancrene Wisse*', in *English and Medieval Studies Presented to J. R. R. Tolkien*, ed. Norman Davis and C. L. Wrenn (London, 1962)

——, 'The Date and Composition of the *Ancrene Wisse*', *Proceedings of the British Academy* 52 (1966)

——, ed., *The English Text of the Ancrene Riwle, edited from B. M. MS Cotton Cleopatra C. vi*, EETS 267 (1972)

——, *The Origins of Ancrene Wisse* (Oxford, 1976)

Doyle, A. I., *The Vernon Manuscript: a Facsimile of Bodleian Library, Oxford, MS Eng. poet. a. 1* (Cambridge, 1987)

Edwards, A. S. G., 'Stephen Batman and *The Book of Privy Counselling*', in *Chaucer in Perspective: Middle English Essays in Honour of Norman Blake*, ed. G. A. Lester (Sheffield, 1999)

Fisher, John H., ed., *The Tretyse of Loue*, EETS o.s. 223 (London 1951)

Furnivall, F. J., *Adam Davy's 5 Dreams about Edward II etc.*, EETS o.s. 69 (1878)

Hanna, R., III, *The Index of Middle English Prose, Handlist XII: Smaller Bodleian Collections* (Cambridge, 1997)

Heuser, W., 'Die Ancrene Riwle – ein aus angelsächsischen Zeit überliefertes Denkmal', *Anglia* 30 (1907)

Hudson, Anne, *The Premature Reformation* (Oxford, 1988)

Jolliffe, P. S., *A Check-List of Middle English Prose Writings of Spiritual Guidance* (Toronto, 1974)

Keiser, George, 'þe holy boke Gratia Dei', *Viator* 12 (1981)

Ker, N. R., *Catalogue of Manuscripts Containing Anglo-Saxon* (Oxford, 1957)

——, *Medieval Libraries of Great Britain*, 2nd edn (London, 1964)

Laing, M., *Catalogue of Sources for an Atlas of Early Middle English* (Cambridge, 1993)

Mack, F. M., ed., *The English Text of the Ancrene Riwle, edited from B. M. MS Cotton Titus D. xviii, together with the Llanhydrock Fragment, Bodleian MS Eng. th. c.70*, EETS o.s. 252 (1963)

McIntosh, Angus, Michael Benskin and M. L. Samuels, eds., with the assistance of Margaret Laing and Keith Williamson, *A Linguistic Atlas of Late Mediaeval English*, 4 vols (Aberdeen, 1986)

Napier, A. S., 'The Ancrene Riwle', *Modern Language Review* 4 (1909)

Parkes, M. B., 'Stephen Batman's Manuscripts', in *Medieval Heritage: Essays in Honour of Tadahiro Ikegami* (Tokyo, 1997)

Robbins, Rossell Hope, and John L. Cutler, *Supplement to The Index of Middle English Verse* (Lexington, 1965)

Scott, Kathleen L., *Later Gothic Manuscripts, 1390–1490*, 2 vols. (London, 1996)

Thompson, Meredith, ed., *þe Wohunge of Ure Lauerd*, EETS o.s. 241 (1958)

Tolkien, J. R. R., '*Ancrene Wisse* and *Hali Meiðhad*', *Essays and Studies* 14 (1929)

——, ed., *The English Text of the Ancrene Riwle: Ancrene Wisse, edited from MS Corpus Christi College Cambridge 402*, with an Introduction by N. R. Ker, EETS o.s. 249 (1962)

Warner, G. F., and J. P. Gilson, *Catalogue of Western Manuscripts in the Old Royal and King's Collections*, 4 vols. (London, 1921)

Wilson, R. M., ed., *The English Text of the Ancrene Riwle, edited from Gonville and Caius College MS 234/120*, with an Introduction by N. R. Ker, EETS o.s. 229 (1954)

Zettersten, A., ed., *The English Text of the Ancrene Riwle, edited from Magdalene College Cambridge MS 2498*, EETS 274 (1976)

——, and Bernhard Diensberg, eds., *The English Text of the Ancrene Riwle, edited from Oxford, Bodleian Library, MS Engl. poet. a. 1*, EETS 310 (2000)

7

Savoring 'Scientia': the Medieval Anchoress Reads *Ancrene Wisse*

ELIZABETH ROBERTSON

Thomas De Quincey made what has become a famous distinction between two forms of literature: literature of knowledge and literature of power: while the former provides invaluable information, the latter offers 'exercise and expansion to your own latent capacity of sympathy with the infinite.'[1] De Quincey assigns the 'cookery' book to the former, Milton's *Paradise Lost* to the latter. Where does the thirteenth-century guide for female recluses, *Ancrene Wisse*, fit in the spectrum between literature of knowledge and literature of power? While *Ancrene Wisse* has been praised for its literary qualities – for the intensity and warmth of its narrator, for its vivid portraits of everyday village life as it enters the window of the anchorhold, and for its range of unusual metaphors describing God's love – it was initially appreciated primarily for its philological interest as a work that filled in a gap between Anglo-Saxon and the florescence of Middle English literature in the fourteenth century.[2] More recently the work has been studied for its Foucauldian regulatory qualities and valued primarily as a cultural artefact that captures a spectacularly rigorous form of religious life for women.[3] As such, it has most often been read for the information it provides, that is as literature of knowledge. Although I am not concerned here to define or defend the literary qualities of this work, I would like to explore what kind of *reading* experience the text may have offered the original anchoritic readers in order to consider the particular ways this text exceeded mere usefulness. Was this text a reference book, a compendium of knowledge, one that embellished a daily practice; or was it crucial to stimulating the anchoress's capacity for self-expansion? What function did it (and other books) have in the anchorhold? How might we reconstruct the scene of reading of the medieval anchoress? How, physically and mentally, was *Ancrene Wisse* read, and how are the physical and mental aspects of reading related for the anchoress? The earliest manuscripts of the text, and the text itself, we shall see, tell us that *Ancrene Wisse* was a text

---

[1] de Quincey, 'Literature of Knowledge', 331.
[2] For summaries of the various forms of criticism devoted to *Ancrene Wisse* see the superb bibliography assembled by Bella Millett with the assistance of Yoko Wada and George B. Jack, *Annotated Bibliographies*.
[3] An excellent example of an essay that explores *Ancrene Wisse*'s regulatory functions is Beckwith, 'Passionate Regulation', 803–24.

designed first and foremost for practical use. Like a cook book, *Ancrene Wisse* provides the knowledge to establish a regulatory practice in which reading, praying, and physical activity are interchangeable and intertwined. The desired end of that practice, however, ultimately is directed towards the expansiveness of the self/soul that results from an intensely focussed confrontation with death. If this is a 'how to' manual, what it teaches is how to die.

To begin to construct a scene of reading, we need to know what the book in the scene looked like. Unfortunately the original manuscript of *Ancrene Wisse* no longer exists and the earliest manuscripts that do survive are, according to E. J. Dobson, at least twice removed from that original.[4] However, it is likely that several of those early manuscripts were in the hands of the group of twenty or more contemplatives that the original three anchoresses are said in the Corpus manuscript (Corpus Christi College Cambridge MS 402) to have become. The seventeen manuscripts that survive can, according to Dobson, be divided into two groups: the alpha group from which descends Corpus alone, probably 'a close copy of the author's own final and definitive revision of his work', and the beta group 'from which descend the sixteen remaining manuscripts.[5] Dobson describes the likely development of this second group as follows:

> [W]e can build up a picture of the sort of community in which the nucleus of the β group must have developed. It had begun with a single unusually accurate, but not perfect, copy of the text, from which it had made certainly two and probably three early transcripts. It valued the book, and took pains to secure the accuracy of its text by the . . . collation of one text with another. It also had a need for an increasing number of copies, and as they were multiplied the processes of collation became more complicated. The community remained in touch with the author, and from him received additions to the basic text . . . The author also wrote additions and explanations in the margins of individual manuscripts and even corrected their errors of copying, which must imply that he visited the community fairly regularly.[6]

At a later date, Dobson surmises that the scribe who initially copied one of the manuscripts (Dobson's Scribe A of the British Library MS Cotton Cleopatra C vi) 'cannot have lived at any great distance, since the [copying] plan depended on the regular delivery to him, and the return by him, of the sections of the exemplar.'[7] Dobson's proposed history creates for us a scene in which the original text must have, from its inception, been a communal text passed among at first three, and then quite soon, a growing community of anchoresses; yet, despite communal sharing, and, since there was so quickly a need for multiple copies even for a small group, it must also have been in demand as a book for solitary reading and contemplation.

---

[4] Dobson, 'Affiliations', 128–63.
[5] Dobson, 'Affiliations', 163.
[6] Dobson, 'Affiliations', 162.
[7] Dobson, *English Text*, p. lv.

This history also captures for us a distinctive authorial presence in the text itself; this was not a book written, then left behind, by the author, but one that he tinkered with as his audience grew before his eyes. (Langland, as is well known, also revised his poem for decades, but not in the presence of a familiar audience.) The author's presence in the text as a guiding voice has been frequently observed, but his presence as an emender only adds to the sense that he is virtually present in the anchorhold with the anchoress as she reads.

We can only extrapolate from the physical appearance of its earliest extant manuscripts what this text might have looked like as a physical object and how it functioned materially within the anchorhold. I shall first consider the manuscripts as a group, then look more closely at a few manuscripts: London, British Library, Cotton MS Cleopatra C vi, Corpus Christi College Cambridge MS 402, and London, British Library Cotton MS Nero A xiv (henceforth Cleopatra C vi, Corpus 402 and Nero A xiv), by reason of their association with the female contemplatives for whom this text was created. The modest appearance of the majority of the extant manuscripts of *Ancrene Wisse* suggests that this is indeed primarily a book designed for use, rather than for aesthetic pleasure or for contemplation aided by imagery. In general, the earlier versions of the text are in relatively small manuscripts (roughly $7\frac{1}{2} \times 5\frac{1}{2}$ inches) that contain only that text with little rubrication and no illuminations, or the text of *Ancrene Wisse* followed by a handful of prayers and devotions to God.[8] A few of the manuscripts, such as Cotton Titus D xviii, include other texts such as saints' lives and sermons, completely in keeping with anchoritic devotional purposes. The small size of most of the early manuscripts, as well as their relative lack of adornment, suggests that *Ancrene Wisse* was to be held in the hands by an individual, perhaps reading privately in her cell, or perhaps reading to her fellow anchoresses or to her servants. (The text itself advises that it should be read from weekly to the servants: '3e ancres ahen þis leaste stucche reden to ower wummen euche wike eanes. aþet ha hit cunnen' ['You anchoresses ought to read this last branch to your servants once each week until they know it.'][9]) Although fairly thick, the early manuscripts (in contrast to the large, heavy Vernon manuscript) might easily be carried around, or tucked into a sleeve or pocket.

The earliest of the extant manuscripts, Cleopatra C vi, may be close in appearance to the original. The manuscript includes annotations which, according to Dobson, may have been drafts of additions included in the text 'in the revision of which MS Corpus Christi College, Cambridge, 402 is a

---

[8] For a discussion of the manuscripts see Millett *Annotated Bibliographies*, 49–61. The manuscripts are housed in Cambridge, Oxford, and London. Most of the manuscripts have been edited for the Early English Text Society.

[9] Tolkien, *The English Text*, 220. All further quotations from the text of *Ancrene Wisse* will be taken from this edition. I have silently expanded the tironian ampersand and the crossed thorn. Translations are my own although I have benefitted from the excellent translations of Salu, *Ancrene Riwle*, Savage and Watson, *Anchoritic Spirituality*, and White, *Ancrene Wisse*.

fair copy.'[10] These two, with the French manuscript, London, British Library, Cotton Vitellius F vii, are the most important witnesses to the original text and, thus, to the text as it may have been experienced by the anchoresses. It is probable that the original text was composed in English, but the anchoresses must have read French with ease and they must have known enough Latin to get through their hours.[11] Given that the dialect of the early manuscripts points to a location near the borders of Wales, they also may well have known a smattering of Welsh.[12] Dated in the first half of the thirteenth century and, thus, probably within the lifetime of the original anchoresses, the Cleopatra manuscript is a small clearly written manuscript showing three hands, one scribe A, believed to have been clerically trained, the second scribe B, perhaps the author himself, providing additions and corrections, and the third, Scribe D, a much later annotator who modernized the text. At one time, Dobson believed Scribe A to be one of the anchoresses; more recently, he argued that the scribe must be male since several masculine pronouns are added in places where one would expect female pronouns if the scribe were an anchoress, a likely, though not definitive, argument.[13] The probability that Scribe A was clerically trained does not rule out the possibility that the scribe was female, perhaps one of the original three anchoresses, since *Ancrene Wisse* acknowledges some clerical training in its audience. There is evidence of highly skilled female scribes at work elsewhere (for instance, the scribe at Nunnaminster), though it is unlikely at this date and locale to find nuns, let alone anchoresses, with such training.[14] The text does indicate that some of the anchoresses knew how to write, since they are forbidden to do so without the leave of the spiritual director and since the text refers to prayers they have written – though perhaps only to prayers that have been written down for them; the author mentions: 'ȝe habbeð of þeos blissen iwriten elleswher mine leoue sustren' ('You have written about these joys elsewhere, my dear sisters,'or, 'you have texts about these joys elsewhere').[15] Nonetheless, it is not at all clear that copying manuscripts would be a part of the anchoritic life. If some anchoresses were involved in copying the text, our re-creation of the scene of reading would be complicated, for reading a text to copy it is

[10] A meticulous discussion of the Cleopatra manuscript is Dobson, *The English Text*. See p. ix for the reference. See also his discussion of the relationship of this manuscript to the others, in Dobson, 'Affiliations'.

[11] For a discussion of the original language of the text see the articles cited in Millett, *Annotated Bibliographies* as well as my summary of them in Robertson, '"This Living Hand"'.

[12] We do not know where the original anchoresses were located. E. J. Dobson argued thoroughly for an Augustinian origin of the text in his *Origins*. More recently, Millett has challenged that position, arguing instead for a Dominican origin for the text: see Millett, 'Origins', 206–28. The dialect of the early manuscripts points towards the Welsh marches and towards the Shropshire/ Herefordshire border, but the actual location is debatable.

[13] In 'Affiliations', Dobson originally thought that Scribe A could possibly have been one of the anchoresses; in his edition, however, he changed his mind because he noticed several places where the scribe substituted masculine for feminine references: see Dobson, 'Affiliations', 163, and Dobson, *The English Text*, p. lvi.

[14] For discussion of this female scribe see Robinson, 'Twelfth-Century Scriptrix', 73–93.

[15] Tolkien, *The English Text*, 209, f. 11a. Bella Millett pointed out to me the possible ambiguity of this comment.

quite different from reading a text as a guide for contemplation. Dobson argues that it is most likely that the scribe was either a professional working for a fee or 'a secular priest or a domestic chaplain, who had undertaken to help the anchoresses by making for them one of the copies which they needed.'[16]

It would, of course, be ideal if the manuscripts themselves revealed something about their early female anchoritic readers through marks or commentary. Unfortunately, the only inscriptions in the manuscript do not guide us to anchoritic readers of the text, although they do tell us a little about some of its later owners, if not some of its readers. Cleopatra C vi is inscribed at the end in a late thirteenth-century hand as a gift from Mathilda de Clare to the nuns at Canonsleigh; dated about 1300, by Dobson, the inscription reads: 'Datus abbatie ant conventu de leghe. per dame.M. de clare.'[17] This inscription tells us the manuscript left the hands of its original owners, perhaps anchoresses, fell into secular hands, and then was passed on to a group of Augustinian canonesses. It is interesting that a text designed with such a particular purpose and audience in mind should be so versatile that it could pass easily into secular hands. An inscription which gives the name Henry Dule of Lancaster also does not indicate a reader since, in Dobson's opinion, this is a pen trial made by one of her clerks when the manuscript was in Mathilda's possession.[18]

The contents of the manuscript other than *Ancrene Wisse* help us pinpoint only where and how the manuscript was used later in its history. Three leaves at the end, perhaps added by Scribe D, contain some Latin antiphons and other liturgical material. The praise of St Etheldreda found in these pages helps us establish a date and locale for this material since St Etheldreda became patron saint of Canonsleigh in 1284. The additional material also includes fourteen lines of French verse on Jesus as lover – a poem in keeping with the particular devotional focus of *Ancrene Wisse*, and in a language they were likely to have been able to read – and directions for devotions that could easily belong in Part 1. Most of this material was probably added while the manuscript resided at Canonsleigh, though it seems close in function to *Ancrene Wisse* itself; if not anchoritic, these added pieces were at least devotional in purpose. The manuscript also includes a fifteenth-century illumination from a book of hours of the Visitation, an addition that suggests late readers associated the text with the hours of the Virgin. Although the early manuscripts eschew such illustrations, an illumination of Mary is in keeping with the emphasis in *Ancrene Wisse* on Mary as a model for the anchoress. The image of Mary, however, could appeal to a variety of devotional audiences, even secular ones.

The appearance of the manuscript can help us to discern that this text may not have been originally created as a meditative text, but rather may have been produced as a copy of the original specifically designed to provide a text that Scribe B could then revise. Its numerous small errors indicate

[16] Dobson, *The English Text*, p. lv.
[17] Dobson, *The English Text*, p. xxv.
[18] Dobson, *The English Text*, p. xxvi.

that it was hastily copied. Given the fact that Scribe B, the annotator, took little interest in these small errors and was much more interested, according to Dobson, in clarifying the sense or in expanding passages, it is possible that this manuscript was used as an exemplar which a reviser or the author himself annotated and from which a clean copy was made. Although it is difficult to determine the original size of margins for the various versions of *Ancrene Wisse* since later bindings may well have cut original margins down, Clepatra C vi seems to have unusually wide margins. It is possible to imagine that such space might have been left for decorations. However, given the fact that the manuscript is hastily produced, and contains many additions and corrections, it is more likely that the space was left deliberately for the reviser.[19] It might well have been a copy prepared either for the author or someone who knew the text well enough to correct it and expand it. It might have been copied by a local canon or by one of the more clerically trained anchoresses, then corrected and expanded by the author himself.

The compilation of the manuscript supports the idea that there was a need for multiple copies of the text to be made quickly, since, in Dobson's view, it seems to have been put together from loose quires, not all of them present at the same time in the copying. Its compilation suggests it was copied in sections out of sequence: 'it seems likely that the scribe of the Cleopatra MS. had his exemplar delivered to him in sections, and that . . . he was not given them in their true order.'[20] It is possible that the growing number of anchoresses created a need for copies of *Ancrene Wisse* to be produced quickly, and thus the Cleopatra exemplar may have been used to produce two copies at once. Dobson posits further: 'if the anchoresses, by reason of the increase in their numbers which is alluded to in a Corpus addition, found themselves in urgent need of additional copies of their Rule, it would follow that they would also find it difficult to spare copies from their existing stock for the time – doubtless months – that it would take to make the new copies . . . only one-third of the exemplar need have been out of the anchoresses' possession at any one time.'[21] This compilation history grants us insight into the form of the text used by the earlier group of anchoresses, since in order to pass parts on, it would have to be easily unbound. As such it would be of most use unbound or loosely collected in a vellum wrapper, rather than in a wooden binding. Although the Cleopatra manuscript might have been produced first and foremost for scribal use, its compilation history suggests that the original text of *Ancrene Wisse* might have been experienced by its readers in pieces rather than as a complete text, or loosely wrapped as a whole.

The Corpus manuscript is probably more typical of the kind of book owned, held and read, if not by the original three anchoresses, then by the

---

[19] Ralph Hanna told me that the vertical spacing in this manuscript is unusual, an observation in keeping with Dobson's thorough measurements of the spaces between lines in his edition of the manuscript, *The English Text*, p. xliii. The irregular spacing seems to have been the result of a scribe more comfortable with wide spacing trying at least initially to write in a more cramped style to match as far as possible the page layout of his exemplar.

[20] Dobson, *The English Text*, p. xxxi.

[21] Dobson, *The English Text*, p. xxxvi.

group of twenty they became. From its earliest date, *Ancrene Wisse* was not intended for a single owner, but rather for a group, first three, then twenty, then larger groups. The late thirteenth-century inscription in the Corpus manuscript tells us the text became a gift from John Purcel to a house of Augustinian canons at Wigmore Abbey. This suggests that this small book, within two generations of its production, became the possession of a group of male readers. Despite its very pointed addresses to the needs, circumstances, and perceived nature of the original female audience, the text early on was equally accessible to the male reader.[22]

Corpus 402 is modest in size and appearance and the text's scribe wrote in a clear, legible hand. The manuscript is relatively unadorned, although divisions are marked by red paragraphs, and sections are marked by initials in red or blue that range from two to six lines high. To Roger Dahood, the original author, or at least, an early scribe, provided specific guidance to the reading of the text through these division markers; in his view, 'placement, size, and ornamentation of initials indicate degrees of subordination among textual divisions.'[23] Although it is difficult to determine whether division markers in a given manuscript were authorial, or the product of the scribe or compiler's imagination, Dahood argues that 'there is a core of agreement across the stemma, indicating that some divisions were already marked in the ancestors of the extant manuscripts.'[24] These markers signal a variety of organizational schemes, the most overarching being the division of the entire text into an introduction and eight parts. The author tells the reader, 'Nu mine leove sustren, þis boc ich todeale on eahte distinctiuns. þet ȝe cleopieð dalen' ('Now, my dear sisters, I have divided this book into eight distinctions which you call parts').[25] The scribe visually reinforces the description of the eight parts that follows by introducing each part with a large capital thorn. Sections are more coherently divided in the first half of the manuscript; in Part 2, 'The Custody of the Senses,' for example, rubricated initials introduce each of the senses in turn as well as an additional section treating speech, sight and hearing together.[26]

Such divisions suggest a variety of reading practices. The emphasis on divisions found in these early manuscripts is in keeping with Hugh of St Victor's proposition that reading proceeds by division ('The method of reading consists in dividing. [*modus legendi in dividendo constat.*]')[27] Bella Millett suggests that the author's appellation of his sections as 'distinctions,' a word significantly not recorded elsewhere in Middle English before the late fourteenth century, was influenced by the mid-twelfth-century prologue of the Premonstratersian Statutes, later retained in the prologue to the early

---

[22] For a discussion of the possible ways in which the author's views of women may have shaped his text see Robertson, *Early English Devotional Prose*.

[23] Dahood, 'Use of Coloured Initials', 81.

[24] Dahood, 'Use of Coloured Initials', 81.

[25] Tolkien, *The English Text*, p. 11, f. 4a.

[26] See Dahood, 'Use of Coloured Initials', 83–4.

[27] Cited in Carruthers, *Book of Memory*, 174.

Dominican Constitutions.[28] The passage similarly introduces and explains a division into parts and reveals the kind of reading division into distinctions is supposed to inspire:

> librum istum, quem librum consuetudinum vocamus, diligenter conscripsimus, in quo quattor distincciones, tam pro rerum varietate, quam pro legencium utilitate, locis suis adnotamus. Prima distinccio continet qualiter se habeat conventus in die . . . Unicuique harum quatuor distinccionum propria capitula assignavimus, et assignata subscripsimus, propria capitula assignavimus, et assignata subscripsimus, ut cum aliquid a lectore queritur, sine difficulte reperiatur

> (We have diligently compiled this book, which we call the book of customs, in which we set out four parts separately, partly because of the diversity of contents, partly for the convenience of the reader. The first part deals with how the community should conduct itself during the day . . . To each of these four parts we have assigned its own chapters, and have listed them below, so that if the reader is looking for anything, it can be found without difficulty.)

This passage, strikingly similar to the opening of *Ancrene Wisse*, suggests a particular interest in a utilitarian reading practice. These divisions make it easier for the reader to find her place. It also suggests discontinuous reading; the reader looks for the division markers when she returns to the book. The division markers help the reader discern the major categories of the text. They might also act to guide a reader who has little time to relevant sections, or, perhaps even to those sentences marked with a colored initial alone, allowing the reader the opportunity to read an outline of the whole passage and to be reminded of the rest. They might also guide a director reading to an anchoress, or an anchoress reading to her servant, to those passages he or she wishes to read out loud.

The initials may in themselves have meaning. For example, the first mark in this manuscript is its opening initial 'marked by a rubric and an ornate blue and red R more than five lines high and extending into the top margin.'[29] This noticeable letter beginning the first word of the text, 'Recti,' seems significant in that it underscores the notion of rule and regulation, at the same time that it escapes the lines it is supposed to occupy. Other early manuscripts similarly begin the text with a noticeable large R. Cleopatra C vi, for example, begins with a four line ornamental initial. While it is, of course, conventional that a scribe would begin a manuscript with a large initial, it is not insignificant that the text was constructed so that its first initial visually reinforces the opening themes of the work. Such a visual play would be in keeping with the author's self-conscious play on words about ruling in the work's opening pages. Indeed, the opening of the text stresses the inadequacy of rules at the very same time that it gives one.

---

[28] Bella Millett kindly passed on this information from her forthcoming edition. The passage is taken from Lefèvre and Grauwen, *Les Statuts*. The translation of the quotation is by Millett.

[29] Dahood, 'Use of Coloured Initials', 82.

Just as this large letter dominates the lines to follow while at the same time escaping its ruled place, so the anchoress is urged to remember that the heart can easily escape its rule.

Although the carefully ordered series of subordinating initials at the beginning of the rule falls away later in the Corpus manuscript, '[c]orrelation between size of initial and degree of subordination is maintained throughout the treatise in the case of primary divisions.'[30] To Dahood 'in the earliest extant manuscripts, *Ancrene Wisse* was in some measure set out as a study text. Whoever first imposed the system of graduated initials was concerned that readers grasp the relationships between divisions and not just focus on discrete passages.'[31] If we accept Dahood's argument, *Ancrene Wisse*, then, from its inception was a text to be engaged in an organized manner.

There are other forms of inscription that indicate passages the Corpus scribe, or perhaps the reader, thought important, that is, the *nota* marks and *nota bene* hands. According to Ker's count, there are 147 *nota* signs as well as some two dozen *nota bene* hands, all probably medieval.[32] It is difficult to determine the logic behind these nota marks and hands, or even whether the marks are those of the author, scribes, or readers. Nonetheless, they do act as guides for other readers to these passages and they do at least indicate concentrated reading. In addition to these intriguing signs of readers of some kind on some occasion, there are words written in the manuscript paleographically dated to the sixteenth century of the same ink as underlinings and numerous crosses throughout the manuscript which tell us it was enthusiastically read centuries later. Given the dearth of such casual marks in earlier hands, the thirteenth-century readers seem to have been more restrained in their reading practices, or at least in recording their responses to their reading. The fact that the manuscript is in relatively good condition – that is, it has only a handful of damp spots and one crease, and that earlier readers chose not to mark up its pages indiscriminately, suggests it was cared for, if not treasured, by its readers.

Although the thirteenth-century Nero A xiv manuscript is considered by Dobson to be an unreliable witness to the original compared to Corpus 402 and Cleopatra C vi, it does testify to aspects of the condition of the presumed original audience that can help us understand how they read. It is the only one to contain an address to the three anchoresses for whom the text was originally intended:

> Muche word is of ou hu gentile wummen ȝe beoð. vorgodleic ant for ureoleic iȝirned of monie. ant sustren of one veder ant of one moder. i ne blostme of ower ȝuweðe uorheten alle worldes blissen; ant bicomen ancren.

> (There is much talk about what noble women you are, sought after for your goodness and generosity, and sisters of one father and one mother.

---

[30] Dahood, 'Use of Coloured Initials', 83.
[31] Dahood, 'Use of Coloured Initials', 97.
[32] See N. R. Ker's introduction to Tolkien, *The English Text*, p. xvii.

In the blossom of your youth, you forsook all the bliss of the world and became anchoresses.)[33]

In the longer passage from which this is taken, we learn also that the anchoresses are supported by one benefactor who provides for them well. The Nero manuscript also includes expanded forms of the prayers and devotions of Part 1, perhaps a reflection of the original non-monastic audience's need to have the prayers of the Little Office spelled out for them because of their lack of liturgical training.

Like the other early manuscripts, this manuscript is small (144×107 mm). It is the work of two scribes, the first who copie *Ancrene Wisse*, the second who copied a series of prayers to God, Christ and Mary, the Apostle's Creed, and twelve lines of Latin verse attributed to St Bernard followed by a Latin prose meditation on the crucified Christ. The ornamentation is simple, an 'economy . . . in keeping with the use of seven single folios in the gatherings, and the presence of many holes and cuts in the parchment which were there before the text was written.'[34] The fact that a rather tattered piece of parchment was chosen upon which to write the text suggests that, in its earliest forms, *Ancrene Wisse* seems never to have been intended to be ornamental or valuable as a material object. The system of division markers is also simpler than that of Corpus. It tends to use initials of uniform size to mark divisions. To Dahood, this system, which eliminates the complexity of the system of graduated initials found in Corpus, 'facilitates reference. The uniform size and placement of initials enables quick scanning of the folios, for the eye need move only down the left-hand side of the page to locate new divisions.'[35] In general, all three of these manuscripts seem to have been designed for use, for easy scanning and reference, for frequent consultation, and not for aesthetic pleasure.

By contrast to these earlier single volume small books, the later Vernon manuscript (Oxford Bodleian Library, Eng. Poet. A.1), which includes *Ancrene Wisse* as one among many devotional works, suggests an entirely different kind of reading practice. The manuscript is very large, originally consisting of more than 420 leaves measuring $23 \times 15\frac{1}{2}$ inches, and is difficult to lift or even open. *Ancrene Wisse* is written in double columns in only eighteen folios. According to Dahood, initials marking divisions are easily lost in the pattern of vines in the page frame. Part Five, a discussion of confession, is the only part with clear division markers, and 'the Vernon scribe seemed to have been particularly concerned to make Part Five accessible for reference.'[36] This suggests that whoever consulted this part of the manuscript valued it particularly as a guide to confession. Clearly this text was a large compilation to be consulted more formally or to be read from to a group by the head of the community. The part of the manuscript which contains *Ancrene Wisse* is, in N. F. Blake's opinion, of a different

[33] Day, *The English Text*, p. 85, f. 50.
[34] Day, *The English Text*, p. xvi.
[35] Dahood, 'Use of Coloured Initials', 93.
[36] Dahood, 'Use of Coloured Initials', 96.

order of intellectual difficulty than that which precedes it; it contains texts as varied as Hilton's *Scale of Perfection, Piers Plowman,* and *Joseph of Arimathea*.[37] Although this manuscript shares the general devotional purposes of the earlier ones and some of its contents may have been written originally for women in the religious life, it seems to have been adapted for a broader audience.

As is well known, *Ancrene Wisse* is also closely associated with a collection of saints' lives and sermons known as the Katherine Group, a group of texts linked dialectally by Tolkien to the Corpus manuscript of *Ancrene Wisse*.[38] Several manuscripts that include *Ancrene Wisse* also include several of these Katherine Group texts or one or more of the works from what is known as the Wooing Group. All these texts seem not only close in dialect, but also close in theme and function, all describing for the female contemplative an intimate, personal, though not particularly mystical relationship to Christ. Dobson has described a situation of manuscript production which suggests a flurry of activity in the early part of the century, with texts being copied and cross-collated, presumably meeting the needs of a quickly growing community of female and male contemplatives. These related manuscripts help expand our sense of the kinds of books one might find in the anchorhold. Anne Savage and Nicholas Watson have described Cotton Titus D xviii, for example, as a 'one-volume library of the anchoritic works, gathering into a single, well-organized collection *Ancrene Wisse,* the three most important Katherine-group works, and . . . *The Wooing of our Lord*.'[39] Since the author of *Ancrene Wisse* recommends that the anchoresses read saints' lives, and especially singles out 'ower englische boc of seinte Margarete' ('your English book of Saint Margaret'), it is possible that the works known as the Katherine Group might well have been circulating with *Ancrene Wisse*.[40] As Savage and Watson point out, however, since the author suggests that they loan books to each other, they may not have been as readily accessible as *Ancrene Wisse* itself.[41]

These paleographic details about these and the other *Ancrene Wisse* manuscripts tease our imagination about how this book was actually read by its anchoritic readers, how it functioned materially in the anchorhold itself, and how reading functioned in the daily life of the anchorhold. Was it read in private in an act of silent, solitary reading? Was it read aloud by one person to a group? Was it one among several books an anchoress might pull down from a shelf at will? When would an anchoress read it? How long might her reading session be? How did the anchoress get her books? Did she own them? How many? Where did she keep them in the anchorhold? How many books might an anchoress have in her cell at any one time? Did she or they have a library of their own? Perhaps most importantly, was this book

---

[37] See Millett's discussion of the Vernon manuscript (Millett, *Annotated Bibliographies,* 57), and Blake, 'Vernon Manuscript', 45–60, as well as the other essays in Pearsall, *Studies in the Vernon Manuscript* (Cambridge: D. S. Brewer, 1990).
[38] Tolkien, '*Ancrene Wisse* and *Hali Meiðhad*', 104–26.
[39] Savage and Watson, *Anchoritic Spirituality,* 29.
[40] Tolkien, *The English Text,* p. 125, f. 66a.
[41] Savage and Watson, *Anchoritic Spirituality,* 29.

simply designed for use as its practical appearance might lead us to believe, or does it also serve a more literary purpose; what was she supposed to *achieve* through reading?

In order to explore the possible answers to these and other questions we must look to the text itself to see what it tells us about reading and books, to the circumstances of the anchoress's daily life described therein, and to the physical circumstances of the anchorhold itself. To begin with, the small space of the anchorhold probably did not allow room for many books, and given the lack of information we have about furnishings, it is not at all clear where books might have been kept. Rotha Mary Clay mentions the difficulty of determining whether or not remains of bookstands found at anchoritic sites were part of the original anchorhold or later additions.[42] It is possible that the books were kept in a book chest, although it is difficult to know how many books an anchoress might have in the anchorhold at any one time. An anchoress might have had many books; Eve of Wilton asks that books be sent to her and Goscelin envies her a life in a room piled high with books.[43] It is unlikely that these anchoresses were like Eve. They certainly did not possess her proficiency in Latin. At this date, even convents possessed only a few books, so it is unlikely that the anchoresses had more than a few books themselves. Limebrook Priory or a similar archeological site, a place that might have housed, if not the original anchoresses, a group like the twenty they became, might well have had room for a small library that included a Bible, *Ancrene Wisse*, saints' lives, and additional prayers and meditations in English or French; or, perhaps the anchoress depended on her advisor or her servants to bring her books from a nearby library, perhaps that of Wigmore Abbey or of Hereford Cathedral.

The text itself gives us some direct information about how *Ancrene Wisse* was supposed to be read and how books or writings were intended to function in the anchorhold. In the very last paragraph of the text, the author instructs the reader:

> Of þis boc redeð hwen ȝe beoð eise euche dei; leasse oðer mare. Ich hopie þet hit schal beon ow ȝef ȝe hit redeð ofte; swiðe biheve . . . ȝef ȝe findeð þet ȝe doð alswa as ȝe redeð; þonckið godd ȝeorne

> (Read from this book each day when you are at leisure, either less or more. I hope that, if you read it often, it will be very profitable to you . . . If you find that you do as you read, thank God earnestly.)[44]

Ancrene Wisse is not to be read through from cover to cover, but is to be turned to repeatedly and read only partially, much as the Bible might have been read. In addition, the reading of the book is seen as a guide to action: '*do* as you read.'

When might an anchoress have the leisure time to dip into this book?

---

[42] Clay, *Hermits and Anchorites*, 84.

[43] See Talbot, ed., *Liber Confortatorius*.

[44] Tolkien, *The English Text*, p. 221, f. 117a.

Drawing on his study of Part 1 of *Ancrene Wisse*, Devotions, Robert
Ackerman has sketched the daily life of the anchoress hour by hour and has
determined that at least five hours of the anchoress's day were devoted to
prayer, thus allowing very little time for the reading of books such as
Ancrene Wisse.[45] There was a period in the afternoon when one might read:
from three to five in the afternoon was set aside for private prayers and
meditation, reading of the Psalter, *Ancrene Wisse*, and other books in
English or French. That time was also to be spent in the instruction of
servants, and work, such as needlework for church vestments or clothing
for the poor. Reading and prayer are assigned interchangeably:

> Euchan segge as best bereð hire on heorte. Verseilunge of sawter.
> Redunge of englisc oþer of Frensch. halie meditatiuns. ower cneolunges
> hwen se ȝe eauer mahen iȝemen. ear mete ant efter.

> (May each one say [their prayers] as her heart inclines her the most,
> reciting verses of the psalter, reading of English or of French, holy
> meditations, your kneelings whenever you can attend to them, before
> food and after.)[46]

Saints' lives were probably a regular part of the anchoress's reading life.
Perhaps next to her copy of *Ancrene Wisse*, the anchoress had a manuscript
such as Bodley 34 containing three saints' lives, a sermon on the soul, and a
guide to virginity. Those two books alone would give the anchoress plenty
of reading material. It is not clear from these instructions whether an
anchoress read alone or to her fellow anchoresses or servants, although
Clay's reconstruction of the likely appearance of the anchorhold suggests
that if the anchoresses did read to each other, they were not doing so in the
same space but rather one anchoress would read at a window that adjoined
the cell of the next anchoress.[47] We do not know precisely where she read:
did she have a chair? Did she sit on the edge of a bed? Did she read the book
while standing looking at it on a bookstand? Did she hold the book on her
knees as she sat on the floor? It also not clear whether she read silently or
out loud. Clearly she prayed aloud since she is warned by the author not to
sing so loud as to interrupt the priest, but the degree of vocalization
involved in her reading is not known.[48]

Reading was not considered a privileged activity in the anchorhold. The
author tells the anchoress that she should either read or perform physical
labor: 'ich bidde ow þat ȝe ne beon neauer idel. ah wurchen oþer reden. oþer
beon i bonen' ('I bid you never to be idle, but to work, or read, or be at
prayer.')[49] These are the fundamental experiences of the anchoress's waking
hours: reading, work, or prayer. The schedule outlined in Part 1 as well as in
these passages tell us reading is to be understood by the anchoress as

---

45 Ackerman, 'Liturgical Day', 734–44. See also Ackerman and Dahood, *Ancrene Riwle*.
46 Tolkien, *The English Text*, pp. 26–7, f. 11a.
47 Clay, *Hermits and Anchorites*, 73–84. See also Warren, *Anchorites*.
48 The classic account of silent reading is Augustine's in *Confessions*. See also the discussion of
   reading practices in Saenger, *Space between Words*.
49 Tolkien, *The English Text*, p. 27, f. 11a.

equivalent to any other activity on the anchorhold, from sewing, to kneeling in prayer, to physical labor such as gardening. As at Brook Farm, where Emerson frustrated his compatriots by wishing to read rather than perform physical labor, here reading and the physical work required to maintain the anchorhold (for example, the repair of window cloths and altar cloths) are not only to hold equivalent amount of time, but are valued as the same *kind* of experience.

Furthermore, reading, she is told, is one among a series of activities that are remedies against temptation – especially temptations of the flesh:

> Aȝein alle temptatiuns. ant nomeliche aȝein fleschliche. Salven beoð ant bote under godes grace. Halie meditatiuns inwarde ant meadlese. ant angoisuse bone. Hardi bileave. redunge. Veasten. wecchen. ant licomliche swinkes.

> (Against all temptations, and especially against fleshly temptations, the remedies and cures are, under God's grace: Holy meditations deeply felt and without restraint, and anguished prayers, steadfast faith, reading, fasts, vigils, and bodily labors.)[50]

Often equated conceptually with eating in monastic literature, reading is here equated with fasting; one form of bodily experience is exchanged for another. This passage lists a series of substitutions – of bodily motions, praying, reading, working – all requiring order, discipline, and regulation. Reading is described as acting on the body, that is, through reading, both in the time it takes away from other more potentially sinful activities as well as in the thoughts it inspires, the anchoress redirects her senses away from temptation. She turns her concerns towards the page, both in what she experiences of the book sensually as she looks and feels the book, and for the experiences of the senses the thoughts expressed on the page inspire. Reading, like fasting, both engages and regulates the senses.

These fragments of information about books and reading suggest that the anchoresses had neither the time nor the training to be studious – reading was not for the purpose of scholarship. Indeed, they were discouraged from being teachers and from scholarly pursuits. The author of *Ancrene Wisse* tells the anchoress: 'Ancre ne schal nawt forwurðe scolmeistre' ('An anchoress must not degenerate into a schoolmistress') and 'ȝe ne schulen senden leattres. ne underuon leattres. ne writen bute leauue' ('You must not send letters or receive letters or write without leave.')[51] *Ancrene Wisse* also tells us, however, that there was a variety of scholarly abilities in the group: 'Sum is clergesse sum nawt. ant moten mare wurchen ant on oþer wise seggen hire bonen.' ('Some are clerics, some not, and must work more or in other ways say their prayers.')[52] It is hard to determine the degree of

---

[50] Tolkien, *The English Text*, p. 123, f. 65a.

[51] Tolkien, *The English Text*, p. 217, f. 114b.

[52] The word 'clergesse,' which means female cleric, is difficult to translate since we don't know specifically what degree of training the author refers here. Tolkien, *The English Text*, p. 7, f. 2a. For further discussion of distinctions between the literate and illiterate see Clanchy, *From Memory to Written Record*, 225–9.

training to which the appellation 'cleric,' refers. Perhaps one or more of the anchoresses, or at least of the larger group of contemplatives, came from a convent. Such a training might indicate some fluency in Latin, although just what degree of Latin literacy women of their upper class background and circumstances could achieve is a matter of debate.[53] Whatever the clerical ability of one or several of the anchoresses, study was clearly not central and not necessarily desirable to the anchoritic life, and those who could not read at all could nonetheless reach the desired state of devotion reading was supposed to inspire.

We also know little about the anchoresses' writing abilities. Some of the anchoresses could write. As I mentioned before, in discussing the joys of heaven, the author comments, 'ʒe habbeð of þeos blissen iwriten elleswher mine leoue sustren' ('You have of these joys written elsewhere, my dear sisters.')[54] It is unclear to what this refers: Anne Savage and Nicholas Watson suggest passages of *Sawles Warde* or *Hali Meiðhad*; perhaps it could refer to one of the prayers of the Wooing Group.[55] It is also not clear whether or not 'writen' here refers to composition or simply inscription. The anchoresses were also, as I have already noted, discouraged from sending letters or writing without leave. This latter prohibition could refer to composition or copying. As mentioned above, the Cleopatra manuscript or one of the early copies of *Ancrene Wisse* now lost may have been made by one of the anchoresses. In Part 1, as the author delineates the prayers the anchoress should say, he directs: 'Euchan segge hire ures as ha haueð iwriten ham' ('May each say her hours as she has written them.')[56] Some anchoresses at least copied down their prayers. The author urges the anchoress who cannot remember her prayers 'leoteð writen on a scrowe hwet se ʒe ne kunnen.' ('Have written on a scroll whatever you do not know.')[57] The anchoress might not have been surrounded by books, but apparently she could carry a scroll, either of her own making, or made for her, with her throughout her day.

Above all, reading is an activity linked to prayer. At some points it is described as similar to a prayer, that is, serving the same devotional purposes as prayer; at other points it is equated directly with prayer. The author writes,

Accidies salue is. gastelich gleadschipe. ant froure of gleadful hope. þurh redunge. þurh hali þoht. oþer of monnes muðe. Ofte, leoue sustren, ʒe schulen uri leasse; forte reden mare. Redunge is god bone. Redunge teacheð hu ant hwet me bidde; ant beode biʒet hit efter. Amidde þe redunge hwen þe heorte likeð. kimeð up a deuotiun þet is wurð monie benen.

(The remedy for sloth is spiritual gladness and comfort of glad hope through reading, through holy thought, or from someone's words. Often,

---

[53] For an excellent discussion of the likely literacy skills of the anchoresses see Millett, 'Woman in No Man's Land', 86–103, as well as Robertson, ' "This Living Hand" '.

[54] Tolkien, *The English Text*, p. 209, f. 111a.

[55] Savage and Watson, *Anchoritic Spirituality*, 402.

[56] Tolkien, *The English Text*, p. 15, f. 6a.

[57] Tolkien, *The English Text*, p. 25, f. 10b.

my dear sisters, you should pray less to read more. Reading is good prayer. Reading teaches you how and what to pray, and prayer achieves it afterwards. Amidst the reading, when the heart is pleased, a devotion arises which is worth many prayers.)[58]

In this passage, reading is described first as an activity that provides the information or knowledge that leads to prayer; as such it acts as a guidebook to prayer. Second, the passage describes reading as equivalent to prayer; it *is* prayer and, exactly as prayer does, inspires devotion.

I would like to explore further here the possible ways reading might be like prayer. Within the monastic tradition, *lectio divina*, that is, the reading of Scripture, is also described as being like prayer; indeed, according to Carruthers 'medieval reading was highly active.'[59] The active prayerful reading described in monastic literature, however, is the Bible. It is not clear that the reading of other materials receives the same high status, although Jean Leclercq does tell us that in some materials, reading of all kinds and prayer are both described as forms of meditation: 'Among texts gathered by Martène (PL 66. 413–14) we find *meditatio* as a synonym for reading, for study, for singing the psalms in private as well as for contemplation. An ancient translation cited there renders *meditari* by "to say the Psalter".'[60] In some senses the general shape of the day for an anchoress is like that of a monk who is supposed to divide the day between *lectio divina*, *opus dei*, and *opus manuum*. However, each of those activities is specifically focussed for the anchoress. The anchoress is urged to read the Bible, but it is unlikely that the anchoress would have engaged in the kind of 'active' study of the Bible that monks might have; nor would she have been likely to have been reading the wide variety of theological, philosophical and literary material read by monks or even by the earlier recluses such as Eve of Wilton, praised for her knowledge of patristic and classical works.[61] The anchoress's day is more likely to have been filled with recitations of prayers, especially the psalms, but within the ideology of this author, the recitation of prayers and reading are interchangeable, at least in terms of their ultimate purpose. For her, praying, like the other kinds of work of the day, as we shall see, has a particular emphasis.

Part 1 of *Ancrene Wisse* tells us what prayers the anchoresses were expected to pray hourly. As Robert W. Ackerman and Roger Dahood have warned us, Part 1 is not easy reading, and it is easy to view the list of prayers as dull, words that the anchoress would utter by rote without feeling or passion.[62] We should not, however, underestimate the tremendous literary variety offered to the anchoress by the psalms alone. A look at the list of prayers the anchoress is urged to recite daily can tell us how profoundly the

---

[58] Tolkien, *The English Text*, p. 148, f. 78a.
[59] See Carruthers, *Book of Memory*, 186, as well as her discussion of monastic conceptions of reading in ch. 5 of her book. See also Leclercq's discussion of monastic reading in his *Love of Learning*, esp. pp. 87–93.
[60] Leclercq, *Love of Learning*, ch. 5, p. 366 n. 8.
[61] See Talbot, ed., *Liber Confortatorius*.
[62] See Ackerman and Dahood, *Ancrene Riwle*, on Part 1.

anchoress's mental life was structured around her engagement with the liturgy. Because the anchoresses for whom *Ancrene Wisse* was composed were unlikely to have come from the monastery or convent (though perhaps some were 'clergesse,') they did not have the training which made liturgical routine second nature to them.[63] Instead, they needed the instruction in the liturgy that Part 1 provides for them. The degree of detail given in Part 1 varies in the manuscripts from the incipits provided in the Corpus manuscript to the extended citations found in the Nero manuscript, suggesting that some readers needed more guidance than others. The structure of prayers provided by Part 1 is based on the Little Office of the Virgin and the Office of the Dead.[64] This seemingly tedious list of prayers is actually rich and varied, ranging in genre from praise poems (Ave Maria) to statements of belief (the Credo) to petitions for salvation to penitential psalms to laments.[65]

A kind of textual experience is thus available to the anchoress daily, what we might call liturgical literacy.[66] Although the anchoresses' primary language of literacy was probably English, the anchoress does enter a world of Latin literature through these prayers. This liturgical literacy, although only partial Latin literacy, should not be underestimated in assessments of the anchoress's 'bookishness,' that is her ability to engage with texts; it is primarily through these texts that the anchoress engages the world of Latin Christian literature. While the anchoress may not have had the opportunities for rumination, meditation, and contemplation of a variety of literary and theological works, as did the monk or university student, she was nonetheless granted access to diverse Latin literary experiences through prayer. Because *Ancrene Wisse* itself is described as interchangeable with the Psalms, the portions of *Ancrene Wisse* read each day, although in English, simply become another liturgical text. *Ancrene Wisse* does not urge the anchoress to study other kinds of Latin texts. The works of the Church Fathers and theological debate are filtered by and translated by the author, one whose specific references are themselves modest, most often to commonly cited passages of authorities such as St Augustine, St Jerome, and St Bernard.[67] The single most powerful engagement with Latin for the anchoress comes through her daily recitation of liturgical prayer.

Furthermore, the recitation of these prayers involves a bodily performance. Part 1 not only lists the prayers that must be said at different times of

---

[63] Ackerman argues that it is because this text provides so much detailed instruction that the original anchoresses could not have come from a convent: 'Such explicit directions about kneeling, beating the breast, signing oneself with the cross, and the like are the best evidence that the original anchoresses were without liturgical training.' See Ackerman, 'The Liturgical Day', 741.

[64] Ackerman describes the prayers in detail in 'The Liturgical Day'.

[65] For a classic introduction to the generic range of the psalms see Gunkel, *The Psalms*.

[66] I am grateful to Bruce Holsinger for stimulating my thinking about the importance of the liturgy to our understanding of vernacular literature.

[67] For the sources to *Ancrene Wisse* see Shepherd, *Ancrene Wisse* introduction, pp. xxv–xxx; essays cited in Millett *Annotated Bibliographies*, and the summary of sources in Hasenfratz, *Ancrene Wisse*, 35–8.

the day, but also describes the bodily positions that must accompany these prayers. For example, the author advises:

> hwen ȝe earst arised; blesci ð ow ant seggeð. In nomine patris et filii et spiritus sancti. Amen. Ant biginneð anan. Veni Creator Spiritus wiþ up ahevene ehnen ant honden toward heovene, buhinde o cneon forðward o þe bedde

> (When you first arise, bless yourself and say 'In nomine Patris et Filii et Spiritus Sancti. Amen,' and begin at once 'Veni, Creator Spiritus' with eyes and hands raised towards heaven, bending forward on your knees on the bed.)[68]

Virtually every prayer is accompanied by a physical action, such as prostration, kneeling, or the raising of head or hands. The anchoress is told to enact the very variety of bodily positions in prayer that we see displayed in Peter the Chanter's *The Christian at Prayer*, which includes illuminations that show the considerable range of possible bodily movements enacted at prayer: hands can be raised in supplication or pointed downwards with the head bent in humility; the body can be bent, prostrate, arched upwards and back, or take the shape of the cross.[69] Prayer, furthermore, is often spoken; sound and sense come together in the act of prayer. Praying is an extension of the body.

The physical movements associated with prayer increase as the anchoress focusses on praise of the cross. At the height of her prayers she crosses herself frequently. The text abandons words at this point, choosing to represent these physical movements with black crosses. Such representation in the text is reproduced outside the text in the anchoress's curtain, a black cloth with a white cross upon it, the negative of the book she has just been pondering; as she moves her eyes from the black cross on the white parchment to the dark walls she will see the inverse image of the white cross on the dark walls, an image also present on the curtain of the anchorhold. Her physical engagement with the material objects around her, including the manuscript, the walls of the anchorhold, and the curtains therein thus replicate synergistically the primary object of her meditation, the cross.

Although reading is likely to take place when the body is more at rest than it is during prayer, nonetheless the body is still part of the reading experience. The reader is told to involve her heart in reading and she is encouraged repeatedly to use the book to help her regulate her senses. Mark Amsler has discussed the importance of this form of literacy, a form of somatic or affective literacy, where the body and the heart are involved in the act of reading.[70] Furthermore, as Amsler has pointed out, the book itself as an object interacts with the body of the reader. The author quotes St Jerome: 'Hali redunge beo eauer i þine honden. Slep ga up o þe as þu lokest

---

[68] Tolkien, *The English Text*, p. 12, f. 4b.
[69] See Trexler, *Christian at Prayer*.
[70] For further discussion of the involvement of the body in reading see Amsler, 'Affective Literacy', 83–109.

þron ant te hali pagne ikepe þi fallinde neb.' ('Let holy reading be ever in your hands. Let sleep come upon you as you look thereon, and let the holy page hold up your falling face.')[71] The book performs a physical function of caressing the reader, holding up her head from sleep. Certainly prayer requires physical performance, and reading, as a form of prayer, is similarly linked to the body.

There are other ways in which the book of *Ancrene Wisse* itself can be seen as an extension of the contemplative's body that needs to be redirected towards Christ. The text itself, written on skin, a parchment, ultimately is a physical manifestation of the regulation and order the anchoress herself must enact daily, a regulation with a specific purpose in mind. The parchment as a skin that is regulated to become a manuscript is analogous to her body; her body must be ruled, just as the parchment page is pricked and ruled. Furthermore, her body is marred like the text and must be corrected as it is. She is told, 'Ful speche is as of leccherie. ant of oðre fulðen þet unweschene muðes speokeð oþerhwiles. þeose beoð alle ischrapede ut of ancre riwle.' ('Foul speech is about lechery and of other filth that unwashed mouths sometimes speak. These are all scraped out of the anchoress's rule.')[72] This command draws the reader's attention to the parchment page, to the places in the manuscript that have been scraped out and corrected, and then metaphorically draws the anchoress's attention to her own need to scrape out her sins, here especially the sins of the flesh, out of her very own body. This is not dissimilar to a passage in a twelfth-century sermon which says: 'Let us consider then how we may become scribes of the Lord. The parchment on which we write for Him is a pure conscience, whereon all our good works are noted by the pen of memory.'[73] In this case, however, it is the act of reading, that is contemplating the parchment as a surface, that activates the conscience. Reading, like the daily prayers the anchoress recites, performs a penitential function that is physically enacted, one that is enacted more extensively throughout the day in the prayers she recites.

In order to explain how the body and the mind are interwoven in the daily life of the anchoress, it is useful to consider the prayers she recited more closely. Although it is difficult to characterize the actual sequence of prayers said daily by the anchoress since they change following the liturgical calendar, there is a pattern to them, especially as they are summarized in Part 1.[74] The anchoress alternates prayers asking for mercy with petitions for peace for the dead. Ackerman points out that 'special emphasis is placed on prayers before the cross and to the Virgin.'[75] Dahood has some difficulty with Janet Grayson's argument that the prayers of Part 1 move towards and away from prayers to the Virgin because 'the prayers to the Virgin are not confined to a single place in the devotional scheme and need not follow, as

[71] Tolkien, *The English Text*, p. 148, f. 78a.
[72] Tokien, *The English Text*, p. 44, f. 21a.
[73] Quoted in Carruthers, *The Book of Memory*, 156.
[74] Roger Dahood has described the structure of prayers found in Part 1 in his 'Design in Part One of Ancrene Riwle': 1–11. See also Ackerman and Dahood, *Ancrene Riwle.*
[75] Ackerman, 'Liturgical Day', 737.

her analysis requires, the celebration of the mass.'[76] Nonetheless, I believe that Grayson is at least correct that the round of prayers themselves reinforces the anchoress's daily progression toward identification with Mary and Christ. As the day progresses, the prayers apparently narrow their focus, becoming primarily those addressed to Mary and Christ. That focus is reinforced by the rubricated large L's in the manuscript drawing the reader's attention to 'Leafdi' Mary, just as a focus on Christ is reinforced by the emphatic black crosses drawn into the manuscript. Thus, whatever the sequence of prayers is as they are enacted, as that structure is read in the manuscript, it is experienced as emphasizing Marian and Christological devotion. The Marian devotion is expressed through prayers of the five joys of Mary, a prayer sequence that is at the center of the author's description of the devotions the anchoress should perform. Her simultaneous culminating prayers to the cross capture the central theme of the inner guide to follow. She prays 'iesu . . . for þe ilke fif wunden þe þu on hire bleddest heal mi blodi sawle of alle þe sunnen þet ha is wið iwundet; þurh mine fif wittes.' ('Jesus, for the same five wounds which you bled on it, heal my bloody soul of all the sins with which she is wounded through my five senses.')[77] Her body and Christ's become one as the day progresses. At the same time that she is taught to imitate Christ on the cross, the anchoress is also taught to imitate Mary; like Mary, she must prepare her nest, her anchorhold, her body, for the entrance of Christ.

The prayers that are added to the text of *Ancrene Wisse* in the Nero manuscript may help us understand how prayers like those listed in Part 1, as well as the other meditations the anchoress read, including *Wisse* itself, furthered the penitential effects of reading. The prayers include the following: 'On god ureisun of ure lefdi,' 'On wel swuðe god ureisun of God almihiti,' 'On Lofsung of ure Lefdi,' and 'On Lofsung of ure Louerde.'[78] Clearly these works are in keeping with the theme of *Ancrene Wisse*. It is not evident who composed these final added pieces, but given the fact that *Ancrene Wisse* also urges the anchoress to recite her prayers 'as she has written them,' it is possible that these texts were at least written down, if not composed, by a female recluse, and were composed with the female anchoritic experience in mind. The prayers might easily have occurred in Part 1 of *Ancrene Wisse* since, in general, they are continuations of the praise poems to God, Christ and Mary found in the liturgy. They can help us understand how prayer functioned for the anchoresses and can be read as the kind of meditation and focus *Ancrene Wisse* is intended to provoke, that is as a form of reader's response to *Ancrene Wisse*.

These prayers have a distinctive character. They are difficult to describe because unlike the psalms, they are relatively devoid of idiosyncratic

---

[76] Dahood, 'Design', p. 2. See Janet Grayson's schematic analysis of Part 1 in Grayson, *Structure and Imagery*, 17–37. See also my discussion of Part 1 in Robertson, *Early English Devotional Prose*, 60–2.

[77] Tolkien, *The English Text*, p. 17, f. 7a.

[78] These titles follow Thompson's list. The first three are named in the manuscript; the second two are named by Richard Morris. See Thompson, *þe Wohunge of Ure Lauerd*, p. ix. See also Day, *The English Text*, p. xxii, and Morris *Old English Homilies*.

imagery, drawing rather on conventional imagery of Jesus as sweet, soft, and bright, and reiterating statements of the abject humility of the speaker. Their simplicity and their dependence on what appear to be clichéd or transparent images are not dissimilar to the kind of intractable imagery we find in many of the poems of the Romantic women poets, recently garnering critical attention after generations of neglect. Critics similarly have tended to overlook these prayers in the Nero manuscript, presumably finding them less interesting than *Ancrene Wisse*, or the longer and seemingly more complex prayer, 'The Wooing of our Lord'. Perhaps because, like the Romantic women's poetry, these thirteenth-century prayers are poems of 'sentiment,' and 'feeling,' they are difficult to analyze. Simple but intense statements of faith, they are relatively devoid of human angst and conflict. They are petitions asking for Jesus's forgiveness and love and contain none of the anguish of the psalms or the ambivalent self-hatred we find in other religious poets, such as Donne. There is no crisis of desire, no conflictual relationship between speaker and God. The prayers establish an intimate, but humble, relationship between the contemplative and Jesus or Mary. As a group they are permeated with simple expressions of love, such as: 'Swete iesu mi leof. mi lif. mi leome. min healewi. min huni ter. þu ert al þet ic hopie.' ('Sweet Jesus, my beloved, my life, my light, my healing oil, my honey drop, you are all that I hope for.')[79] Devoid of theological speculation, such as that found in the writings of Julian of Norwich, or erotic imagery such as that of Rolle or Hilton, they seem like chant, but unlike Buddhist chant, these are chants of desire, although desire without an emphasis on the pain of separation or longing that one finds in later religious poetry, and even in more affective medieval poetry.

What might be the function of these simple, reiterated statements of praise of and desire for God? The prayers repetitively assert both the presence and absence of Christ, thus capturing the central paradox of Christianity. Paul Jones summarizes: 'Without the reality of Christ's presence, redemption would be unavailable to the faith community. Without the reality of Jesus' absence, the assertion of Christ's death, resurrection, ascension and *parousia* would be undermined. Both presence and absence are required simultaneously.'[80] The lines at times alternate between the assertion of presence in direct addresses to Christ: 'Swete iesu mi leof,' and statements of longing for the absent Christ, 'Woa is me þet ich am so freomede wið þe.' ('Woe is me that I am so estranged from you.')[81] But even the repetition itself captures the paradoxical simultaneity of presence and absence. In what might be called a Derridean play of signifiers calling God into the present, the lines assert the inevitable absence of the transcendental signified, that is, God. Repetition is key to the prayer's meaning; as Derrida asserts, 'the absence of the transcendental signified extends the domain and

---

[79] Thompson, *þe Wohunge of Ure Lauerd*, 5. Translations are my own, but I have consulted Savage and Watson's translations of three of the prayers.
[80] Quoted in Beckwith, *Signifying God*, 72–3.
[81] Thompson, *þe Wohunge of Ure Lauerd*, 5.

the play of signification infinitely.'[82] The Center, which here we would call God, 'closes off the play which it opens up and makes possible.'[83] Derrida's comments about the emotions involved in such a play of signifiers can perhaps help us understand the lack of agon in these meditations: '[a]nd on the basis of this certitude [that there is a center] anxiety can be mastered, for anxiety is invariably the result of a certain mode of being implicated in the game, of being caught by the game, . . . [a]nd again on the basis of what we call the center (and which, because it can be either inside or outside, can also indifferently be called the origin or end, *archē* or *telos*) repetitions, substitutions, transformations, and permutations, are always taken from a history of meaning . . . whose origin may always be reawakened or whose end may always be anticipated in the form of presence.'[84] These prayers are marked by certitude expressed through repetition.

All of the prayers in the Nero manuscript have a similar pattern: they proclaim adoration and then they petition God, Mary, or Christ to remove the contemplative's sins. They end in meditations on Christ's suffering on the cross, a suffering the contemplative wishes devoutly to recreate in her daily life. Unlike monastic meditations, these poems are neither theological nor eschatological; and unlike mystical works, although Christ is present in the anchorhold, the text focusses on the sinful condition of the anchoress rather than on the bliss of mystical union with Christ. While celebrating the contemplative's intensely personal relationship with God, Mary, and Christ, and while emphasizing the sufferings of Christ as a reminder to the anchoress of her purposes, the prayers, like *Ancrene Wisse* itself, eschew the jouissance of a mystical celebration of union with God found in the work of mystical writers such as Richard Rolle and Walter Hilton. The relationship is often more companionate than erotic:

> hwoa so euer wule habben lot wið þe of þine blisse; he mot delen wið þe; of þine pine on eorðe. nis he nout treowe ifere þet nule nout scotten iþe lure.

> (whoever wants to have a part with you in your joy must share with you in your pain on earth. Someone is no true companion who will not take their share of the loss as well as the gain.)[85]

Just as the speaker contemplates union with Christ, the text veers from celebrating or contemplating that union and instead focusses on Christ's suffering in this world. This sequence in the prayer to God is typical:

> hwoa wule beon biclupped? . . hwi nam ich iþin ermes so istreihte. ant ispred on rode? And weneð ei to beon bi clupped bitweonen þine blisfulle ermes in heovene. bute he worpe er him her. bitweonen þine rewðful ermes oðe rod?

> (Who wishes to be embraced? . . . Why am I not in your arms so stretched and spread on the cross? And does anyone believe they will be embraced

---

[82] Derrida, 'Structure', 85.
[83] Derrida, 'Structure', 83.
[84] Derrida, 'Structure', 84.
[85] Thompson, *þe Wohunge of Ure Lauerd*, 7.

between these joyful arms in heaven, unless they first throw themselves between your pitiful arms on the cross?)[86]

It may be that it is in the nature of prayer to manipulate space and time; throwing oneself into the arms of the dead Christ stops time. The speaker beseeches the dead Christ to embrace her. The focus here is oddly very much in the world. This seems central to the anchoritic experience: rather than being oriented to the future bliss of heaven, it is focussed on this present life, a present life that must be solely focussed on death, that is the death of Christ, and the anchoress's recreation of that experience in her own death in the anchorhold: 'hwi nis me unwurð everich wordlich þing aȝein þe muchele delit of þine swetnesse?' ('Why is not every worldly thing worthless in comparison with the great delight of thy sweetness?')[87] Worldly things are replaced by an image of Christ, present in the anchorhold, not in some future union. She is prevented from experiencing that presence only by her sins which she asks to be removed. 'þi passiun acwenche þe passiun of sunnen þet wunieð wið inne me.' ('May your suffering quench the passion of sin that dwells within me.')[88] Although the contemplative meditates on the wounds of Christ, the suffering of Christ is not grotesque as it is in later affective literature; instead the suffering of Christ is directly mapped on to the anchoress's body. In the prayer to our Lord, the speaker asks:

þeo sterke stremes ant þet flod þet fleaw of þine wunden. moncun uor to helen; clense and peasch [*sic*] mine sunfule soule þuruh þine fif wunden iopened o rode. wið neiles uor drivene and seoruh fulliche fordutte. hel me uor-wunded þuruh min fif wittes wið deadliche sunnen. and opene ham heovenliche king touward heouenliche þinges.

(May the fierce streams and the flood that flowed from your wounds to heal mankind, cleanse and wash my sinful soul. Through your five wounds, opened on the cross, sorrowfully pierced through with nails, and filled up, heal me, wounded through my five senses with deadly sins, open them, oh heavenly king, toward heavenly things.)[89]

The body of Christ is mapped onto the body of the anchoress who is found lacking; his five wounds become her five senses, senses to be turned away from this world and directed to heavenly things. Like the reading of *Ancrene Wisse* itself these prayers guide the anchoress to recreate Christ's death daily in her own body.

Within the anchorhold, it seems that prayer had a more specific function than prayer in the monastery, that is, prayer reinforces both an identification with Christ and Mary, and a remembrance of them. A word used repeatedly throughout *Ancrene Wisse* is 'munegunge,' remembrance. Reading and prayer are a means to remembrance, remembrance of Christ's suffering and the salvation that suffering promises. Mary Carruthers has

---

[86] Thompson, *þe Wohunge of Ure Lauerd*, 6.
[87] Thompson, *þe Wohunge of Ure Lauerd*, 7.
[88] Thompson, *þe Wohunge of Ure Lauerd*, 11.
[89] Thompson, *þe Wohunge of Ure Lauerd*, 11.

illuminated for us the primary function of reading in the middle ages as memorial. Here this text is memorial in a very strict sense. It acts as a 'munegunge,' a memory of Christ, one that replaces the anchoresses' physical experiences of deprivation and temptation with the experiences of Christ, especially Christ's death.

What then does reading achieve? Hélène Cixous says of reading: 'Not everyone carries out reading in the same way . . . Reading is eating the forbidden fruit, making forbidden love, changing eras, changing families, changing destinies and changing day for night, reading is doing exactly as we want and on the sly . . . And what books do we read? . . . Those that teach us how to die.'[90] To Cixous, reading is a form of dying because to her reading is a way of letting go of the self, a dissolution of the self through an immersion into the text as other. By contrast, writing is an assertion of the ego and an attempt to forestall death. Reading *Ancrene Wisse*, like praying and interchangeable with praying, also teaches the anchoress to die. As she reads, the anchoress forgets herself and the boundaries of the self dissolve. Yet, the anchoress experiences the meaning of death much more consciously. For the anchoress, dying was of particular significance, for her central role in the contemplative life was to be dead to the world. She reads and prays in order to join Christ in suffering and in death. The work reiterates her role: she is told 'ȝe beoð deade ant ower lif is ihud mid criste' ('you are dead and your life is hidden in Christ') and 'is euch religius dead to þe worlde; ant cwic þah to criste' ('each religious is dead to the world and nevertheless alive to Christ').[91] In Part 1, the anchoress is told to ask Mary, 'ȝef me deien wið him ant arisen in him. worltliche deien. gasteliche libben' ('allow me to die with him and arise in him; to die in the world, to live in the spirit').[92] In Part 2, every sense experience is to be redirected to recreating Christ's sensual experiences in her body; if she feels thirst she must consider his thirst on the cross, if she feels discomfort, think of his discomfort, etc. She is told 'haueð eauer hire deað as biuoren hire ehnen' ('she who has her death always as it were before her eyes').[93] Her death and Christ's are one and the same: 'Mors tua. mors Christi . . . þench of þin ahne deað of godes deað o rode. þe grimme dom of domesdei. munneð ofte ofte i mode.' ('your Death; the Death of Christ . . . think of your own death, of God's death on the cross. Recall often in your mind the grim doom of Judgment Day.')[94] Prayers, while aiding her in her death, at the same time can save the dead; her prayers for herself and for others are 'cwic bone' ('live prayers'); reading to die and praying to die, paradoxically then is reading and praying to live.[95] *Ancrene Wisse* curiously retreats from a celebration of that future life, however, and eschews, as a number of critics have

[90] Cixous, *Three Steps*, 21–2.
[91] Tolkien, *The English Text*, pp. 179, 180, f. 95a.
[92] Tolkien, *The English Text*, p. 23, f. 9b.
[93] Tolkien, *The English Text*, p. 63, f. 31b.
[94] Tolkien, *The English Text*, p. 123, f. 65a.
[95] Tolkien, *The English Text*, p. 88, f. 45b.

observed, focus on mystical union.[96] Rather, the anchoress learns by regulating her body to map it on to that of Christ; her body dies with his as she reads.

The habitus of the anchorhold reinforces the role of the anchoress as dead. Anchorholds were often constructed on the north side of the church, and, according to the archeologist Roberta Gilchrist, there is evidence that some were built in graveyards.[97] We know, for example, of the recluse Alice, who, in 1397, was housed in the cemetery by John Dodyngton, canon of Exeter.[98] The narrow dimensions of the anchorhold mimic the grave. As Paulette L'Hermite-Leclercq summarizes:

> La logette est très souvent installée au flanc nord, froid et humide, des églises, dans le cimetière, ou à côté d'une chappelle dédiée à saint michel, l'ange psychopompe. Ou bien elle flanque une léproserie ou sont parqués ces autres morts au monde qui épouvantaient les gens: c'est le cas de reclusoir de Juette de Huy.
>
> (The cell is very often installed on the north side, cold and humid, of churches, in the cemetery, or next to a chapel dedicated to St. Michael, the psychopompe. Or else it flanks a leper colony where those other dead of the world are placed who horrify people: that is the case of the anchorhold of Juette of Huy.)[99]

The anchorhold is described in *Ancrene Wisse* and in related texts, such as Aelred of Rievaulx's guide for his sister, as a sepulcher. L'Hermite-Leclercq describes the medieval understanding of the anchorhold:

> souvent défini comme une prison, son reclusoir n'est que la projection hors de lui de son 'corps de mort,' prison de son âme qui attend l'expansion.
>
> (often defined as a prison, his anchorhold is nothing but a projection outside of himself of his 'body of death,' prison of his soul which awaits release.)[100]

Often anchoresses and anchorites were buried in the very cell in which they were enclosed. Wulfric of Haselbury, for example, devoted himself to anchoritism 'burying himself in Christ in a cell adjoining the church,' and when he died in 1154, was buried in his cell by the Bishop of Bath'.[101] In some enclosure rites, a requiem mass was said at the installation of the anchoress, and ashes were cast over the floor of the anchorhold.[102] Clay vividly captures for us the emphasis on death that occurs at enclosure in her summary of the conclusion of the Exeter pontifical's rite of enclosure:

---

[96] See, for example, the discussions in the introductions to Shepherd, *Ancrene Wisse*, and Savage and Watson, *Anchoritic Spirituality*; and also Georgianna, *Solitary Self*.

[97] Gilchrist, *Gender*, 177. Clay lists evidence of recluses from the eleventh to the fifteenth centuries, most of whom were enclosed on the north side of the church: see pp. 73–84 of *Hermits and Anchorites*.

[98] Clay, *Hermits and Anchorites*, 76.

[99] L'Hermite-Leclercq, 'La femme', 154.

[100] L'Hermite-Leclercq, 'La femme', 155.

[101] Clay, *Hermits and Anchorites*, 74.

[102] Clay, *Hermits and Anchorites*, 96.

The bishop then began to perform rites which were designed to impress upon the devotee the fact that in a strict sense he was henceforth dead to the world. The office of extreme unction was performed, with the commendation of the soul, lest death should anticipate the last rites.

"These things being done, let the grave be opened, entering which, let the recluse himself, or another in his name, sing: 'This shall be my rest forever.' Dust was scattered with the words: 'From dust wast thou created, etc.'" Before going, the bishop made a final exhortation, and the door of the house was built up.[103]

Anchoresses, like lepers, were treated as legally dead; as L'Hermite-Leclercq writes,

Mise à mort symbolique, l'inclusion des reclus n'a d'équivalent que la séparation des lépreux présente souvent dans les mêmes pontificaux. Eux aussi sont des morts-vivants.[104]

(Put to death symbolically, the enclosure of the recluses has no other equivalent than the separation of lepers often present in the same pontificals. They also are the living dead.)

The focus on death is distinctive to the contemplative experience of the anchoress. Although the death of Christ is at the center of Christian meditation and liturgy, other aspects of the Christian ideology occupy monastic meditation – the resurrection, ascension, the joys of heaven, etc. Furthermore, a nun's entrance to a convent was marked by a marriage ceremony rather than the ceremony for the dead. L'Hermite-Leclercq distinguishes the morbid experience of the anchoress upon entering the anchorhold to the joyous one of the consecration of nuns:

On voit combien la tonalité funèbre de l'inclusion diffère de la profession des moines ou de la consécration des vierges. Le moine ne meurt au monde que pour une renaissance et le renoncement au vieil homme est plus une mue qu'une mort. Quant à la consécration des vierges elle exalte les noces mystiques.

(One sees how much the funereal tone of enclosure differs for the profession of monks or for the consecration of virgins. The monk dies from the world only to be reborn and the renunciation of the old man is more a shedding than a death. As for the consecration of virgins, it exalts the mystical marriage.)[105]

Although heaven is hoped for, the focus of meditation in the anchorhold advocated in *Ancrene Wisse* is just that found in the prayers in the Nero manuscript, the redirection of the senses of the anchoress to Christ's suffering; her body becomes Christ's body on the cross. Reading and prayer in the anchorhold or reading that is prayer thus further an expression

---

[103] Clay, *Hermits and Anchorites*, 96.
[104] L'Hermite-Leclercq, 'La femme', 154.
[105] L'Hermite-Leclercq, 'La femme', 153.

of, and erasure of, longing in their culminating evocations of images of the crucified Christ, at once an image of God's absence and presence, a doubleness enacted further by the mapping of the anchoress's body on to the dead body of Christ. Although the insistent repetitive evocation of the image of the dying Christ might seem like a perverse, melancholic attachment to the dead body of Christ, in Christian terms, this remembrance, this 'munegunge' is a form of mourning rather than melancholy, one that releases the ego from its obsessive attachments. Contemporary readers may recoil from the morbid reiteration of images of the lacerated dying body of Christ, but rather than a compulsive repetition, such a focus liberates the ego; the anchoress, rather than regressing 'from object cathexis to the still narcissistic oral phase of the libido,' is freed from narcissism through a continual practice of empathy.[106] Freud says, 'when the work of mourning is completed the ego becomes free and uninhibited again.'[107] In contrast, 'in grief the world becomes poor and empty; in melancholia it is the ego itself.'[108] The anchoress is taught to leave the world, the world of objects perceived through the senses, and to transform these objects into connections to the transcendental signified, God. The repetition of a chain of signifiers empties the signifiers, that is the world of objects, of meaning, leading the contemplative to the Other, and this focus on the dying God is an engagement with the Other that seriously disturbs the narcissistic ego. This profound confrontation with Otherness allows the anchoress to, in Catherine Pickstock's terms, 'stand open to the surprize of what arrives, according to the non-totalizing gaze of faith.'[109]

Such an achievement of mental balance and such an enactment of faith can only be realized through the repetition of daily practice. The saying of prayers like those found at the end of the Nero manuscript, or even those better known prayers of her daily hours, or the repetitive reading of passages from *Ancrene Wisse*, may seem mere rote performance, but in fact these acts of reading are the expression of faith; as Sarah Beckwith writes: 'Peter Carnley has spoken recently about how resurrection beliefs often concentrate on the cognitive element, making prayer and worship a 'dutiful consequence' rather than a response to his personal presence.' But it is impossible to speak of the resurrection in a dualist anthropology, just as it was impossible to tell by looking at Christ who he really was. The disciples could believe only when they acceded to, recognized in self-recognition, his demand. In this sense, faith is a virtue, a habit that must be endlessly practiced if it is to exist at all, and not simply a belief.'[110] Reading these meditations or vocalizing them as prayer, reading *Ancrene Wisse* itself or other holy meditations, or saying daily hours, each in their way is a practice within which resides faith. The knowledge

---

[106] Freud, 'Mourning and Melancholia', 160.
[107] Freud, 'Mourning and Melancholia', 154.
[108] Freud, 'Mourning and Melancholia', 155.
[109] Pickstock, 'Signs of Death', 110.
[110] Beckwith, *Signifying God*, p. 75.

the anchoress gains from *Ancrene Wisse*, her 'scientia,' then, is more than just knowledge, it is a guide to practice that enables expansiveness.

The primary purpose of reading, as we have seen above, is to remind the anchoress of Christ. Unlike other affective texts of this period, this one draws the anchoress not to contemplation of her mystical union with Christ, but repeatedly to an *imitatio Christi*; her bodily sufferings become one with Christ's and they die together. The last folio of the Nero manuscript contains twelve lines of Latin verse ascribed to St Bernard, followed by a piece of Latin prose which brings the manuscript to a close with an image of the crucified Christ with 'manus perforatos' ('pierced hands').[111] If the reader of this passage has just finished reading *Ancrene Wisse*, then the image of Christ's pierced hands will already be in her mind. At the end of part two, the author urges the anchoress to forgo a contemplation of her own white hands, and, instead, to dig with those white hands the grave in which she will rot, and to imagine nails piercing her hand just as they did Christ's: 'ha schulden schrapien euche dei þe eorðe up of hare put þet ha schulien roten in.' ('She should scrape each day the earth out of the grave in which she shall rot.')[112] The concluding Latin lines in Nero are a reminder of that startling image and thus epitomize the experience of reading a work such as *Ancrene Wisse*. The reader holding this manuscript might easily glance from the lines of the text to her own hands, especially as she closes the book. From her own hands, the reader then might glance at the *nota bene* hands drawn on the manuscript page. She might then become conscious of the hand that inscribed the manuscript; finally she might think of all those hands specifically as they relate to Christ's hands. This hand that holds the text, the *nota bene* hands, the hand that inscribed the manuscript, and Christ's hands become one. And the goal of these multiple mappings? To bring to our mind simultaneously death and transcendence, the mortality of the flesh, yet the persistence of the *nota bene* hands, the hand that wrote the manuscript that we can now witness, and the hand that once held it as God's hand reaches down from heaven to draw the anchoress up.

St Paul warns against the dangers of too much knowledge: 'scientia inflat.'[113] The Cistercian Arnoul of Boherris gives this advice: 'When he reads let him seek for savor, not science.'[114] Reading *Ancrene Wisse* teaches the anchoress to seek the practical knowledge to learn how to be dead to the world. She turns to the book, however, not to increase her knowledge, but to increase her understanding, that is to savor her alignment with the dead Christ. The physical act of reading, like physically enacted prayer, redirects the anchoress's senses to Christ. The Christian knowledge of crucifixion, however, is not to be experienced once, but repetitively; it is to be savored. To Derrida, 'Religion presumes access to the responsibility of a free self,'

---

[111] See Day, *The English Text*, xxii.
[112] Tolkien, *The English Text*, p. 62, f. 31b. I discuss this passage at length in Robertson, ' "This Living Hand" '.
[113] Leclercq, *Love of Learning*, 256.
[114] Quoted in Leclercq, *Love of Learning*, 90.

and faith is 'a form of involvement with the other that is a venture into absolute risk.'[114] Derrida describes death as a gift, 'the gift of death that puts me into relation with the transcendence of the other, with God as selfless goodness . . . [r]esponsibility and faith go together, however paradoxical that might seem to some, and both should, in the same movement, exceed mastery and knowledge.'[116] Through contemplation of death, the anchoress does indeed experience an expansion of self that exceeds the regulatory knowledge the work teaches. One learns to die, as Derrida says, 'in order to attain the new immortality.'[117] A contemplation of death thus liberates the self: 'This concern for death, this awakening that keeps vigil over death, this conscience that looks death in the face is another name for freedom.'[118] Far from being a morbid denial of life, the anchoress's contemplation of death awakens her senses and focusses her attention on each one of the sense's experiences. We have seen that while *Ancrene Wisse* might appear to be an instance of De Quincey's literature of knowledge in the guidance to daily practice it provides, it in fact possesses all the expansive qualities of literature of power; paradoxically it is through the enactment of the knowledge that the power is achieved. Reading *Ancrene Wisse* is not like reading most books. Mind and body are essentially interwoven in the anchoritic reading experience and mutually defining; reading is linked to the physicality of the manuscript itself as an object, and the goal of the reading experience both emphasizes the physical realization of religious truths and values that physicality. Religious literature of the Middle Ages has a tremendous range of type and purpose; this text is unusually single-minded in its focus on death, yet it is in that very intensity that its power resides. Through the contemplation of the Other *Ancrene Wisse* facilitates, the anchoress is released from the limits of her own body, of her ego, of the walls of the anchorhold, even from the walls of the grave, while experiencing the boundaries of the self to their fullest. In her prayerful reading, by mapping her sensual experiences on to Christ's who, as *Ancrene Wisse* author said, felt more than anyone, she savors the world as she immerses herself in the infinite.[119]

[115] Derrida, *Gift of Death*, 2 and 5. I am grateful to Sue Zemka for drawing my attention to this essay.

[116] Derrida, *Gift of Death*, 6.

[117] Derrida, *Gift of Death*, 12.

[118] Derrida, *Gift of Death*, 15.

[119] I would like to thank Ralph Hanna for graciously answering questions about the manuscripts of *Ancrene Wisse* on short notice, Mark Amsler for helpful comments about reading practices, Sister Mary Clemente Davlin for her thoughtful comments about prayer, Bruce Holsinger for comments about the liturgy, Gerda Norvig for discussing the Psalms with me, Kate Crasson for a thoughtful response on performativity, Jana Mathews for accompanying me to see the manuscripts, Stephen Shepherd and Karen Palmer for a meticulous editing of the whole manuscript. I am especially indebted to Jeffrey Robinson for thoughtful advice about the essay as a whole. Finally, I am very grateful to Bella Millett who kindly agreed on very short notice to review the manuscript before it went to press.

Works Cited

Ackerman, Robert W., 'The Liturgical Day in *Ancrene Riwle*', *Speculum* 53, issue 4 (October 1978)

Ackerman, Robert W., and Roger Dahood, *Ancrene Riwle: Introduction and Part I* (Binghamton, New York: Medieval and Renaissance Texts and Studies, 1984)

Amsler, Mark, 'Affective Literacy: Gestures of Reading in the Later Middle Ages', *Essays in Medieval Studies* 18 (2001). Published electronically by the Muse Project at http://muse.jhu.edu

Beckwith, Sarah, 'Passionate Regulation: Enclosure, Ascesis, and the Feminist Imaginary', in *Materialist Feminism*, ed. Toril Moi and Janice Radway, *The South Atlantic Quarterly* 93, no. 4 (Fall 1994)

——, *Signifying God: Social Relation and Symbolic Act in the York Corpus Christi Plays* (Chicago: University of Chicago Press, 2001)

Blake, N. F., 'Vernon Manuscript: Contents and Organisation', in *Studies in the Vernon Manuscript*, ed. Derek Pearsall (Cambridge: D. S. Brewer, 1990)

Carruthers, Mary, *The Book of Memory: a Study of Memory in Medieval Culture* (Cambridge: Cambridge University Press, 1990)

Cixous, Hélène, *Three Steps on the Ladder of Writing: the Welleck Library Lectures at the University of California, Irvine*, trans. Sarah Cornell and Susan Sellers (New York, 1993)

Clanchy, M. T., *From Memory to Written Record: England 1066–1307*, 2nd edn (Oxford: Blackwell, 1993)

Clay, Rotha Mary, *The Hermits and Anchorites of England* (London: Methuen & Co., 1914)

Dahood, Roger, 'Design in Part One of Ancrene Riwle', *Medium Ævum* 56 (1987)

——, 'The Use of Coloured Initials and Other Division Markers in Early Versions of *Ancrene Riwle*', in *Medieval English Studies Presented to George Kane*, ed. Edward Donald Kennedy, Ronald Waldron, and Joseph S. Wittig (Cambridge: D. S. Brewer, 1988)

Day, Mabel, ed., *The English Text of the* Ancrene Riwle: *Edited from Cotton MS Nero A. xiv*, EETS o.s. 225 (London: Oxford University Press, 1952; repr. 1957)

de Quincey, Thomas, 'The Literature of Knowledge and the Literature of Power', in *Confessions of an English Opium Eater and Other Writings* (New York: The New American Library, 1966)

Derrida, Jacques, *The Gift of Death*, trans. David Wills (Chicago: University of Chicago Press, 1995)

——, 'Structure, Sign and Play in the Discourse of the Human Sciences', in *Critical Theory since 1965*, ed. Hazard Adams and Leroy Searle (Tallahasee: University Presses of Florida, 1986)

Dobson, E. J., 'The Affiliations of the Manuscripts of *Ancrene Wisse*', in *English and Medieval Studies Presented to J. R. R. Tolkien on the Occasion of his Seventieth Birthday*, ed. Norman Davis and C. L. Wrenn (London: Allen, 1962)

——, *The English Text of the* Ancrene Riwle: *Edited from B.M. Cotton MS. Cleopatra C. VI*, EETS o.s. 267 (London: Oxford University Press, 1972)

——, *The Origins of* Ancrene Wisse (Oxford: Oxford University Press, 1976)

Freud, Sigmund, 'Mourning and Melancholia', in *Collected Papers, Volume IV* (London: The Hogarth Press, 1953)

Georgianna, Linda, *The Solitary Self: Individuality in the Ancrene Wisse* (Cambridge: Harvard University Press, 1981)

Gilchrist, Roberta, *Gender and Material Culture: the Archeology of Religious Women* (London and New York: Routledge, 1994)

Grayson, Janet, *Structure and Imagery in Ancrene Wisse* (Hanover, New Hampshire: University Press of New England, 1974)

Gunkel, Hermann, *The Psalms: a Form-Critical Introduction*, trans. Thomas M. Horner (Philadelphia: Fortress Press, 1967)

Hasenfratz, Robert, *Ancrene Wisse* TEAMS (Kalamazoo, Michigan: Medieval Institute Publications, 2000)

Leclercq, Jean, *The Love of Learning and the Desire for God*, trans. Catharine Misrahi (New York: Fordham University Press, 1961)

Lefèvre, Pl. F., and W. M. Grauwen, ed., *Les Statuts de Prémontré au milieu du XIIe siècle*, Bibliotheca Analectorum Praemonstratensium 12 (Averbode, 1978)

L'Hermite-Leclercq, Paulette, 'La femme, la recluse et la mort', in *Muerte, Religiosidas Y Cultura Popular Siglos XIII–XVIII*, ed. Eliseo Serrano Martin (Zaragoza: Institucion 'Fernando el Catolico', 1994)

Millett, Bella, with the assistance of George B. Jack and Yoko Wada, *Annotated Bibliographies of Old and Middle English Literature, II:* Ancrene Wisse, *the Katherine Group, and the Wooing Group* (Cambridge: D. S. Brewer, 1996)

——, 'The Origins of Ancrene Wisse: New Answers, New Questions', *Medium Ævum* 61 (1992)

——, 'Woman in No Man's Land: English Recluses and the Development of Vernacular Literature in the Twelfth and Thirteenth Centuries', in *Women and Literature in Britain: 1150–1500* ed. Carol Meale (Cambridge: Cambridge University Press, 1993)

Morris, Richard, *Old English Homilies and Homiletic Treatises of the Twelfth and Thirteenth Centuries*, EETS o.s. 29 and 34 (London, 1868)

Pearsall, Derek, ed., *Studies in the Vernon Manuscript* (Cambridge: D. S. Brewer, 1990)

Pickstock, Catherine, 'Signs of Death,' ch. 3 of her *After Writing: On the Liturgical Consummation of Philosophy* (Oxford: Blackwell, 1998)

Robertson, Elizabeth, *Early English Devotional Prose and the Female Audience* (Knoxville: University of Tennessee Press, 1990)

——, ' "This Living Hand": Thirteenth-century Literacy and the Naturalist Innocence of the *Ancrene Wisse*', *Speculum* (January, 2003)

Robinson, P. R., 'A Twelfth-century Scriptrix from Nunnaminster', in *Of the Making of Books: Medieval Manuscripts, their Scribes and Readers. Essays Presented to M. B. Parkes*, ed. P. R. Robinson and Rivkah Zim (Aldershot, 1997)

Saenger, Paul, *Space between Words: the Origins of Silent Reading* (Stanford: Stanford University Press, 1993)

Salu, M. B., trans., *Ancrene Riwle (The Corpus MS: Ancrene Wisse)* (London: Burns & Oates, 1955)

Savage, Anne, and Nicholas Watson, *Anchoritic Spirituality: Ancrene Wisse and Associated Works*, with a preface by Benedicta Ward (New York: Paulist Press, 1991)

Shepherd, Geoffrey, *Ancrene Wisse: Parts Six and Seven* (London: Thomas Nelson & Sons, 1959)

St Augustine, *Confessions*, trans. R. S. Pine-Coffin (London and New York: Penguin, 1961)

Talbot, C. H., ed., *The Liber Confortatorius of Goscelin of Saint Bertin*, Studia Anselmiana 37 (Rome, 1955)

Thompson, W. Meredith, ed., þe Wohunge of Ure Lauerd, EETS o.s. 241 (London: Oxford University Press, 1958; repr. 1970)

Tolkien, J. R. R., 'Ancrene Wisse and Hali Meiðhad', Essays and Studies 14 (1929)

——, ed., The English Text of the Ancrene Riwle: Ancrene Wisse: Edited from MS Corpus Christi College Cambridge 402, EETS o.s. 249 (Oxford: Oxford University Press, 1962)

Trexler, Richard C., The Christian at Prayer: an Illustrated Prayer Manual Attributed to Peter the Chanter (d. 1197) (Binghamton, New York: Medieval and Renaissance Texts and Studies, 1987)

Warren, Ann K., Anchorites and their Patrons in Medieval England (Berkeley: University of California Press, 1985)

White, Hugh, Ancrene Wisse: Guide for Anchoresses (London: Penguin, 1993)

8

The Legacy of *Ancrene Wisse*: Translations, Adaptations, Influences and Audience, with Special Attention to Women Readers[1]

CATHERINE INNES-PARKER

Recently, I purchased a piece of art from an artist who styles her work 'Stitches in Time'.[2] The work uses several different materials and techniques; a fabric background, which provided the inspiration for the piece, has been painted and then stitched to form a picture. The background is in soft blues and greens, suggesting a mist, and the obscure light of late evening or night. Two figures, a man and a woman, stand in the center of the picture, washed in gold, which creates an almost unearthly light. The man's feet are obscured in the mist. The figures stand on a stitched foreground, which suggests the flagstones of a church or courtyard. The flagstones are either fragmented, or whole and irregular in shape. Behind the figures is the outline of a building – a ruin, or a memory? – a manor house or a church. A window is illuminated by the same pale glow that highlights the central figures, and a tree stands to one side, suggesting that they are outside. The piece is entitled 'Apparitions'.

When I bought this haunting picture, the artist told me that in its creation she had attempted to portray our fragmentary relationship with the past. It struck me then that this picture, which drew me in such a compelling way, was a perfect metaphor for the work I was doing in this article, as I searched for information about the readers and owners of *Ancrene Wisse* and the texts that are descended from it. Like the picture, I am drawing on many different kinds of materials, often scattered in unlikely places and put together in unlikely combinations, in an attempt to construct a picture of the past. Like all history, but particularly women's history, much of the information I find is in fragments, or lost in the mists of time. Most of these fragments are found outside the 'main stream' of historical or literary criticism. Many bits and pieces are irregular, and need to be carefully arranged in order to find a pattern that 'fits'. Like my 'Apparitions', the literary picture I construct is

[1] Funding for the research summarized in this article was provided by the Social Sciences and Humanities Research Council of Canada, and the University of Prince Edward Island Senate Committee on Research.
[2] The artist is Margaret England, from Kensington, Prince Edward Island. Her work can be viewed at various locations across Prince Edward Island.

sometimes fragmentary, necessarily conjectural, but nevertheless often suggestive. Indeed, my picture, like my painting, changes when viewed in different 'lights' and from different perspectives. When I brought the painting home and hung it on my living room wall beside a dusty rose curtain, the rosy highlights in the background, which I had not seen before, stood out in a whole new way, forcing me to revise my first impression of a night-time scene, and conjecture that the picture portrayed twilight, or even dawn. So, too, the fragments of information collected here will look different in the light of different questions, or in different combinations, changing our reconstructed view of the past.

With this apt, if somewhat whimsical, metaphor in mind, then, I want to attempt to reconstruct a literary picture of the legacy of *Ancrene Wisse* and its influence on two centuries of readers and authors. I want to address questions of what the admittedly fragmentary evidence which survives can tell us about who read *Ancrene Wisse* and how it was used and adapted to suit the needs of varied audiences; and what this might suggest, in particular, about the women readers for whom *Ancrene Wisse* and its descendants seem to have held a particular appeal.

The 'dynamic character' of *Ancrene Wisse* has long been recognized (the term is Doyle's, 'Survey', 1:234). Its popularity in its own time is attested by the facts that it was translated into both French and Latin (at a time when the direction of translation was usually the other way), and that it survives in seventeen medieval manuscripts or fragments. Yet, the significance of *Ancrene Wisse* does not end in its own day. In the centuries that followed, the demand for vernacular devotional texts increased dramatically, as lay piety flourished and a growing middle class provided an audience that was literate (or semi-literate) but untutored in Latin. Among these texts, the number of borrowings and adaptations of material from *Ancrene Wisse* illustrates a continuing influence which cannot be underestimated. *Ancrene Wisse* was expanded on and incorporated into a number of later texts from the mid-thirteenth century until well into the fifteenth century, including þe *Wohunge of Ure Lauerd* (mid-thirteenth century), *A Talkyng of the Love of God* (fourteenth century, via *Wohunge*), the Vernon Manuscript's *Life of Adam and Eve*, þe *Holy Boke Gratia Dei* (fourteenth century), *The Chastising of God's Children* (late fourteenth century), *Disce Mori* and the related *Ignorancia Sacerdotum* (mid-fifteenth century, via *Chastising*), *The Pore Caitiff* (late fourteenth century), *The Book of Vices and Virtues*; *The Treatise of the Five Senses* (fifteenth century), *The Tretyse of Loue* (late fifteenth century), an anonymous fifteenth-century 'Sins Tract' identified by Diekstra ('Fifteenth-century Borrowings'), and a passion meditation in BL Harley 1740, edited by Marx ('Harley MS 1740'). Many of these texts, like *Ancrene Wisse*, were extremely popular and often survive in multiple manuscripts (over thirty, in the case of *The Pore Caitiff*). Some, including *The Pore Caitiff*, *The Chastising of God's Children*, and *The Tretyse of Loue*, were among the earliest texts printed by Wynkyn de Worde in the fifteenth century. While many of these texts were originally directed, as was *Ancrene Wisse*, to devout women, some of them were adapted for a more general audience of men or laypersons (as indeed was *Ancrene Wisse* itself in the version represented in BL Cotton Titus D.xviii). The wide appeal of such texts is indicated by their use, not only by 'professional religious', but also as guides for pious laypersons, a type of text that was increasingly in demand in the fourteenth and fifteenth centuries (Gillespie, 'Vernacular Books').

The continuing influence of *Ancrene Wisse* is also indicated by texts such as Nicholas Love's *Mirror of the Blessed Life of Jesus Christ*, which makes reference to *Ancrene Wisse* in a way that assumes the reader's familiarity with the text. In addition, there is some evidence that the fourteenth-century anchoress Julian of Norwich read and used *Ancrene Wisse*, and her reading of *The Chastising of God's Children* is clearly reflected in her *Revelations*. There is also evidence that other authors, such as Richard Rolle, and Walter Hilton, were influenced by *Ancrene Wisse*, even though there are no direct borrowings to indicate clear literary dependence. *Ancrene Wisse* and the texts of the Katherine Group, associated with it by dialect and manuscript tradition, thus stand at the beginning of a thriving tradition of vernacular devotional literature in England.

Yet, aside from identifying borrowings and adaptations, little attention has been paid to the continuing influence of *Ancrene Wisse* in the development of vernacular devotional literature. Surveys such as Doyle ('Survey'), Sargent ('Minor Devotional Writings') and Millett (*Ancrene Wisse*) have usefully gathered information about such influence which has hitherto been scattered, yet no extensive studies have been undertaken. H. E. Allen pointed out the need for such research years ago in two articles in which she identified a number of texts from the fourteenth and fifteenth centuries that draw upon *Ancrene Wisse* (Allen, 'Fourteenth Century Borrowings', 'Further Borrowings'). When Allen began her pioneering studies of vernacular devotional literature in England, few of the texts that she identified had been edited in any form. Since Allen's study, however, diplomatic editions of many of the manuscripts have been produced, and in some cases critical editions are available. Texts that draw upon *Ancrene Wisse* have been edited by, among others, Westra, *Talkying*; Fisher, *Tretyse of Love*; Brady, 'Pore Caitiff'; Baugh, *The English Text*; Bazire and Colledge, *Chastising*; Thompson, *Wohunge*; and Arntz, *Richard Rolle*. While some manuscripts remain unedited, the existence of editions for most of the texts identified as dependent upon *Ancrene Wisse* has made possible a sustained study of the nature of the influence of *Ancrene Wisse* on later texts and its place in the development of vernacular devotional prose.

An important part of such a study is the opportunity to examine the reception of the text amongst various audiences. As Patterson (*Negotiating*) has pointed out, the ways texts are represented or appropriated by later texts provides an important field of study in itself. The extensive copying and adaptation of *Ancrene Wisse* presents the literary analyst with a particularly rich opportunity for such a study. In addition, the textual tradition growing out of *Ancrene Wisse* provides an opportunity to study the influence of gender on the development of literary tastes and attitudes, including as it does texts written by both male and female authors for both male and female audiences. The popularity of these later texts among women readers make them a crucial element in the study of medieval English women's literacy. Studies of individual texts have begun to appear, but as Meale ('oft siþis') points out, there is a need for broader studies which make connections between the texts and manuscripts. This article is an attempt to provide a beginning by looking at the audiences to which *Ancrene Wisse* and some of its descendants are directed (the intended audience) and surviving evidence concerning readers and owners (the actual audience). As we will see, the intended audience and the actual audience did not always coincide; *Ancrene Wisse* and its descendants reached a broad audience which included both men and women, both religious and lay.

In many cases, there is a great deal of internal evidence available in the texts themselves which makes it is possible to identify their intended audience: whether they were directed at specifically male or female audiences (or simply addressed to general audiences); and whether the intended audiences were professional religious or devout laypersons. Many texts contain addresses (such as 'dear sister'), the alteration of such addresses, or other details that indicate the audience for which the author originally composed or adapted his or her work. Such indications should not be taken as restrictive – even texts such as *Ancrene Wisse*, which was directed in the first instance to a very specific audience of three enclosed sisters, contain indications of the author's awareness that the text would reach a wider audience. Yet, the original intended audience has a great influence upon form and content, and must be taken into account.

The determination of the actual readership of texts is more complicated, and depends heavily on evidence of manuscript ownership and transmission, such as names inscribed in the manuscripts and bequests of specific books in wills. Due to the partial nature of the evidence, such a study is necessarily limited and incomplete,[3] and information about individual readers is not always easy to find. In addition, many manuscripts that bear inscriptions indicating female ownership are not mentioned in the surviving wills of those owners and, by the same token, many books mentioned in wills cannot be linked to extant manuscripts, indicating that the picture painted from such sources will always be incomplete. Such information as does survive is often scattered; and, as Tarvers ('Thys ys my mystrys boke') has pointed out, indications of female ownership and readership, in particular, have often been overlooked by previous editors and cataloguers, and must be painstakingly gathered. Nevertheless, there is a great deal to be learned. While the information is still scattered, the current expansion in studies of manuscript ownership and transmission, including bequests of manuscripts in wills (e.g. Doyle, 'Survey'; Ker, *Medieval Libraries*, *Medieval Manuscripts*; Rosenthal, 'Aristocratic Cul-

---

[3] For some of the difficulties involved in such a study, see Harris, 1989.

tural Patronage'; Tarvers, 'Thys ys my mystrys boke'; Meale, '. . . alle the bokes' and 'oft siþis'; Bell, *What Nuns Read*), has made such information more accessible, and one consequence is that we now know that the female readership of many texts was much wider than has been recognized.

The Ancrene Wisse *Manuscripts*

The manuscripts of *Ancrene Wisse* themselves provide a great deal of information about early owners and audiences. This information has been admirably summarized by Doyle ('Survey'), Sargent ('Minor Devotional Writings') and Millett (*Ancrene Wisse*). Yet, I would like to take a moment to address the question of what these manuscripts suggest about the complex relationship between actual and intended audiences. The manuscripts indicate that, whatever the original intended audience, *Ancrene Wisse* was read and owned by people of both sexes, from a variety of social classes and geographical locations. For example, BL Cotton Nero A.xiv, dating from the mid-thirteenth century or earlier, is the only surviving manuscript to retain the passage which addresses the original three anchoresses and indicates the identity of the first audience of *Ancrene Wisse*. More than any other surviving copy, this manuscript suggests a precise and narrow audience of female recluses. Yet, marginal notations suggest that the manuscript eventually passed into male hands, perhaps owned by the Benedictine abbey of Winchcombe before the dissolution, and later by a rising yeoman family in the neighborhood of Winchcombe. From there, it seems to have been taken to London (Day, *The English Text* xii–xv; Millett, *Annotated Bibliographies* 52). Similarly, BL Cotton Cleopatra C. V. passed through a number of hands. Its earliest identifiable owner was the great Marcher lady, Matilda de Clare, Countess of Gloucester, who gave it to the house of Augustinian canonesses at Canonsleigh, Devon (a house which was re-founded under her patronage), sometime between 1284 and 1289. It likely remained there for some time (possibly until the dissolution), but at some point it crossed the breadth of England and passed into the hands of Robert Talbot, prebendary of Norwich (d. 1558) (Dobson, *The English Text* xxv–xxix; Millett, *Annotated Bibliographies* 51–52).

Ownership by religious houses is to be expected and, indeed, copies of *Ancrene Wisse* were owned by both male and female houses. Sometimes, as in the case of the Cleopatra manuscript, these were gifts from secular patrons; sometimes manuscripts seem to have passed down through clerical hands. In both cases, the manuscripts often ranged far indeed from their original audience. As the only surviving copy of the author's final revision for a wider audience of 'twenty or more' anchoresses, Corpus Christi College Cambridge 402 is the most important extant manuscript of *Ancrene Wisse*. Dating from the early thirteenth century, it must have been copied very soon after the revision was made, yet it seems nevertheless to have been copied not for the larger group, but for a solitary anchoress. By c.1300, it had passed into the hands of John Purcel, who presented it to the abbey church of Wigmore at the request of the current precentor, brother Walter of Ludlow (Ker in Tolkien, *The English Text* xvii; Millett, *Annotated Bibliographies* 49). While there is no way of knowing for whom the Corpus manuscript was originally copied, it is interesting that there was an anchoress at the castle of Ludlow, under the patronage of Walter de Lacy (d. 1240) (Allen, 'Wynkyn de Worde' 204–205). The existence of this anchoress at the right time and, given the intercession of 'Walter of Ludlow', in the appropriate place is even more interesting given that there may also have been a family connection between Walter de Lacy and the author and/or translator of *Ancrene Wisse*. Walter de Lacy was married to Margaret, or Margery, de Braose. Margaret de Lacy's patronage of religious women is evident in her founding of a convent at Aconbury in memory of her mother, Maude or Matilda de Braose, who, with her eldest son, was starved to death on the orders of King John. Margaret had two sisters who became anchoresses: Annora, Lady Mortimer (who, with other members of her family, was imprisoned at the time of her mother's death), and Loretta, Countess of Leicester. Dobson (*Origins*) has suggested that the patron of the original three anchoresses to whom *Ancrene Wisse* was originally addressed may have been Annora's husband, Hugh de Mortimer, Lord of Wigmore.[4] Dobson further suggests that the first French translation of *Ancrene Wisse* may have been made for Annora, who became an anchoress at Iffley, near Oxford, after her husband's death (in about 1232). Interestingly, among the decorations at the church in Iffley where Annora was enclosed, is a carving of King John, included amongst the devils and demons which decorate the south door.

Loretta, Countess of Leicester, was enclosed at Hackington, near Canterbury, from 1221 until her death in 1266. She was an important patron of the first Franciscans, suggesting a further, although speculative, connection with *Ancrene Wisse*, given that among the revisions in the Corpus text is a reference to the Dominican and Franciscan friars (and, indeed, that reference is one of the keys to dating the revision of the text). All of this is, of course, conjecture; however, the possibility of such connections between *Ancrene Wisse* and the de Braose women opens up fascinating avenues of exploration, suggesting that the text enjoyed a high degree of female patronage. It may never be known whether the Corpus manuscript was copied for the anchoress at Walter de Lacy's castle of Ludlow, interesting though the possibility may be. Whoever owned it during these years seems to have read it carefully, as suggested by the annotations found in the text (Ker in Tolkien, *The English Text* xvi–xviii; Millett, *Annotated Bibliographies* 49).

Other manuscripts show evidence of having been composed or adapted for a wider audience, suggesting that the range of ownership summarized

---

[4] This has recently been questioned by Millett ('Origins'). However, the existence of these three anchoresses connected to the region where *Ancrene Wisse* originated, as well as the family's religious patronage, is certainly suggestive. For further information about Annora and Loretta de Braose, see Powicke, *Historical Essays*; Allen, 'Wynkyn de Worde'; Dobson, *Origins*; and Labarge, 'Three Medieval Widows'.

above indicates a wider demand which later copyists attempted to satisfy. The immediate ancestor of BL Cotton Titus D.xviii (second quarter of the thirteenth century) seems to have been adapted for a male religious community, and the Titus manuscript itself shows evidence of sporadic modification for use by men. Overall, the alterations in this version seem to suggest adaptation for a more general audience, rather than the original and specific audience of recluses (Mack, *The English Text* xiv–xvii; Millett, *Annotated Bibliographies* 53). Yet, Mack concludes, 'the essential character of the *Ancrene Riwle* as a work written primarily for the instruction of women recluses has been only superficially disturbed' (Mack, *Ancrene Wisse*, p. xvii).[5] On the other hand, Cambridge Gonville and Caius College, 234/120, copied during the mid to late thirteenth century, contains a collection of extracts from the inner rule, in an apparently haphazard order, more carefully adapted for a male readership (Millett, *Annotated Bibliographies* 50). The continuing popularity of *Ancrene Wisse* amongst male readers is also indicated by BL Royal 8. C. i (dating from the early or mid fifteenth century) a manuscript which seems directed at a male audience and contains Lichfield's *Treatise of the Five Senses*, a 'free adaptation' of *Ancrene Wisse* parts 2 and 3 for a more general, lay audience (Baugh, *The English Text* ix; Millett, *Annotated Bibliographies* 55). Yet that the text remained popular amongst women readers is also clear. The Vernon manuscript (Bodl. eng. poet. a 1, fourteenth century), for example, which preserves a later version close to the Corpus text, seems to have been commissioned by a wealthy patron, possibly for a house of nuns. Yet, along with a number of works originally written for women religious, the manuscript includes others which have been adapted or composed for a lay audience (Doyle, 'Survey' n. 60, 136–8; III.234; Millett, *Annotated Bibliographies* 57), suggesting that the work continued to have a broad appeal.

Translations into French and Latin

The varied audience for *Ancrene Wisse* is also indicated by the translations into French and Latin which were made very early in its history. The surviving copies of French translations, which indicate the existence of at least three French versions, date from the late thirteenth and early fourteenth centuries, suggesting that the translations themselves were made even earlier. As Doyle ('Survey' III.233) suggests, it is likely that the translations

---

[5] This is an interesting point for the question of the influence of gender on authors and readers of medieval texts. Clearly, someone felt it worthwhile to attempt to alter both details of language (substituting masculine for feminine pronouns and nouns) and content (such as the original address to the three sisters, which is greatly reduced to a simple statement). Yet, the issue of gender was not pressing enough for the adaptor to do more than a superficial and sporadic job; in other words, it was not felt that the feminine associations of the text were a barrier to a male reader. Further study needs to be done into the question of whether this worked both ways; whether female audiences might have been considered equally flexible and adaptable as readers. If this is so, perhaps it might suggest that issues of gender were less important to medieval readers than modern readers, however they may have been viewed by clerical authors.

were undertaken for women readers; and, as noted above, Dobson (*Origins*) suggests that the first French translation was made at the time of the copying of the Cleopatra manuscript (i.e. before c.1250), possibly for Annora de Mortimer. This suggested female readership is, indeed, borne out by the manuscript evidence. BL Cotton Vitellius F.vii, dating from about the beginning of the fourteenth century, is the only surviving copy of the earliest French translation and is remarkably close to the sense of the original (Millett, *Annotated Bibliographies* 54). The manuscript was damaged in the Cottonian fire of 1731, and later restored. A damaged inscription indicates a fascinating history, which tells us a great deal about at least one circle of readers. The inscription reads:

> . . . m. . Duchesse de Gloucester du doun d . . .
> . . . kent: Plesance
> Al en vn   (Herbert, *The French Text*, xii)

This suggests that the manuscript was owned by Joan Holand, the wife of Thomas Holand, the eighth Earl of Kent. Joan Holand gave the manuscript to Eleanor Cobham, the second wife of Humphrey, Duke of Gloucester, sometime between 1433 (when he began to build 'Plesance', now Greenwich Palace) and 1441 (when Eleanor was indicted for sorcery) (Herbert, *The French Text* xii–xiii). Although Herbert laments that nothing further is known of the book's early history, this alone provides some fascinating clues. Joan Holand also owned, and probably commissioned, Takamiya 8 which contains, amongst other things, a copy of Nicholas Love's *Mirror of the Blessed Life of Jesus Christ* (another text which indicates the abiding influence of *Ancrene Wisse*).[6] Joan gave this manuscript to 'Allyse Belacyse', a gift which is recorded in an elaborate inscription, and Alice passed the book on to her servant, Elizabeth (Meale, 'oft siþis' 35). Both Joan Holand and Alice Belasys spent much of their lives in religious seclusion, Joan from the time of her widowhood and Alice seemingly from her youth. Alice's piety seems to have been rather more public than Joan's; she gave gifts of lands and rents for masses to be said for her soul and the souls of her family. Joan spent the years from 1410 until her death in the Cistercian house of Beaulieu in Hampton, and it is there that she must have been living at the time of her gifts to Alice Belasys and Eleanor Cobham (Alice Belasys was born c.1410 or slightly earlier) (Meale, 'oft siþis' 35–36). Together, these two manuscripts illustrate the kind of 'reading circle' which, it is becoming clear, was common amongst fourteenth- and fifteenth-century aristocratic women.[7] But Cotton Vitellius F.vii suggests other possibilities. Joan's wit

---

[6] As noted above, Love refers to *Ancrene Wisse* in a way that assumes his readers' knowledge of the text; the case of Joan Holand indicates that such an assumption is thoroughly justified.

[7] Other such 'circles' will be discussed below. Meale ('oft siþis') points out similar circles of readers indicated by the passing of manuscripts between women. Other studies (such as Tarvers, 'Thys ys my mystrys boke'; Boffey, 'Women Authors'; Riddy, 'Women talking'; Meale, '. . . alle the bokes'; and Erler, 'Exchange'), have shown that lay women read, owned and commissioned texts in larger numbers than has previously been assumed. Bell ('Medieval Women Book Owners'), Finke (*Feminist Theory*) and Meale ('. . . alle the bokes') have studied the influence of women patrons on the contents of the manuscripts they commissioned, suggesting that women may have had a far

may be indicated in the 'Al en vn' which Herbert suggests 'is probably a sort of punning motto for Eleanor' (Herbert, *The French Text*, p. xiii, who cites a letter by Mrs Clotilda Marson, *Times Literary Supplement*, 12 April 1934). But it is also interesting to speculate on the motivation for her gift. Was this just another instance of a woman passing on a book to a friend with similar interests? Or is this the gift of a devout woman to an acquaintance who was dabbling in suspect activities?[8]

Although Cotton Vitellius F.vii indicates the continuing popularity of *Ancrene Wisse* amongst aristocratic women, other manuscripts of French translations indicate a breadth of audience similar to the Middle English copies. Cambridge Trinity College R. 14.7, for example, contains an adaptation copied in the late thirteenth or early fourteenth century. The text consists of extensive borrowings from *Ancrene Wisse* which are independent of the earlier French translation. As Tretheway points out 'the original text is broken up, rearranged, inflated, and embedded in a lengthy Compilation or series of treatises constituting a sort of handbook or manual of religious living', addressed to an audience that includes both men and women, lay and religious.[9] Tretheway suggests that 'as an historic document it illustrates the process of generalization, expansion and adaptation of the original *Ancrene Riwle* text during the thirteenth century' (Trethewey, *The French Text*, 1971, ix). The text is a good indication of the extent of the early circulation of *Ancrene Wisse* and the number of manuscripts which are now lost; its source is not *Ancrene Wisse* itself, but an intermediate text based on a version of *Ancrene Wisse* related to the Middle English Titus manuscript, which had already been expanded and generalized (Trethewey, *The French Text*, 1971). The manuscript was acquired by Norwich Cathedral Priory sometime between 1272 and 1325, where it remained until at least the sixteenth century (Millett, *Annotated Bibliographies* 51). An inscription suggests that it was owned by a monk, Geoffrey of Wroxham (d. 1322), who was the refectorer of Norwich priory in 1311 and 1313–1314. Allen suggests that, although it is possible that the book was used for private devotional reading, the incipits suggest that the work may have been intended to be read aloud, possibly at meals. As we shall see, the manuscripts of *Chastising* also support such a conclusion. Allen cites the work of Saunders (1930) who 'shows that the Norwich

---

greater influence on the subject matter of vernacular literary production than has been recognized in the past. Meale ('oft siþis') suggests a number of ways in which such studies can shed light on women's reading practices, but points out the need for further study of male- and female-authored works composed for a female audience.

[8] Eleanor Cobham was indicted on charges of sorcery for employing a necromancer to cast the horoscope of Henry VI, allegedly in order to calculate the date of his death. The charges seem largely aimed at her husband, Humphrey, Duke of Gloucester, who was, at the time, heir presumptive to the throne. Nevertheless, it is interesting to speculate why a devout widow living in religious seclusion would give a manuscript containing *Ancrene Wisse* and other devotional material to another woman who would, in a very few years, face such charges.

[9] Trethewey points out that the same compilation occurs in BN fonds fr 6276 (late thirteenth or early fourteenth century, written in England but later sold or taken to France) and Bodl. 90 (a manuscript of the late thirteenth or early fourteenth century written in England, the early history of which nothing is known).

refectorer procured certain books of a type which . . . suggest that a small reference library may have been kept in the refectory'. She concludes, 'probably . . . the Norwich refectorer had some responsibility for the provision of books to be read at meals (according to the explicit prescription of the Rule of St Benedict)' (Allen, 'Wynkyn de Worde', 200–201).[10]

The existence of another French translation is indicated by *The Tretyse of Loue*, an adaptation of extracts from *Ancrene Wisse* Parts 4 (on Temptation) and 7 (on Love), combined with additional material, which was re-translated from French into English in the late fifteenth century and printed by Wynkyn de Worde in 1493 or 1494. Five of the last six items in the *Tretyse* also occur in Bibliothèque Royale MS Français 2292, transcribed by David Aubert in 1475 for Margaret of York, a patroness of Caxton, for whom Aubert made many compilations. While the Brussels manuscript is not the direct source of the *Tretyse*, its existence suggests a common source current in Burgundian circles, and also suggests that *Ancrene Wisse* circulated on the continent in at least one form. Fisher speculates that the French source of the *Tretyse* may also be of Burgundian origin, and that there might, indeed, have been other copies or versions of *Ancrene Wisse* in Belgium or Northern France which have not survived. However, the *Tretyse* may also have been of Anglo-Norman origins (Fisher, *Tretyse* xiv–xxi). Nothing further is known about the translator, readers or owners of this text.

Ancrene Wisse was also translated into Latin. The manuscripts containing Latin versions vary in form and content. BL Cotton Vitellius E.vii (early fourteenth century with later additions) was badly damaged in the Cottonian fire of 1731 and survives in fragmentary form. Yet, it is the only version which includes Part 8 of *Ancrene Wisse*, which is either omitted or nearly so in all other Latin versions (Millett, *Annotated Bibliographies* 53; d'Evelyn 1944, *The Latin Text* xiii). It is interesting to speculate as to why this might be so, and whether the Latin versions were intended for an audience which would require a different form of 'outer rule' than that presented in *Ancrene Wisse* 8. In both Smith's catalogue of Cottonian manuscripts and the version preserved in Oxford, Magdalen College, Latin 67 (fourteenth century), the Latin version is attributed to Simon of Ghent, Bishop of Salisbury (d. 1314), and it is indicated that he wrote it for recluses at Tarrant who were under his care (Millett, *Annotated Bibliographies* 53–54; d'Evelyn, 1944, *The Latin Text* xiii), an attribution which, incidentally, indicates that the Cistercian nuns at Tarrant were literate in Latin.[11] The

---

[10] As Allen points out, the Trinity manuscript also suggests that copies of *Ancrene Wisse* were owned in Norwich during the mid and late thirteenth century.

[11] Bell (*What Nuns Read*) cautions against too-easy assumptions about the Latin literacy, or lack thereof, of English nuns. After a detailed consideration of the surviving manuscripts linked to English nunneries, he concludes that 'more nuns than we suppose might have been able to construe a Latin text, and more nunneries than we suspect might have taught the language . . . In short, although it is undoubtedly true that from the early fourteenth century onwards, most nuns (and probably most lay-monks) were unable to read and understand a non-liturgical text in Latin, I would contend that the minority who could may well have been greater than has hitherto been supposed' (pp. 63, 66).

early ownership of Oxford, Magdalen College, Latin 67 and the Latin version in Oxford, Merton College, C.1.5 (early fourteenth century) is unknown, as is the ownership of the Latin BL Royal 7 C.x (sixteenth century). BL Cotton Vitellius E.vii, however, was presented to the Benedictine abbey of Bardney by Robert of Thornton, a former prior, and at the dissolution passed into the library of Henry VIII (Millett, *Annotated Bibliographies* 59).

The extant manuscripts thus indicate that *Ancrene Wisse* enjoyed a wide readership, including both men and women, both lay and religious. It circulated in a variety of forms, and was owned by royalty, nobility, and yeomen. It passed from religious houses to lay owners and back again, and was translated for the use of readers of widely varied levels of education and differing cultural milieus. It was also read across a wide geographical area, crossing England by the end of the thirteenth century and eventually making its way to the continent.

Borrowings and Adaptations

The popularity and adaptability of *Ancrene Wisse* is also indicated by the number of borrowings and adaptations incorporated into later texts. These range from excerpted material, such as those found in the sixteenth-century Bodl. Laud misc. 201 (containing prayers from Part 1) and Bodl. Laud misc. 381 (containing excerpts from Parts 2–7), to full scale borrowings (such as the opening chapters of *The Chastising of God's Children*) and adaptations (such as *þe Wohunge of Ure Lauerd*). As Millett (*Ancrene Wisse*) points out, many of the 'borrowings' that have been suggested over the years are inconclusive, and one must be cautious about attributing direct influence where perhaps only an intermediary source is indicated. Nevertheless, the evidence that such 'intermediary sources' existed, and that the images and ideas of *Ancrene Wisse* found their way into the works of authors into the fifteenth century and beyond, whether directly or indirectly, suggests a range of influence that, in itself, has much to say about the legacy of *Ancrene Wisse*.

There are many texts which have been identified as derivative from or dependent upon *Ancrene Wisse*. Again, these are summarized by Doyle ('Survey'), Sargent ('Minor Devotional Writings') and Millett (*Ancrene Wisse*), and further discussion is found in the various editions and articles cited here. A detailed examination of these texts, their owners and readers, is beyond the scope of this paper, but a few examples will suffice to illustrate the audiences to which they appealed. Many of these later texts are, like *Ancrene Wisse*, addressed to female audiences. For example, *þe Pater Noster of Richard Ermyte* (ed. Aarts, 1967), composed in the early fifteenth century (and probably before 1408 [Millett, *Annotated Bibliographies*]), is addressed to a 'dere sistir'. Although there is no information about who this 'sister' was, it is likely that the text was written for a nun, and that the author at least envisioned a wider audience which would include women religious who were literate in English, but not in Latin. Yet, of the surviving manuscripts, only one, CUL Ii.vi.40, can be identified as belonging to a nun. This manuscript, which also contains *Fervor Amorist*, material from *The Pore Caitiff* (see below), Rolle's *Form of Living* and *Commandment* and various other Middle English devotional texts, as well as a long Latin prayer, belonged to Joan Moureslegh, a nun at Shaftesbury abbey in the mid-fifteenth century (Doyle, 'Survey' n. 46; Bell, *What Nuns Read* 130). It also belonged to an unidentified 'Annys' or 'Agnette Dawns filie Thome Grene' in the early sixteenth century and a Thomas Worth in the early to mid sixteenth century (Doyle, 'Survey' n. 46). Other manuscripts, however, indicate again a wide readership. Westminster School Library MS 3 (early fifteenth century), which also contains Rolle's *Form of Living*, and *Ego Dormio*, was owned in 1472 by a layman, Richard Cloos, who may have been one of the churchwardens of St Mary-at-Hill, London, from 1491–1493 (the name appears frequently in parish records from 1483–1502). One Johannes Levell, who may have been a parish priest, owned Cambridge, Trinity College O.1.29 (Aarts, *Pater Noster* xi–xiv).

While the existence of such borrowings is of interest in itself, the nature of the borrowings is also suggestive, and it is to two particular kinds of borrowings that I now wish to turn. Many (although by no means all) of the borrowings from *Ancrene Wisse* found in later texts fall into two main categories: the image of God as a mother who disciplines her children in a game, or 'pley of love' (found primarily in the context of temptation and sin); and the image of God as a divine lover who woos the human soul, or the Christ-knight (found in the context of mystical or devotional material). Both sets of images are first introduced into Middle English by the author of *Ancrene Wisse*. But, by the end of the fourteenth century, both sets of images are fairly common, and occur in other contexts that provide an opportunity for comparisons with their use in texts that draw upon *Ancrene Wisse*. These two images thus provide an opportunity to address the question of influence, as well as direct borrowing and adaptation.

The Christ-Knight

The parable of Christ as a lover-knight, found in *Ancrene Wisse* Part 7, is adapted and expanded upon in the early thirteenth-century poem, *þe Wohunge of Ure Lauerd* (ed. Thompson, *Wohunge*), the text which gives the title to the 'Wooing Group'.[12] Like *Ancrene Wisse*, *Wohunge* sets the image in the context of a passion meditation, giving a fascinating interpretation of the parable, re-written in a first-person, female voice and addressed to a female anchoritic audience. The poem is clearly intended to provide a feminine reading of the parable which would appeal to female readers.[13]

---

[12] *Ancrene Wisse* 7 is also among the excerpts found in *The Tretyse of Loue*, discussed above under 'translations'.

[13] I have discussed the implications of this 'feminine' reading of the parable in *Wohunge* in my '*Ancrene Wisse*'.

Yet, interestingly enough, the sole surviving copy is found in BL Cotton Titus D.xviii, described above, which also contains a version of *Ancrene Wisse* sporadically modified for a male readership.

Wohunge itself was further adapted and incorporated into *A Talkying of þe Loue of God* (ed. Westra, *Talkying*), which also draws upon *On wel swuðe god ureisun of God Almihti*, another text of the Wooing Group, extant with *Ancrene Wisse* in BL Cotton Nero A.xiv (discussed above), and in Lambeth 487. *Talkying*, like *Wohunge*, falls squarely into the tradition of affective devotion, and incorporates the figure of the Lover-Knight into a passion sequence. In the ways in which it adapts its sources, *Talkyng* is reminiscent of the affective writings of Richard Rolle, to the extent that it has been called an imitation of Rolle in both manner and style (Westra, *Talkying* xxx, citing Horstmann). The text thus serves as a link between the more conservative *Ancrene Wisse* and the fully developed affective mysticism of the fourteenth-century mystics. Indeed, Allen ('Mystical Writings') has suggested that 'the whole development of English mysticism may turn out to be indicated in the genealogy of the "talking of the love of God" '.

On the basis of internal evidence, it seems that *Talkying* was, unlike *Wohunge*, compiled by a man for a primarily male audience (or, as Westra puts it, 'in any case not exclusively for women'). Masculine forms (such as son and brother) are used of the soul, suggesting that the treatise was either written or adapted for the use of men. It seems likely that the original audience consisted of either monks or friars. Yet, *Talkyng* is preserved only in the Vernon manuscript (Bodl. eng. poet. a 1, discussed above), and the related Simeon manuscript (BL Add. 22283, discussed below), both of which are associated with female readers. Nothing further is known of the text's purpose or audience; yet, its inclusion in two deluxe manuscripts with works such as *Ancrene Wisse*, the Middle English *Stimulus Amoris* and the writings of Hilton and Rolle, and suggests 'that it ranked with the most popular devotional works of the 14th century' (Westra, *Talkying* xxxl).

The image of the Christ-Knight was widely used in fourteenth-century literature, and Woolf ('Theme') provides an excellent survey. Many of these instances, such as the appearance of the Christ-Knight in *Piers Plowman*, are clearly independent of *Ancrene Wisse*. Others, such as the Latin analogue in the fourteenth-century preaching text found in Harley 7322 may be indirectly influenced by *Ancrene Wisse*. Woolf suggests that the image in Harley 7322 derives from a common source but, as with the image of the playful mother discussed below, no such source has been identified (Woolf, 'Theme' 5–6). A final example is the passion meditation in Harley 1740, which is specifically addressed to a woman (edited by Marx, 'Harley MS 1740'). While there are no verbatim borrowings, this text contains enough verbal echoes of *Ancrene Wisse* to suggest a direct influence, if not slavish literary dependence. The widespread popularity of the image in other texts and contexts attests to its appeal to male and female authors and audiences alike.

The Mother-God

The image of God as a mother who plays with her wayward child provides a more complex tangle to the student of *Ancrene Wisse* and its descendants, in part because the image often occurs in contexts which are close enough to its use in *Ancrene Wisse* to make direct influence possible (although at times only remotely so), but not close enough to make direct literary dependence clear. This image thus provides a fascinating 'case study' of how complex the inter-relationships between texts can become, but also of how common the images found in *Ancrene Wisse* had become by the end of the fourteenth century. The mother-God's 'play' of love is used in *The Pore Caitiff* and *The Chastising of God's Children* in a way that suggests their authors' independent use of *Ancrene Wisse* in one of its incarnations. *Chastising* itself is among the sources of the compilations *Disce Mori* and its derivative *Ignorancia Sacerdotum*, which are also dependent on Rolle and Hilton (Hudson, 'Chapter'; Jones, 'Chapter'). But the image is also found in James of Milan's *Stimulus Amoris* (which was translated into Middle English as *The Prickynge of Love*, sometimes attributed to Hilton); William Flete's *De Remediis contra Temptaciones* and its Middle English translations; *The Book of Tribulation*; and *The Doctrine of the Heart*. Such independent use of similar images provides a 'control' group of texts with which to compare the texts that draw more directly upon *Ancrene Wisse*, but it also complicates the question of influence by suggesting the possible existence of common sources and illustrating the difficulties of establishing direct dependence, as will be seen in the discussion below.

The *Chastising of God's Children* makes independent use of the same Latin source as *The Pore Caitiff*. The opening chapter begins with a lengthy quotation from *Ancrene Wisse*. Bazire and Colledge argue that 'there can be little doubt that the author is here translating from a Latin compilation similar to the fragment found in Ms Laud misc. 111, f. 187r' (*Chastising* 259–260), a fragment also found in Lincoln Cathedral C.4.6, Bibliothèque Royale 1485, Prague University 814, and Vienna Nationalbibliothek 4483, which was first identified by Allen ('Fourteenth Century Borrowings'), and is cited by Sargent ('Minor Devotional Writings') as the 'Quandoque Tribularis'. Bazire and Colledge suggest that this particular fragment may not be the direct source, as *Chastising* retains some features from *Ancrene Wisse* which the Latin has lost, concluding that 'the Latin is a survival of some fuller Latin compendium made from the *Ancrene Riwle*, from which lost source *The Chastising* and *The Pore Caitiff* borrow independently' and that other material in *Chastising* may also have been borrowed from this source (*Chastising* 263).

The evidence of such a lost, intermediate, Latin source suggests a far wider circulation of the Latin translation of *Ancrene Wisse* than might have been supposed from the extant manuscripts. As well, the fact that it was circulating in Latin means that it would have entered into clerical circles and have been encountered by readers who might have disdained to read it in the vernacular. Indeed, the use of this 'lost' Latin source by the author of

Chastising is an interesting comment on the shifting attitudes towards the vernacular in the fourteenth century. In the opening pages of his work, in a statement which employs a conventional humility topos, the author laments that the needs of his female reader, a 'religious sister', compel him to write in English, for, although he is unfit to write such a treatise in Latin or English, the vernacular poses particular difficulties to one who would write of divine things:

> Also, my sistir, y drede sore to write of suche hiȝe matiers, for y haue neiþer felynge ne knowynge opinli to declare hem in englisch ne in laytn, and nameli in englisch tunge, for it passiþ fer my wit to shewe ȝou in any maner vulgare þe termes of diuinite. (Bazire and Colledge, *Chastising*, 95)

It is a delightful irony that the Latin source upon which he slavishly depends for the title and first section of his treatise is itself a translation from the very 'vulgar' tongue which he feels is inadequate for the project.

Chastising also shows the influence (although again, possibly indirect) of James of Milan's *Stimulus Amoris* and William Flete's *De Remediis contra Temptaciones*, both of which were translated into Middle English in the fourteenth century, and both of which use the metaphor of God as a mother playing with her child which *Chastising* borrows from *Ancrene Wisse*. Like *Ancrene Wisse*, all three texts use the metaphor in the context of dealing with temptation, yet, with the exception of *Chastising*, these cannot be identified with certainty as direct 'borrowmgs'. As Bazire and Colledge (*Chastising*) point out, 'there are no textual or verbal similarities to suggest that *The Chastising* and the English version of *Stimulus Amoris* borrow from one another' (p. 265). If James of Milan or William Flete were familiar with the metaphor from its use in *Ancrene Wisse*, they have adapted it in ways that suggest the authors' independence of thought rather than direct 'copying'. Indeed, while *Ancrene Wisse* may well have been translated into Latin before James of Milan wrote the *Stimulus Amoris* (late thirteenth century), there is little evidence of the Latin *Ancrene Wisse*'s circulation in the thirteenth century, although, as we have seen, it may well have been wider than supposed. We thus have no way of knowing whether James of Milan could have encountered it. This lack of evidence has led to speculation about a lost 'common source'. However, if such a lost source could be adapted differently by various authors, so too could *Ancrene Wisse* itself, and no such common source has yet been identified. The earliest identifiable use of this particular metaphor (although not of the broader metaphor of God as mother, which, as Bynum [*Jesus*] has shown, was widespread) is *Ancrene Wisse* itself.

William Flete, on the other hand, writing in England, was almost certainly familiar with *Ancrene Wisse* in either its Latin or vernacular forms. *De Remediis* was written before Flete's departure for the continent in 1359, probably in an East Anglian Augustinian convent (Hackett, 'William Flete'). It was copied and owned by men and women, lay and religious, and translated into at least three Middle English versions (Colledge and

Chadwick, '*Remedies*'; Hackett, Colledge and Chadwick, '*De Remediis*'). Bazire and Colledge (*Chastising* 263) argue that Flete is dependent upon James of Milan's *Stimulus Amoris* for the metaphor of God as a mother, and that their version of the metaphor is independent of the version in *þe Chastising of God's Children* and *The Pore Caitiff* which descend directly from a translation of *Ancrene Wisse*. Hackett (1961) supports this conclusion, arguing that the sections of *De Remediis* which include the metaphor are drawn verbatim from *Stimulus Amoris*. Hackett, however, argues that Flete is dependent on *Ancrene Wisse* elsewhere in his text (Hackett, 'William Flete'; Hackett, Colledge and Chadwick, '*De Remediis*'). Sargent ('Minor Devotional Writings'), on the other hand, suggests that *De Remediis* and *Chastising* derive from the same source, the Latin translation of *Ancrene Wisse* found in 'Quandoque Tribularis'. Millett (*Ancrene Wisse*) rejects this possibility, and argues that the evidence of *Ancrene Wisse* having influenced Flete is not strong. Caution is therefore needed when drawing conclusions about direct literary influence.

A further point of interest lies in the way in which *De Remediis* was itself used by later authors. *Chastising* bears a number of resemblances to *De Remediis* and may well have been influenced by it (Hackett, Colledge and Chadwick, '*De Remediis*'). But even more suggestive, for my purposes, is that one passage of Thomas More's 'A Dialogue of Comfort against Tribulation', composed in prison, is clearly derived from *De Remediis*. It is not, however, transcribed from any extant version, Latin or English, suggesting that More is writing from memory (Colledge and Chadwick, '*Remedies*'). This suggests that literary influence does not always take a direct form, and even when it does, it will not always appear in the form of direct verbal parallels.

More's use of *De Remediis* raises questions for the determination of literary influence which are especially important when considering the metaphor of God as a mother playing with her wayward child. Whether the metaphor was 'borrowed' (directly or indirectly) from *Ancrene Wisse* or a lost common source, its occurrence in such a wide variety of texts with such a varied circulation means that it would have been familiar to a wide range of fourteenth- and fifteenth-century readers. The occurrence of the metaphor in the *Pore Caitiff*, *Chastising*, *De Remediis*, and *Stimulus Amoris*, like More's use of *De Remediis*, suggests the possibility of a wider range of adaptation and influence, looser than direct literary dependence, but nonetheless real. This kind of influence is as useful as evidence of direct literary borrowing, for it indicates the kind of adaptation and interpretation of texts which reveals the interests and needs of readers. In addition, such influence can reflect the oral transmission of texts that was common amongst small 'communities' of reading women, who might have read aloud and discussed a wide variety of texts (Bell, 'Medieval Women Book Owners'; Riddy, 'Women talking'; Boffey, 'Women Authors'; and Erler, 'Exchange').[14] Riddy ('Women talking') argues that much of Julian of

---

[14] This would include the kind of 'reading circles' identified above in connection with Joan Holand,

Norwich's knowledge of devotional and mystical texts would have come from such oral sharing of the written word and discussion of its meaning. The influence of memory in the adaptation of sources (as opposed to direct literary dependence) is not, of course, limited to women readers and authors, as More's use of *De Remediis* clearly shows. Yet, the example of Margery Kempe shows that such influence is central to women 'readers', even when they are illiterate. Indeed, it is such oral transmission, and the memory of what has been read to women, that permeates Kempe's *Book*, and her responses to the theological climate of her times. Recognizing such influence thus expands the scope of the study of women's responses to literary and devotional works (see, for example, Baker, 'Julian').

The question becomes even more complicated when one considers an author like Julian of Norwich, who uses the metaphor of God as a mother in vastly different ways from the authors of the texts cited above, yet whose writing shows evidence of her wide reading.[15] It is possible that Julian had read *Ancrene Wisse*, although this cannot be conclusively proven (Baker, 'Julian'). Indeed, her exposure to the ideas and images found in *Ancrene Wisse* may have been indirect, through reading texts which were themselves influenced by it. Her writings show the influence of works such as *A Talkying of the Love of God*, and the Middle English *Stimulus Amoris*. It is likely that she read *Chastising*, and she may also have been familiar with a Middle English version of Flete's *De Remediis*, which, along with the metaphor of God as mother, includes a reference to the two wills (godly and evil) in each man, similar (but not identical) to Julian's 'bestely' and 'godly' wills (Long Text, Chapter 37). Taken together, what these texts show is how far the ideas and images which are first introduced into Middle English in *Ancrene Wisse* had spread by the late fourteenth century, and how common and influential they had become. In the survey below, I will not attempt to discuss all of the many manuscripts containing these texts; however, even a brief look at the owners and readers of the manuscripts in which the later texts occur indicates just how wide the influence of these ideas on readers and authors might have been.

The Middle English *Stimulus Amoris* (*The Prickynge of Love*) circulated with both Flete's *De Remediis* (CUL Hh.i.11) and *Chastising* (Trinity College Cambridge B 14 19) and, like them, clearly appealed to a female audience. The rubric in Cosin V.iii.8 and the Stonor Park manuscript of *Prickynge* suggests that the text was made for a religious audience, possibly nuns and, indeed, the *Treatise of the Ghostly Tree*, written for nuns in the East Midlands in the first half of the fifteenth century, specifically refers its readers to the *Stimulus Amoris* as appropriate reading (Doyle, 'Survey'). Two copies belonged to Dartford in the mid-fifteenth century. One,

---

or below, in connection with the nunneries of Barking and Dartford. The fact that a number of these texts had common owners also indicates the breadth of reading which such circles may have encompassed, especially when one considers that other texts may have been, and, indeed, likely were borrowed from other, now unidentified, owners.

[15] I have made a detailed comparison of the uses of the metaphor of God as mother in *Ancrene Wisse*, *Chastising*, and Julian's *Revelations* in my 'Subversion and Conformity'.

Downside 26542, also contains *The Pore Caitiff*. It was given to Betryce Chaumber, who bequeathed it to Sister Emma Wynter and Sister Denyse Caston, nuns of Dartford (Doyle, 'Survey' I.52). The second Dartford manuscript, Harley 2254, also contains Hilton's *Mixed Life*. Three names, Alice Braintwaith, Elizabeth Rede, and Joanna Newmarch, are inscribed on the front flyleaf. Joanna Newmarch was likely the original owner; an armorial shield on f. 1, containing the arms of Shirley and Brewes, suggests that she should be identified as Joan Shirley Newmarch, the daughter of Sir Hugh Shirley (d. 1403) and Beatrice Brewes Shirley (d.c. 1440). Joan Newmarch had family connections to Dartford, which was founded in 1346 – her maternal grandfather was a benefactor – and it may be that she gave the manuscript to Dartford during her lifetime. Joan herself was a gentlewoman of Isabel, Countess of Warwick, who bequeathed her sufficient funds to retire into religious seclusion (Erler, 'Exchange' 361–2). Alice Braintwaith was the prioress of Dartford in 1461. Elizabeth Rede is unidentified (Doyle, 'Survey' n. 51; Bell, *What Nuns Read* 131).

Evidence of lay ownership of *Prickynge* comes from the Simeon manuscript (BL Add. 22283), which may have been compiled for Joan Bohun, the grandmother of Henry V, and was eventually owned by an 'Awdri Norwood' (Tarvers, 'Thys ys my mystrys boke'). *Prickynge* is the only item in Bodley 480, which is inscribed 'My lady Marques' Dorsettes Book', possibly referring to either Cecily or Margaret Dorset (fl. 1477–1530) (Kane, *Prickynge* vi–vii).

The Middle English translations of Flete's *De Remediis* survive in at least three versions, and show the same mixed readership as the other texts we have discussed. For example, Bodley 131 (mid-fifteenth century), which also contains Love's *Mirror*, was written by a layman, John Morton of York, possibly for a middle class audience. It eventually was owned by a member of the regular clergy (Meale, 'oft siþis'; Doyle, 'Survey' III.184, n. 33). But, like *Prickynge*, with which it is found in CUL Hh.i.11, *De Remediis* seems to have held particular appeal for the female audience to which it was originally directed. CUL Hh.i.11 seems to have been produced in a nunnery (Colledge and Chadwick, '*Remedies*'), possibly a contemplative nunnery in East Anglia (Doyle, 'Survey' n. 47), and contains *Prickynge* and two versions of the Middle English *De Remediis*. Harley 2409 was given by Maude Wade, the prioress of Swine (c. 1473–82) to Joan Hyltoft of Nuncoton (both Cistercian nunneries) (Gillespie, 'Vernacular Books'). The Foyle manuscript (see below), which also contains Love's *Mirror*, belonged to Sybilla de Felton, abbess of Barking (d. 1419). Another copy, Harley 1706, which also contains tracts from the *Pore Caitiff* may have once belonged to Barking; it was certainly owned by Elizabeth de Vere (see below), indicating an appeal to lay readers as well as religious. BL Royal 18.A.x contains a version of Flete's treatise adapted by a female author as an epistle to a 'religious sister', similar to the version in Trinity College Dublin 154, addressed to a 'good sister' and possibly originating in an East Anglian nunnery (Doyle, 'Survey' I.70). Holkham Misc. 41 contains the same version as Trinity College Dublin 154, along with another compilation of meditations and prayers on the passion compiled by one religious sister at the request of another (Tarvers, 'Thys ys my mystrys bok'; Colledge and Chadwick, '*Remedies*'; Doyle, 'Survey'; see also Barrett, *Women's Writing*; Pollard, 'Mystical Elements').

The Pore Caitiff, which survives in over thirty manuscripts (in both its complete form and in fragments), was addressed to both religious and lay people, and seems to have been particularly intended for women readers (Doyle, 'Survey'; Brady, 'Pore Caitiff'). It shows signs of Lollard influence, but also circulated amongst orthodox owners. Once again, the manuscripts indicate a broad readership. Hunterian V.7.23 may have been part of a monastic library: it is preserved in a medieval binding, with a label 'G.30.' CUL Ff.vi.55 was owned by Canon William Cotson in 1489 (Doyle, 'Survey' n. 13). Bodley 938 is of a scope that would suggest a priestly owner, but contains criticism of clerics and their ways. Contemporary annotations noting heterodox passages suggest an orthodox owner, and a Latin inscription suggests an educated lay owner at some time (possibly late fifteenth or early sixteenth century [Doyle, 'Survey' n. 15]). Lambeth Palace 541 was given by 'Johanni Petyrsfeylede' (a cleric) to 'Mr. T Eyburhall' (presumably a layman) in the mid-fifteenth century, although it likely had previous owners (Doyle, 'Survey' n. 51). Rylands Eng. 98 belonged to a Thomas Roberts and family (Doyle, 'Survey' II.148). Cambridge, Trinity College B. 14.53 was owned in the mid-sixteenth century by a Thomas Philips. Rylands Eng.85 was owned by 'Johanni Ade', 'Wyllyam Vicary' and 'Margett Kyghtley', all presumably lay. Stowe 38 was owned by a Denis Beke and Isabelle Beke. Notes in the margins suggest a curate or churchwarden's activities (Doyle, 'Survey' n. 10). Rawlinson C 882 is inscribed with the names of two women: Dame Margaret Erley 'cum magno gaudio et honore' and Agnete (surname illegible) who is aggressive about her ownership, adding 'He hoo thys boke steleth scall have cryst curse and myne' (Doyle, 'Survey' n. 11). Doyle suggests that Ashmole 1286, which also contains the English *Stimulus Amoris*, was most likely made for devout women perhaps nuns, as is also likely for Hh.i.12. *The Pore Caitiff* is also found in a number of manuscripts which also contain other texts deriving from *Ancrene Wisse*, some of which are included below.[16] Many of these were owned by women.

The Chastising of God's Children was written between 1382 and 1408 and was, like many of the texts discussed here, addressed to devout women, probably nuns. It was a popular text throughout the fifteenth century, and nine manuscripts of the complete text survive. It was also adapted in the compilation *Disce Mori*, which was addressed to a 'Dame Alice', a religious woman, probably a nun.[17] *Disce Mori* and the *Ignorancia Sacerdotum* (a condensed adaptation of *Disce Mori*) survive in four manuscripts, and a collection of extracts also survives in Harley 1288. *Chastising* was also printed by Wynkyn de Worde, and reprinted several times. As Bazire and

---

[16] See also CUL Ii.vi.40, discussed above.
[17] *Disce Mori* also draws upon Hilton and Rolle, among other sources.

Colledge (*Chastising*) point out, even more extensive copying is indicated by the complex textual relations between the extant manuscripts, suggesting that many more copies were lost than survive.

The ownership of the extant manuscripts has been detailed by Bazire and Colledge (*Chastising*), and needs only to be summarized here. Once again, a wide readership is evident, as is the fact that the text was put to a variety of uses: As Bazire and Colledge point out, the surviving manuscripts of *Chastising* suggest a number of things about how the text was used. Some are so full of errors that Bazire and Colledge conclude that they could not serve the needs of the 'serious student' (which suggests private owners and private reading). St John's College Cambridge E.25 is very difficult to read, suggesting that it was a copy made for private use, while Add 33971 has been annotated by a scribe in the margins and is a 'beautifully legible copy' that would be easy for readers to use. Bodley 505 has been carefully corrected by two hands in a way that suggests that the revisions were made for a religious house, and in a way that would present no difficulty to a lector. The interlinear annotations in Pepys 2125 suggest that the manuscript was intended to be read aloud, while Trinity College Cambridge B.14.19 is annotated in such a way to suggest silent reading (often in the margins or in footnotes). Rawlinson C.57 contains annotations that consist of detailed instructions which appear to be aimed at a scribe producing a short treatise intended for a house of women religious, similar to the type of text produced in *Disce Mori* and *Ignorancia Sacerdotum* (Bazire and Colledge, *Chastising*).

In spite of being originally addressed to a female audience, *Chastising* found a substantial male readership. Bodley 505 and Rawlinson C.57 were owned by Carthusian houses (London and Sheen, respectively), and there is an undated memorandum which indicates the existence of another copy which was taken from the Charterhouse at London to Hull by John Spalding. Pepys 2125 has been annotated by a contemporary corrector in order to make the text appropriate for a male religious house (Bazire and Colledge, *Chastising*).

Not surprisingly, *Chastising* was also popular in women's houses. A number of extant copies are traceable to Syon; Jesus 39 (containing the *Disce Mori*) was owned by Dorothy Slyghe (a nun at Syon in the sixteenth century), and two of the surviving printed editions were also owned by Syon nuns: Sidney Sussex College Cambridge Bb.2.14 belonged to Edith Morepath and Katherine Palmer, and Göttingen UL 4^0 Theol. Mor. 138/53 was owned by Awdrey Dely and Mary Nevell (Bazire and Colledge, *Chastising* 6; Bell, *What Nuns Read* 196–197).[18] Although most of *Chastising*'s concerns seem more appropriate to a religious community, it seems to have been considered suitable for recluses, as well as devout women in

---

[18] Both Sidney Sussex College Cambridge Bb.2.14 and Göttingen UL 4^0 Theol. Mor.138/53 also contain *The Tretyse of Loue*, which is often found bound with *Chastising*. In fact, eight of the ten extant copies of *The Tretyse of Loue* are bound with *Chastising* and it is likely that a ninth, John Rylands Library no. 15541, was originally bound with the Huth copy of *Chastysing* (Fisher, *Tretyse* xi–xii).

religious houses. Heneage 3084 (which also contains the ME *Stimulus Amoris*) may also have belonged to Syon, although there is no direct evidence (Kane, *Prickynge* xiv).[19] The version in Heneage 3084, which is related to the form of *Chastising* circulating among the nuns of Syon, ascribes *Chastising* to Hilton and identifies it as a text written for 'a religious woman lyuing solitarie' (Sargent, 'New Manuscript').

There is also evidence that *Chastising* was owned by laywomen. Mercy Ormesby bequeathed a primer and a copy of *Chastising* to the Benedictine nuns at Easebourne Priory in 1451 (Bazire and Colledge, *Chastising* 38), and Lady Peryn Clanvowe left a copy to Elizabeth Joye in 1422 (Tarvers, 'Thys ys my mystrys boke'; Doyle, 'Survey'). Another lay owner, about whom we know a bit more, is Agnes Stapilton. Like Joan Holland, Agnes Stapilton seems to have chosen a devout widowhood after her husband's death in 1417. She left many bequests to female religious houses in her will, dated 27 March 1448 and proved 1 April 1448, among them ten books in English and French, including a Psalter, a Primer, the *Stimulus Amoris*, the *Pricke of Conscience*, and the *Book of Vices and Virtues*. She left 'librum meum vocatum Bonaventure' to the nuns of Sinningthwaite in Yorkshire, which is probably Love's translation, a book of saints' lives in French to a granddaughter, Elene Ingelby, and a copy of *Chastising* to the Cistercian nuns at Esholt, near Leeds (Doyle, 'Survey'; Bazire and Colledge, *Chastising*; Bell, *What Nuns Read*).

Reading Circles: Barking, Dartford and their Patrons

The texts which use the metaphor of the mother-God, including *Chastising*, *The Pore Caitiff*, and the Middle English versions of *Stimulus* (the *Prickynge of Love*) and Flete's *De Remediis*, are also associated with the Benedictine convent of Barking and the Dominican convent of Dartford, and it is to the circle of readers and manuscripts which can be connected with these two houses that I wish to turn next. Inter-connections between texts is suggested in a number of ways besides direct borrowings: texts are bound together; texts refer to each other; texts are shared amongst a circle of readers. The convents of Barking and Dartford offer an opportunity to explore such inter-connections amongst the texts with which this article is concerned.

Although there is no extant manuscript linking *Chastising* to Barking, it is clear that the text was familiar to its inhabitants. *The Cleansing of Man's Soul*, an anonymous text extant in two manuscripts, makes reference to *Chastising* in a way that assumes its readers' familiarity with the text, and, indeed, it is this reference which provides one of the clues to the date of *Chastising*. *The Cleansing of Man's Soul* is found in Bodley 923, which contains an inscription, dated 1401, indicating that the manuscript was

---

[19] Bell (*What Nuns Read*) also records the existence of a (now lost) copy of the de Worde edition of *Chastising* which was given by a nun of Campsey, Elisabeth Willowby, to another nun, Catherine Symonde.

owned (and possibly commissioned) by Sybille de Felton, who was abbess of Barking from 1394. Sybille de Felton also owned the Foyle manuscript (Beeleigh Abbey), which contains, among other things, Rolle's *Form of Living*, Love's *Mirror*, and a Middle English version of Flete's *De Remediis*. Since Sybilla de Felton died in 1419, this manuscript must have been copied very shortly after the licencing of Love's *Mirror* by Archbishop Arundel in 1410 (see Gillespie, 'Vernacular Books'; Doyle, 'Reflections'). As Doyle points out, these two manuscripts suggest that Sybille de Felton and the nuns at Barking 'were in the forefront of the public for such English theology, and readily supplied' ('Survey' n. XX). More recently, in a detailed survey of surviving manuscripts from English nunneries, Bell has expanded upon this point, noting that a number of English nunneries in the fifteenth century (including Barking, Dartford, Syon and Denney) owned a surprising number of texts that were new and up to date. Bell concludes:

> It was precisely at this time that English achieved (as Vincent Gillespie puts it) a 'new-found respectability' in religious contexts, and to a very large extent, English spirituality was transmitted in the English language. But since it was the nuns . . . who, by choice or necessity, seem to have evinced the greatest interest in this vernacular literature, it was the nuns, not the monks, who stood at the fore-front of English spirituality.
> (Bell, 1995, pp. 75–76)[20]

The Foyle manuscript is an excellent example of the kind of 'reading circle' mentioned above; as Meale points out, it 'is richly suggestive of the kind of relationships, often encompassing a shared piety which joined women together . . .' (Meale, 'oft siþis' 35). The manuscript evidently remained in Barking until the dissolution; an inscription records that the book was given by Margaret Scrope, who was a nun at Barking prior to the dissolution, to Mistress Agnes Goldwell, a gentlewoman in the household of her sister, Elizabeth Scrope Peche. This inscription connects the manuscript with the book-owning female Scropes. The need for a detailed study of the reading habits of the female Scropes has been pointed out before, and such a project is clearly beyond the scope of this article. However, a brief summary is not amiss. The children and grandchildren of Henry, Fourth Baron Scrope of Bolton and his wife, Elizabeth Scrope (a distant cousin) were avid readers and patrons of vernacular literature, especially the women. The Scrope women, in particular, provide evidence of the extent to which manuscripts passed between lay and religious women readers, suggesting that the needs and tastes of devout laywomen were not so very different from their religious sisters. If this is so, then the conclusions drawn by Bell and Doyle concerning the up-to-date reading and intellectual aspirations of nuns are also applicable to their lay counterparts.

One daughter, Agnes Scrope Boynton Ratcliffe, chose a life of religious seclusion at Marrick after her second husband, Sir Richard Ratcliffe, was killed at Bosworth in 1485. She is recorded as the owner of New York

---

[20] Bell here cites Gillespie, 'Vernacular Books'.

Public Library Spenser 9. On f. 3v, there is an inscription, written by her daughter, 'Here beginnith the boke cald grace dieu Giffin vnto the Monestarye of Marrik By Dame Agnes Radcliffe on/ Whose sowl Jhesu haue mercy Amen/ Per me Ilsabell Lumley' (Erler, 'Exchange' 364). As Erler points out, this inscription suggests that Agnes' daughter may have been carrying out instructions from her mother after her death. The fact that these instructions are not found in Agnes' will confirms the problem of tracing women's ownership of manuscripts. While a great deal of evidence can be gleaned from wills, as seen above, many manuscripts known to have been owned by noble women are not mentioned in their wills (see, for example, Elizabeth de Vere, below). Similarly, many of the manuscripts mentioned in wills are either unidentifiable or no longer extant. Thus, the paucity of such evidence is by no means an indication that women owned books only in rare cases.

Agnes Ratcliffe is mentioned in the 1498 will of her sister-in-law, Anne Harling Wingfield Scrope, although not as the recipient of a book (Erler, 'Exchange'). Anne Scrope was the second wife of John, fifth Lord Scrope (the son of Henry and Elizabeth Scrope, and Agnes' brother). Anne Scrope owned Harley 4012, a compilation similar to Harley 1706, owned by her cousin, Elizabeth de Vere (below), which contains, among other material suitable for female readers, the second extant copy of *The Cleansing of Man's Soul*, and tracts from *The Pore Caitiff*. An inscription in the book records her name as 'Dame Anne Wyngfeld of harlyng' (Doyle, 'Survey' n. XXII), indicating that she owned the manuscript during her second marriage to Sir Robert Wingfield (d. 1480/81), before her marriage to John Scrope in 1490/91.

Margaret Scrope, the Barking nun who gave the Foyle manuscript to Agnes Goldwell, was a niece of Agnes Ratcliffe and Anne Scrope. Another niece, Joan Scrope, was prioress of Dartford in 1471/2. The female Scropes thus had family associations with both Barking and Dartford.[21] A third niece was Elizabeth Scrope Beaumont de Vere, who, on her second marriage to John De Vere, became the Countess of Oxford. Elizabeth de Vere's connections with Barking and Dartford, and her books, have been discussed in detail by Doyle ('Survey' and 'Books'). Elizabeth de Vere was the owner of Harley 1706, which contains, among other things, a Middle English version of Flete's *De Remediis*, and fragments from both *The Pore Caitiff* and *þe Holy Boke Gratia Dei*; this manuscript, along with Douce 322, from which it seems to have been copied, associates her with the group of texts under discussion here.

There is some evidence (not indisputable) that Harley 1706 may once have belonged to Barking. Nevertheless, it was clearly in the hands of Elizabeth de Vere during both her first marriage to William Beaumont, and her second, to John de Vere, Earl of Oxford; both forms of her married

---

[21] Indeed, such connections between the patrons of female houses, and indeed, between the houses themselves, were not isolated. In fact, there is evidence that books did pass between houses; BL Add. 10596 may have migrated from Dartford to Barking (Doyle, 'Survey'), and Harley 2409 passed from Swine to Nuncoton (see above).

name appear (more than once) in the manuscript. Given the close relations between the female Scropes and Barking, it is not unlikely that a manuscript might have passed from one of the nuns to a lay friend or relative (as, indeed, is the case with the Foyle manuscript). The names of Edmond Jernyngham (a nephew) and Elysabeth Rokewod (one of her 'maidens') also appear in the book. Again, the book is not mentioned in Elizabeth de Vere's will, and its subsequent history is unknown until the seventeenth century, when it came into the hands of Henry Worsely of Lincoln's Inn (Doyle, 'Survey' and 'Books').

A further connection is suggested by Douce 322, which bears an inscription stating that it was copied as a gift from William Barron to Dartford, for the use of his niece (or granddaughter), Petronilla Wrattisley, an nun of Dartford (Doyle, 'Survey'; Bell, *What Nuns Read* 133). The fact that the first half of Harley 1706 was copied from Douce 322, probably after Douce 322 was given to Dartford, is an example of the 'complex network of associations between Dartford and Barking that, typically, involved movement of books and texts through family, and often lay, intermediaries' (Gillespie, 'Vernacular Books', 331).

Conclusion

The manuscripts which we have traced, however briefly, yield an immense amount of information. When the bits and pieces are put together, a picture emerges of a broad range of readers, whose interests and tastes are reflected in the variety of texts which they owned and read. It is apparent that the ideas and images drawn from *Ancrene Wisse* circulated freely, and that texts using these images circulated together in the same manuscripts or in different manuscripts owned or read by the same people. These images and ideas would thus have become very familiar to the reading audiences of the fourteenth and fifteenth centuries. Their widespread influence becomes even more apparent when one considers the exchange of texts and the oral transmission indicated by reading circles. It is clear that the influence of *Ancrene Wisse* on future generations is much broader even than that indicated by evidence of direct literary dependence.

The texts that we have examined clearly held a wide appeal; they were read by men and women, religious and lay, noble and middle class, orthodox and not-so-orthodox. Some were adapted to 'suit' new and varied audiences; others were simply read by audiences other than those to whom they originally directed. The gaps between intended and actual audiences suggest that we cannot draw wholesale conclusions from addresses such as 'dear sister', which suggest a gendered approach, and that men and women frequently read texts originally directed at the opposite sex. Yet, there is substantial evidence that these texts, originally composed for a specifically female audience, were widely read and owned by women, who passed them on to other women. Such patterns of ownership and transmission suggest that their authors had a keen sense of what would appeal to their intended readers.

This suggests the need for further research into the influence of socially and culturally constructed notions of gender on reading practices and assumptions about reading in the thirteen to fifteenth centuries, studying medieval women as readers, as consumers of texts produced for and about them. The vast majority of texts owned and commissioned by such women were, like the texts surveyed here, vernacular devotional texts, most of them written or compiled by men. It is true that male authors of devotional works often made sharp distinctions between male and female audiences, clearly indicating that the gender of their intended readers affected both the style and content of their works. The attitudes of male authors towards their female readers have been explored in a number of recent studies (e.g. Frost, 'Attitude'; Bartlett, *Male Authors*; Carruthers, 'No womman'; Robertson, *Devotional Prose*), but there is a need for further study of how women actually read and understood the texts written for and about them. Did the ambivalence of male authors towards women as both readers and writers affect women's perceptions of themselves as readers, writers, and thinkers? Or were medieval women able to develop reading strategies that enabled them to read, write, and think in an atmosphere that discouraged not only their writing (and often reading), but even, as in *Chastising*, their very language? What were these strategies, and how did they influence medieval women's responses to and interpretations of the gendered imagery which permeates vernacular devotional texts?

The reading patterns uncovered here suggest that the women readers whom we have encountered were not, as has sometimes been assumed, passive readers, so firmly embedded in what we, in the twentieth century, have perceived as the negative cultural and intellectual milieu of their times that they simply 'internalized' the misogyny that characterized medieval clerical writings. Indeed, the texts surveyed above suggest that the attitudes of the male clerical elite did not, as the lopsided survival rate of their writings might suggest, define the attitudes of society at large, that readers, male and female, religious and lay, were far more flexible and adaptable than has been previously assumed. The kinds of texts that we have seen, and the patterns of ownership we have traced, also indicate that, contrary to received opinion, women were not relegated to the marginal wastelands in their devotional reading, but were, on the contrary, on the cutting edge of things. New developments in vernacular devotional writings rapidly found their way into the hands of women who, it is increasingly evident, were intelligent and sophisticated readers. Nor were their reading habits and materials substantially different from many men, particularly laymen. As well, it seems clear that the distinctions we make, as twentieth-century scholars, between different types of vernacular religious texts were, in the middle ages, less rigid than we would like to believe. Lay and religious readers often used the same texts, indicating that the line between contemplative readers and those engaged in the active life was not clearly drawn. Similarly, the distinction between didactic material, such as *The Chastising of God's Children*, and affective devotion, such as that found in *Wohunge*, was not sharp enough to prevent such texts from circulating amongst the same readers and, often, as with *Chastising* and *The Tretyse of Loue*, in the same manuscripts. Indeed, *The Tretyse of Loue*, borrowing as it does from the didactic *Ancrene Wisse* Part 4 (on Temptation) and the more affective Part 7 (on Love), combines both streams in the same text. The circulation of many of these texts amongst the same readers, as indicated by the kinds of reading circles discussed above, indicates that the women who shared these books were exposed to a wide variety of texts, even if they did not own them. Indeed, as the case of Eleanor Cobham and Joan Holand suggests, these texts were shared by women who ranged from the deeply devout to the marginally heretical. The uses to which medieval readers put such texts were clearly varied and dynamic.

The legacy of *Ancrene Wisse*, then, includes a vast array of texts, ideas, and attitudes. Themes and images which are introduced into the English language in *Ancrene Wisse* have, by the fifteenth century, become widespread and immensely popular. *Ancrene Wisse* and its sister texts stand at the beginning of a thriving tradition of vernacular devotion in England, a tradition which continued up to, and even beyond, the Reformation. By including women readers in this tradition, *Ancrene Wisse* and its descendants opened up vast new avenues to their audiences, placing them, indeed, in the forefront of many of the religious trends which led to the Reformation. But we, in the twentieth century, are also heirs to the tradition generated by *Ancrene Wisse*, given as we are a means of exploring the history of women's literacy and history in a dynamic context, which extends for over two centuries of women's reading and writing. *Ancrene Wisse* has thus left a valuable legacy indeed.

Works Cited

Aarts, F. G. A. M., *þe Pater Noster of Richard Ermyte: a Late Middle English Exposition of the Lord's Prayer* (The Hague, 1967)

Allen, Hope Emily, 'Some Fourteenth Century Borrowings from "*Ancrene Riwle*"', *Modern Language Review* 18 (1923), 1–8

——, 'Further Borrowings from "*Ancren Riwle*"', *Modern Language Review* 24 (1929), 1–15

——, 'Mystical Writings of the *Manuel des Péchiez*', *Romanic Review* 9 (1918), 154–193

——, 'Wynkyn de Worde and a Second French Compilation from the "Ancren riwle" with a Description of the First (Trinity Coll. Camb. Ms 883)', in *Essays and Studies in Honor of Carleton Brown* (Freeport, New York, 1940), 182–219

Arntz, Sr Mary Luke, ed., *Richard Rolle and þe Holy Boke Gratia Dei* (Salzburg, 1981)

Baker, Denise N., 'Julian of Norwich and Anchoritic Literature', *Mystics Quarterly* 19:4 (1993), 148–160

Barratt, Alexandra, *Women's Writing in Middle English* (London, 1992)

Bartlett, Anne Clark, *Male Authors, Female Readers and Middle English Devotional Literature* (Ithaca, NY, 1995)

Baugh, A. C., ed., *The English Text of the Ancrene Riwle, British Museum Ms. Royal 8 C.i (The Treatise of the Five Senses)*, EETS o.s. 232 (London, 1956)

Bazire, Joyce, and Eric Colledge, eds., *The Chastising of God's Children and the Treatise of Perfection of the Sons of God* (Oxford, 1957)

Bell, David N., *What Nuns Read: Books and Libraries in Medieval English Nunneries* (Kalamazoo, 1995)

Bell, Susan Groag, 'Medieval Women Book Owners: Arbiters of Lay Piety and Ambassadors of Culture', in *Women and Power in the Middle Ages*, ed. Mary Erler and Maryanne Kowaleski (Athens, GA, 1988), 149–187

Boffey, Julia, 'Women Authors and Women's Literacy in Fourteenth- and Fifteenth-century England', in *Women and Literature in Britain, 1150–1500*, ed. Carole M. Meale, Cambridge Studies in Medieval Literature 17 (Cambridge, 1993), 159–182

Brady, Sr Mary Teresa, ed., 'The Pore Caitiff, Ms. Harley 2336', Dissertation (Fordham, 1954)

Bynum, Caroline Walker, *Jesus as Mother: Studies in the Spirituality of the High Middle Ages* (Berkeley, CA, 1982)

Carruthers, Leo, ' "No womman of no clerk is preysed": Attitudes to Women in Medieval English Religious Literature', in *A Wyf Ther Was: Essays in Honour of Paule Mertens Fonck*, ed. Juliette Dor (Liège, 1992), 49–60

Colledge, Edmund, and Noel Chadwick, '*Remedies Against Temptations*: the Third English Version of William Flete', *Archivo italiano per la storia della pietà* 5 (1968), 199–240

Day, Mabel, ed., *The English Text of the Ancrene Riwle, Cotton Nero A.XIV*, EETS o.s. 225 (London, 1952)

d'Evelyn, Charlotte, ed., *The Latin Text of the Ancrene Riwle, edited from Merton College Ms. 44 and British Museum Ms. Cotton Vitellius E. vii*, EETS o.s. 216 (London, 1944; repr. 1957)

Diekstra, F. N. M., 'Some Fifteenth-century Borrowings from the *Ancrene Wisse*', *English Studies: A Journal of English Language and Literature* 71:2 (1990), 81–104

Dobson, E. J., ed., *The English Text of the Ancrene Riwle, B.M. Cotton MS Cleopatra C.VI.* EETS o.s. 267 (London, 1972)

——, *The Origins of 'Ancrene Wisse'* (Oxford, 1976)

Doyle, I. A., 'Books Connected with the Vere Family and Barking Abbey', *Transactions of the Essex Archaeological Society* 25 (1958), 222–243

——, 'Reflections on Some Manuscripts of Nicholas Love's Myrrour of the Blessed Lyf of Jesu Christ', *Leeds Studies in English* 14 (1983), 82–93

——, 'A Survey of the Origins and Circulation of Theological Writings in English in the Fourteenth, Fifteenth and Early Sixteenth Centuries with Special Consideration of the Part of the Clergy Therein', Ph.D. Dissertation (Cambridge, 1954) 2301–2302

Erler, Mary C., 'Exchange of Books between Nuns and Laywomen: Three Surviving Examples', in *New Science out of Old Books: Studies in Manuscripts and Early Printed Books in Honour of A. I. Doyle* ed. Richard Beadle and A. J. Piper (Aldershot, 1995), 360–373

Finke, Laurie, *Feminist Theory, Women's Writing* (Ithaca, NY, 1992)

Fisher, John H., ed., *The Tretyse of Love*, EETS o.s. 223 (London, 1951)

Frost, Cheryl, 'The Attitude to Women and the Adaptation to a Feminine Audience in the *Ancrene Wisse*', *Journal of the Australasian Universities Language and Literature Association* 50 (1978), 235–50

Gillespie, Vincent J., 'Vernacular Books of Religion', in *Book Production and Publishing in Britain 1375–1475*, ed. Jeremy Griffiths and Derek Pearsall (Cambridge, 1989), 317–344

Hackett, Benedict, 'William Flete and the *De Remediis Contra Temptaciones*', in *Medieval Studies presented to Aubrey Gwynn, S.J.*, ed. Watt J. B. Morrall and F. X. Martin (Dublin, 1961), 330–348

——, Eric Colledge and Noel Chadwick, 'William Flete's *De Remediis Contra Temptaciones* in its Latin and English Recensions: the Growth of a Text', *Medieval Studies* 16 (1964), 210–230

Harris, Kate, 'Patrons, Buyers and Owners: The Evidence for Ownership, and the Role of Book Owners in Book Production and the Book Trade', in *Book Production and Publishing in Britain, 1375–1475*, ed. Jeremy Griffiths and Derek Pearsall (Cambridge, 1989), 163–200

Herbert, J. A., ed., *The French Text of the Ancrene Riwle*, EETS o.s. 219 (London, 1944)

Hudson, Anne, 'A Chapter from Walter Hilton in Two Middle English Compilations', *Neophilologus* 52 (1960), 416–421

Innes-Parker, Catherine, '*Ancrene Wisse and þe Wohunge of Ure Lauerd*: the Thirteenth-century Female Reader and the Lover-Knight', in *Women, the Book and the Godly*, ed. Jane Taylor and Lesley Smith (London,1995), 137–147

——, 'Subversion and Conformity in Julian of Norwich: Authority, Vision and the Motherhood of God', *Mystics Quarterly* 23:2 (1997), 7–35

Jones, E. A., 'A Chapter from Richard Rolle in Two Fifteenth-century Compilations', *Leeds Studies in English* n.s. 27 (1996), 139–162

Kane, Harold, ed., *The Prickynge of Love*, Elizabethan and Renaissance Studies (Salzburg, 1983)

Ker, N. R., *Medieval Libraries of Great Britain: a List of Surviving Books*, 2nd edn (London, 1964)

——, *Medieval Manuscripts in British Libraries*, 3 vols. (Oxford, 1969)

——, *Books, Collectors, and Libraries: Studies in the Medieval Heritage* (London, 1985)

Labarge, Margaret Wade, 'Three Medieval Widows and a Second Career', in *Aging and the Aged in Medieval Europe: Selected Papers from the Annual Conference of the Centre for Medieval Studies, University of Toronto, held 25–26 February and 11–12 November 1983*, ed. Michael M. Sheehand, Papers in Medieval Studies 11 (Toronto, 1990), 159–172

Mack, Frances M., ed., *The English Text of the Ancrene Riwle, edited from B. M. MS Cotton Titus D. xviii, together with the Llanhydrock Fragment, Bodleian MS Eng. th. c.70*, EETS o.s. 252 (1963)

Marx, C.W., 'British Library Harley MS 1740 and Popular Devotion', in *England in the Fifteenth Century*, ed. Nicholas Rogers (Stamford, Lincolnshire, 1994), 207–222

Meale, Carol M., ' ". . . alle the bokes that I haue of latyn, englisch, and frensch": Laywomen and their Books in Late Medieval England', in *Women and Literature in Britain, 1150–1500*, ed. Carol M. Meale (Cambridge, 1993), 128–158

——, ' "oft siþis with grete deuotion I þought what I miȝt do pleysyng to god": the Early Ownership and Readership of Love's *Mirror*, with Special Reference to its Female Audience', in *Nicholas Love at Waseda: Prodeedings of the International Conference 20–22 July 1995*, ed. Shoichi Oguro, Richard Beadle and Michael G. Sargent (Cambridge, 1997)

Millett, Bella, *Annotated Bibliographies of Old and Middle English Literature, Vol. 2: Ancrene Wisse, the Katherine Group, and the Wooing Group* (Cambridge, 1996)
——, 'The Origins of *Ancrene Wisse*: New Answers, New Questions', *Medium Aevum* 61:2 (1992), 206–228
Patterson, Lee, *Negotiating the Past: the Historical Understanding of Medieval Literature* (Madison, WI, 1987)
Pollard, William F., 'Mystical Elements in a Fifteenth-century Prayer Sequence: "The Festis and the Passion of Oure Lord Ihesu Crist"', in *The Medieval Mystical Tradition in England*, ed. Marion Glasscoe (Cambridge, 1987), 47–61
Powicke, F. M., *Historical Essays in Honour of James Tait* (Manchester, 1933)
Riddy, Felicity, ' "Women talking about the things of God": a Late Medieval Subculture', in *Women and Literature in Britain, 1150–1500*, ed. Carol M. Meale (Cambridge, 1993), 104–127
Robertson, Elizabeth, *Early English Devotional Prose and the Female Audience* (Knoxville, TN, 1990)
Rosenthal, Joel, 'Aristocratic Cultural Patronage and Book Bequests, 1350–1500', *Bulletin of the John Rylands Library* 64 (1982), 522–548
Sargent, Michael G., 'Minor Devotional Writings', in *Middle English Prose: a Critical Guide to Major Authors and Genres*, ed. A. S. G. Edwards (New Brunswick, 1984), 147–175
——, 'A New Manuscript of *The Chastising of God's Children* with an Ascription to Walter Hilton', *Medium Aevum* 46 (1977), 49–65
Saunders, H. W., *An Introduction to the Rolls of Norwich Cathedral Priory* (Norwich, 1930)
Tarvers, Josephine Koster, ' "Thys ys my mystrys boke": English Women as Readers and Writers in Late Medieval England', in *The Uses of Manuscripts in Literary Studies: Essays in Memory of Judson Boyce Allen*, ed. Charlotte Cook Morse, Penelope Reed Doob and Marjorie Curry Woods, Studies in Medieval Culture 31 (Kalamazoo, MI, 1992), 305–327
Thompson, W. Meredith, ed., *þe Wohunge of Ure Lauerd*, EETS o.s. 241 (London, 1958)
Tolkien, J. R. R., ed., *The English Text of the Ancrene Riwle: Ancrene Wisse, edited from MS Corpus Christi College Cambridge 402*, EETS o.s. 249 (London, 1962)
Trethewey, W. H., ed., *The French Text of the Ancrene Riwle, Trinity College Cambridge MS R.14.7*, EETS o.s. 240 (London, 1958)
Westra, M. Salvina, ed., *A Talkying of þe Loue of God* (The Hague, 1950)
Woolf, Rosemary, 'The Theme of Christ the Lover-Knight in Medieval English Literature', *Review of English Studies* n.s. 13 (1962), 1–16

9

The *Recluse* and its Readers: Some Observations on a Lollard Interpolated Version of *Ancrene Wisse*

CHRISTINA VON NOLCKEN

For many readers of the present volume, the *Recluse* or, as its final rubric would have it, 'þis good book Recluse' (184/27) will mainly exemplify *Ancrene Wisse* disintegrating under 'the pressures of time and transmission' (Millett, 19).[1] But partly thanks to its very disintegration it also raises pressing questions in its own right. Perhaps most pressingly, it raises questions about its meaning. That it may never have communicated particularly effectively with its readers has recently been intimated by Millett (19), who sees its text as having reached just about that point where, in Paul Zumthor's words, 'il n'y a plus de communication possible.' Yet even in as unpromising a case as this we should remain alert to the sometimes startling ways in which, again in Zumthor's words, 'les déco- dages successifs actualisent les potentialités toujours nouvelles du texte' (Millett, 19). In what follows I will be mainly concerned with how, thanks to a distinctive approach to language, certain medieval readers could indeed have actualized new meanings in the *Recluse*. But because the *Recluse* remains one of our least familiar versions of *Ancrene Wisse*, I will first consider its scholarly history to date.

Some quarter to a third shorter than *Ancrene Wisse*, the *Recluse* is the sixth item in Magdalene College Cambridge Pepys MS 2498, a collection labeled 'Wickleef's Sermon's MS' on its Pepysian binding (Zettersten, x).[2] Like the more elaborate Vernon and Simeon manuscripts with which it is remotely related (Doyle, 'Shaping', 7), this collection must have been prepared for some devout company; a pro-secular and even pro-lay bias in the *Recluse* points towards the gentry (Doyle, 'Survey', II:67). That its texts were for reading aloud is indicated by verse tags at their beginnings and ends; the one at the end of the *Recluse* can stand for them all:

---

[1] Except where otherwise indicated, all references to the *Recluse* will be to Zettersten's edition by page and line. I am grateful to Mrs A. Fitzsimons, Assistant to the Pepys Librarian, for providing me with a microfilm of the manuscript. References to *Ancrene Wisse* (*AW*) will normally be to Morton's edition, also by page and line.
[2] For a description of the collection, see McKitterick and Beadle, 86–88.

þis good book Recluse/ here now makeþ ende.
Vn to þe blis of heuen/ god graunte vs grace to wende.   (184/27–28)

Later annotations aside, the whole collection is in a single hand, one Samuels has identified as also responsible for British Library MS Harley 874, which contains a slightly interpolated English translation of an Anglo-Norman Apocalypse with commentary, and Bodleian Library MS Laud Misc. 622, which contains mainly English romances and sermons (Samuels, 'Some Applications', 87).[3] This hand worked in a dialect that, again according to Samuels, was of the Waltham Abbey area, in west Essex (Zettersten, xvii–xviii). Paleographic datings have ranged between c.1340 and 1370 (Fridner, vii) and xiv ex. (Doyle, 'Survey', I:232); some of the texts in Pepys may push towards the later part of this period.[4] These texts include:

a.   pp. 1–43. The unique copy of *The Pepysian Gospel Harmony* (ed. Goates).

b.   pp. 45–212. The late fourteenth-century prose translation of the thirteenth-century Anglo-Norman *Miroir*, a rhymed set of gospel sermons made by Robert of Greatham to wean a certain Aline or Eleanor away from minstrels (Deanesly 149–51). The translation addresses a lay reading public (Spencer, 36).

c.   pp. 212–26. An account of the Pains of Sin, also in the Vernon manuscript, ff. 392–93, and in part in Bodleian MS Bodley 938, ff. 17–24 and 61–63. It is followed in Pepys (p. 217) by the unique copy of an exposition of the Ten Commandments beginning, 'Now vnderstondeþ þe comaundementis of god þat al þe folk of þe werlde & of religioun schulden perfytlich kepen.'

d.   pp. 226–263. The same translated Apocalypse with commentary as is contained in British Library MS Harley 874 (ed. Fridner) and at least eleven further manuscripts.

e.   pp. 263–370. The glossed Psalter in Latin and English now known as 'The Midland Prose Psalter' (ed. Bülbring).

f.   pp. 371–449. The *Recluse*.

g–h.   pp. 449–463. *The Prose Complaint of Our Lady*, followed by an account of the resurrection from *The Gospel of Nicodemus* (ed. Marx and Drennan). These constitute an established sequence in both Anglo-Norman and English (Marx and Drennan, 7–8). Its editors have tentatively dated the sequence post 1377 and perhaps post 1380 (Marx and Drennan, 15).

i.   pp. 463–64. Five prayers, to the 'Swete fader of heuene,' 'Swete lorde

---

[3] On the collection's later annotations, see Zettersten, x–xvi. On British Library MS Harley 874, see Fridner, vii–ix; on Bodleian Library MS Laud Misc. 622, see Smithers, 1–4.
[4] Although Samuels originally considered 1360 late for this dialect ('Some Applications,' 87), he later described it as 'late fourteenth century' ('Chaucer's Spelling,' 18).

Jhesu crist,' 'Swete lorde Jhesu crist fader & son & holy gost,' 'Lefdi seint marie,' and 'Alle halewen.'

That the *Recluse* had its beginnings in *Ancrene Wisse* was first remarked in 1902 by Paues:

> The '*Recluse*' so called is nothing but a version of the *Ancren Riwle* in the language of the latter half of the XIVth century. The text is, however, at times strongly abridged and differently arranged from that printed by Morton. In several places the translator introduces some entirely new matter, either of his own making or from other sources. (345)

But although the work follows its antecedent quite closely in places, it would not prove particularly interesting to *Ancrene Wisse* scholars. It has been diplomatically edited twice, by Påhlsson (1911, repr. with notes 1918) and, as the penultimate volume in the Early English Text Society's printings of *Ancrene Wisse* texts, by Zettersten (1976). Its textual relations with the *Ancrene Wisse* have also been explored, by Macaulay, who grouped it with Corpus Christi College Cambridge MS 402 and the Vernon manuscript (151); by Påhlsson, who noted its close affinities with BL MS Cotton Titus D. XVIII and Magdalen College Oxford Latin MS 67 (329–30); and by Dobson, who also associated it with Titus (134), and therefore with a version that was early – and somewhat inconsistently – modified towards a generalized and depersonalized audience (Mack, xiv–xvi). On the whole, however, *Ancrene Wisse* scholars could afford to be dismissive:

> We have here [. . .] an adaptation or paraphrase rather than a copy of the original text, and some of the characteristic features are lost by an attempt to make the Rule applicable to men as well as women. In many places the text is so much altered, or so corrupt, as to be almost unrecognisable, and there is much omission, especially in the seventh and eighth parts. Also many passages, some of considerable length, are added, especially one on the visions of the Apocalypse. (Macaulay, 147)

They have left it largely for others to define its interest.

As Påhlsson anticipated, this interest would importantly lie in the *Recluse*'s fourteenth-century additions:

> As soon as I began to work at the MS, these [additional] passages struck me as clashing in part with the general tenor of the Ancren Riwle as I knew it from Morton's text, and I saw in them the outcome of ideas prevalent in the turbulent times from which the MS apparently dates. As far as I am a judge, the inference can hardly be doubted that the man by whose hand these alterations were made must have embraced ideas typical of the spiritual life of England at the close of the 14th. cent. and I do not consider the labelling of the volume – *Wickleef's Sermons* – as altogether misleading. It would have been a matter of interest to deal with the subject in detail. (332)

It was not Påhlsson but Colledge who first explored this interest, however, in 1939, in the only full-length article on the *Recluse* to date. Colledge's findings would stand unchallenged until Hudson briefly reconsidered the work in 1988 (*Premature Reformation*, 27–28).

Colledge based his discussion on thirty-two of the *Recluse*'s longer additions.[5] They now seem quite various. Some mainly extend and update *Ancrene Wisse*, by introducing elements of the mysticism popularized by Richard Rolle, for example, or by giving space to late fourteenth-century liturgical developments (Colledge, 130–41). Others are more reformist, like the passage on the Apocalypse noted by Macaulay, which Colledge thought was probably scribal (8–10).[6] And others indeed sound Wycliffite or Lollard (terms largely synonymous in their time).[7] On the strength of the last Colledge grouped the work with what has since proved an expanding class of texts, one comprising seemingly Lollard interpolated versions of such orthodox works of instruction as Richard Rolle's *English Prose Psalter*, Gaytring's *Catechism* (now better known as the *Lay Folks' Catechism*), and *The Prick of Conscience* (Colledge, 1).[8]

Colledge was well aware that the *Recluse* contains inconsistencies – he commented, for example, on how a passage praising only Martha has been interpolated immediately after one praising Mary over Martha (Colledge, 7–8). His was an intellectual climate far more interested in continuities than in discontinuities, however, and what he mainly wanted to demonstrate was the work's unity. The most egregious of its inconsistencies he accordingly assigned to hasty revision: 'It may be that the work as we have it here represents a first draft, produced in haste and never revised' (3–4). The rest he explained in terms of date. He noted how, while the work anticipates persecution, it does not do this with any urgency (134 and n. 4) – it dwells, indeed, with some relish on how Christ and the apostles were persecuted (*Recluse*, 43/10–13, 117/3–14), on how those who speak of God will be done to death by hypocrites (50/6–8), on how clerks tried to make Paul swear on a book that he wouldn't speak of Christ (67/33–35), and on how such clerks put Paul and the disciples out of what would now be called Holy Church (67/36–68/2). So, suggesting a date somewhere between the Peasants' Revolt in 1381 and the first burning of a Lollard in 1401 (134 n. 4), Colledge placed the *Recluse* just before Lollard discourse had fully defined itself.[9] I quote from his concluding paragraph:

---

[5] Colledge's references (13–14) are to Påhlsson 1918; in Zettersten the passages are 2/17–28, 4/21–5/11, 6/3–8, 15/23–17/16, 18/25–19/7, 20/28–36, 22/7–14, 27/27–29/12 except for 28/18–20, 43/3–46/2, 47/1–16, 49/21–52/30, 53/10–22, 54/34–57/19, 59/8–60/5, 60/19–61/19, 62/28–63/5, 66/19–73/33 except for 70/12–17, 84/23–85/26, 86/8–88/5, 89/22–91/10, 101/21–102/4, 103/19–36, 111/8–20, 112/24–113/13, 124/35–125/16, 130/17–25, 136/23–137/8, 142/20–144/6, 146/4–147/8, 149/23–150/31, 176/4–20, 177/30–182/29.

[6] This seems to represent an independent translation from the same Anglo-Norman Apocalypse and commentary whose translation also appears in Harley MS 874 and as the fourth item in Pepys.

[7] On these terms, see Hudson *Premature Reformation*, 2–4.

[8] On such texts, see Aston, 209–12; on the difficulty of defining these and other texts as Lollard, see Hudson, *Premature Reformation*, 421–30.

[9] The work could also belong a few years earlier. Cannon plausibly suggests Wyclif's Poor Priests began their preaching in roughly 1376–77 (451–55), and William Thorpe, questioned for heresy in 1407, claims dealings with true priests since at least 1377 (Hudson, *Two Wycliffite Texts*, 38/470–77).

[I]n *The Recluse* we have a truly devotional product of the early Lollard movement, which serves to bridge the gap between the reformers and the mystics of the fourteenth century, a gap which, though it exists, is not so wide as might be thought by those whose only knowledge of Lollardy is derived through a study of the later period, when open schism and cruel persecution had finally alienated the Lollards from that communion in which, we cannot doubt, such men as the author of *The Recluse* would gladly have remained. (145)

We are now in an intellectual climate rather better able to deal with discontinuities than Colledge's was; we have also been adding to our knowledge of early Lollardy. Even so, Colledge was surely right to associate the *Recluse* with the Lollards.[10] Admittedly, as he observed, it seems quite orthodox on that hallmark of Wycliffite belief, the Eucharist (130). It also seems quite orthodox on images and pilgrimages, as well as on penance, despite a couple of statements to the effect that one should only confess to a good priest or, more colorfully, that one should not confess to any old sot unable to maintain himself in a pure life (145/8–13 – a slight elaboration of *AW*, 336/10–12; see also *Recluse*, 26/18–19). But some of its views come very close to ones regularly condemned as Wycliffite – that any pope, bishop, monk or friar in deadly sin is out of orders (89/26–28), for example, or that knowingly giving alms to someone in deadly sin only sustains him in his sin (56/5–12), or its disparagement of the canon law concerning clerical celibacy (69/4–24), or its view that every member of the clergy should earn his living with his hands (68/21–32, 72/34–37), as Our Lady did (69/32–33), as Peter did (68/16–17), as Peter and Paul did (4/27–29, 69/30–32, 153/19–22), or at least as the latter did when he had time during his preaching tours (68/19–21).[11]

Colledge was also very probably right to invoke date to help explain the *Recluse*'s inconsistencies. Certainly, something very like its mix of the

---

[10] Colledge's criteria for Lollardy (129–30) come from a summary in some versions of the *Chronicon Angliae*; the summary appears under the year 1377 when Wyclif first appears in the chronicle, though it was probably written some years later. Colledge's claim (130) that except on the Eucharist the *Recluse*'s interpolations contain all the elements of Lollard doctrine described in the summary seems exaggerated – the point that no pope or prelate should have prisons, for example, is unparalleled in the *Recluse*.

[11] The first resembles item VIII in the list of heresies and errors drawn up against Wyclif by the Blackfriars Council in 1382, 'Item quod si papa sit praescitus, et malus homo, ac per consequens membrum diaboli, non habet potestatem supra fideles Christi ab aliquo sibi datam, nisi forte a Caesare' ('that if the pope is foreknown, and an evil man, and as a result a limb of the devil, he has no power over Christ's faithful given him by anyone, except perhaps the Emperor'), for example (*Fasciculi*, 278; see also Hudson, *Premature Reformation*, 27); the second, though not specifically directed against the friars, resembles item XXIV in the same list, 'Item quod conferens eleemosynam fratribus, vel fratri praedicanti, est excommunicatus; et recipiens' ('that a person giving alms to friars, or to a preaching friar, is excommunicate; also the one receiving,' *Fasciculi*, 282); the last, item XXIII (ibid.), 'Item quod fratres teneantur per laborem manuum, et non per mendicationem, victum suum acquirere' ('that friars should be required to gain their living by the labor of their hands and not by mendicacy'). William Ramsbury, a layman examined as a Lollard 'priest' in 1389, was advocating clerical marriage by that date (Hudson, *Premature Reformation*, 357–58); the question 'an licitum sit sacerdoti habere vxorem' (whether it is permissible for a priest to have a wife) would later feature in at least one standardized list of questions that might be asked of a suspect (Hudson, *Lollards and their Books*, 134).

apparently conventional and the apparently reformist also characterizes such early Lollard works as the *Floretum/Rosarium theologie*, a widely disseminated group of preachers' handbooks originally compiled between 1384 and 1396.[12] It also characterizes the piety of those members of the gentry who seem to have constituted the Wycliffites' early patrons – persons like Sir John Clanvowe (d. 17 October 1391), whose *Two Ways* shows him very probably identifying with those meek livers regarded by the world as 'lolleris and loselis' (Scattergood, 70), but who also ended his days either while on pilgrimage or while preparing to fight the Turks, hardly activities calculated to appeal to Lollards.[13] And the *Recluse* is hardly the only Lollard-sounding interpolated work to seem hastily revised: in 1922–23 Everett noted how the interpolations into Rolle's *Psalter* frequently ignore Rolle altogether, thus (218, 385), and Hudson has pointed to how the possibly Lollard-influenced version of the *Lay Folks' Catechism* in Lambeth Palace Library MS 408 'simply lacks any kind of theological consistency' ('New Look', 258).

But the *Recluse* can't even make up its mind about the way of life it most wants to endorse.[14] Some of the time it concentrates approvingly on 'Men & wymmen þat ben bischett' (182/30). Some of the time it concentrates on 'onelich men & wymmen' as well as 'alle oþer þat desiren forto seruen god' (2/11–12; see also 22/9). Some of the time it addresses men and women who want to be spiritual (112/29–30), or who want to be perfect in God's service (148/25–26); once it declares that what it means by a solitary man or anchoress is Everyman (43/29–31). And for quite a lot of the time it considers living among men in the world to be the only way to love God perfectly (44/29–33) – after all, Moses and Elijah weren't enclosed (64/30–34), John the Baptist wasn't (66/19–29); the disciples weren't (44/29–33). When it admits an exception to its general rule that all members of the clergy should earn their livings with their hands (68/21–32, 72/34–37), the exception is not for some anchorite confined to his cell – anchorites, it seems, would be better off keeping pigs or geese (5/30). It admits it for an itinerant preacher rapidly traveling from town to town (72/27–32).[15] I could continue.

It is hardly surprising, therefore, that when Hudson reconsidered the *Recluse*, she raised the possibility that Colledge had underestimated the extent of its inconsistencies. She did this only in a footnote (*Premature Reformation*, 28 n. 117). But in her text she also implicitly questioned several of Colledge's other assumptions. Pointing to a long exhortation to observe the canonical hours in Part 1 that he (141–44) had identified as

---

[12] On this work and its background, see von Nolcken, *Rosarium*, 9–51.

[13] On those early patrons known as the 'Lollard Knights,' see McFarlane; Wilks. On their piety, see Tuck; Thomson, 'Orthodox Religion,' 44–46; Thomson, 'Knightly Piety.' On Clanvowe, see Scattergood, 25–27. For the Lollards' views on pilgrimage, see Hudson, *Premature Reformation*, 301–9; for their views on war, *Premature Reformation* 367–70.

[14] As remarked by Hudson in a brief reference to 'some disparaging remarks about the way of life that the body of the text is designed to promote' (Hudson, *Premature Reformation*, 27).

[15] Thorpe will similarly comment on how the apostles earned their livings except when they were too busy preaching (Hudson, *Two Wycliffite Texts*, 68/1432–37).

coming from St Edmund Rich's *Merure de Seint Eglise*, she questioned whether all the *Recluse*'s additional material could possibly have come from a single Lollard redactor (27–28). And far from accepting *Ancrene Wisse* as a likely text for Lollard reworking, she referred to it as one 'which, one would think, was about the most intractable to Lollard purposes that could be found' (*Premature Reformation*, 27). She did not attempt to deal with this latter oddity (28). But she did suggest a reason for some of the *Recluse*'s other oddities, by providing a rather more complicated transmission than had hitherto been suspected:

> [I]t seems likely that this version of *Ancrene Riwle* has been through at least two stages of modification [she presumably means after the initial widening of its audience], the first by an orthodox reviser who added material reinforcing the intentions of the original author, the second by a perfunctory and unorthodox redactor who endeavoured rather sporadically to convert the text to a secular purpose. (*Premature Reformation*, 28)

In the page and a half she allotted the *Recluse*, Hudson did not explore her suggestion. But it makes excellent sense, textually as well as historically. Textually, it helps explain some of the work's overall inconsistencies, as well as some of the inconsistencies between its added passages. It also helps explain some inconsistencies within these passages, a feature I have not yet remarked upon. Without source texts we can seldom be sure of the details. But in the passage from the *Merure de Seint Eglise* what seems to have been the *Merure*'s usual text (for this, see Colledge, 141–44) has itself been interpolated, first with a passage blaming clerks rather than simple folk for killing Christ (16/21–23), then with one discussing when best to sow the Word of God (16/31–17/16). For Colledge, the passage shows in the reviser's additions 'many of the chief preoccupations of the Lollard text – the reviser's devotion to the Passion, his orthodoxy so far as the sacrifice of the Mass is concerned, and his praise of the 'simple folk' at the expense of the 'clerks' (144). But praising simple folk at the expense of clerks is not quite the same as blaming clerks for killing Christ. And just how much the discussion of when best to sow the Word of God is at odds with the *Merure* is suggested by Walter Brut's scornful words when he was questioned for heresy in the early 1390s: 'And, whereas Christ and his apostles do command the preaching of the word of God, the priests now be more bound to celebrate the mass, and more straitly bound to say the canonical hours; whereat I cannot but greatly marvel' (Foxe, III:181).[16] Two fourteenth-century redactors would indeed seem called for.

Hudson's suggestion also makes sense historically. When Colledge described his single redactor he came up with a man of some learning, a student of the Vulgate and of various mystical writers, someone whom an access of Lollard sympathies had driven to become an itinerant preacher but whose devotional sympathies, knowledge of the liturgy and decision to work on *Ancrene Wisse* argue a connection with some religious house

---

[16] On Brut, see Hudson, '"Laicus litteratus."' Knighton describes the well-known Lollard John Purvey as holding a similar view at much the same time (290–92, 291–93).

(145).[17] Such a profile is not entirely implausible: we could perhaps look for its owner among the apostate friars who got involved with Lollardy in its early years, like the ex-Augustinian Peter Pateshull who bought a chaplaincy in 1387 and '[t]henceforth thought that he was freed from all control and began openly to support the Wyclifites' (Emden, III:1434, quoting Walsingham). But things become much more plausible once we turn Colledge's one redactor into two (we could turn him into more, but two would seem to suffice). Then we have an earlier redactor rather like Colledge's but without the Lollard sympathies, and a later one whose career and preoccupations were very much what we might expect of an early Lollard.

Like Colledge's single redactor, this later redactor was certainly a cleric (90/2), though very probably a member of the secular rather than the regular clergy (Doyle, 'Survey', II:67). He was also well acquainted with the Vulgate, looking for his models to its versions of Christ (66/29–31), John the Baptist (66/22–24), and Paul (67/26–27). Given his sympathy with itinerant preachers it is almost inconceivable that he wasn't such a preacher himself: as Påhlsson put it: '[W]e seem to see John Ashton [*sic*] travelling on foot, staff in hand, through all the towns of England preaching with the zeal of an apostle' (333). But like many such preachers, he doesn't overtly proselytize; rather, he addresses his comments as if to persons already somewhat acquainted with his thinking.[18] Given the overall nature of the Pepys manuscript, he was probably enjoying the patronage of the upper laity.[19] And his vehemence on the need for preachers to earn their livings suggests that even while on tour he was careful to do this, perhaps by preparing up-to-date reading matter out of locally available books. Indeed, his choice to rework some version of *Ancrene Wisse* may seem less odd if we assume he was simply making the best of what was available in the provinces, so to speak.

The Recluse is the only book we can certainly assign this redactor, although I hope to argue elsewhere that he might also have reworked the Anglo-Norman Apocalypse. But his main preoccupation must always have been with his preaching. Like many early Lollards, he is much interested in who may or may not do this, maintaining that a man can preach only if he be sent by God (28/20–31).[20] But he does not necessarily associate this sending

---

[17] Despite Allen's 1923 discussion of the wide availability of *Ancrene Wisse* in the later fourteenth century, Colledge continued to locate it almost exclusively within the religious houses.

[18] The extent to which he does this is partly obscured by the *Recluse*'s layered textual history: sometimes a didactic voice addresses some undefined reader in the singular (as at 2/29, 47/7, 63/1), sometimes such a voice addresses either this reader in the polite plural or a group of such readers (as at 4/4, 6/14, 13/29–30, 62/34); especially in the added passages, however, the voice can be less didactic and the readers more informed (as at 68/2–3, 71/15–20). On the Lollards' avoidance of any proselytizing rhetoric, see Hudson, 'Wycliffite Prose,' 249; *Lollards and their Books*, 62; on their tendency to write as if for persons already well acquainted with their thinking, see von Nolcken, '"A Certain Sameness,"' 199–201.

[19] Colledge comments (without references) on how the *Recluse* compares the religious orders unfavorably with the lay nobility (131).

[20] The issue is discussed in ways he would have approved in the *Rosarium* under *Prechour* (von Nolcken, *Rosarium*, 92/4–41).

with the established church. Rather, he believes God will more readily allow a good layman to speak of him 'þan any of hem as ȝe han in þis boke tofore' (89/37); he also carefully notes that Peter and Paul were not priests (72/34–35). So upset is he by clerks who say no-one can preach unless he be in orders (89/23–25), indeed, that not once but twice he leaves room even for a woman to preach, 'ȝif sche be þe ouer holyer' (28/18–19; also 29/14).[21] And he is so convinced that true religion has come to reside almost exclusively with the laity, that – again twice – he interpolates a garbled version of the parable of a man with two sons (Matt. 21:28–32), interpreting the son who said he would work in the vineyard and didn't as a clerk, and the one who said he wouldn't work and did as a simple man too modest to assume religious orders and yet living the true religious life (61/2–19, 71/20–72/4). 'Whi, ne haþ nouȝth a lewed man als gret myster come to god as a Clerk' (43/32–33).

Aided by Hudson's suggestion, thus, we can now tentatively answer some of the *Recluse*'s textual and historical questions. But further questions define themselves. With our knowledge of *Ancrene Wisse* and various fourteenth-century writings we could continue locating the *Recluse*'s meaning primarily in a series of more authoritative if sometimes hypothetical earlier versions. But the intellectual climate that has helped us deal with the *Recluse*'s discontinuities also reminds us that its medieval readers would normally have encountered it only as it emerges from a manuscript like Pepys.[22] Before we again set this work aside – perhaps for another half-century – we should surely try to relate it with these readers.

Not that we will ever know who these readers were or what they were like, although given the nature of the Pepys manuscript and the *Recluse*-redactor's interests it seems reasonable to place them amongst the gentry and assume their Wycliffite sympathies. Beyond this, we cannot go except very hypothetically. We do have one early fifteenth-century comment about a work resembling the *Recluse*, in a preface to an interpolated version of Rolle's *Psalter Commentary*; its tone is rabidly anti-Lollard, however, and any readers it would provide would be far too simple-minded to look for any sense in what they read:

> Copyed has this Sauter ben, of yuel men of lollardry:
> And afturward hit has bene sene, ympyd in with eresy.
> They seyden then to leude foles, that it shuld be all enter,
> A blessyd boke of hur scoles, of Rychard Hampole the Sauter.
> Thus thei seyd, to make theim leue, on her scole thoro sotelte:
> To bryng hem in, so hem to greue, ageyn the feyth in grete fole:
> And slaundird foule this holy man, with her wykkyd waryed wyles:
> Hur fantom hath made many a fon, thoro the fend that fele begiles.
>
> (Ed. Bramley 2/49–56, from Bodleian Library MS Laud Misc. 286)[23]

---

[21] See also 5/4–6, though Colledge believes there is textual corruption here (4). On Lollard claims that women were capable of priesthood, see Aston, 49–70.

[22] For discussion of this intellectual shift and some of its effects see, for example, the essays edited by Nichols.

[23] On this passage's rhetoric, see Kuczynski, 165–68. Aston, among others, takes it relatively

We would probably do better, therefore, to look towards the sometimes astonishingly well-informed implied readers of the Wycliffites' own writings. Admittedly, these well-informed readers are no less idealized than the 'leude foles' of the fifteenth-century preface. But as we shall see, early Lollard writers do often seem to have been able to assume a considerable academic sophistication on the part of their actual readers.[24] It seems fairer to the Lollards, therefore, as well as potentially more fruitful in relation to the *Recluse*, to consider it in relation to readers such as these. This, at any rate, is what I will attempt in the rest of this essay.

There has been little modern discussion of how the Lollards read their texts.[25] They evidently did this in ways that seemed distinctive to contemporaries, however.[26] All too often these contemporaries refer to little more than their disregard for the accumulated interpretive authority of the established church. But some are more informative, including John Trefnant, Bishop of Hereford, in a complaint he made in about 1391 about Lollard preachers; this complaint also helps show how originally learned reading practices could quickly make their way to more popular environments:

> [P]ublice predicare nequiter presumpserunt et presumunt, [. . .] exponendo videlicet sacram scripturam populo ad litteram more moderno aliter quam spiritus sanctus flagitat, ubi vocabula a propriis significacionibus peregrinantur et novas divinari videntur, ubi non sunt iudicanda verba ex sensu quem faciunt sed ex sensu ex quo fiunt, ubi construccio non subjacet legibus Donati, ubi fides remota a racionis argumento sed suis principiis, doctrinis, et dogmatibus publicis et occultis virus scismatum inter clerum et populum ebullire. (Capes 232)

> (They have wrongly undertaken and undertake to preach in public, [. . .] by expounding Holy Scripture to the people according to the letter in a modern way otherwise than as the Holy Spirit demands, where designations wander from their proper significations and new meanings seem guessed at, where the words must not be judged from the sense that they make but from the sense from which they are made, where the construction is not bound by Donatus' rules, where faith is far removed from the capacity of reason, but they labor with their first principles, doctrines and teachings both public and private to boil up the poison of schisms between the clergy and the people.)[27]

---

literally: 'Under cover of an ostensibly unimpeachable author or title it might be possible to pass off the views of the sect or infiltrate them into the hands of unsuspecting readers. [. . .] Insinuating Lollard views into Rolle's *Psalter* or the *Prick of Conscience* was a means of climbing onto the laps of people – including the gentry – who had come to fight shy of heresy' (211); less trenchant are Kellogg and Talbert, 349; Swanson, 291.

[24] On how dauntingly well-informed these readers sometimes had to be, see Hudson, 'Wycliffite Prose,' 262–63; *Premature Reformation*, 218–19.

[25] An outstanding exception is Copeland's discussion of the subversive reading practices of certain Lollard women ('Women,' 270–80).

[26] Hurley 311–33 has gathered some of the things they said; the writers he quotes are mainly concerned with Wyclif, but those who worked after his death also had his followers in mind.

[27] Copeland uses this passage to show how the Lollards saw rhetoric as 'an obstruction of the literal

No less than his contemporaries, Trefnant is here preoccupied with what he sees as the Lollards' desire to evade all normal intellectual restraints. But he also betrays his awareness that their approach derived from sophisticated intellectual roots. His allusion to Donatus precisely counters Wyclif's own subordination of humanly authored grammars to the grammar and logic of the Bible:

> [O]portet in scripturam sacram exponendo vel intelligendo adiscere novam gramaticam ac novam logicam, sicut patet per beatum Gregorium et alios sanctos, qui exponunt autoritate scripture novos sensus terminorum scripture, qui nusquam originantur ex libris gramatice. ubi, queso, nisi ex doctrina scripture reperiretur, quod
>
> > Terra sit infernus, virgo, deus ac elementum,
> > Celica vita, caro, prothoplastum, machina mundi
>
> et sic de singulis similibus equivocatis nunc ad literam et nunc ad sensum misticum. debemus ergo intelligendo scripturam sacram sensum puerilem abicere ac sensum, quem deus docet, accipere [. . .]. (Wyclif, *De Veritate Sacrae Scripturae*, I:42)

> In expounding or interpreting Scripture one must learn a new grammar and a new logic, as is made clear through the Blessed Gregory and other saints who, on Scripture's authority, expound new senses of Scripture's terms which are not to be found in books of grammar. Where, I ask, except in the teaching of Scripture, is it found that the earth is hell, a virgin, God, the elements, heavenly life, flesh, protoplasm, and the machine of the world? The same is the case with each and every similar equivocation which are [*sic*] taken now in the literal sense and now in the mystical. So when interpreting Holy Scripture we should reject the childish sense and accept the sense which God teaches [. . .]. (Jeffrey, *Law of Love*, 333)[28]

And his reference to the Wycliffites interpreting words 'not [. . .] from the sense that they make but from the sense from which they are made' accurately describes what happens when one reads through lenses originally provided by Wyclif's own idiosyncratic blend of philosophical Realism and fervent biblicism.[29] They are lenses, I shall be suggesting, that could turn even the *Recluse* into a relatively meaningful work.

As Kenny has emphasized, both Wyclif and his immediate philosophical predecessors were linguistic philosophers in the sense that they paid great attention to language (*Wyclif*, 6). Where they parted company was over what they thought language could objectively signify. Wyclif's most important predecessors – as well as those Wyclif liked to see as his current

---

sense' while their adversaries saw it as 'an obstructive and perverse literalism' ('Rhetoric,' 22). Hudson refers to it when discussing what the Wycliffites meant by 'literal sense' ('Lollard Preaching,' 143–44).

[28] On Wyclif's views on the grammar and logic of the Bible, see Jeffrey, 'Chaucer and Wyclif,' 117–123. On *De Veritate Sacrae Scripturae*, see Tresko.

[29] On Wyclif's realism, see Leff, II:500–10; Kenny, *Wyclif*, 1–30; Kenny, 'Realism'; Catto, 190–93; on his biblicism, see Smalley; Leff, II:511–16; Minnis, 13–16; Kenny, *Wyclif*, 56–67; Catto, 195–98, 209.

opponents – tended towards the view that human language can signify objective reality only in the case of particular things.[30] For them, the conceptual categories or universal terms into which we organize our perceptions of such things remain the products of our own minds. Wyclif, by contrast, tended towards the view that, when rightly used, these categories also correspond with independently existing realities.[31] He was not Platonist enough to make these realities autonomous. But he endowed them with what he termed intelligible (as opposed to potential or actual) being and located them eternally in God (Leff, II:501–3).

No less than his opponents, Wyclif regarded human language as multivalent and therefore potentially ambiguous. But unlike these opponents, he did not regard it as objectively fixed only in relation to things here. He also regarded it as fixed at higher conceptual levels. Evans has put the point well:

> This way of thinking required an approach which rested on the assumption that the ways in which a word signifies form a connected system with the ways or modes of being of the things signified, and of rational understanding, human or divine. [. . .] But though the name of the thing may be artificially chosen, the thing it names is inseparably linked with a concept, and that means that the operations of language are firmly fixed in reality. (55–56)

She has also noted how such thinking might cause one to privilege the more universal or conceptual over the more particular: 'For those who held a Realist view of the nature of language, the primary signification of a term (*quod primo et principaliter apprehenditur toto signo*) was the universal or concept to which it referred, and the secondary signification the particular thing to which it referred' (56). Persons influenced by such thinking might indeed seem to be judging words 'not [. . .] from the sense that they make but from the sense from which they are made.'

For Trefnant, such processes would have involved a refusal to read 'as the Holy Spirit demands.' For the Wycliffites, quite the reverse was true. This was mainly thanks to how Wyclif reconciled his thinking about the Bible with his philosophical Realism.[32] He fully accepted that we encounter the Bible only as written by human authors in words that might often seem self-contradictory (*De Veritate Sacrae Scripturae*, I:107/6–15, 189/12–23). But he also believed that at its highest or most essentialized level of being, that is, as the Word, or God's Law, or Holy Scripture, it exists eternally whole and perfect (*De Veritate Sacrae Scripturae*, I:268/12–269/7). As good readers, therefore, we should strain towards understanding the Bible's words at as high a level as we can. We should also learn to privilege such

---

[30] For a brief account of some of the views Wyclif was reacting against, see Tresko, 156–59.

[31] On universals, see Kenny, *Wyclif*, 7–9.

[32] On the connection between Wyclif's realist metaphysics and his view of Scripture, see Smalley, 79–80, Tresko 159–62; on the Bible as eternal Word, see Smalley, 83–84; on Wyclif's rejection of the human rhetoric of the Bible in favor of the language of Scripture, see Copeland, 'Rhetoric,' 14–23.

an understanding in our own lives and discourse (*De Veritate Sacrae Scripturae*, I:34/26–35/5).

As Wyclif was the first to admit, good reading was only possible for those already possessing Wisdom: '[I]mpossibile est, quemquam aliquid adiscere sine sapiencia prima docente' (*De Veritate Sacrae Scripturae*, I:201/18–19).[33] But in addition to donning Wycliffite lenses, its practitioners had to do some hard interpretive work of their own. First they had to scrutinize the Bible's equivocal terms, that is, those of its terms that can signify different things in different senses (Evans, 115).[34] Then they had to consider the various significations that the Bible provides for those terms and identify the ones that approximate most closely to its meaning at its higher levels.[35] Then, on the principle that '[t]here can be no contradiction between statements where the same term is used in different senses' (Evans, 116), they had to explain away any apparent verbal ambiguities and contradictions they might encounter (*De Veritate Sacrae Scripturae*, I:23/21–27/30); this seems mainly to have involved their reading 'now in the literal sense and now in the mystical.'[36] In all these undertakings they could have received help from right-minded teachers, biblical concordances and the like; as Somerset has argued (197–201), they could also have drawn on the *Floretum/Rosarium theologie*, which structures its discussion around the various significations of key scriptural terms. But when they 'reject(ed) the childish sense and accept(ed) the sense which God teaches,' they had to do it in their lives as well as in their interpretations.

In an unpublished paper on Wyclif's 1372–4 pamphlet war with the Oxford Carmelite John Kenningham, Levy has pieced together an example of Wyclif's approaching biblical language in just this way; his example also reveals what Trefnant probably meant when he described the Lollards as allowing designations to 'wander from their proper significations.'[37] At issue is the term 'antiquitas.' Wyclif believes the antiquity (*antiquitas*) of Scripture establishes it as supremely authoritative (*Fasciculi*, 4).[38] Kenningham objects, partly on the ground that the Old Testament would then have greater authority than the Gospel, and the prophets greater authority than the apostolic epistles (*Fasciculi*, 5). Wyclif claims that *antiquitas* should primarily be understood with reference to the eternity of God (*Fasciculi*,

[33] For Wyclif's views on the moral virtue necessary for reading well, see Jeffrey, 'Chaucer and Wyclif,' 115–16.

[34] Somerset points out in her discussion of Thorpe's use of equivocation (195–96 n. 46), that in his *De Logica* Wyclif provides the most basic definition of an equivocal term, as one that 'according to different definitions signifies different things' ('propter raciones diversas significat res diversas').

[35] As we can deduce from Wyclif's understanding of *antiquitas* and Wyche's of confession in the examples discussed below.

[36] On the language theory driving medieval theories of equivocation, see Ashworth. On Wyclif's seeking out of equivocations and resolving apparent contradictions, see Evans, 114–20; Tresko.

[37] I am grateful to Dr Levy for a copy of his paper, 'The Wyclif-Kenningham Debate Reconsidered,' which he presented in May 1998 at the 33rd International Congress on Medieval Studies, Kalamazoo, Michigan.

[38] *Fasciculi* contains four of Kenningham's determinations against Wyclif together with a reply and short codicil by Wyclif (4–103, 453–80).

15). Kenningham dismisses his claim (*Fasciculi*, 15) on the ground that such an understanding is not in keeping with the commonly accepted manner of speaking ('nec salvat communem modum loquendi'). But, Wyclif responds (*Fasciculi*, 479), the holy philosophers follow Daniel in speaking of God as the *antiquus dierum* (Dan. 7:9). While he accepts that *antiquitas* conventionally means longevity, therefore, in understanding it in less obviously temporal terms he is emulating the *modus loquendi Scripturae* (*Fasciculi*, 454–55).

More likely to feature in Wycliffite discourse than the term *antiquitas*, however, and therefore more likely to be telling in relation to a work like the *Recluse*, is the term 'church.' The *Rosarium theologie* provides four possible significations for this, all grounded in the Bible. It is a material temple hallowed by the bishop (Ps. 67:27, 'In chirchez blessez ȝe our Lorde'). It is the number of the chosen (Ecclus. 3:1, 'þe childer of wisdom bene þe chirche of riȝtwis menn'). It is the number of the reproved (Ps. 25:5, 'I hated the chirch of wicked men'); the compiler later refers to Augustine on how this is the church headed by the devil (*De Doct. Christ.*, III:37). And it is the number of the chosen and reproved together who will finally be separated on the Day of Judgement (with reference to the net of Matt. 13:47–48) (von Nolcken, *Rosarium*, 66–68). Opponents normally privileged the last signification; for them, the church was most usefully defined in terms that were primarily institutional, temporal, and contingent. But it is the second signification, of the Church as the number of the chosen, or as the 'universitas predestinorum,' that Wyclif claims is privileged in Scripture and by the holy doctors ('aput auctores scripture et sanctos doctores ipsa specialiter intelligitur' (*De Ecclesia*, 439/22–23)).[39] And it is this definition that the *Rosarium theologie* treats most fully, supporting it not only with further biblical citations (Eph. 1:22, 4:15, 5:23, Col. 1:18) but with passages from Augustine, Grosseteste, Bernard, Hilary of Poitiers and Gregory (von Nolcken, *Rosarium*, 67–68). It would also be this definition that the institutional church would declare heretical: from at least 1428 the question 'an mali sint pars ecclesie catholice' would feature in heresy trials (Hudson, *Lollards and their Books*, 134).[40]

The difference between conventional language and this other, higher language, or what William Thorpe, questioned for heresy in 1407, was to term the difference between 'vnperfit speche' and speaking 'propirli' (Somerset, 196), also explains the Lollards' preferred understanding of a multitude of other terms likely to feature in a work like the *Recluse*, not least those signifying the officers of the church. For opponents, such terms primarily signified persons whose only certain affiliations lay with the institutional church: even if ultimately headed for perdition, such persons maintained their title here by virtue of their office. For the Wycliffites, such terms more properly signified members of the eternal Church of Christ: the *Rosarium theologie* distinguishes priests in both letter and spirit (ordained

---

[39] On Wycliffite understandings of the Church, see Hudson, *Premature Reformation*, 314–27.

[40] In a trial using the list containing this question the suspect's answer is that they are not; the suspect was declared a heretic (Maxwell-Lyte and Dawes, I:124).

priests who properly carry out their duties of preaching the Gospel and the like), from priests in letter only (corrupt earthly priests who are therefore not really priests), from priests in spirit only (laymen who, while counting among the predestinate, should only preach and administer the sacraments in times of emergency). As Pseudo-Chrysostom put it in a passage collected into the *Rosarium theologie*, 'Many bene prestez and few bene prestez' (Cambridge, Gonville and Caius College MS 354/581, f. 113).[41]

That the Wycliffites privileged this other language did not prevent them from also deploying 'vnperfit speche' when it suited them. As early as 1382, for example, Wyclif's immediate university followers, Nicholas Hereford, Philip Repingdon and John Aston, perhaps inspired by a passage that would also later appear in the *Rosarium theologie*, 'Heretikes ar wont for to calle trewe men heretikes' (Cambridge, Gonville and Caius College MS 354/581, f. 45v), were equivocating over terms like 'haeresis' and 'error' (*Fasciculi*, 319–33) and generally depending on 'the subtlety of words' (*uerborum subtilitate*) to get around their accusers (Knighton, 280, 281). And in c.1389–91 William Swynderby was constantly playing on the various possible significations of such terms as church, priest, law of God, and true Christian man in his exchanges with the authorities.[42] Worth mentioning too, given the anchoritic origins of the *Recluse*, is a Leicester anchoress named Matilda who, when accused of Lollardy in 1389, was found 'not to answer plainly and directly to the same, but sophistically and subtilely' (Foxe, III:199). Examples could be multiplied.

These Lollards seem to be using equivocation as we primarily think of it today, as a device for shifting between meanings with an intention to mislead. But they would have considered they were 'openly' transferring the meaning of their terms, by paying due attention to what the users of these terms intended by them.[43] Certainly, this is what the suspect Richard Wyche comes close to stating in the letter he wrote a lay friend in 1402–3 about his own questioning and condemnation by Walter Skirlaw, Bishop of Durham.[44] Important here is an oath of obedience to the laws and constitutions of the church as contained in the Decretum, Decretals, Sext and Clementines (Matthew, 531/19–22) that Wyche repeatedly refuses to swear. Finally a knight persuades him to formulate a version he could accept. Predictably, it leaves plenty of room for interpretation: 'I know the law of God is the law of the Catholic church and far be it but that I should obey the law of our God insofar as it applies to me' ('scio quod lex Dei est lex ecclesie catholice et absit quin obedirem legi Dei nostri in quantum ad

---

[41] In the *Opus Imperfectum in Matthaeum*, probably the work of a Latin author in the sixth century but attributed to Chrysostom from at least the eighth century. It was much used by the Wycliffites, and forms one of the two bases of Wyclif's *Opus Evangelicum*. Wyclif saw its philosophical tendencies as akin to his own (*Opus Evangelicum*, II:4); passages in the *Floretum/ Rosarium theologie* suggest that the Wycliffites particularly approved of its author's approach to language.

[42] For this exchange, see Capes, 231–78; most of the material is translated into English by Foxe (III:107–31).

[43] On the open transference of meaning, see Tresko, 163; on views concerning the relationship between use and authorial intention, see Ashworth, 61–63.

[44] On this case, see von Nolcken, 'Richard Wyche.'

me pertinet', Matthew, 534/27–28). But Wyche also reveals himself much
concerned with intentions, remarking to the knight as he formulates this
version: 'But you know well that if I go ahead with the oath from the judge,
I ought to go ahead with it according to the intent of the judge and not
according to my own' ('Sed vos scitis bene, dixi, si reciperem iuramentum a
iudice, oportet me recipere secundum intentum iudicis et non secundum
meum', Matthew, 534/30–32); he also tries to convey his own intentions
when he finally swears the oath before the bishop (Matthew, 535/18–20).

However carefully deployed, such equivocation could involve its users in
considerable intellectual contortion, as Wyche's letter also reveals. Early in
the proceedings, Wyche makes the very un-Lollard-sounding concession
that auricular confession is necessary for salvation (Matthew, 533/2). He
doesn't immediately tell his readers what was in his mind. But he later
observes that whereas the good Wyclif ('bonus Wicleff'), in denying the
need for such confession (Matthew, 536/14), was speaking in the manner of
the sophists ('ad modum loquendi sophistarum', Matthew, 536/15), Wyche
himself was speaking in terms of Scripture ('Et ego concessi ad modum
loquendi scripture', Matthew, 536/15–16).[45] Again he doesn't explain. But
the *Rosarium* provides the clue: 'Confession of feþe is be wiche wiþ hert we
trew to riȝtwisnes. Wiþ mouþe, forsoþe, we confesse to hele, Rom. 10.: Vnde
saluator. Mr. 8.: He þat confesse me & my wordes in þis generacion
avowterere & a synner [*peccatrice*] & þe son of man schal knowlech hym
[. . .]' (Cambridge, Gonville and Caius College MS 354/581, f. 23). Where
Wyclif was referring to illegitimate confession as members of the institutional church on earth would have understood this, Wyche was referring to
Christ's scriptural injunctions that we acknowledge him before men.

Lay persons like Wyche's addressee must have learned their equivocations in some version of a Lollard school.[46] It nevertheless remains that for
the Wycliffites just as for Wyclif, 'proper' reading ultimately depended on
whether or not one had grace, or the Holy Spirit (Minnis, 24–27; Somerset,
201). For only if one was working with this might one gain any real access
to the Truth – my favorite illustration of this point comes from the General
Prologue to the Wyclif Bible translation:

> Therfore a translatour hath greet nede to studie wel the sentence [. . .], and
> he hath nede to lyue a clene lif, and be ful deuout in preiers, and haue not
> his wit ocupied about worldli thingis, that the Holi Spiryt, autour of
> wisdom, and kunnyng, and truthe, dresse him in his werk, and suffre him
> not for to erre. [. . .] Bi this maner, with good lyuyng and greet trauel, men
> moun come to trewe and cleer translating, and trewe vndurstonding of
> holi writ, seme it neuere so hard at the bigynnyng.
>
> (Forshall and Madden, I:59–60)

And if one were not, one would be like the Saducees: 'Gessist thou that
prestis of Saduceis redden not scripturis? but thei mygte not fynde God in

---

[45] For Wyclif and his followers' views on confession, see Hudson, *Premature Reformation*, 294–301.
[46] On Lollard schools, see Hudson, *Premature Reformation*, 174–200.

hem, for thei wolde not lyue worthili to God,' observes a tract on Biblical translation (Deanesly, 450/13–15). As the *Recluse*-redactor himself puts it, even Jerome, Ambrose and Gregory, not to mention Peter and Paul, had real knowledge only because the Holy Ghost was with them (90/9–17). It is time to return to his text.

As we have seen, a good place to begin when considering whether or not we can usefully read such a text through Wycliffite lenses is with the term 'church.' For the *Recluse* or, rather, for what was surely its last redactor, this is 'a gaderynge of goode folk in goddes name' (44/23–24); it is a definition we could read as exclusively temporal and therefore contingent in its application. But its rider that churches built by men are no more than houses of prayer (44/24–25) suggests we are being invited to read in higher way, as do the several indications that Antichrist has found a place in the *Recluse*'s scheme – clerks are even now going over to his Church (70/4–9), and those who seek ease of body are Antichrist's prophets because 'her lyf is contrarie aȝein ihesus cristes lyf' (40/18–20).[47] And that the redactor was quite capable of maneuvering between various possible significations is suggested by an added passage elaborating on earthly and heavenly poverty and wealth:

> þere ben in þis werlde foure manere folk. Riche and riche. And þere ben Pouer. and pouer. þat is pouer here and in helle boþe. And Riche and riche. þat is Riche here and Riche in the blisse of heuene boþe. And þere ben Riche and Pouer. þat ben hij þat ben Riche here and gon to helle. And þere ben Pouer & Riche. þat ben hij þat ben Pouere here and gon to heuene. (52/24–30).

It would indeed seem that when we see such equivocal words as 'rich' or 'poor' in less explicit contexts we need to decide whether we should read them from a conventionally temporal or some more conceptual perspective – a perspective whereby temporal rich can really mean Poor, and temporal poor can really mean Rich.

It would have suggested a great deal about the ultimate allegiances of those who read the *Recluse*, of course, whether they approached its text in this distinctive way. But if they did not, it is not very likely that they would have ever made much sense of its text. Rather, like the Saducees (and some modern scholars), they would have found themselves bogged down in words – in all those conflicting words about how they ought to conduct their lives, for example. Whereas if they indeed read the *Recluse* 'propirli,' they would have found themselves cooperating in the construction of what its latest redactor would surely have considered a 'right' reading even of those parts of his original that he has left seemingly untouched.[48] They

---

[47] On the Lollards' liking for this somewhat essentialized version of Antichrist, see von Nolcken, 'A Certain Sameness,' 195–97.

[48] Even Colledge, who scarcely mentions audience, suggests that the reviser might at times have relied on an interpretation by his Lollard readers different from that intended by the original without any revision on his part (12–13).

would have found themselves assimilating what both *Ancrene Wisse* and the *Recluse* say about only confessing to a good priest to various Wycliffite tenets denying real authority to those living in mortal sin.[49] And on a larger scale, they would have found themselves applying what is left of *Ancrene Wisse*'s positive treatment of recluses not necessarily to persons who have embraced a religious discipline the Wycliffites didn't in fact much approve of, but to persons really dead to that 'gaderyng of wicked folk' (4/21–22) that constitutes the World (18/25–29, 19/1).[50] Dare I add that they would have found themselves endorsing women's preaching, and less because of any feminist views they might have had on the subject than because of a Wycliffite conception of the equality of all real believers?[51]

Whether *The Recluse* ever actually found readers able to read in this way we cannot know. The one reader we can track, the Pepys scribe, seems only to have added to its disintegration; whether this was because he recklessly privileged its real meaning above the more conventional meaning of its words or because he found these words well-nigh incomprehensible we cannot know.[52] Of his own medieval readers we have hardly a trace. But from the ranks of the gentry there would emerge some whose piety was more consistently Lollard than, say, Clanvowe's. They include Walter Brut, who in 1391–93 defended among other things the view that a just laywoman can preach (Capes, 345–47), or Sir Lewis Clifford who in 1402 abjured some very extreme sounding tenets, claiming he had been taken in by the Lollards' ambiguous language (Walsingham, II:252–53). A generation later they would include that most notorious member of the gentry ever to be associated with the movement, Sir John Oldcastle.[53] Perhaps some of these were nurtured on a 'propir' reading of 'þis good book Recluse.'

---

[49] See, for example, the fourth heresy in the list drawn up against Wyclif in 1382, 'Item quod si episcopus vel sacerdos existat in peccato mortali: non ordinat, conficit, nec baptizat' ('if a bishop or priest is in mortal sin he does not ordain, confess or baptize,' *Fasciculi*, 278).

[50] Hudson refers to Wyclif as 'roundly' condemning the anchoritic way of life (*Premature Reformation*, 27); he did, however, have some good words for recluses, especially when they were like John the Baptist (*De Civili Dominio*, I:173). Under *Religio* the *Rosarium* distinguishes true from feigned religion and discusses private religions under the latter head; noteworthy is a passage from Chrisostom on how our Lord asks people to keep the faith and not to be enclosed in cells or dungeons or pits (Cambridge, Gonville and Caius College MS 354/581, f. 110v).

[51] On the Lollards' views concerning the equality (or priesthood) of all real believers, sometimes including women, see Hudson, *Premature Reformation*, 325–27.

[52] Påhlsson largely blames the Pepys scribe for the *Recluse*'s corruption (xi, 323); Zettersten remarks on his carelessness (xx) and Millett on his 'habitually high tolerance for nonsensical readings' (11). As Colledge points out, though, its redactor must also have been remarkably careless (3–5), so both he and the scribe may have deprivileged the actual words on the page in favor of their real meaning. On such privileging of prior meaning over words, see Wyclif, *De Veritate Sacrae Scripturae*, I:21/12–14.

[53] On Oldcastle, see Waugh; Powell, 141–67. For a revisionary account of his 'Rebellion,' see Strohm, 65–86. Hargreaves discusses his advocacy of clerical marriage.

Works Cited

Allen, Hope Emily, 'Some Fourteenth Century Borrowings from "Ancren Riwle"',
  Modern Language Review 18 (1923), 1–8

Ashworth, E. J., 'Signification and Modes of Signifying in Thirteenth-Century
  Logic: a Preface to Aquinas on Analogy', *Medieval Philosophy and Theology* 1
  (1991), 39–67

Aston, Margaret, *Lollards and Reformers: Images and Literacy in Late Medieval
  Religion* (London, 1984)

Bramley, H. R., ed., *The Psalter or Psalms of David and Certain Canticles, with a
  Translation and Exposition in English by Richard Rolle of Hampole* (Oxford,
  1884)

Bülbring, Karl D., ed., *The Earliest Complete English Prose Psalter together with
  Eleven Canticles and a Translation of the Athanasian Creed*, Early English Text
  Society o.s. 97 (London, 1891)

Cannon, H. L., 'The Poor Priests: a Study in the Rise of English Lollardry', *Annual
  Report of the American Historical Association* 1 (1900 for 1899), 451–82

Capes, William W., ed., *Registrum Johannis Trefnant, Episcopi Herefordensis A.D.
  1389–1404*, Canterbury and York Society 20 (London, 1916)

Catto, J. I., 'Wyclif and Wycliffism at Oxford 1356–1430', in *The History of the
  University of Oxford, Vol. II: Late Medieval Oxford*, ed. J. I. Catto and Ralph
  Evans (Oxford, 1992), 175–261

Colledge, Eric, '*The Recluse*: a Lollard Interpolated Version of the *Ancren Riwle*',
  Review of English Studies 15 (1939), 1–15 and 129–45

Copeland, Rita, 'Rhetoric and the Politics of the Literal Sense in Medieval Literary
  Theory: Aquinas, Wyclif, and the Lollards', in *Interpretation: Medieval and
  Modern. The J. A. W. Bennett Memorial Lectures, 8th Series, Perugia 1992*
  (Cambridge, 1993), 1–23

——, 'Why Women Can't Read: Medieval Hermeneutics, Statutory Law, and the
  Lollard Heresy Trials', in *Representing Women: Law, Literature, and Feminism*,
  ed. Susan Sage Heinzelman and Zipporah Batshaw Wiseman (Durham, 1994),
  253–86

Deanesly, Margaret, *The Lollard Bible and Other Medieval Biblical Versions*
  (Cambridge, 1920)

Dobson, E. J., 'The Affiliations of the Manuscripts of *Ancrene Wisse*', in *English
  and Medieval Studies Presented to J. R. R. Tolkien on the Occasion of his
  Seventieth Birthday*, ed. Norman Davis and C. L. Wrenn (London, 1962),
  128–63

Doyle, A. I., 'The Shaping of the Vernon and Simeon Manuscript[s]', in *Studies in
  the Vernon Manuscript*, ed. Derek Pearsall (Cambridge, 1990), 1–13

——, 'A Survey of the Origins and Circulation of Theological Writings in English in
  the Fourteenth, Fifteenth, and early Sixteenth Centuries with Special Consideration of the Part of the Clergy therein', 2 vols., Ph.D. Diss. (University of
  Cambridge, 1953)

Emden, A. B., *A Biographical Register of the University of Oxford to A.D. 1500*, 3
  vols. (Oxford, 1957–59)

Evans, G. R., *The Language and Logic of the Bible: the Road to Reformation*
  (Cambridge, 1985)

Everett, Dorothy, 'The Middle English Prose Psalter of Richard Rolle of Hampole',
  Modern Language Review 17 (1922), 217–27, 337–50; 18 (1923), 381–93

Fasciculi Zizaniorum Magistri Johannis Wyclif cum Tritico, ed. Walter Waddington Shirley, Rolls Series 5 (London, 1858)

Forshall, Josiah and Frederic Madden, eds., *The Holy Bible, [. . .] in the Earliest English Versions made from the Latin Vulgate by John Wycliffe and his Followers*, 4 vols. (Oxford, 1850)

Foxe, John, *The Acts and Monuments*, ed. Stephen Reed Cattley, 8 vols. (London, 1837–41)

Fridner, Elis, ed., *An English Fourteenth Century Apocalypse Version with a Prose Commentary, edited from MS Harley 874 and ten other MSS*, Lund Studies in English 29 (Lund, 1961)

Goates, Margery, ed., *The Pepysian Gospel Harmony*, Early English Text Society o.s. 157 (London, 1922)

Hargreaves, Henry, 'Sir John Oldcastle and Wycliffite Views on Clerical Marriage', *Medium Aevum* 52 (1973), 141–46

Hudson, Anne, '"Laicus litteratus": the Paradox of Lollardy', in *Heresy and Literacy, 1100–1530*, ed. Peter Biller and Anne Hudson, Cambridge Studies in Medieval Literature 23 (Cambridge, 1994), 222–36

——, *Lollards and their Books* (London, 1985)

——, 'A New Look at the Lay Folks' Catechism', *Viator* 16 (1985), 243–58

——, *The Premature Reformation: Wycliffite Texts and Lollard History* (Oxford, 1988)

——, '"Springing cockel in our clene corn": Lollard Preaching in England around 1400', in *Christendom and its Discontents: Exclusion, Persecution, and Rebellion, 1000–1500*, ed. Scott L. Waugh and Peter D. Diehl (Cambridge, 1996), 132–47

——, ed., *Two Wycliffite Texts: The Sermon of William Taylor 1406, The Testimony of William Thorpe 1407*, Early English Text Society o.s. 301 (Oxford, 1993)

——, 'Wycliffite Prose', in *Middle English Prose: a Critical Guide to Major Authors and Genres*, ed. A. S. G. Edwards (New Brunswick, 1984), 249–70

Hurley, Michael, S. J., '"Scriptura Sola": Wyclif and his Critics', *Traditio* 16 (1960), 275–352

Jeffrey, David Lyle, 'Chaucer and Wyclif: Biblical Hermeneutic and Literary Theory in the XIVth Century', in *Chaucer and Scriptural Tradition*, ed. David Lyle Jeffrey (Ottawa, 1984), 109–40

——, *The Law of Love: English Spirituality in the Age of Wyclif* (Grand Rapids, 1988)

Kellogg, A. L., and Ernest W. Talbert, 'The Wyclifite *Pater Noster* and *Ten Commandments*, with Special Reference to English MSS 85 and 90 in the John Rylands Library', *Bulletin of the John Rylands Library* 42 (1959–60), 345–77

Kenny, Anthony, 'The Realism of the *De Universalibus*', in *Wyclif in his Times*, ed. Anthony Kenny (Oxford, 1986), 17–29

——, *Wyclif* (Oxford, 1985)

Knighton's Chronicle 1337–1396, ed. and trans. G. H. Martin, Oxford Medieval Texts (Oxford, 1995)

Kuczynski, Michael P., *Prophetic Song: the Psalms as Moral Discourse in Late Medieval England* (Philadelphia, 1995)

Leff, Gordon, *Heresy in the Later Middle Ages*, 2 vols. (Manchester, 1967)

Macaulay, G. C., 'The "Ancren Riwle"', *Modern Language Review* 9 (1914), 63–78, 145–60, 324–31 and 463–74

Mack, Frances M., ed., *The English Text of the Ancrene Riwle edited from Cotton MS Titus D.xviii*, Early English Text Society o.s. 252 (London, 1963)

Marx, C. William, and Jeanne F. Drennan, *The Middle English Prose Complaint of Our Lady and Gospel of Nicodemus*, Middle English Texts 19 (Heidelberg, 1987)

Matthew, F. D., 'The Trial of Richard Wyche', *English Historical Review* 5 (1890), 530–44

Maxwell-Lyte, H. C., and M. C. B. Dawes, eds., *The Register of Thomas Bekynton, Bishop of Bath and Wells 1443–1465*, 2 vols., Somerset Record Society 49–50 (Frome and London, 1934)

McFarlane, K. B., *Lancastrian Kings and Lollard Knights* (Oxford, 1972)

McKitterick, Rosamond, and Richard Beadle, *Catalogue of the Pepys Library at Magdalene College Cambridge, Vol. 5, Manuscripts, Part i, Medieval* (Cambridge, 1992)

Millett, Bella, '*Mouvance* and the Medieval Author: Re-Editing *Ancrene Wisse*', in *Late-Medieval Religious Texts and their Transmission: Essays in Honour of A. I. Doyle*, ed. A. J. Minnis (Cambridge, 1994), 9–20

Minnis, A. J., ' "Authorial Intention" and "Literal Sense" in the Exegetical Theories of Richard FitzRalph and John Wyclif: an Essay in the Medieval History of Biblical Hermeneutics', *Proceedings of the Royal Irish Academy* 75 sect. C (1975), 1–31

Morton, James, ed. and trans., *The Ancren Riwle: a Treatise on the Rules and Duties of Monastic Life*, Camden Society 57 (London, 1853)

Nichols, Stephen G., ed., *The New Philology*, *Speculum* 65 (1990), 1–108

Påhlsson, Joel, ed., *The Recluse, a Fourteenth Century Version of the Ancren Riwle* (Lund, 1911, repr. with notes, Lund, 1918). All references will be to the 1918 version.

Paues, A. C., 'A XIVth Century Version of the *Ancren Riwle*', *Englische Studien* 30 (1902), 344–46

Powell, Edward, *Kingship, Law, and Society: Criminal Justice in the Reign of Henry V* (Oxford, 1989)

Samuels, M. L., 'Chaucer's Spelling', in *Middle English Studies Presented to Norman Davis*, ed. Douglas Gray and E. G. Stanley (Oxford, 1983), 17–37

——, 'Some Applications of Middle English Dialectology', *English Studies* 44 (1963), 81–94

Scattergood, V. J., ed., *The Works of Sir John Clanvowe* (Cambridge, 1975)

Smalley, Beryl, 'The Bible and Eternity: John Wyclif's Dilemma', *Journal of the Warburg and Courtauld Institutes* 27 (1964), 73–89

Smithers, G. V., ed., *Kyng Alisaunder, Volume 2, Introduction, Commentary and Glossary*, Early English Text Society o.s. 237 (London, 1957)

Somerset, Fiona, *Clerical Discourse and Lay Audience in Late Medieval England* (Cambridge, 1998)

Spencer, H. Leith, *English Preaching in the Late Middle Ages* (Oxford, 1993)

Strohm, Paul, *England's Empty Throne: Usurpation and the Language of Legitimation, 1399–1422* (New Haven, 1998)

Swanson, R. N., 'Literacy, Heresy, History and Orthodoxy: Perspectives and Permutations for the Later Middle Ages', in *Heresy and Literacy, 1100–1530*, ed. Peter Biller and Anne Hudson, Cambridge Studies in Medieval Literature 23 (Cambridge, 1994), 279–93

Thomson, J. A. F., 'Knightly Piety and the Margins of Lollardy', in *Lollardy and the Gentry in the Later Middle Ages*, ed. Margaret Aston and Colin Richmond (Stroud, 1997), 95–111

——, 'Orthodox Religion and the Origins of Lollardy', *History* n.s. 74 (1989), 39–55

Tresko, Michael, 'John Wyclif's Metaphysics of Scriptural Integrity in the *De Veritate Sacrae Scripturae*', *Dionysius* 13 (1989), 153–96

Tuck, J. Anthony, 'Carthusian Monks and Lollard Knights: Religious Attitude at the Court of Richard II', in *Studies in the Age of Chaucer, Proceedings no. 1, 1984: Reconstructing Chaucer*, ed. Paul Strohm and Thomas J. Heffernan (Knoxville, 1985), 149–61

von Nolcken, Christina, 'A "Certain Sameness" and Our Response to it in English Wycliffite Texts', in *Literature and Religion in the Later Middle Ages: Philological Studies in Honor of Siegfried Wenzel*, ed. Richard G. Newhauser and John A. Alford (Binghamton, 1995), 191–208

——, ed., *The Middle English Translation of the Rosarium theologie: a Selection ed. from Cbr., Gonville and Caius Coll. MS 354/581*, Middle English Texts 10 (Heidelberg, 1979)

——, 'Richard Wyche, a Certain Knight, and the Beginning of the End', in *Lollardy and the Gentry in the Later Middle Ages*, ed. Margaret Aston and Colin Richmond (Stroud, 1997), 127–54

Walsingham, Thomas, *Historia Anglicana*, ed. Henry Thomas Riley, 2 vols., Rolls Series 28 (London, 1863–4)

Waugh, W. T., 'Sir John Oldcastle', *English Historical Review* 20 (1905), 434–56 and 637–58

Wilks, Michael, 'Royal Priesthood: the Origins of Lollardy', in *The Church in a Changing Society, CIHEC Conference in Uppsala, 1977* (Uppsala, 1978), 63–70

Wyclif, John, *De Civili Dominio*, ed. Reginald Lane Poole, 4 vols., Wyclif Society (London, 1885–1904)

——, *De Ecclesia*, ed. Johann Loserth, Wyclif Society (London, 1886)

——, *De Veritate Sacrae Scripturae*, ed. Rudolf Buddensieg, 3 vols., Wyclif Society (London, 1905–7)

——, *Opus Evangelicum*, ed. Johann Loserth, 2 vols., Wyclif Society (London, 1895–96)

Zettersten, A., ed., *The English Text of the Ancrene Riwle, edited from Magdalene College, Cambridge MS Pepys 2498*, Early English Text Society o.s. 274 (London, 1976)

10

Ancrene Wisse, Religious Reform and the Late Middle Ages

NICHOLAS WATSON

The Surprising History of an Early Middle English Text

As a volume like this testifies, *Ancrene Wisse* and the works associated with it set some of the most intransigent puzzles Middle English scholars have faced, posing endless questions while tantalizing us with the hope that works as rich as these *must* yield their secrets. With three early versions and later English, French, and Latin ones of *Ancrene Wisse* to consider, many source texts to uncover and much philological information to assess, scholars have naturally paid more attention to some issues than others. As used to be the case with *Piers Plowman* studies, labourers in the vineyard are few, and much that seems of less than the first significance is left to one side (Millett, *Bibliography*; Dahood).

This essay takes up one of the neglected topics in *Ancrene Wisse* studies: that of the work's importance to vernacular writers and readers in the period c.1370–1450, when most of the surviving Middle English religious prose was written. Several generations of scholars have established the fact of that importance in this period (especially Allen, 'Some Fourteenth-Century Borrowings', 'On "Some Fourteenth-Century Borrowings"', 'Further Borrowings', 'Wynkyn'; Colledge, '*Recluse*'; Diekstra, 'Some Fifteenth-Century Borrowings', *Book*).[1] The text was copied into the great Vernon manuscript alongside the works of Rolle and Hilton (Doyle, *Vernon*), and twice adapted for a mixed or lay audience, in *The Pepys Rule* and *The Simple Tretis* (Zettersten; Baugh). It was a source for five compilations – *Book for a Simple and Devout Woman, þe Pater Noster of Richard Ermyte, þe Holy Boke Gratia Dei, Pore Caitif*, and *The Chastising of God's Children* (Diekstra, *Book*; Aarts; Arntz; Brady, '*Pore Caitif*'; Bazire and Colledge) – and was probably cited in Walter Hilton's

---

[1] Adaptation of *Ancrene Wisse* for new audiences of course started much earlier than the fourteenth century, and may have begun with the author himself. Thirteenth-century adaptations for male religious include the 'Titus' version and the 'Gonville and Caius' compilation (Mack; Wilson). Parts of the text were included in an Anglo-Norman *compileisun*, written for a mixed religious and lay audience, that urgently needs study (Trethewey). Early fourteenth-century adaptations of *Ancrene Wisse* aimed at anchoresses, nuns, or monks include the *Latin Rule* (D'Evelyn) and possibly *The Dublin Rule* (Oliger; queried by Millett, *Bibliography*, 33). Analysis of these works necessarily lies outside the scope of this essay. See also Catherine Innes-Parker's and Christina von Nokken's essays in this volume.

Scale of Perfection and certainly in a version of Nicholas Love's *Mirror of the Blessed Life of Jesus Christ* (Sargent, 1992).[2] It may not have been quite the most influential work of the period: one thirteenth-century text, Edmund of Abingdon's *Speculum religiosorum*, was better-known in Anglo-Norman and English versions (Forshaw; Lagorio and Sargent, 3116), and by 1400 *Ancrene Wisse* was being supplanted by guides to holy living by Richard Rolle, Walter Hilton, and others. But it had a greater impact than its major predecessor, Aelred's *De institutione inclusarum* (Ayto and Barratt), and an incomparably greater one than anything else in English before the *South English Legendary*, a text that, unlike *Ancrene Wisse*, was written for a general readership (c.1280; Görlach 1974). Indeed, *Ancrene Wisse* is the earliest substantial Middle English text we know to have achieved a national readership or be translated into Anglo-Norman and Latin.[3] Yet, partly because its quality seems so obvious, the singularity of its history has never given the surprise it should have – with the result that we have only a broad sense of why this one Early Middle English work was accorded such respect.

In this essay, then, I attempt a reconstruction of how the Middle English writers who drew on *Ancrene Wisse* thought about the text. *Ancrene Wisse* was perhaps the first long Middle English work written for anchoresses – a group emblematic of insular religiosity in much the way the beguines were emblematic of the religiosity of northern continental Europe (Bolton, 'Some Thirteenth Century Women', 'Thirteenth-Century Religious Women') – whom the work treats in opposing ways: as fragile vessels, who must exert utmost vigilance in guarding their lives from their carnal female nature; and as tough-minded and ambitious descendants of the heroic desert solitaries of the early Church. Written after the Fourth Lateran Council of 1215 (Millett, *Bibliography*, 6–13), at the end of a hundred-year period of reform and experimentation – a period in which many different assumptions about the world, salvation, and holy living were articulated, often in opposition to one another (Constable, *Reformation*) – this foundational exposition of the female solitary life is full of the excitements and tensions of its era. As a vernacular text that implies such contradictory attitudes about the spiritual and professional status of its main intended readers, and that indirectly addresses two subsidiary audiences (the author's learned colleagues and the anchoresses's perhaps illiterate servants), *Ancrene Wisse* has an especially involved understanding of what it means – practically, rhetorically, historically, and theologically – to advocate a life of perfection to a vernacular readership.

[2] See below for Hilton's probable use of *Ancrene Wisse*, which has not previously been noticed. Claims for the work's influence on William Flete's *De remediis* and Julian of Norwich's *Revelation of Love* are inconclusive (Millett, *Bibliography*, 33), but it also contributed brief passages to several Middle English sermons, *The Book of Vices and Virtues* (Spencer, 86, 309) and the Vernon *Life of Adam and Eve* (Crawford), featured in a fifteenth-century will, and was in at least one convent library (Doyle, 'Survey,' 234; Dobson, xx–xxv).

[3] Compare the fate of the *Orrmulum*, Layamon's *Brut*, and *The Owl and the Nightingale* (Cannon; Hahn). Apart from two *Wooing*-Group works and *Sawles Warde*, *Ancrene Wisse*'s satellites also seem to have had only brief and local careers (Millett, *Bibliography*, 33).

My argument is that this understanding was as significant a factor in the work's success as its literary brilliance, and may have been what turned it from an exceptional foray into Middle English prose into the important resource it became. Despite many changes, fourteenth-century vernacular theology revisited several twelfth-century reformist themes in a new idiom: the tension between salvation and perfection as religious goals, the spiritual status of the *literati* and *illiterati*, the meaning of profession, and the place of the institutional life were all fourteenth-century themes as much as they were earlier ones (Watson, 'Censorship'). Although there were many conduits by which these themes reached the fourteenth century, *Ancrene Wisse* was exceptional, I suggest, because it provided reflections on such themes as they applied to the most theoretically problematic category of devout person, female solitaries, and did so in a vernacular medium that by the later period had itself become a bone of theological contention. The mother tongue is not overtly an issue in *Ancrene Wisse* – even if it is the object of a sustained experimentation that could well be read as a commentary on the paradoxically specialized and generalized nature of the profession the work describes. Yet because the work had quasi-official status for anchoritic readers, because of its interest in historicizing its understanding of the life it advocates, and because of the distinctively early thirteenth-century ways in which it alludes to issues still alive in the late fourteenth century, it could stand as an authoritative account of the life of female solitaries which could, nonetheless, be used to advance very complex agendas by later writers. Above all, the work's canonical status meant that borrowing from it or rewriting it could have *symbolic* import, especially for the moderate reformists whose reconception of lay religiosity as a version of the anchoritic life makes them – more than devotional writers such as Rolle and Hilton – *Ancrene Wisse*'s immediate intellectual descendants, and whom this essay sees as the most careful and sophisticated readers of the work.[4] Rather as Rolle's *English Psalter* was cited as a precedent by proponents of Bible translation at the turn of the fifteenth century, while being radically reshaped as an example of how a vernacular Psalter commentary should work (Hudson, 25–27), *Ancrene Wisse* could function for later vernacular writers as a textual synecdoche for the life of holiness as it might be practiced by women and other notionally uneducated Christian people.

The Twelfth-Century Reformation and the Ascetic Ideal

Despite the remarks just made, *Ancrene Wisse* has sometimes been seen as a traditionalist work, dedicated to confirming, more than challenging, exist-ing cultural structures in ways it is hard to associate with reform (e.g. Bennett, 264–75). Even though Geoffrey Shepherd long ago argued for the

---

[4] Contrast Watson, 'The Methods,' which tries to draw *Ancrene Wisse* into the prestigious ambit of mystical writing by associating it with writers like Hilton and even the author of *The Cloud of Unknowing*, who conceive of the holy life as a progressive ascent to God.

work's originality (Shepherd; compare Millett, 'Women'), there are obvious reasons why this picture persists. After all, the work's imagined readers are locked away from the world, shoring up the Church with their constant prayers; keeping eyes, mouths, limbs, thoughts under strict control; sustained only by the prospect of future (and sporadic present) reward, and by the example of the imagined community of earlier solitaries and preachers the author draws together for their comfort. Although the *auctores* it cites include such figures as Bernard of Clairvaux – whose works often depict the ascent to the advanced spiritual states some twelfth-century thinkers considered the true goal of the perfect life – it avoids the topic of union with God (Watson, 'Methods'), just as it does formal theology (Baldwin). If we compare the work's sense of the dangers of the spiritual life with the confidence of Rolle's *Form of Living*, or set its theological allusions alongside the analyses Hilton provided in *The Scale of Perfection*, *Ancrene Wisse* can seem cautious to the point of restrictive-ness. Along the same lines, its assertions that the way of life it describes represents the highest state its women readers will attain can seem to reveal attitudes nothing short of misogynist (Robertson; Bradley; compare Wogan-Browne, 'Chaste Bodies'). Since such views have an inevitable impact on our understanding of the work's influence, I need to give space to a consideration of its reformist agenda, before going on to ask how this was perceived in the two centuries after its composition.

Ancrene Wisse announces at once its interest in finding its own way through the complex of contemporary thinking about religious profession. Bella Millett has devoted two ground-breaking articles to the work's discussion of the 'outer rule,' to the affiliation of its liturgical instructions with the Dominicans, and to its sense of its readers as semi-official, not members of a formal order (Millett, 'Origins', '*Ancrene Wisse* and the Book of Hours'). She argues that the text reflects the Lateran Council's demand that all religious follow an existing rule, but (in its substitution of the Hours of the Virgin Mary for the canonical hours) is also part of the process by which the liturgy was adapted for extra-monastic religious (as in the early Books of Hours), to suit this new cadre of 'semi-educated' contemplatives: a group we should see as defined less by lack of Latinity than by lack of a *guarantee* of Latinity. That is, *Ancrene Wisse* participates at the same time in a tendency to formalize religious profession – anchoresses here take vows rather than simply declaring a *propositum*, as most hermits did and as had earlier been common among all religious professionals (Constable, 'Ceremonies', *Reformation*, 15–18) – and in the opposite tendency to bridge what had once been the clearer conceptual divide between religious and lay Christians.

As will become evident, the paradoxical place *Ancrene Wisse* ascribes itself and its readers is a key to its mediation between twelfth- and fourteenth-century perfectionist and extra-institutional thought. In its opening section, anchoritic readers are told to see the outer rule (the subject of Parts I and VIII) as wholly subordinate to the demands of the inner – a mere handmaid, by no means a habit of living (*conversatio*) that can generate anything of itself, or has more intrinsic usefulness than the laws of mechanics ('*regula recti mechanici*,' f. 1v:7–8). The anchoresses are then given a witty rejoinder to those who ask them to what order they belong, and a historical defence of their lack of institutional status:

> ȝef ei unweote askeð ow of hwet ordre ȝe beon – as summe doð, þe telleð me, þe siheð þe gneat and swolheð þe flehe – ondswerieð: 'Of Sein Iames, þe wes Godes apostel [. . .]' ȝef him þuncheð wunder and sullich of swuch ondswere, easkið him hwet beo ordre, and hwer he funde in Hali Writ religiun openlukest descriue[t] and isutelet þen is i Sein Iames canonial epistel. He seiþ what is religiun, hwuch is riht ordre: *Religio munda et immaculata apud Deum et patrem hec est: visitare pupillos et viduas in necessitate sua et immaculatum se custodire ab hoc seculo* – þat is: 'cleane religiun and wiþute wem is iseon and helpen widewen and federlese children and from þe world witen him cleane and unwemmet.' þus Sein Iame descriueþ religiun and ordre. þe leatere dale of his sahe limpeð to reclusen. [. . .] Pawel, þe earste ancre, Antonie and Arsenie, Makarie and te oþre, neren ha religiuse and of Sein Iames ordre? Alswa Seinte Sare and Seinte Siclecice, and monie oþre swucc, hewepmen ba and wummen, wið hare greate matten and hare hearde heren: neren ha of god ordre? And hweðer hwite oðer blake – as unwise ow askeð, þe weneð þe ordre sitte i þe curtel – Godd wat noðeles ha weren wel baðe: nawt tah onont claðes, ah as Godes spuse singed bi hire seoluen, *Nigra sum set formosa*, 'Ich am blac and tah hwit,' ha seið. (Tolkien, ff. 2v:27–3v:12; punct. modernized)

> If any ignorant person asks you to what order you belong – as you tell me some do, who strain out the gnat and swallow the fly (Matthew 23:24) – answer: 'Of St James, who was God's apostle [. . .]' If such an answer seems strange and wonderful to him, ask him what an order is, and where he finds religion more plainly described and made clear in Holy Writ than it is in St James's canonical epistle. He says what religion is, what makes proper order: *Religio munda et immaculata apud Deum et patrem hec est: visitare pupillos et viduas in necessitate sua et immaculatum se custodire ab hoc seculo* – that is: 'religion pure and without stain is to see and help widows and fatherless children, and to keep oneself from the world, pure and unstained.' Thus St James describes religion and order. The latter part of his saying has to do with recluses. Paul the first anchorite, Anthony and Arsenius, Macarius and the others, were they not religious, and of St James's order? Also St Sarah and St Syncletica and many other such, both men and women, with their rough sleeping-mats and their harsh hair shirts: were they not of good order? And whether they were white or black – as the foolish ask you who believe that the order lies in the habit – God indeed knows that they were truly both: though not in their clothing, but in the sense God's spouse sings of herself, *Nigra sum set formosa* (Canticles 1:5): 'I am black and yet white,' she says.
> (Savage and Watson, 49–50, modified)

Millett may be right to suggest that the author imagines his readers's lack of formal status as a source of anxiety (Millett, '*Ancrene Wisse* and the Book of Hours'). But this passage actually makes the anchoresses into exemplary religious, who more than others preserve the indifference to matters of habit and order felt by the desert hermits and can teach a sharp lesson to anyone who assumes their lives must be defined in merely institutional terms. Giles Constable finds a similar resistance to the concept of order in some twelfth-century reformers, and notes that the *Libellus de diversis ordinibus* regards solitaries as holy *because* of their diversity (Constable, *Reformation*, 58, 60). Just as the beguines, another group of semi-formal religious with pretensions to radical perfection, kept alive through the thirteenth century the dangerous sense that holiness could be anti-institutional by definition (Grundmann, 139–52, 237–45), so *Ancrene Wisse* here suggests an absolute equation between the anchoritic life and the lady (not the servant), the inner (not the outer) rule. And if the practical regulations in Parts I and VIII qualify this equation, the rest of the text reinforces it. So focussed must the anchoresses be on the inner life that to look outside, even to talk to a bishop, unless they must, has grave dangers – for simply glancing out of the window can turn the holiest Judith or Esther into a weak woman, an Eve or a Dinah (Parts II and III).

Such language has been read as mere condescension towards women (Robertson). But *Ancrene Wisse* consistently asserts that the danger anchoresses are in, and the attitude of abject humility they need to maintain in consequence (f. 4r:2–14), is a mark of their importance: elevated to the top of the tower of holiness; pledged to act day and night, through their very being, as an anchor on which the Church depends (ff. 61v:9–19; 38v:26–39r:12). If the text avoids Bernard's elaborations of the perfect life as a systematic ascent to God, this is not because its readers are thought spiritual beginners but because *Ancrene Wisse* is using a different model for the perfect life: one still as alive for the twelfth-century reformers as it was for the fourth-century desert fathers, based on the imitation of Christ through daily ascesis. Bernard and other theorists – Victorines and, later, Franciscan, Dominican, and beguine writers – built up elaborate models of spiritual ascent out of the topos of 'violent love,' in which the entire spiritual life is organized around a single aspect of the self, love (McGinn). But these ascent models always coexisted with ascetic ones that saw the path to perfection in the processes of conversion, penitence, and victory over temptation. Accounts of this path balance the idea of ascent with that of *vicissitude*, an important theme for English spiritual writers, even those influenced by Bernard. Rather than having the soul and God blend like water and wine, this tradition sees the Christian life as martyrdom; as sharing in Christ's suffering; as the always incomplete conquest of world, flesh, and devil (Constable, *Three Studies*, 143–248, *Reformation*, 257–95; Bynum). *Ancrene Wisse* is full of such language. Here, the holy life never moves beyond a fundamental riskiness, as the soul, spurning sin, self, and world, delving for spiritual gold with 'ȝeornful, sechinde þoht: hwer hit beo, hwuch hit beo, hu me hit mahe ifinden,' and busily seeking to 'waden up of unþeawes, creopen ut of flesch, breoken up ouer hire,' all 'wið heate of hungri heorte,' reaches up over and over 'wið heh þoht toward heouene' (f. 29v:5–11).[5]

---

[5] 'And what is that delving? Eager, seeking thought: Where it is; what it is; how it can be found. This

Ascent models of the spiritual life tend to make theoretically strict distinctions between those few who attain perfection and the much larger number who must remain content with mere salvation. Ascetic models often also allow that not all receive equal heavenly reward (as does *Hali Meidhað*); yet the maps of salvation they draw do not thereby treat the ways of salvation and perfection as essentially distinct. A major tool for teaching the Christian life to the late-medieval laity, the Seven Deadly Sins, was partly developed out of Cassian's ruminations on the heroism of the desert fathers, and continued to function at once as part of a minimal account of what the whole Christian community must know to be saved and as a reminder that all are called to holiness (Bloomfield; Constable, *Reformation*, 289–95). One reason *Ancrene Wisse* has been thought to offer only basic instruction is that it is in the advance guard of thought about Christian pedagogy, devoting the whole of Part V (on confession) to material relevant to 'alle men iliche' (f. 93r:3–4; Millett, '*Ancrene Wisse* and the Conditions'), and (especially in Parts IV–VII) presenting the anchoritic life as a version of the life all who desire salvation must live. This stance is compatible with the work's elevation of anchoresses to a position of special attainment. But paradoxically it still acknowledges that, in some respects, they have as much in common with lay-people as they do either with monks and nuns or with the clerics the work regularly satirizes (ff. 12r:1–35, 15v:13): after all, like the laity, anchoresses govern their own spiritual lives without much learning or the security of living under a communal rule. Much as the promotion of 'semi-liturgical devotions' (like those in Book I) among informal religious caused the spread of these devotions to the laity (Millett, '*Ancrene Wisse* and the Book'), so the work's articulation of an ascetic ideal in the vernacular gave it from the start a pioneering role as a conduit of all aspects of anchoritic spirituality beyond the cell into the world. In other words, *Ancrene Wisse* points directly forward to a four-teenth-century world in which the laity, not the female solitary, slowly becomes the object of vernacular anxiety and attention.

Ancrene Wisse *and the Professional Religious*

Ancrene Wisse's argument that order and the outer rule are of small importance for its semi-religious readers is echoed in different ways by the two great anchoritic guides of the fourteenth century, Rolle's *Form of Living* and Book I of Hilton's *Scale of Perfection*, both of which emphasize the interior life over the exterior to the extent that they are close to undoing all distinction between the female solitary and the devout lay-person. As such, these guides are part of a laicizing trend towards thinking of any vernacular religious writing as aimed at a general Christian readership: a

---

is the delving: to be busily and eagerly always about it, with a constant yearning, with the heat of the hungry heart; to wade up out of sin; to creep out of the flesh; to break up above her; to rise above her on your own with high thought toward heaven' (Savage and Watson, 89). *Ancrene Wisse* only once suggests that spiritual peace can be found in this life (f. 59v:9–10).

trend in which, despite fierce disagreements over its implications, most vernacular theologians after 1370 participate, reformist and conservative alike (Watson, 'Middle English Mystics', 'Politics'). All but three of the works that make use of *Ancrene Wisse* explicitly address a general audience (or a single member of the laity), and to that extent acknowledge its relevance to those who are not solitaries – although several of them borrow only a few passages of the work. Even the three works written for solitaries or nuns (Book I of *The Scale of Perfection*, *The Chastising of God's Children*, and *þe Pater Noster of Richard Ermyte*), are aware of (and were read by) the laity. Yet the works that use *Ancrene Wisse* do not always share the same views about the intellectual or spiritual capacities of their readers, lay or religious, and their attitude to their source varies accordingly. The rest of this paper divides responses to *Ancrene Wisse* into three groups: works that, whatever their intended audience, treat it as a specialized guide for professional religious or semi-religious; works that tap it for expositions of Christian living aimed, usually, at the devout laity; and finally works that consist of adaptations of all or part of the text, also for the devout laity. Such was the intensity of debate, however, about the role of vernacular theology, the place of the laity in religious practice, and the nature of authentic religious living itself, that even within these groups there is variety, and sometimes disagreement.

Three works conceptualize *Ancrene Wisse* as a specialized text for professional religious. All of these works are variously committed to an understanding of the perfect life as a progressive ascent to God, not as the ascetic imitation of Christ, and all assume respectful familiarity with *Ancrene Wisse*. But their attitude to their joint source is different. One seeks to protect lay readers from material too advanced for them. Another uses passages of *Ancrene Wisse* to introduce an exposition of the perfect life which has a specialized original audience but invites a broader readership. And a third disagrees with *Ancrene Wisse* about how an anchoress should conduct herself, in a way that threatens to break down the distinction between professional and lay audiences altogether.

Nicholas Love's *Mirror of the Blessed Life of Jesus Christ* (c.1409) is a paraphrase of the popular *Meditationes vitae Christi*, a devotional life of Christ originally written for a nun by a Franciscan, Johannes de Caulibus. Love, prior of the Carthusian house of Mount Grace (Yorkshire), conceived his adaptation as a conservative response to the Wycliffite Bible and designed it to compete for the attention of the same general lay audience targeted by the Lollards. It became a quasi-official devout book after receiving endorsement from Archbishop Arundel, was widely copied and read in its revised form, and was printed early and often (Salter; Sargent, 1992).

An early draft of the *Mirror* contains an allusion to Part I of *Ancrene Wisse* at the end of one of Love's substantial additions to his source: a schematic account of the five joys of Mary, in which each is linked to a clause of the prayer *Ave Maria* and the virtues of meekness, chastity, faith, hope, and charity. Love sums up his account in a brief, alliterative mnemonic prayer ('*Heil Marie*, maiden mekest, / Gret of angel Gabriel in Jesu graciouse conceyuyng./ *Ful of grace*, as modere chast/ without sorow or peyne þi son, Jesu blessed beryng,' etc. [Sargent, 1992, 29:33–36]). He then adds a note that seems to apply not simply to the prayer but to the entire addition:

> Thus þinketh me may be had contemplacion more conueniently after þe ordre of þe fyue ioyes of our lady, Seynt Marye, in þe forseide gretynge, *Aue Maria et cetera*, þan was bifore writen to þe Ankeresse, as it scheweþ here. Chese he þat liste to rede or write þis processe as him semeþ best, or in oþer manere ȝif he kan, so þat – be it one, be it oþere – þe ende and þe entente be to þe worshippe and plesynge of oure lord Jesu and his blessed moder, Marye. (Salter, 33)

This note is omitted in the final draft of the text, which allows readers and copiers no such freedoms.

Behind Love's composition of a 'more conuenient' exposition of the *Ave Maria* than *Ancrene Wisse*'s – despite the pressure he feels to follow the latter – seems to lie anxiety about the suitability of the earlier prayer for a general audience. The main difference between the two passages is that, where *Ancrene Wisse* creates a play of identifications between the anchoress, Gabriel, and the Virgin – echoing standard practice in many kinds of prayer or meditation – *The Mirror* gives a historical exposition of the five joys which keeps present and past, reader and subject, firmly separate:

> Leafdi seinte Marie, for þe ilke muchele blisse þet tu hefdest inwið þe i þet ilke time þet Iesu Godd, Godes sune, efter þe engles gretunge nom flesch and blod in þe and of þe: underfeng mi gretunge wið þe ilke *Aue*. And make me telle lutel of euch blisse utewið, ah froure me inwið and ernde me þeo of heouene. Ant ase wis as i þe ilke flesch þet he toc of þe nes neauer sunne – ne i þin as me leueð efter þe ilke tacunge, hwet se biuore were – clense mi sawle of fleschliche sunnen.
> (*Ancrene Wisse*, Tolkien, f. 9r:27–9v:7)[6]

> In þe first part of þis gretyng þat stant in þees tweyn wordes, *Heyl Marie*, þow maiȝt vndirstond þe first ioy þat she hade in hire Annunciacion of Jesu gracious conceyuyng, of þe which mekenes was þe grounde [. . .] And as þees wordes, *Heil Marie*, bene þe first and þe bygynnyng of þis gretyng, so þis fest was þe bygynnyng and þe gronde of al oþere.
> (*Mirror*, Sargent, 1992, 28:15–21)

Despite its early instruction to the reader to 'make þe in þi soule present to þoo þinges þat bene here writen, seyd, or done of oure Lord Jesu, and þat bisily, likyngly and abydyngly' (13:1–3), Love's text is far from offering

---

[6] 'O Lady St Mary, for the same great joy that you had within you in that time that Jesus God, God's Son, after the angel's greeting, took flesh and blood in you and of you, accept my greeting with the same *Hail*. And make me count every outward joy as little; but comfort me within, and send me the joys of heaven. And as surely as in the same flesh that he took from you there was never sin, nor in your own after that same taking, whatever may have been before, cleanse my soul from fleshly sins' (Savage and Watson, 61). Perhaps Love also objected to 'hwet se biuore were,' with its implication that even the Virgin required purification from sin.

readers the intimacy with the scene of Christ's life and death Part VI of *Ancrene Wisse* conveys in presenting anchoresses as 'niht and dei up o Godes rode' (f. 94r:16–17). Indeed, in his treatment of the *Ave Maria*, we see Love, a professional contemplative, flinching from the idea that the laity can ever do more than observe, rather than imitate, the characters in the sacred drama.

The Chastising of God's Children (c.1395) is a treatise on tribulation and contemplation partly compiled from recent continental sources – Jan van Ruusbroec's *Spiritual Espousals*, Alphonse of Pecha's *Epistola solitarii*, and Henry Suso's *Horologium sapientiae* – partly from passages of Isidore, Gregory, Cassian, Anselm, Bernard, and Aelred. The work is addressed to a 'religious sister' (Bazire and Colledge, 95:1), perhaps a nun of Barking, a convent that according to another treatise, *The Cleansing of Man's Soul*, had a copy in its library before 1401.[7] Its fifteenth-century readership may have consisted mainly of professional religious, but it survives in twelve manuscripts, and was excerpted in later compilations and printed in 1491 (Bazire and Colledge).

The Chastising is divided into chapters suitable for refectory reading, each ending with the verse: '*Uigilate et orate, ut non intretis in temptacionem*; wakeþ and preieþ, þat ȝe entre nat into temptacion' (Bazire and Colledge, 96:12–13; Matthew 26:41). The chapters deal with many issues – the stages of contemplative ascent, predestination, visions and their validity – which are discussed in an apparently cautionary way as so many spiritual tests. The first chapter of the work describes God's tendency to apply such tests in terms derived from Part IV of *Ancrene Wisse*:

> þerfore he is disceyued þat weneþ he be hooli for he is nat tempted. For soþ it is, goode men and wymmen þat trauelen to be parfite bien more tempted þanne oþer whiche bien recheles of lyuynge. And a skille whi: for þe hiȝer þat a mounteyn is, þere is the gretter wynd. In þe same maner, þe hiȝer a mannes lyuynge be, þe strennger is þe temptacioun of his goostli enemye. Wherfore if men or wymmen of religion or of any parfeccion fele no temptacioun, þanne ouȝten þei sorrest to drede, for þanne bien thei most tempted whanne þei felen hem nat tempted [. . .] Also whanne oure Lord suffrith us to be tempted, in oure bigynnynge he pleieþ wiþ us as þe moder with hir child, whiche sumtyme fleeth awei and hideþ hir, and suffreþ þe child to wepe and crie and beseli to seke hir wiþ sobbynge and wepynge. But þanne comeþ þe moder sodeinli wiþ meri chier and lauȝhynge, biclippynge hir child and kissynge, and wipeþ awei þe teeris. þus fariþ oure Lord wiþ us [. . .] (97:12–98:9)[8]

---

[7] 'Of this mater ȝe haue in a boke of Englisch, I trowe, which is cleped amonges ȝow *þe Chastising of Goddes Children*' (Regan, 220). 'ȝow' here is likely either the Barking nuns or a group of nuns associated with Sibylle de Felton, abbess of Barking in 1401, the date given at the end of the manuscript (Oxford, Bodleian Library MS 923), along with a colophon identifying the book as hers.

[8] See *Ancrene Wisse*, f. 47v:21–29 and 62v:1–16. As Bazire and Colledge point out, the immediate source for this part of the *Chastising* may be a brief Latin compilation known as *Quandocumque tribularis*, also used by the author of *Pore Caitif*. Chapter 2 of *The Chastising* is drawn directly from this same section of *Ancrene Wisse* (Part IV), establishing that the author knew the work independently of the compilation (Bazire and Colledge, 259–66).

The second part of this passage also gives the work its title and is carefully extrapolated in chapter 5, which imagines the harsher discipline the mother metes out to the child as it grows older.

By contrast with *The Mirror*, *The Chastising* – written for a self-consciously specialized readership – is secure in its relationship with its predecessor, borrowing passages that emphasize the difference between those who seek for perfection and ordinary Christians, and describing how God's 'queynt pleie' with the soul becomes fiercer as the soul progresses in virtue, as God smites the soul if it tries to 'walke abrode' in vanity or negligence (115:1). The structuring role given the passages from *Ancrene Wisse* in this sophisticated compilation can be read two ways. On the one hand, the emphasis on temptation evoked by chapter-by-chapter repetition of *Vigilate et orate* and described at the work's outset serves to contain the speculative tendencies the work at once instructs its readers to resist and struggles to resist itself. Thus *Ancrene Wisse*, representative of an ancient insular spiritual tradition, here acts to normalize an effervescent mixture of material daringly imported from the continent. On the other hand, however, *The Chastising* also presents itself as an *extrapolation* of the earlier work: as though all it takes from the Dutch and Rhineland schools of mysticism, or from Alphonse on the visionary experiences of Bridget of Sweden, is latent in the earlier work's discussion of the difficulties and comforts of the perfect life. Here, then, the canonical status of *Ancrene Wisse* as a paradigmatic account of the trials of the contemplative life and its emphasis on the ascetic rather than the mystical are acknowledged at once. By using *Ancrene Wisse* to make the space within which it can come into being, *The Chastising* not only offers further testimony to the earlier work's status in late fourteenth-century England, but suggests how flexibly it could be understood and updated.

Walter Hilton's *Scale of Perfection*, Book I (c.1385–90) is a religious guide consisting of descriptions of the kinds of contemplative experience and detailed expositions of how to confront the image of sin in the self. Hilton, an Augustinian canon at Thurgarton (Northamptonshire), wrote the work for an unnamed anchoress, but later (before 1396) added a second book which turned the work as a whole into a guide to holy living and the fundamentals of theology for a broader audience, again written partly in opposition to Lollard and reformist writings. Book I circulated widely, both on its own and with Book II, and the complete work was printed by Wynkyn de Worde as early as 1494. Although it has its peculiarities, the work is often taken as an exemplary essay in moderation, and seems to have held the interest of a range of readers – including, for example, the author of *The Cloud of Unknowing*, Margery Kempe, and the Carmelite Thomas Fyslake, who translated both books into Latin – from the time of its composition on (Hussey; Clark and Dorward).

Chapters 78–82 of Book I of *The Scale* describe the senses as windows of the soul, which must be kept shut in order not to feed the image of sin that overlays the soul's divine nature. Clark and Dorward (182–84) note parallels with Bernard's *De gradibus humilitatis et superbiae*, also the source of a similar passage at the opening of Part II of *Ancrene Wisse* (f. 12v). But Hilton seems to be thinking of the vernacular work as well, for chapter 83 concerns the reception of visitors: a topic not mentioned by Bernard but which *Ancrene Wisse* (f. 15) juxtaposes with its discussion of the windows of the soul. Hilton's advice is completely different from *Ancrene Wisse*'s injunctions to avoid contact with the outside world. Just as earlier chapters (75–77) insist that only love can direct decisions as to what food to eat, so this passage puts love, not fear, at the centre of its thinking:

> þou art bounden (as ilk man and woman is) to loue þin euencristen principaly in þi hert, and also in dede forto schewe hym tokens of charité as reson askez, up þi my3t and þi knowyng. Now syn it is so þat þou ow3ez no3t go out of þi house forto seke occasion how þou my3t profite þin euencristen by dedes of mercie, bycause þat þou art enclose, neuerþeles þou art bounden forto [loue] hem all in þi hert, and to hem þat comen to þe forto schewe [hem] tokens of loue sothfastly. And þerfor whoso wil speke with þe (what þat he be, in what degré he be), and þou knowe no3t what he is ne whi he comez, be sone redy with a gode will forto witt what [h]is will is. Be no3t doungerous, ne suffre hym no3t long forto abide þe . . . (Bliss, Hussey and Sargent, forthcoming)

This is almost the only passage in *The Scale* to discuss what *Ancrene Wisse* calls the outer rule.

Hilton's objection to *Ancrene Wisse*'s injunctions against receiving visitors should be read in light of a broad fourteenth-century English reaction against asceticism and tendency to emphasize *discretio* at the expense of physical penance.[9] Yet this tendency was itself part of the process of laicization, making the lives of solitaries and religious less harsh and so less distinct, and it is notable that Hilton refers to the enclosed state of his reader here only because he is advising her to overcome, so far as possible, the differences between her way of life and that of those who can 'profite [their] euencristen by dedes of mercie' – the laity. Enclosure is here a formality or even a disadvantage, as Hilton imagines a version of the solitary life in which the anchoress busies herself with both halves of St James's definition of 'cleane religiun,' not only keeping herself 'cleane and unwemmet' but also striving to 'helpen widewen and federlese children' (as *Ancrene Wisse* has it). Hilton was a defender of religious orders (author of a treatise *De utilitate et prerogativis religionis* [Clark and Taylor]), as well as of distinctions between the obligations of the laity and others (as in his *Mixed Life* [Ogilvie-Thomson], and *Epistola ad quemdam seculo renunciare volentem* [Clark and Taylor]). But his unwillingness to justify the solitude of the solitary here anticipates the shift of imagined audience between the two books of *The Scale of Perfection* – from solitary anchoress to any devout

---

[9] This reaction is evident in the writings of Rolle, who denies all value to self-mortification (Watson, *Richard Rolle*, chapter 2). *Ancrene Wisse* is itself a harbinger of this reaction: its prescriptions are much softer than those of its most important insular source, Aelred's *De institutione inclusarum*, and the prominence it gives to the virtue of *discretio* much more pronounced.

and reasonably well-informed member of the laity – and the collapse of the sense of distinctiveness he at first sought to attribute to the figure of the anchoress.[10]

Pore Caitif *and Other Anonymous Compilations*

All the other works that make significant use of *Ancrene Wisse* in the period 1370–1450 assume or argue the conclusion to which *The Scale of Perfection* tends: that the life of perfection followed by anchoresses is directly relevant to the devout laity. Yet in these other works, as not for Hilton, this position is the result of two reciprocal processes: not only a process of *generalization*, in which the notion of spiritual perfection comes to be thought of as detachable from its professional base in the contemplative life and so available to everyone, particularly the laity; but also a process we can term *puritanization*, in which devout members of the laity are invited to imagine themselves as separated from the wider Christian community – often redefined in such texts as 'the world,' the enemy of virtuous living – by their adoption of a form of perfect living that turns them into spiritual equivalents of solitaries. These processes are worked out differently in different texts – sometimes in more radical ways, sometimes in less – but in some combinations their effect is to suggest opposite constructions of the imagined lay audience: as incorporating a group that notionally consists of everybody, since all should listen to the call to a holy life; but also as including only the few who actually heed this universal appeal. In other words, the audience of these works tends to be understood simultaneously as a community of the chosen and as the representatives of the entire Church militant on earth. In most of *Ancrene Wisse*'s late-medieval derivatives, it is this imagined community of serious-minded lay-people, not anchoresses, who are the direct descendants of the semi-regular contemplatives for whom the work was originally written. It is they who inherit the paradoxically mixed status that *Ancrene Wisse* attributes to female solitaries – holy but frail, potentially rich in spiritual experience but lacking in formal religious knowledge – and they who by their lack of external signs of religious status (habits, vows, Latinity) represent the culmination of that work's stated indifference to the outer rule.

Four of the six works concerned are compilations which use excerpts of *Ancrene Wisse* in their address to a lay audience (or, in one case, a nun). Although these works are theologically and structurally very different – one is a stage-by-stage ascent to God, one a rule, one a pastoral treatise, one a

---

[10] Mention should be made of the Vernon copy of *Ancrene Wisse* (*The Roule of Reclous*), as this manuscript may have been made for nuns (Doyle, *Vernon*; Zettersten, 2000). *Ancrene Wisse* is the last major prose work in the manuscript, after works by Rolle, Hilton (including Book I of *The Scale*) and others. Its placement suggests its niche in the tradition of devout, non-polemical treatises Vernon sought to create, but the carefulness of the copy – by contrast, e.g., with Vernon's two adaptations of Edmund's *Mirror*, which are much freer – paradoxically suggests it may have been included in part for completeness' sake. The work is omitted from Vernon's partial twin, Simeon, which substitutes a copy of the pastoral treatise *The Book of Vices and Virtues* (Francis).

commentary – they share a conception of themselves as compendia: complete guides to holy living that suggest equally complete visions of the nature and status of their audiences.

Pore Caitif (c.1370s) is a collection of pastoral and affective tracts said to have been compiled to 'teche symple men and wymmen of good will þe riȝt weie to heuene,' in the form of 'a laddir of dyuerse rongis,' up which the reader ascends 'fro vertu into vertu' (Brady, *'Pore Caitif'*, 1:1–2:9). The ladder consists of expositions of the faith (the Creed, the Ten Commandments, the Lord's Prayer), followed by a set of 'short sentencis excitinge men to heuenli desiir,' grouped under the rubric 'þe Councel of Crist,' and again organized as a ladder. Where the first part of the compilation expounds the truths necessary to salvation – which for this text consist of orthodox belief, rules for Christian living, and due reverence to God in prayer – the second part is organized as an ascent to the perfect life, adapting relatively specialized material for the devout lay reader, who is instructed to 'stie up fro oon to anoþir as he is clepid of [God], sum in hier, sum in lower, as he is ablid of God þerto' (174:6–7) – that is, to use as much of this second part as she or he finds applicable. Addressing a plural audience whose members are expected to attain different levels of perfection, *Pore Caitif* is the most generously inclusive – if also the least specific in its instructions – of the works considered in this essay. Moreover, the surviving copies of *Pore Caitif*, mostly consisting of extracts, suggest that the work did appeal to a wide variety of lay readers, including some well below the social level of the gentry, while the fact that the work also survives in a Lollard-interpolated version suggests there was a radical side to its inclusiveness (Lagorio and Sargent, 3135, 3470; Brady, 'Lollard Interpolations').

The brief tract derived from Part IV of *Ancrene Wisse* (via the Latin *Quandocumque tribularis*, see note 8), 'Off temptacioun,' is one of the earliest of the 'short sentencis' in the second section of the work, located after penitential extracts on conversion from Rolle's *Emendatio Vitae* and *Form of Living*, and before a pair of allegories ('þe Chartre of Oure Heuenli Eritage' and 'Off Goostli Batel') which move the work towards more affective material. Where *The Chastising* uses the same passages from Part IV as a preliminary statement of an entire ambitious thesis, *Pore Caitif* treats them as a stage on the way to holiness, in theory implying that readers who progress beyond this 'sentence' on their way to God leave this stage behind.[11] We could take this as a sign that the *Pore Caitif* compiler viewed *Ancrene Wisse*, built on an ascetic rather than an ascent model, as a limited, even primitive, guide to perfect living compared to the writings of Rolle. Yet the last section of *Pore Caitif*, a '[Myrour] off Chastite' written by the compiler, returns lay readers to the very mode of asceticism the 'short sentencis' ostensibly leave behind, discussing virginity, chastity, and continence as essential religious ideals, and introducing them with an account

---

[11] The compiler's model here may be Rolle's *Emendatio vitae*, organized along similar lines, from which *Pore Caitif* borrows much material (Watson, *Richard Rolle*, 207–21; Brady, 'Rolle').

of the custody of the senses that contains several possible reminiscences of Part II of *Ancrene Wisse* (Brady, '*Pore Caitif*', 176, 179). Not only is *Ancrene Wisse* thus a more important presence in the text than it at first seems. *Pore Caitif*'s use of an ascent model is revealed as partly a heuristic device which finally leaves the earlier work's ascetic understanding of the spiritual life as struggle and vicissitude largely intact.

þe *Holy Boke Gratia Dei*, þe *Pater Noster of Richard Ermyte* and *Book for a Simple and Devout Woman* are so closely related they can be discussed together. F. N. M. Diekstra has shown how these works – which may originate from a centre in the north-east Midlands – draw not only on each other but on 'a common fund of source material' that includes: Peraldus's *Summa de vitiis et virtutibus* (a main source for the *Book*, with the *Somme le Roi* and two other pastoral compilations); pseudo-Chrysostom's *Opus imperfectum in Matthaeum* (also a source for the last section of *Pore Caitif*); Edmund's *Speculum religiosorum*; and various passages of *Ancrene Wisse*, especially Parts II and III (Diekstra, *Book*, 316–28).[12] Although the compilations tend to hold orthodox views on such matters as confession and priesthood, the 'network of connections' that emerges as the very complex relationships between them and their sources are traced associates all three of them with other texts and manuscripts of reformist or Lollard derivation, which tend to share their puritanical outlook.[13] These compilations also testify to a clerical milieu in which *Ancrene Wisse* was closely read – perhaps in more than one form (Diekstra, *Book*, 319) – accorded equal status with Latin and French writings, and internalized to the point where its rhythms and images arose unbidden in the minds of compilers.

þe *Holy Boke Gratia Dei* (1370–1400) is a tripartite guide to devout living for a lay readership, which develops a set of instructions about prayer, the use of time, meditation, and daily conduct, out of a discussion of divine grace and its relation to the vigorous exercise of free will. Although its brief is narrower, it can be taken as a 'lay rule' on the model of *Ancrene Wisse*, with an emphasis on the outer rule. Instead of the instructions for life in the cell given in Part VIII of *Ancrene Wisse*, for example, þe *Holy Boke* ends with advice on how to live in the world without mingling with it, how to avoid contact with sin when travelling, even what sort of inn to use (Arntz, 112–16). The work survives in three manuscripts, always in partial form (Arntz; Keiser).

þe *Pater Noster of Richard Ermyte* (1370–1400) is a long exposition of the Lord's Prayer, attributed to (although not by) Rolle, which is addressed to a nun, a 'dere sistir in God, Goddis hondemayden and his spouse' (Aarts,

---

[12] þe *Holy Boke* also shares material with the Middle English *Ladder of Four Rungs*, *Abbey of the Holy Ghost*, *Sawles Warde*, *Three Arrows*, and *Milicia Christi*, probably borrowing from all of these, as the *Book* borrows from the last of them (Arntz, xliv–lix).

[13] For example, the group has some connection with the sermons in Cambridge, Sidney Sussex MS 74, copied by a scribe who also copied the important West Midland reformist treatise *Book to a Mother* and supervised the production of a manuscript of the Wycliffite Bible (Fletcher; Watson, 'Devotion'). By way of þe *Pater Noster*, it can be linked with another network of texts Ralph Hanna has identified in his study of London, Westminster School MS 3, a network that also includes *Book to a Mother*, þe *Lyfe of Soule*, and some other controversial works (Hanna).

3:1). Like the previous work, þe Pater Noster has encyclopaedic pretensions (since the Lord's Prayer 'biloukeþ al þat we haue nede of to lyf or to soule' [4:2]), offering an overview of theology and salvation history and a sometimes satirical view of Church and society, in its attempt to provide a clause-by-clause 'vndirstondynge' of the Lord's Prayer presently available only to 'men of religioun and oþer clerkis.' (3:11, 7–8). The work survives in six manuscripts, several of them with reformist or Lollard connections (Aarts; Fletcher).

Book for a Simple and Devout Woman (1370–1400) is a lengthy exposition of the Seven Deadly Sins (figured by the seven heads of the beast in chapter 13 of Revelation), addressed in its sole complete manuscript (London, British Library MS Harley 6571) to a lay woman, but of broader relevance. With its many subdivisions, the work in some ways resembles the Sins section of a manual like The Book of Vices and Virtues (Francis). However, rather as in Piers Plowman (Schmidt, B, passus V), the whole of Christian society is scrutinized under the heading of one sin or another, with the effect that much of the work consists of commentary or satire on Church and society, not personal instruction. A partial copy of the work in a second manuscript (London, British Library MS Additional 30944), contains a number of additional passages that take the work's satirical tendency to a radical extreme, and have clear parallels with Lollard polemic (Diekstra, Book, 49–51).

The specific borrowings from Ancrene Wisse in these three works are identified by their editors but are too many to enumerate here. The compilers used various short passages as rhetorical colouring; longer descriptions like those of the backbiter and jangler; and a few more systematic didactic discussions, seamlessly weaving all these into discussions taken from other sources. What is most interesting for my purposes, though, is how often all these works, in evoking Ancrene Wisse, give themes typical of twelfth-century reformism a fourteenth-century reformist twist.

For example, the longest borrowings from Ancrene Wisse in þe Holy Boke – a passage on keeping silence from Part II (Arntz, 32:9–35:7, Ancrene Wisse, ff. 17–20) and the 'nightbird' passage with eight reasons for keeping vigil from Part III (67:11–69:12, Ancrene Wisse, f. 39) – are central to this text's attempt to organize the lay reader's life as far as possible along anchoritic or conventual lines. Such a project is often discussed by modern scholarship under the heading of 'mixed' life, on the model of Hilton's treatise Mixed Life. Yet even though þe Holy Boke does acknowledge that different demands are made on different kinds of Christian – early rising for prayer is especially the job of 'mene of relegione [. . .] men of haly kyrke [. . .] and also maydens and wedous' (62:16–20) – the work assimilates the lay Christian to the life of holiness more fully than does Hilton. Here, grace and abundant heavenly reward are granted to 'ilk a mane of what state he be' whose behaviour is appropriate to his status: who does 'honeste werke withowttene lettynge of his tyme'; and whose 'uttire berynge, whareso he comes, so honeste be and faire þat louynge be to God and stirryng of gude all þat hym seese' (15:13–21). The author supplements the material he takes from *Ancrene Wisse* with passages on the same subjects from other sources, and some of the middle part of the work strikes off in its own direction with material on private devotion, the need for an affective relation with Jesus, and the terrors of the Day of Judgement (75–100). But the structure of *þe Holy Boke*, and the tenor of its argument, are suggestive of how closely he had read *Ancrene Wisse* as a whole, meditated on its ambition and refusal to define its readers in institutionalized terms, then used this refusal to recast the idea of a religious rule and the idea of the laity in new forms.

þe Pater Noster also rethinks the idea of a rule, and does so in such a manner as to challenge any notion its first intended reader, a nun, may have had that her status made her special or different from others. The work's opening justifies its vernacular project by using a common topos about how 'women þat beþ religious, al ʒif þei kun rede and synge and here preier make as falliþ to religious, noʒt forþi vndirstondynge hem wantiþ,' as though the work is going to contain material specific to the conventual life (Aarts, 3:9–11).[14] But although a later passage of *þe Pater Noster* does describe a rule, this proves not to be the Benedictine or any other formal religious rule, but a series of injunctions extrapolated from the curse laid on Adam after the fall – 'in swoot of þi face þou schalt ete þi breed' (13:35) – which all alike, religious and lay, are obliged to obey. Before the fall, Adam 'was in an ordre softe and ful of likyng al at his wille'; with sin, however, God imposed this 'reule, wheraftir he and al his osprynge schulde reule here fleisch . . . a new reule, swiþe hard to þole' (13:25–26, 21–2, 32–3), consisting of laws against 'idilnes, glotenye [and] gelous kepynge and tendre ouer þe fleisch' (14:1). The penitential life *þe Pater Noster* demands of readers – consisting of hard work, self-restraint, and sobriety, especially in matters of food, sex, and clothing – thus in practice has little to do with the conventual life except on the level of imagery.

However, where *þe Holy Boke* – developing its argument from its early discussion of the need to prepare the soul for God's grace – offers a relatively mechanical picture of the devout life, *þe Pater Noster* follows *Ancrene Wisse* by juxtaposing its discussion of the need for bodily discipline with an account of the inner virtue of charity: even if someone should 'do bodily werkis as tiliand men don, or wastiþ hymself wiþ swynk as werkmen don, or goostly werkis deliten hym to don as to pyne his fleisch wiþ fastynge, [. . .] þe hungri to fede, þe nakede to cloþe, and oþer dedis of mercy to do hem alle on row, [. . .] but þei in loue be don and in charite, to þe pyne of helle dampned may he be' (16:34–17:2). For 'charite is þat oon weiʒte þat schal weiʒen oure mede þat we schulen haue' (17:36–37, echoing *Ancrene Wisse*, f. 104v:19–20: 'luue ane schal beon ileid i Seinte Mihales weie'). This emphasis on love is important to remember, because the devil, finding direct methods unsuccessful, is especially likely to tempt 'goode religious' to climb the ladder to heaven unwarily by egging her or him on to 'werkis of penaunce' so harsh that 'his kynde enfeblischiþ and his spirit

---

[14] Compare the prologues to *The Mirror of Our Lady* and Richard Fox's translation of *The Benedictine Rule* (Wogan-Browne *et al.*, excerpts 2.8 and 3.12).

bicomiþ al dul and his loue keliþ' (48:4–8, a passage that echoes *Ancrene Wisse*, ff. 60r:19–60v:21). Although its borrowings from *Ancrene Wisse* are relatively few, *þe Pater Noster* thus weaves one of the earlier work's central motifs into its extrapolation, from a single prayer, of the whole of Christian history and ethics, written not only to enforce obedience to a set of commandments in 'Goddis seruauntis' but to assist 'Goddis louers,' for whom 'fastyng, wakyng and oþere hardschipes' are merely 'lomes that helpiþ as to þe ende' which is 'þe loue of God' (54:15–18, echoing *Ancrene Wisse*, f. 104r:1–18).

This interplay between love and obedience to a rule grows out of a more complex reading of *Ancrene Wisse* than is found in *þe Holy Boke* or *Pore Caitif* – and it is has theological consequences in the form of an especially rigorous theology of salvation. *þe Holy Boke* views God as always ready to bestow saving grace, if only it were not true that 'of als mykell folk as now is, of lered and lewd, so foue will swynke to wyne þis grace of God' (Arntz, 99:7–8). By contrast, *þe Pater Noster*'s analysis of '*Adueniat regnum tuum* [. . .] come to us þi rewme' (Aarts, 30:28–30) describes the devout life as a brutal competition between Christians for an unknown but small number of seats at the heavenly banquet (34–35), and ends with a thought 'þat wondirfully greueþ: þat noon may wyterly vndirstonde ȝif he be in charite – for alle þe werkis þat he doiþ he may do hem þoruȝ pride' (56:10–12). Although *Ancrene Wisse*'s caution over salvation is much more carefully particularized than this (compare f. 4r), the exclusivity of this position – which we will meet again – has roots in that work's elevation of its readers to a position of exemplary, if imperilled, holiness, and is part and parcel of the puritanizing tendency at work in this body of texts. Here again, then, we see a version of the process of theological translation that typifies later responses to *Ancrene Wisse* in operation.

Book for a Simple and Devout Woman is the longest of the three works and makes the most extensive use of *Ancrene Wisse*: sometimes to colour or elaborate material derived from Peraldus or the *Somme le Roi* but several times to structure a discussion of some branch of a sin.[15] Drawing extensively on *þe Pater Noster* as it does on *þe Holy Boke* (unless the borrowings are the other way around, or involve an undiscovered common source), the *Book* uses one passage of *Ancrene Wisse*, on how 'hope and dred schulen aa beon imengt togederes' (Tolkien, f. 90r:24–25) to articulate a salvation theology that is cautiously more optimistic than *þe Pater Noster* (Diekstra, *Book*, 1332–56) – although sharing with that work, and with *Ancrene Wisse*, a particular fear of vainglory, the sin that 'kenly [. . .] assayleþ' even 'Godis derworthe children' (909; see also 888–93, which echoes *Ancrene Wisse*, f. 36r:1–4). But its most sustained use of *Ancrene Wisse* and its ascetic model of the spiritual life is more particular than that of its fellow compilations. Like these, the *Book* focusses on topics relevant to all Christians in its depiction of the Church as a community of souls

---

[15] For the first see, e.g., the discussion of anger (*Book*, chapters 22–27); for the second, the discussion of the sins of the mouth (*Book*, especially chapter 92).

working their way in hope towards salvation, while also offering advice specific to different constituencies within the framework of its address to a particular reader. The last section of the work, on the Sins of the Mouth, several times makes this particular reader – named in the last chapter as 'my dere suster,' and in a closing rubric as *'cuisdam muleris simplicis et deuote'* (7620, 7661) – the object of instruction on the basis of her gender, and twice invokes *Ancrene Wisse* for this purpose. Whereas chapter 95, on the sin of 'vnwise silence,' names priests as having a duty 'þurh cure þe peple to teche' (7569–70), chapter 92's account of the sin of 'muchel speche' repeats the contrast between Eve and Mary found in *Ancrene Wisse*, Part II (f. 16), which it introduces with: 'So to wommen hit semeþ vuel to be of myche speche' (7478). This chapter is indeed more insistent on silence as a feminine virtue, speech as a feminine vice, than *Ancrene Wisse*, which moves between gendered and general instances of both.[16] Again, in the *Book*'s penultimate chapter, 'silence of religion' is described using another passage of *Ancrene Wisse*, Part II (f. 20). Here, the injunction to silence is partly directed at monks, who are contrasted with the talkative teaching priests of the previous chapter. But the chapter's placement so near both the discussion of Eve and the work's end have the effect of making the injunction read as a summation of what the *Book* says to devout women in particular: that 'riȝtwisnesse of silence brynguþ fruyte of pes' (7593–95, echoing *Ancrene Wisse*, f. 20r:10).

So far, the *Book*'s use of *Ancrene Wisse* seems to revolve around simple gender stereotyping. Yet there is something anxiously incongruous about a work that imparts so much information not simply about personal sin but about social wrongdoing to a woman reader who is then enjoined to a silence that would prevent her from passing any of it on, and it may be that these final chapters should be read as problematizing the notion of an undifferentiated, essentially ungendered devout readership the rest of the *Book* accepts. Specifically, the *Book* may be reacting to a late fourteenth-century debate about the teaching roles of women: a debate that sporadically issued in suggestions that women should even be allowed to preach, as well as to teach other women in private (Cross; Aston), and that has been argued to lie behind Chaucer's depiction of the Wife of Bath as a preacher (Blamires).[17] For the *Book*'s final chapter (chapter 97) is an address to the reader that appeals to her to avoid the very variety of contemporary female spirituality – one centred around visionary experiences – most likely to result in women's annexation of the right to preach or teach:

My dere suster, my counsaile is þat þu fiȝte aȝeyn vayneglorie, for þerof þu art moste fondud. Dremes and siȝtes þat þu seest in þi slepe, ȝeue to

---

[16] Compare, e.g., *Ancrene Wisse*'s quotation from Seneca, *'ad summam uolo uos esse rari loquas tuncque pauciloquas,'* which applies this advice not only to the anchoresses but to Job's counsellors (Tolkien, f. 18r:11–12), with the *Book*'s redirection of the same saying: 'Forþi Senek spekeþ to wommen and techeþ hem what þey scholde be' (Diekstra, *Book*, 7478–79).

[17] *The Pepys Rule* includes two references to women as preachers, both of which offer them hope of preaching authority: 'Ac womman ne owe nouȝt to prechen bot ȝif sche be þe ouer holyer' (28:18–19; compare 29:13–14, 5:4–6) is restrictive, but less so than contemporary canon law, even with the addition 'for seinte Poule forbedeþ hem.'

hem no feipe. Lyft þyn herte holiche from hem and haue hem alle
suspecte, ne tel no worde bi hem to non to wite that þey wolde mene.
Soþfaste siȝte is, and of parfite mede, knowynge of þyself, þorw þe whiche
quykeneþ knowyng of God and vnyte wiþ hym [. . .] Be þu blynde to þyn
owne gode as Tobie was [. . .] Of penaunce and of hardschip siker buþ þe
weyes, and of contemplacion vnstabele and somdel to drede. So perlus hit
is on hyȝ to clymbe, and siker wei to God hit is þat mon holde hym lowe.
Aungelus office hit is heuenliche þyngus to knowe and to wite þe pryuytes
þat mow not be departed. Hit is inow to mon to se his owne lodliche
synnes. (7620–7638, echoing *Ancrene Wisse*, f. 24r:11–14, and perhaps
f. 60v:24–26)

In an environment where news of contemporary continental women visionaries such as Bridget of Sweden and Catherine of Siena was perhaps being
supplemented by rumours of insular visionaries such as Julian of Norwich,
the *Book* gives traditional advice a new edge by directly combatting the
attitudes of a text like *The Chastising of God's Children*, in which visions
must precisely *not* be concealed but rather discussed with a spiritual advisor,
and in which valid visions are explicitly stated to be usable as the basis for
teaching and writing, by women as well as by men.[18] This passage attempts
to set bounds to the process of laicization in which it is also a participant by
insisting that the old ascetic model is safer for vain women than the fashion
for visions, which had given a newly literal meaning to the idea of the ascent
to God. Here, then, *Ancrene Wisse*'s praise of silence and elevation of a
penitential way of life again furthers a project of lay puritanization. In this
case, however, it also declares war on a contemporary religious trend – the
trend towards acceptance of visionary experiences found in a work like *The
Chastising* – and does so in spite of the fact that, as we saw, *The Chastising*
is equally concerned to draw on *Ancrene Wisse* as a legitimating forebear.

The Simple Tretis *and* The Pepys Rule

In light of the powerful impact *Ancrene Wisse* makes in a number of
compilations written for or read by the laity, it need come as no surprise
that two texts attempt a partial or wholesale adaptation of the work for this
same lay audience. *The Simple Tretis* is a careful rewriting of *Ancrene Wisse*,
Parts II and III that survives in a single manuscript of Latin and English
religious writings (London, British Library MS Royal 8 C.i) which attrib-

---

[18] 'Many men and wymmen haue hadde and haue reuelacions and visions, and sum han a spirite of
profecie. Also sum han deuocion and grete plente of teeris, and comforten moche oþer folke, and
counceilliþ and conuertiþ hem wiþ her hooli and deuoute speche and wiþ her techyng, as eiþer
wiþ deuout speche or prechyng, or wiþ hooli teermes in writyng and makynge of bookes in Latyn
or in Ynglisshe' (Bazire and Colledge, 182:19–183:1), the opening of the last of several chapters in
The Chastising (chapters 18–21) that deal with visions, often (though not here) drawing on
Alphonse of Pecha's *Epistola solitarii*. Characteristically, the passage continues more cautiously
('but alle þese and suche oþer preuen nat a man ne womman hooli ne parfite' [183:1–2]), but only
after having introduced the notion that women might teach, preach, and write on the basis of
their revelations. For English suspicion of visions, see Watson, 'Composition,' 647–48.

utes the text to 'lichef[eld]'; three candidates who flourished between the 1380s and the 1440s have been suggested, although none from the Nottingham area where the copy's dialect can be localized (Millett, *Bibliography*, 55). *The Pepys Rule*, which remarkably rethinks the entirety of *Ancrene Wisse* as a rule for the laity, is probably earlier. This work survives in a single manuscript (Cambridge, Pepys Library MS 2498) which contains several vernacular texts aimed at a lay readership and seems to have been copied near Waltham, Essex, around 1360–90 (Zettersten, ix–xix). Although the two works are very different, *The Simple Tretis* being less radical in tendency than *The Pepys Rule*, both of them make explicit the connection between the solitary ideal and the devout laity I have argued is the strongest thread in *Ancrene Wisse*'s later reception. As such, they often bring us back to the reformist world of *þe Holy Boke Gratia Dei* and its colleagues.

The Simple Tretis is much the more consistent of the two works, constructed as a two-part discourse that carefully irons out references to the anchoress's cells in its version of Part II while adding or substituting material (some of it from Nicholas of Lyra's *Postillae*) relevant to the new audience. Examples here include: an opening account of how the senses can properly be described as gateways of the soul (Baugh, 1); an explanation of Latin *cor* as an acronym for *camera omnipotentis regis* (13:16–23); and a long passage on gluttony added to *Ancrene Wisse*'s discussion of taste (17–19). These and other additions recognize the needs of a general audience to have things explained to them and to have the complex texture of the original simplified. They turn Part II into yet another version of the outer rule, a guide to discreet and self-contained behaviour.

In adapting Part III, however, which is more explicitly concerned with the solitary life, the author confronts the relationship between his readers and solitaries more directly in fashioning an inner rule for lay people out of an extended parallel between them and solitaries. After the omission of the whole opening account of pelicans and anger (*Ancrene Wisse* ff. 32–35r), the earlier work's discussion of foxes (bad anchoresses in the original) is rewritten to apply to 'fals men [. . .] þat setten al her hert in tresuryng of worldly gode,' then made the cause for a satirical digression on worldly religious that sounds briefly like a Lollard attack on private religion:

> Many prestes, many monkys, chanons, freres, ankyrs and ankeresses, nunnys and heremytes, are more worldly, lifen more lustily, are more delauy in curiose talkyng of þe world, an luken more after worldly reuerense and honour, þen þay shold haue done dwellyng stil in þe state of þe world þat þey were first in or ellys in any worldly state þat euer þay shold haue commen to. In such priuate astates may þay do many preuey vnleueful þinges more þen þay myȝt do if þey were in myddys þe world. (Baugh: *Simple Tretis*, 24:15–25)

These bad religious are immediately contrasted with good ones who seek solitude for proper reasons, and who correspond to *Ancrene Wisse*'s birds of the air (much reduced) (f. 35v:22). Such a contrast redeems professional religious in the eyes of the lay audience, but also includes that audience in

the possibility of living in the same state of honourable detachment from
the world: this by means of an ingenious analogy between the circular
nests made by these birds and the circle of integrity people fashion when
using God as the stable centre around which the compass of their lives is
drawn (25).

The climax of the second part of *The Simple Treatise* is at the close of a
long discussion of solitude and the need to keep good deeds private (36–43,
compare *Ancrene Wisse*, ff. 38v–44r, the *nicticorax*), and begins as a defence
of the treatise's emphasis on solitude. The author voices the objection that
'for to write or speke so mych of solitari lijf amang þe comen people of þe
world is bot foly. Forwhy? And all men were solitary, þen shold no men be
marchantes, plughmen, ny men of craft, and so sholde þe world be
confounded and at an end' (43:15–20). The objection is answered by the
comment that 'vnnethes may any man or woman be broght to such maner
of lyfyng' (43:31–32): a comment that sets the solitary apart from the
reader. But the underlying point of the objection is addressed in the
following passage that describes 'how al men and wymmen shold in party
be solitary' (43:33), a passage that again elides the difference between
solitaries and others. Some people are so worldly that they sin in thought
even when they are alone (44:1–18). However:

> Anoþer peple þer is þat desiren noþing þat is in þis warld, bot as to be a
> mene to b[r]yng þem to endles blis [. . .] For þou3 þey haue besines
> outeward – as gouernance of houshold, cure of paryshens as parsones
> haue, gouernance of contres and cytees as sherefes, maires, and baylees –
> 3it her intent is euer set [opon] 'on þing': to do right and lawe of God,
> kepyng clene her conscience. And many a tyme such men, when þey are
> by hemselue, þey examyn her conscience, and if þey fynd anyþing amys,
> þey amenden it by trew penance: þus þey are solitary in her intent, settyng
> her hert [op]on 'on þing,' þat is on rightwisnes and Goddes plesance, wich
> ar alon. (44:19–33, echoing Luke 10:42)

Solitude here is defined both as inner withdrawal from the world and as
unity of attention, such as Mary, not Martha, was able to give Christ (see
also 48:28–49:1). Such solitariness in the world is hard, when it involves the
company of worldly folk who use 'þe comyn spech of men: as veyn sweryng,
wariyng, ribaudy and such oþer' (45:20–21). 'But a man most in his wil –
þou3 pershaunce he may not with his body – be fer fro such condicioned
peple [. . .]; and þus may euery man, if he will, be in sum maner solitari and
fer from synful condicions of þe world' (45:24–34). To flee the world in the
full sense is 'a ded of perfeccion' to which not all are 'bounden.' 'Bot euery
man þat wil be saued most forsake þe world on þis wise' (48:2–5), and build
a city of conscience in their soul, far from others, which they must then
learn to read, correct, and rewrite like a book (49–54). Finally (in a
peroration evocative of Hilton's *Mixed Life*), the alternation between
active and contemplative deeds inherent in this model is compared to the
mixed life of 'prelates and folke of religion,' who mingle prayers with good
works: 'It is a gode dede a tilman or a crafty man to do his labour treuly; it

is a better dede to here a messe or a sermon; and ȝit most such a man go fro þe messe heryng or fro þe sermon to his occupacion ageyn' (58:15–18). Such is the ideal of lay solitude in the world as enunciated by *The Simple Tretis*: an ideal of detachment from the world that is enunciated in essentially passive terms – like the anchoress, the devout layperson here has no mission to preach or teach God's law to others, or even to reprove sinners. As such, it has a clear relationship not only with Hilton's influential model of lay religiosity but with that of the so-called *devotio moderna* in the Low Countries, which later in the fifteenth and sixteenth centuries was to find its English articulation in the many translations and editions of Thomas à Kempis's *Imitation of Christ* (Biggs).

The Pepys Rule is discussed at length elsewhere in this volume by Christina von Nolcken, and my brief remarks here focus on the single issue of its laicizing of the notions of 'rule' and 'order.' For all the visual care of its manuscript presentation, the text itself – possibly the product of more than one phase of revision and in places, I suspect, of a blending of the text with a set of marginalia in the scribe's exemplar – is often so puzzling, even on the level of syntax, that it is hard to imagine the work had any impact. But in its rewriting of *Ancrene Wisse* as a rule for all Christians – since 'alle men and wymen moten holde o reule wiþinne' (Zettersten, 2:14–15) – it does represent the most extreme extension of the processes described in this paper, by which the work was made relevant to fourteenth-century conditions. Many of its attitudes resemble those of *The Simple Tretis*. Like that work, for example, it concedes that the lives of solitaries and preachers may garner greater heavenly reward than the lives of the laity (4:29–5:3), while cautioning against a premature ascent to 'heiȝe lyf and to ordre' (61:12), and protesting any automatic link between state of life and state of virtue: 'Wene ȝe þan þat a man schal come to parfit lyf for þat he bicomeþ a man of ordre? Nay! þe heiȝer þat he clymbeþ þe ferrer he is þerfro bot ȝif he rewle hym by wisdom and by queyntise' (43:22–26). Like that work, too, it is constructed around the insight that all Christians need to live like solitaries:

> Now vnderstondeþ þat a mannes body is cleped in holy wrytt sumtyme an hous, and sumtyme a citee, and sumtyme Goddes temple and Holy Chirche. þan riȝth as ȝee see þat an ancre is bischett in an hous and may nouȝth out, riȝth so is vche mannes soule bischett in his body as an ancre. And þerfore vche man, lered and lewed, ȝif he wil queme God and be his deciple, helde hym in his hous, schete his dores and his wyndowes fast þat ben his fyue wyttes, þat he take no likyng to synne ne to werldelich þynges. And þan he is an ancre and wel better quemeþ God þan hij þat byschetten hem and taken hem to heiȝe lyf and ben werldelich.
>
> (Zettersten: *Pepys Rule*, 44:2–12)

Yet *The Pepys Rule* takes these and other ideas several steps further than *The Simple Tretis*, sometimes into territory associated with Lollard and reformist radicalism (Colledge, '*Recluse*'). Like *Book for a Simple and Devout Woman*, it is uneasy about the claims that enclosed religious make to represent the highest spiritual calling, and several times interrupts expositions of the solitary life to assert that preachers have an equal or superior claims to be regarded as holy. For example, its exposition of St James's definition of true religion (quoted in its original form above, p. 201) spends as much time on the first part of this definition ('*Visitare pupillos et viduas in tribulacione*' [4:11–12]) – which *Ancrene Wisse* ignores, as relevant only to the active life – as it does on the second part; here the preaching apostles, Peter and Paul, are implicitly elevated above the solitary desert fathers (4–5). The same reversal of a traditional hierarchy is made explicit after the discussion of all Christians as solitaries in Part III, which also elevates the lay reader to the role of preacher. Here, the apostles are praised because they 'were proued in þe werlde – *hij nere nouȝt bischett* – and duelleden amonges men in sorouȝ and in wo in þis werlde, and tauȝtten þe folk and lyueden after her techynge [. . .] *And ne schal a man neuer loue God parfitelich bot ȝif he do so*' (44:29–33, my italics). Thus while solitaries still have a place in the world-view of *The Pepys Rule* (see, e.g., 4:2–3, 27:2–5), as in the *Simple Tretis*, they largely function here as mere symbols of a devout lay lifestyle. Indeed, even as symbols, they need critiquing and supplementing with material about the need to 'aunter þe forto saue Ihesus Cristes lyf and his worschipp' (45:4–5) by taking on an apostolic preaching role in the world. Again, sinful members of religious orders are not just criticized, as in the *Simple Tretis*, but said to be excommunicate from their order ('out of ordre') – 'þeiȝ þat he be a pope, oiþer a bisschope, monk, oiþer frere' (89:25–27) – a position often associated with Lollardy (Hudson, chapter 7). Obdurate sinners among the laity are likewise exiles from God's law (compare *Book to a Mother* [McCarthy, 73]) whom it is deadly sin, not a work of mercy, to help in any way: 'and understonde wel ȝif þou susteyne a wicked man oiþer a womman, and þou it wost, þou dooste more harme to God þan þou susteyned oiþer Iew oiþer Sarazene' (56:38–57:1).

In one sense, the work holds the exclusiveness potentially associated both with the solitary life and with its own radical tendencies at bay: thus the illiterate laity are told not to despair at their initial failure to understand 'Goddes lawȝe' but to exercise their spiritual 'cunnyng' with his help (86). Yet the work's interest in this group is far from implying a generously inclusive view of the company of the elect that is the Church ('þat is: a gaderynge of goode folk in Goddes name: þat is holy chirche and non oþere' [44:23–24]). On the contrary, it is 'wicked men and commune synners,' not the good, who assert that 'God tooke alle out of helle and att Domesday he schal make alle goode' (57:10–11), and flattering mendicants, not true preachers, who are said to elevate God's mercy above his justice – so that, for anyone who believes them, 'it were inpossible þat þise schulden ben ysaued' (50:29–30). Like other works discussed in this essay that share its attitude to the world as an evil from which the devout must separate themselves, *The Pepys Rule* extrapolates a restrictive view of God's willingness to forgive sinners from *Ancrene Wisse*'s attention to the perils of even the holiest form of life.[19] If *The Simple Tretis* (in this like *þe Holy Boke Gratia Dei*) leaves the notion of order intact by treating its lay readers as recipients of instruction whose concern for holy living is merely personal, *The Pepys Rule* seeks to fashion its readers into subjects as actively engaged in the process of reforming the world as is the work itself. In this, it points forward not to *On Mixed Life* or *The Imitation of Christ* but to separatist attacks on the evils of world and institutional Church such as the early fifteenth-century *Lanterne of Liȝt* (Swinburn), or its sixteenth-century descendants.

Conclusion

In this essay I have surveyed the later Middle English texts known to have borrowed substantially from *Ancrene Wisse*.[20] The variety of uses to which the text was put dooms to over-simplification any straightforward argument as to the nature of its influence, and I have been anxious not to smooth out the bumpy contours of the evidentiary landscape. However, where accounts of the history of Middle English religious prose tend to imagine a line of development from *Ancrene Wisse* to the so-called 'fourteenth-century mystics' (Colledge, *The Mediaeval Mystics*; Watson, 'Methods'), this analysis locates the work's major impact elsewhere: in a group of writings associated with what I call a puritanizing tendency in late fourteenth-century vernacular theology, which can sometimes (although by no means always) be linked to the reformist thinking that crystallized in the Lollard movement.

With the arguable exception of *The Pepys Rule* and the Additional version of *Book to a Simple and Devout Woman*, there is nothing heterodox about any of these works, and – since these two works seem to have been written at different times in different parts of the country both from the compilations discussed in section IV and from one another – it may be tendentious to group *The Pepys Rule* or *The Simple Tretis* with the compilations at all. Just how these five works and *Pore Caitif* are to be configured in relation to one another, or to the writings of Hilton, Love, and the author of *The Chastising* – let alone to vernacular Lollard prose, *Piers Plowman*, or the works of the *Gawain*-poet (compare Watson,

---

[19] For a universalist tendency in English vernacular theology that texts like *The Pepys Rule* may be concerned to combat, see Watson, 'Visions'. The idea that if Christ took all souls from hell at the Harrowing of Hell (theoretically, only souls in the *limbus patrum* were taken) he will do so at the Last Judgement is related to the account in *The Gospel of Nicodemus* (see *Piers Plowman* B, passus XVIII). *Book for a Simple and Devout Woman* also contains two more explicit attacks on what it treats as a superficial and worldly universalist position (Diekstra, *Book*, 1323–30, 3958–4010), both related to a brief tract on the topic also edited by Diekstra ('British Library').

[20] The main exception, apart from the Vernon copy of *Ancrene Wisse* (see note 10), is *The Tretyse of Loue*, a late fifteenth-century translation of a French original that includes extensive excerpts from Parts V and VII of the work and was printed by Wynkyn de Worde around 1493 (Fisher). *The Tretyse* was translated too late to be considered here, and seems to stand outside the lines of development suggested by *Ancrene Wisse*'s earlier derivatives. It also displays no sign of being aware that one of its ultimate sources is *Ancrene Wisse* – although it is suggestive that between 1491 and 1494 de Worde also printed *The Scale of Perfection* (1494) and *The Chastising of God's Children* (1491) (Fisher, ix; Allen, 'Wynkyn').

'Visions', '*Gawain*-Poet') – is a matter for further research. Yet these works do have one distinct thing in common: an interest in translating the spiritual ambition *Ancrene Wisse* associates with the solitary life into terms accessible to the devout laity. To some extent, this interest runs parallel to Hilton's agenda in *The Scale of Perfection* or *Mixed Life* and finds analogues in other affective texts like *Contemplations of the Dread and Love of God*, with its roots in the eremitic spirituality of Rolle (Connolly). The parallels are especially striking in the two most cautious works of the group, *The Simple Tretis* and *þe Holy Boke Gratia Dei*, both of which expound versions of lay solitude that involve withdrawal into a life of private virtue, rather than the paradoxically evangelical self-separation from the world *The Pepys Rule* advocates. But the resonances that follow from thinking of the devout laity as though their lives were translations of the anchoritic ideal, varied as these are, nonetheless stamp all these works with the imprint of an ambition that – for all the talk of lowliness several of the works take over from *Ancrene Wisse* – has the tendency to view the laity as equals of the clerics, monks, and solitaries traditionally regarded as their spiritual superiors. As we saw, this view is anticipated by *Ancrene Wisse* itself, in its own translation of theological ideas associated with the twelfth-century reformation into an idealization of the semi-regular religious life. There are many other versions of this view in fourteenth-century religious thought. Yet insofar as the puritanical elitism of these works anticipates the puritanism of the sixteenth-century reformation, and their levelling of old hierarchies anticipates the Protestant declaration of 'the priesthood of all believers,' it might be possible to see them as a bridge between religious worlds four hundred years apart.[21]

Works Cited

Aarts, Florent G. A. M., ed., *þe Pater Noster of Richard Ermyte: a Late Middle English Exposition of the Lord's Prayer* (Nijmegen, 1967)

Allen, Hope Emily, 'Further Borrowings from *Ancren Riwle*', *Modern Language Review* 24 (1929), 1–15

——, 'On "Some Fourteenth-Century Borrowings from *Ancren Riwle*"', *Modern Language Review* 19 (1924), 95

——, 'Some Fourteenth-Century Borrowings from *Ancren Riwle*', *Modern Language Review* 18 (1923), 1–8

——, 'Wynkyn de Worde and a Second French Compilation from the *Ancren Riwle*

[21] I wish to thank Alison Conway, Fiona Somerset, and Jocelyn Wogan-Browne for their careful readings of this paper; Bella Millett for generously sharing her published and unpublished work with me; Christina von Nolcken for the gift of a preliminary version of her essay on *The Pepys Rule*; and Stan Hussey and Michael Sargent for the gift of the text of their forthcoming edition (with the late A. J. Bliss) of *The Scale of Perfection*. This essay was completed in the fall of 1999; Arne Zettersten and Berhard Diensberg's edition of the Vernon text of *Ancrene Wisse* (2000) was thus published too late for me to make use of it.

with a Description of the First', in *Essays and Studies in Honor of Carleton Brown* (New York, 1940), 182–219

Arntz, Mary Luke, ed., *Richard Rolle and þe Holy Boke Gratia Dei: an Edition with Commentary*, Salzburg Studies in English Literature: Elizabethan and Renaissance Studies 92:2 (Salzburg, 1981)

Aston, Margaret, *Lollards and Reformers: Images and Literacy in Late Medieval Religion* (London, 1984)

Ayto, John, and Alexandra Barratt, eds., *Aelred of Rievaulx's De Institutione Inclusarum: Two English Versions*, EETS o.s. 287 (1984)

Baldwin, Mary, '*Ancrene Wisse* ands its Background in the Christian Tradition of Religious Instruction and Spirituality', Diss. (University of Toronto, 1974)

Barratt, Alexandra, 'Anchoritic Aspects of *Ancrene Wisse*', *Medium Aevum* 49 (1980), 32–56

Baugh, A. C., ed., *The English Text of the 'Ancrene Riwle', edited from British Museum MS Royal 8.C.1*, EETS o.s. 232 (1956)

Bazire, Joyce, and Eric Colledge, eds., *The Chastising of God's Children and the Treatise of the Perfection of the Sons of God* (Oxford, 1957)

Bennett, J. A. W., *Middle English Literature*, ed. and completed Douglas Gray (Oxford, 1986), 264–75

Biggs, B. J. H., ed., *The Imitation of Christ: the First English Translation of the 'Imitatio Christi'*, EETS o.s. 309 (1997)

Blamires, Alcuin, 'The Wife of Bath and Lollardy', *Medium Aevum* 58 (1989), 224–42

Bliss, A. J., S. S. Hussey and Michael Sargent, eds., *Walter Hilton's 'Scale of Perfection'*, unpublished typescript of forthcoming EETS volume

Bloomfield, Morton W., *The Seven Deadly Sins* (East Lansing, MI, 1952)

Bolton, Brenda, 'Some Thirteenth Century Women in the Low Countries: a Special Case?', *Nederlands Archief voor Kerkgeschiedenis* 61 (1981), 7–29

——, 'Thirteenth-Century Religious Women: Some Further Reflections on the Low Countries "Special Case" ', in *New Trends in Feminine Spirituality: the Holy Women of Liège and their Impact*, ed. Juliette Dor, Lesley Johnson and Jocelyn Wogan-Browne, Medieval Women: Texts and Contexts 2 (Turnhout, 1999), 129–58

Bradley, Ritamary, 'In the Jaws of the Bear: Journeys of Transformation by Women Mystics', *Vox Benedictina* 8 (1991), 116–75

Brady, Mary Theresa, 'Lollard Interpolations and Omissions in Manuscripts of *The Pore Caitif*', in *De Cella in Seculum: Religious and Secular Life and Devotion in Late Medieval England*, ed. Michael G. Sargent (Cambridge, 1989), 183–203

——, ed., 'The *Pore Caitif*: edited from MS Harley 2336 with Introduction and Notes', Diss. (Fordham University, 1954)

——, 'Rolle and the Pattern of Tracts in *The Pore Caitif*', *Traditio* 39 (1983), 456–65

Bynum, Caroline Walker, *Jesus as Mother: Studies in the Spirituality of the High Middle Ages* (Berkeley, 1982)

Cannon, Christopher, 'Monastic Productions', Chapter 12 of Wallace 1999, 316–48

Chambers, E. K., 'On the Continuity of English Prose from Alfred to More and his School', EETS o.s. 191A (1957) (first published 1932)

Clark, John P. H., and Rosemary Dorward, trans., *Walter Hilton, The Scale of Perfection*, Classics of Western Spirituality (New York, 1991)

Clark, John P. H., and Cheryl Taylor, eds., *Walter Hilton's Latin Writings*, 2 vols., Analecta Cartusiana 124 (Salzburg, 1987)

Colledge, Eric, ed. and introd., *The Mediaeval Mystics of England* (New York, 1961)

——, '*The Recluse*: a Lollard Interpolated Version of the *Ancren Riwle*', *Review of English Studies* 15 (1939), 1–15, 129–45

Connolly, Margaret, ed., *Contemplations of the Dread and Love of God*, EETS o.s. 303 (1993).

Constable, Giles, 'The Ceremonies and Symbolism of Entering Religious Life and Taking the Monastic Habit, from the Fourth to the Twelfth Century', *Segni e riti nella chiesa altomedievale occidentale*, Settimane di studio del Centro italiano di studi sull'alto medioevo 33 (Spoleto, 1987), 771–834

——, *The Reformation of the Twelfth Century* (Cambridge, 1996)

——, *Three Studies in Medieval Religious and Social Thought* (Cambridge, 1995)

Crawford, S. J., 'The Influence of the "Ancren Riwle" in the Late Fourteenth Century', *Modern Language Review* 25 (1930), 191–92

Cross, Claire, ' "Great Reasoners in Scripture": the Activities of Women Lollards, 1380–1530', in *Medieval Women*, ed. Derek Baker, Studies in Church History, Subsidia 1 (Oxford, 1978), 359–80

Dahood, Roger, 'The Current State of *Ancrene Wisse* Group Studies', *Medieval English Studies Newsletter* 36 (University of Tokyo, 1997), 6–14

D'Evelyn, Charlotte, *The Latin Text of the 'Ancrene Riwle': edited from Merton College MS 44 and British Museum MS Cotton Vitellius E vii*, EETS o.s. 216 (1944 for 1941)

Diekstra, F. N. M., ed., *Book for a Simple and Devout Woman: a Late Middle English Adaptation of Peraldus's 'Summa de Vitiis et Virtutibus' and Friar Laurent's 'Somme le Roi'*, Mediaevalia Groningana 24 (Groningen, 1998)

——, ed., 'British Library MS 37049, f. 96r–96v: a Mutilated Tract on God's Mercy and Justice and Material for its Reconstruction', *English Studies* 75 (1994), 214–22

——, 'Some Fifteenth-Century Borrowings from the *Ancrene Wisse*', *English Studies* 71 (1990), 81–104

Dobson, E. J., ed., *The English Text of the 'Ancrene Riwle': edited from B.M. Cotton MS Cleopatra C.vi*, EETS o.s. 267 (1972)

Doyle, A. I., 'The Shaping of the Vernon and Simeon Manuscripts', in *Studies in the Vernon Manuscript*, ed. Derek Pearsall (Cambridge, 1990), 1–13

——, 'A Survey of the Origins and Circulation of Theological Writings in English in the Fourteenth, Fifteenth, and early Sixteenth Centuries with Special Consideration of the Part of the Clergy therein', 2 vols., Diss. (Cambridge University, 1953)

——, ed., *The Vernon Manuscript: a Facsimile of Bodleian Library, Oxford, MS Eng. Poet. a. 1* (Cambridge, 1987)

Fisher, John H., ed., *The Tretyse of Loue*, EETS o.s. 223 (1951 for 1945)

Fletcher, Alan J., 'A Hive of Industry or a Hornet's Nest? MS Sidney Sussex 74 and its Scribes', in *Late-Medieval Religious Texts and their Transmission: Essays in Honour of A. I. Doyle*, ed. A. J. Minnis, York Manuscripts Conferences: Proceedings Series 3 (Cambridge, 1994), 131–55

Forshaw, Helen P., ed., *Edmund of Abingdon's 'Speculum Religiosorum' and 'Speculum Ecclesie'* (London, 1974)

Francis, W. Nelson, ed., *The Book of Vices and Virtues: a Fourteenth-Century English Translation of the 'Somme le Roi' of Lorens d'Orléans*, EETS o.s. 217 (1942)

Grundmann, Herbert, *Religious Movements in the Middle Ages: the Historical Links* between Heresy, the Mendicant Orders, and the Women's Religious Movement in the Twelfth and Thirteenth Century with the Historical Foundations of German Mysticism*, trans. Steven Rowan (Notre Dame, 1995; orig. pub. in German, 1935; rev. edn 1961)

Gürlach, Manfred, *The Textual Tradition of the South English Legendary*, Leeds Texts and Monographs n.s. 6 (Leeds, 1974)

Hahn, Thomas, 'Early Middle English', Chapter 3 of Wallace 1999, 61–91

Hanna , Ralph, III, 'The Origins and Production of Westminster School MS 3', *Studies in Bibliography* 41 (1988), 197–218

Hudson, Anne, *The Premature Reformation: Wycliffite Texts and Lollard History* (Oxford, 1988)

Hussey, S. S., 'Walter Hilton: Traditionalist?', in *The Medieval Mystical Tradition in England: Dartington 1980*, ed. Marion Glasscoe (Exeter, 1980), 1–16

Keiser, George, ' "Noght how lang man lifs; bot how wele": the Laity and the Ladder of Perfection', in *De Cella in Seculum: Religious and Secular Life and Devotion in Late Medieval England*, ed. Michael G. Sargent (Cambridge, 1989), 145–59

Lagorio, Valerie M., and Michael G. Sargent, 'English Mystical Writings', in *A Manual of the Writings in Middle English, 1050–1500*, vol. 9., ed. Albert E. Hartung (New Haven, 1993), 3049–137

Mack, Frances M., ed., *The English Text of the 'Ancrene Riwle': edited from Cotton MS Titus D.xviii*, EETS o.s. 252 (1963 for 1962)

McCarthy, Adrian James, ed., *Book to a Mother: an Edition with Commentary*, Salzburg Studies in English Literature: Elizabethan and Renaissance Studies 92:1 (Salzburg, 1981)

McGinn, Bernard, *The Presence of God: a History of Western Christian Mysticism*, Volume 2, *The Growth of Mysticism*, Volume 3, *The Flowering of Mysticism* (New York, 1994, 1998)

Millett, Bella, '*Ancrene Wisse* and the Book of Hours', in *Writing Religious Women: Female Spiritual and Textual Practices in Late Medieval England*, ed. Denis Renevey and Christiania Whitehead (Cardiff, 2000), 21–41

——, '*Ancrene Wisse* and the Conditions of Confession', *English Studies* 80 (1999), 193–215

——, *Annotated Bibliographies of Old and Middle English Literature, Vol. 2: Ancrene Wisse, the Katherine Group, and the Wooing Group* (Cambridge, 1996)

——, 'The Origins of *Ancrene Wisse*: New Answers, New Questions', *Medium Aevum* 61 (1992), 206–28

——, 'Women in No Man's Land: English Recluses and the Development of Vernacular Literature in the Twelfth and Thirteenth Centuries', in *Women and Literature in Britain, 1150–1500*, ed. Carol M. Meale, Cambridge Studies in Medieval Literature 17 (Cambridge, 1993), 86–103

Ogilvie-Thomson, S. J., *Walter Hilton's 'Mixed Life', edited from Lambeth Palace MS 472*, Elizabethan and Renaissance Studies 92:15 (Salzburg, 1986)

Oliger, Livarius, ed., 'Regulae tres reclusorum et eremitarum Angliae saec. XIII–XIV', *Antonianum* 3 (1928), 151–90, 299–320

Regan, Charles, ed., 'The Cleansing of Man's Soul: edited from MS Bodl. 923, with Introduction, Notes, and Glossary', Diss. (Harvard University, 1963)

Robertson, Elizabeth, *Early English Devotional Prose and the Female Audience* (Knoxville, TN, 1990)

Salter, Elizabeth, *Nicholas Love's 'Myrrour of the Blessed Lyf of Jesu Christ'*, Analecta Cartusiana 10 (Salzburg, 1974)

Sargent, Michael G., *Nicholas Love's Mirror of the Blessed Life of Jesus Christ* (New York, 1992)

Savage, Anne, and Nicholas Watson, trans., *Anchoritic Spirituality: 'Ancrene Wisse' and Associated Works*, Classics of Western Spirituality (New York, 1991)

Schmidt, A. V. C., *Piers Plowman: a Parallel-Text Edition of the A, B, C, and Z Versions* (London, 1998)

Shepherd, Geoffrey, ed., *Ancrene Wisse: Parts Six and Seven*, Nelson's Medieval and Renaissance Library (London, 1959)

Spencer, H. Leith, *English Preaching in the Late Middle Ages* (Oxford, 1993)

Swinburn, Lilian M., ed., *The Lanterne of Liȝt*, EETS o.s. 151 (1917)

Tolkien, J. R. R., ed., *The English Text of the 'Ancrene Riwle': edited from MS Corpus Christi College Cambridge 402*, EETS o.s. 249 (1962)

Trethewey, W. H., ed., *The French Text of the 'Ancrene Riwle': edited from Trinity College Cambridge MS R. 14. 7*, EETS o.s. 240 (1958 for 1954)

Wallace, David, ed., *The Cambridge History of Medieval English Literature* (Cambridge, 1999)

Watson, Nicholas, 'Censorship and Cultural Change in Late-Medieval England: Vernacular Theology, the Oxford Translation Debate, and Arundel's Constitutions of 1409', *Speculum* 70 (1995), 822–64

——, 'The Composition of Julian of Norwich's *Revelation of Love*', *Speculum* 68 (1993), 637–83

——, 'Fashioning the Puritan Gentrywoman: Devotion and Dissent in *Book to a Mother*', in *Medieval Women: Texts and Contexts in Late Medieval Britain: Essays for Felicity Riddy*, ed. Jocelyn Wogan-Browne *et al.* (Turnhout, 2000)

——, 'The *Gawain*-Poet as Vernacular Theologian', in *A Companion to the Gawain-Poet*, ed. Derek Brewer and Jonathan Gibson, Arthurian Studies 38 (Cambridge, 1997), 293–313

——, 'The Methods and Objectives of Thirteenth-Century Anchoritic Devotion', in *The Medieval Mystical Tradition in England: Exeter Symposium 4: Papers Read at Dartington Hall, July 1987*, ed. Marion Glasscoe (Cambridge, 1987), 132–53

——, 'The Middle English Mystics', Chapter 21 of Wallace 1999, 539–65

——, 'The Politics of Middle English Writing', in Wogan-Browne 1999, 331–52

——, *Richard Rolle and the Invention of Authority*, Cambridge Studies in Medieval Literature 13 (Cambridge, 1991)

——, 'Visions of Inclusion: Universal Salvation and Vernacular Theology in Pre-Reformation England', *Journal of Medieval and Early Modern Studies* 25 (1997), 145–87

Wilson, R. M., ed., introd. N. R. Ker., *The English Text of the 'Ancrene Riwle': edited from Gonville and Caius College MS 234/120*, EETS o.s. 229 (1954 for 1948)

Wogan-Browne, Jocelyn, 'Chaste Bodies: Frames and Experiences', in *Framing Medieval Bodies*, ed. Sarah Kay and Miri Rubin (Manchester, 1994), 24–42

——, Nicholas Watson, Andrew Taylor Ruth Evans, eds., *The Idea of the Vernacular: an Anthology of Middle English Literary Theory, 1280–1520* (University Park, 1999)

Zettersten, A., ed., *The English Text of the 'Ancrene Riwle': edited from Magdalene College, Cambridge MS Pepys 2498*, EETS o.s. 274 (1976)

——, and Bernhard Diensberg, *The English Text of the Ancrene Riwle: The 'Vernon' Text, edited from Oxford, Bodleian Library MS Eng. poet. a. I*, EETS o.s. 310 (2000)

11

Ancrene Wisse and the Identities of Mary Salome

ROGER DAHOOD

The story of the Easter morning visit of the three Marys to Jesus' empty tomb is a familiar one.[1] In the late Middle Ages it was a commonplace. Theodorich, a twelfth-century pilgrim to the Holy Land, reports that over the entry to the tomb was a mosaic showing 'the Three Marys, well-known from the Gospel, with their phials of ointment, and presiding over them the angel himself' (Folda, 232).[2] The author of *Ancrene Wisse* also alludes to the three Marys:

[þ]e þreo Maries bohten deorewurðe aromaz his bodi forte smirien.
(Tolkien, 190–91, f. 101a1–2)

(The three Marys bought precious spices to anoint his body.)

He soon identifies them as Mary Magdalene (f. 101a7–8), Mary of James (f. 101a15), and Mary Salome (f. 101b5). No editor of *Ancrene Wisse* has commented on the presence of three Marys. Shepherd, for example, cites Mark 16:1 and Luke: 24:1 as 'texts often used in Eastertide sermons, and providing the basis for the famous *Quem quaeritis* trope of the liturgical drama.' He devotes the rest of his brief notes to the allegorical interpretation and the etymologizing in the passage (46–47). Savage and Watson likewise address issues of allegory and etymology (396–97). It may come as a surprise, therefore, that, Theodorich's confident assertion and modern editorial silence notwithstanding, the visit of three Marys is not scriptural. The only woman named in all four Gospel accounts of the Easter morning visit is Mary Magdalene:

Vespere autem sabbati quae lucescit in primam sabbati venit Maria Magdalene et altera Maria videre sepulchrum. (Mt 28:1)

(Now after the sabbath, toward the dawn of the first day of the week, Mary Magdalene and the other Mary went to see the sepulchre.)[3]

---

[1] I am grateful to Robert A. Burns and Herbert Schneidau for providing helpful advice and bibliography for the present essay, to Jon Solomon for answers to questions about Greek passages, and to Carl Berkhout, H. A. Kelly, Peter Medine, and Cynthia White for careful reading of the typescript. To Cynthia White I am grateful for helpful critique of my translations from Medieval Latin.

[2] Folda cautions that iconography of two Marys at the tomb was usual in the East, whereas three were usual in the West. Theodorich, a Westerner, in reporting three Marys, may be describing 'what he expected to see,' not what was actually there.

[3] Unless otherwise noted I quote the English from the Revised Standard Version.

Et cum transisset sabbatum Maria Magdalene et Maria Iacobi et Salome
emerunt aromata ut venientes unguerent eum. (Mk 16:1)

(And when the sabbath was past, Mary Magdalene, and Mary the mother
of James, and Salome, bought spices, so that they might go and anoint
him.)

. . . [M]ulieres quae cum ipso venerant de Galilaea . . . viderunt
monumentum et quemadmodum positum erat corpus eius . . . et sabbato
quidem siluerunt secundum mandatum. Una autem sabbati valde diluculo venerunt ad monumentum portantes quae paraverant aromata. . . .
Erat autem Maria Magdalene et Iohanna et Maria Iacobi et ceterae quae
cum eis erant quae dicebant ad apostolos haec . . . (Lk 23:55–24:10)

(The women who had come with him from Galilee . . . saw the tomb, and
how his body was laid. . . . On the sabbath they rested according to the
commandment. But on the first day of the week at early dawn, they went
to the tomb, taking the spices which they had prepared. . . . Now it was
Mary Magdalene and Joanna and Mary the mother of James and the
other women with them who told this to the apostles . . .)[4]

Una autem sabbati Maria Magdalene venit mane cum adhuc tenebrae
essent ad monumentum et videt lapidem sublatum a monumento.
Cucurrit ergo et venit ad Simonem Petrum et ad alium discipulum
quem amabat Iesus et dicit eis tulerunt Dominum de monumento et
nescimus ubi posuerunt eum. (Jn 20:1–2)

(Now on the first day of the week Mary Magdalene came to the tomb
early, while it was still dark, and saw that the stone had been taken away
from the tomb. So she ran, and went to Simon Peter and the other
disciple, the one whom Jesus loved, and said to them, 'They have taken
the Lord out of the tomb, and we do not know where they have laid
him.')[5]

The Gospels name only one or two Marys at the tomb, and none names
Mary Salome. What is more, no Mary Salome appears anywhere in the
Bible. Where, then, did the author of *Ancrene Wisse* find her? Because the
reference to the three Marys occurs also in the earliest extant version of
Ancrene Wisse, which by all estimates dates from well before mid-century,[6]
neither of the two most widely known medieval accounts of Mary Salome,
that of Vincent of Beauvais in the *Speculum Historiale* (c.1250; Book 6, ch.
12, p. 225), nor that of Jacobus de Voragine in the *Legenda Aurea* (c.1260;
The Golden Legend, 'The Birth of the Blessed Virgin Mary,' 2:150), can be a
source. The three Marys, however, were well known to learned writers of

---

[4] Luke is not precise about which women saw the empty tomb, only about which women reported
it.
[5] The use of the first person plural 'nescimus' in verse 2 has been taken to imply the presence of
other women at the tomb (Knox, trans., fn. to John 20:2).
[6] London, British Library MS Cotton Nero A. xiv, ff. 102v–103 (Day, 169–70); MS Nero contains
the version of *Ancrene Wisse* addressed to three consanguineous sisters (f. 50r; Day, 85:12, 23–26).
Scholarly consensus has assigned *Ancrene Wisse* to the first quarter of the thirteenth century. Bella
Millett has recently suggested 'the beginning of the 1230s' as a probable *terminus ad quem* for the
original version (Millett, 12).

the twelfth century, including Vincent's acknowledged source, Peter Comestor (d. 1178; *PL*, 198:1563C–64A). The three Marys were also early established in popular tradition. There can be little doubt that the *Ancrene Wisse* author's knowledge of Mary Salome derives from twelfth-century learned writings, popular tradition, or both.

The origins of Mary Salome are obscure. The evidence, much of which Max Förster, Beda Kleinschmidt, and M. R. James gathered early in this century, is spotty at best. It falls into two main categories, the writings of the Greek Fathers and secular historians to the fifth century, and Western Latin and vernacular writings from the ninth century on. Between the fifth and ninth centuries, information is wanting. My object, as my title indicates, is to call attention to Mary Salome's multiple identities in late antiquity and the Middle Ages and to comment on some implications of her presence in *Ancrene Wisse*.

The evidence suggests that Mary Salome is the product mainly of two concerns of the early Church. The first was to harmonize the Gospels, especially where harmony could be achieved without much strain. The second, from the time of Jerome (d. 420), was to maintain the doctrine of the perpetual virginity of Mary the mother of Jesus. Of the Gospels the two pertinent to the creation of Mary Salome are Matthew and Mark. At the end of the crucifixion narrative Matthew says, 'There were also many women there, looking on from afar, who had followed Jesus from Galilee, ministering to him; among whom were Mary Magdalene, and Mary the mother of James and Joseph, and the mother of the sons of Zebedee' (27:55–56). The corresponding passage in Mark reads, 'There were also women looking on from afar, among whom were Mary Magdalene, and Mary the mother of James the younger and of Joses, and Salome, who when he was in Galilee followed him, and ministered to him; and also many other women who came up with him to Jerusalem' (15:40–41). For the sake of harmony, post-scriptural writers beginning with Tatian (d. c. 170), *Diatessaron*, at Mt 27:56 (p. 325), and more important Origen (d. c. 254) identified the mother of the sons of Zebedee with Salome:

> Sin autem oportet opinari, et dicere etiam nomen matris filiorum Zebedaei, dico quoniam haec ipsa fuerat Salome, *pacifica*, appellata. Opinatus sum autem hoc, videns apud Matthaeum et Marcum tres praecipuas mulieres nominatas, de quibus praesens sermo habetur. Et duas quidem esse praesens evangelista exponit, Mariam Magdalenam, et Mariam Jacobi: tertiam autem dici matrem filiorum Zebedaei. Apud Marcum autem tertia illa Salome appellatur. . . . Et hoc observa quoniam superius duae istae Mariae, et mater filiorum Zebedaei, quam existimamus ipsam esse Salomem, de longe spectabant mirabilia quae in passione Christi fiebant et corpus eius suspensum in ligno. (*PG*, 13:1796A, 1797C)

> (If indeed it is fitting to have an opinion and to speak the name of the mother of the sons of Zebedee, I say that she had been named Salome, 'peacemaker.' I have supposed this, moreover, observing in Matthew and Mark three principal women named, with whom the present discussion has to do. And indeed Matthew writes, two are Mary Magdalene, and

Mary of James: the third is called the mother of the sons of Zebedee. But in Mark the third is called Salome. . . . And note this, that earlier the two Marys and the mother of the sons of Zebedee, whom we judge to be Salome, watched from a distance the wondrous things that were happening in the passion and his body hung on the cross.)

Origen's cautious rhetoric indicates that his identification of Salome with the mother of the sons of Zebedee is conjectural, as recent scholarship stresses it must be (Brown, 2:1017). Still, it is one of the foundations on which later tradition erected Mary Salome.

By the fourth century evidence emerges associating the name 'Mary' with the sons of Zebedee. The Codex Sinaiticus, a fourth-century Greek Bible, at Mt 27:56 reads, 'Among whom was Mary the mother of James and the Mary of Joseph and the Mary of the sons of Zebedee' (Tischendorf, 517).[7] The reading of the Codex Sinaiticus puts three Marys at the crucifixion, although in sharp contrast to the canonized reading the Codex excludes Mary Magdalene. It is unknown how in the Codex the name Mary came to be linked with the sons of Zebedee. Syrian tradition in the twelfth century, as we shall see from the testimony of William Le Mire, identifies the third Mary as the mother of the sons of Zebedee. Whether the Syrian tradition, however, should be connected to the Codex narrative is unknown. Also unknown is whether the author of the Codex variant identified this Mary with Mark's Salome and whether he thought of her as one of the women at the tomb.

The first explicit association of the name Mary with Salome occurs also in the fourth century in Basil's *Menologium*. In the entry for 25 July Basil supplies a genealogy for Anna (St Anne), mother of the Virgin Mary. Anna is not canonical. She first appears in the apocryphal Protevangelium of James (composed after 150),[8] which clearly models her on her Old Testament namesake Hannah in I Samuel 1 (Kleinschmidt, 11). In the Protevangelium Anna is married to Joachim. In Eastern Christendom the Anna stories had taken hold from an early date. Epiphanius (c. 315–402) provides the detail that Anna died at age seventy-two in Jerusalem, and in Eastern tradition Anna was descended from Levi. Also, in Eastern tradition Anna died before the Annunciation (Algermissen, cols. 230–34, esp. 231). In the West there is evidence of an early tradition that Anna remained alive until after the birth of Jesus. A mosaic, dated c. 432–40, in the church of Santa Maria Maggiore in Rome shows Anna with the Magi at the nativity (Kleinschmidt, 28 and Bild 5). Under the influence of Jerome and Augustine (d. 430), however, the Western Church for the most part long resisted the Anna legend.

According to Basil, Anna was of the tribe of Levi. She, Mary, and Soben were daughters of Matthan, a priest during the reign of Cleopatra, before

---

[7] Förster prints the Greek (125). A brief account of the Codex Sinaiticus, London, British Library MS Additional 43725, is available in Milne and Skeat.

[8] The Protevangelium has gone by many names. The established designation 'Protevangelium' or 'Protoevangelium' lacks ancient authority (Cullmann, 423–24, 426).

Herod's reign. Mary married in Bethlehem and gave birth to Σαλώμην τὴν
Μαρίαν 'Salome, who is also Mary.' Soben likewise married in Bethlehem
and gave birth to Elizabeth, mother of John the Baptist. Anna married in
Galilee and gave birth to the Virgin. Basil stresses that Salome, Elizabeth,
and the Virgin Mary are daughters of three sisters (*PG*, 117:557).[9] Basil's
account of Anna's genealogy can be represented as follows:

Tribe of Levi

Matthan

Mary   Soben   Anna

Salome/Mary   Elizabeth   Virgin Mary

John the Baptist   Jesus

Basil's genealogy reflects the parallel implied between Elizabeth and the
Virgin in the first chapter of Luke's Gospel, where in the space of a few
verses both receive angelic blessing and miraculously conceive. The genealogy brings Salome/Mary into the holy family as a cousin of the Virgin Mary
and provides not quite symmetrical sets of three related women (three
daughters of three sisters). Salome/Mary is the odd woman out, with no
annunciation, no miraculous conception, and no reported offspring. Basil
offers no grounds for his assertion that Salome is also Mary. We cannot be
sure that Basil supposed Salome/Mary to be the mother of the sons of
Zebedee or the Salome at the tomb. In any case, after Basil, Salome/Mary
niece of Anna disappears from the record. There is no evidence that she was
ever known to the late medieval West.

Sometime before the ninth century, Mary Salome enters Western church
lore. Haimo of Auxerre (d. c. 855), who provides the earliest extant
accounts of Mary Salome in the West (Glorieux, 57), knew three different
explanations of her name.[10] In his *Historiae Sacrae Epitome*, Haimo
presents the account that predominated after the eleventh century and by
the end of the Middle Ages prevailed. According to this story, Mary Salome
is Anna's third daughter and a half-sister of the Virgin:

Sciunt etiam qui diligenter exploraverunt, quia frater Domini sit dictus,
tanquam cognatus sit. Hic enim mos Hebraeorum, cognatos vel propin-
quos fratres dicere vel appellare. Frater igitur Domini sic dictus est, quia
de Maria sorore matris Domini, et patre Alpheo genitus est; unde Jacobus
Alphei appellatur. Sed, quoniam nunc se ingessit occasio, de duobus
Jacobis omnem quaestionem rescindamus, et altius generis eorum repe-
tamus originem. Maria mater Domini, et Maria mater Jacobi, fratris
Domini, et Maria fratris Joannis evangelistae, sorores fuerunt, de diversis
patribus genitae, sed de eadem matre, scilicet Anna. Quae Anna primo

[9] Förster was the first to call attention to Basil's linking of Salome and Mary (125).
[10] The works now assigned to Haimo of Auxerre were formerly attributed to Haymo, Bishop of
Halberstadt (d. 853). The chronicle imputed to a fifth-century Flavius Lucius Dexter (*PL*, 31:49),
which mentions a Mary Salome, is now thought to be a forgery (Glorieux, 22).

nupsit Joachim, et de eo genuit Mariam matrem Domini. Mortuo
Joachim, nupsit Cleophae, et de eo habuit alteram Mariam, quae dicitur
in Evangeliis Maria Cleophae. Porro Cleophas habebat fratrem Joseph,
cui filiastram suam beatam Mariam desponsavit; suam vero filiam dedit
Alpheo, de qua natus est Jacobus minor, qui et Justus dicitur, frater
Domini, et Joseph alius. Mortuo itaque Cleopha, Anna tertio marito
nupsit, scilicet Salome, et habuit de eo tertiam Mariam, de qua,
desponsata Zebedaeo, nati sunt Jacobus major, et Joannes evangelista.

(PL, 118:823D–824C)

(They know who have diligently sought that [James] was called the
brother of the Lord, insofar as he was related.[11] This was the custom of
the Jews, to call or name relations or relatives 'brothers.' He was indeed
therefore called the brother of the Lord, because he was sprung from
Mary, the sister of the Lord's mother, and Alphaeus; whence he is called
James of Alphaeus. But now, since the occasion presents itself, let us
reopen the whole question of the two Jameses, and let us more deeply
revisit the origin of their birth. Mary the mother of the Lord, and Mary
the mother of James, brother of the Lord, and Mary of the brother John
the Evangelist were sisters, born of different fathers but of the same
mother, namely Anna. This Anna first married Joachim, and from him
bore Mary, the Lord's mother. When Joachim died, she married
Cleophas, and by him had a second Mary, who is called in the Gospels
Mary Cleophas. Next, Cleophas had a brother, Joseph,[12] to whom he
betrothed his stepdaughter, the blessed Mary; to Alphaeus, however, he
gave his daughter, from whom was born James the minor, who is called
Justus, the brother of the Lord, and another Joseph.[13] And when
Cleophas died, Anna married a third husband, namely Salome, and
had from him a third Mary, from whom, after she had married Zebedee,
James the major and John the Evangelist were born.)

According to Haimo, Anna had three husbands. By each she had a
daughter named Mary. The Virgin Mary was born to Anna and Joachim,
Mary Cleophas to Anna and Cleophas, and a third Mary to Anna and
Salome. Each Mary in turn took a husband and had offspring. The Virgin
Mary gave birth to Jesus. The others were his cousins, who in Jewish
tradition, Haimo explains, would have been called his brothers.[14] We may
represent the relationships as follows:

[11] According to an alternative explanation, which Haimo attributes to Clement and mentions only
to reject, James is a son of Joseph, 'qui Christi quasi pater habebatur' (PL, 118:823C–D) 'who
was regarded as if he were the father of Christ.'

[12] According to ancient tradition as early as Hegesippus (d. c. 180), Cleophas and Joseph were
consanguineous brothers (Eusebius Bk 3, ch. 11).

[13] The identification of the disciple James of Alphaeus (Mt 10:3, Mk 3:18, Lk 6:15, and Acts 1:13)
with James the minor, which implies the marriage of this Mary and Alphaeus, can be found as
early as Jerome, who in the same passage identifies this Mary with the Mary 'whom John
surnames Mary of Cleophas.' De Perpetua Virginitate Beatae Mariae adversus Helvidium (PL,
23:205B–206A; hereafter Adversus Helvidium); translated in Jerome, Dogmatic and Polemical
Works, 29. Jerome is referring to Jn 19:25: '. . . [B]ut standing by the cross of Jesus were his
mother and his mother's sister, Mary the wife of Clopas, and Mary Magdalene,' but the Gospel
sentence is ambiguous, and Jerome's inference is open to question (Brown, 2:1014–15).

[14] Jerome gives this explanation of 'brothers' and cites earlier writers in Adversus Helvidium, PL,
23:206C–212A; translated in Jerome, Dogmatic and Polemical Works, 30–37.

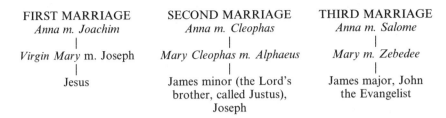

FIRST MARRIAGE	SECOND MARRIAGE	THIRD MARRIAGE
Anna m. Joachim	*Anna m. Cleophas*	*Anna m. Salome*
|	|	|
Virgin Mary m. Joseph	*Mary Cleophas m. Alphaeus*	*Mary m. Zebedee*
|	|	|
Jesus	James minor (the Lord's brother, called Justus), Joseph	James major, John the Evangelist

There are two points of especial interest in Haimo's use of the Anna legend. First, Haimo narrates a version that is in its gross outlines fully developed (Kleinschmidt, 254), although details continued to be fluid. Haimo's imputation to James of the epithet 'the Just,' for example, diverges from later usage, which reflects Acts 1:23: 'Joseph called Barsabbas, who was surnamed Justus.' Most Anna stories in which the cognomen 'Justus' appears apply it to James' brother Joseph (Förster, passim). Gnostic apocrypha, such as the Gospel of Thomas, and the historian Eusebius, among others apply the epithet to James (Bienert, 473). It is possible that Haimo's attribution if not simply an error is a non-canonical but ancient vestige that canonical tradition later elbowed aside. Some later versions add Simon and Judas (not Judas Iscariot) or Thaddeus to the descendants of Mary and Alphaeus and some omit Joseph (Förster, passim). Second, the context is a discussion of the blood relations of Jesus. Haimo's source is unknown, but the story of the thrice-married Anna is not likely to antedate the fourth century, when a need arose to reconcile scriptural references to the brothers and sisters of Jesus (for example, Mt 13:55–56) with the newly solidifying doctrine of Mary's perpetual virginity.

What has not as far as I know been noticed before is Haimo's other reference to Mary Salome. It occurs in an Easter homily on Mk 16.1, where Haimo noncommittally offers the alternative explanations that Mary Salome was named either from a village or a husband. Those who say that Mary Salome had two husbands, Haimo reports, identify her with Mary Cleophas. Neither alternative is consistent with the account supplied in the Anna legend, about which Haimo is here silent:

> Et hoc est quod Marcus ait: 'Maria Magdalene, et Maria Jacobi, et Salome, emerunt aromata,' etc. Et pulchre mulieres uno nomine censentur, ut quibus una erat voluntas, parque desiderium, unum esset et vocabulum. Quarum nominum distinctionem evangelica lectio ostendit, per adjectiva nomina, cum ait: 'Magdalene, Jacobi, et Salome'. Maria Magdalene a Magdalo dicta est castello. . . . Maria Jacobi a filia sua Jacob dicta est, quae matertera fuit Domini, id est soror matris, et mater Jacobi et Joseph. Maria Salome, vel a vico, vel a viro dicta est. Tradunt enim eam habuisse duos viros, Cleopham scilicet et Salomem: ipsam volunt esse, quae alibi Maria Cleophae appellatur. (*PL*, 118:446B, C)

> (And this is what Mark says: 'Mary Magdalene, and Mary the mother of James, and Salome, bought spices,' etc. And the blessed women are called by one name, so that as they had one will, and like desire, they had one

name. Of their names the Gospel passage makes a distinction, through
additional names, when it says: 'Magdalene, mother of James, and
Salome.' Mary Magdalene was named from the village Magdalum. . . .
Mary of James, who was the maternal aunt of the Lord, that is the sister
of his mother, and mother of James and Joseph, was named from her son
James. Mary Salome was named either from a village or a husband. For
they say that she had two husbands, Cleophas and Salome: they hold that
she is the one who elsewhere is called Mary Cleophas.)

There is nothing in the above passage about Salome as the third Mary's
father. Also, the identification of Mary Salome with Mary Cleophas
conflicts with the account in the Anna legend. The conflicting accounts of
the *Epitome* and the Easter homily suggest that Haimo was uncertain about
Mary Salome's precise identity. There seems to be no question, however,
that for Haimo Mary Salome is one of the women at the tomb.

Förster, the first modern scholar to focus attention on the legend of the
thrice-married Anna, assembled a wealth of evidence in Latin and vernacular literature demonstrating awareness of Mary Salome in Western
Europe beginning in the eleventh century.[15] In his *Elementarium* or, as it is
sometimes known, *Vocabularium*, Papias the Lombard (mid-eleventh century), who does not mention Anna and her husbands but presents the
Marys, their husbands, and offspring as in the Anna legend, following
Haimo wavers between competing explanations of the name 'Mary
Salome'.[16]

I. Maria mater Domini; II. Maria Cleophae sive Alphei uxor, quae fuit
mater Iacobi episcopi et apostoli et Symonis et Thadei et cuiusdam
Ioseph; III. Maria Salome, uxor Zebedei, mater Ioannis evangelistae et
Iacobi; IV. Maria Magdalena. Istae quatuor in evangelio reperiuntur.
Iacobus et Iudas et Ioseph filii erant II., materterae Domini. Iacobus
quoque et Ioannes III., alterius materterae Domini, fuerunt filii. II.
Maria, Iacobi minoris et Ioseph mater, uxor Alphei, soror fuit Mariae
matris Domini, quam Cleophae Ioannes nominat, vel a patre vel a
gentilitatis familia vel alia causa. III. Maria Salome vel a viro vel a vico
dicitur; hanc eandem Cleophae quidam dicunt, quod duos viros habuerit.
(Förster, 125–26)

(I. Mary mother of the Lord; II. Mary Cleophas or the wife of Alphaeus,
who was the mother of James the bishop and apostle and of Simon and of
Thaddeus and of a certain Joseph; III. Mary Salome, wife of Zebedee,
mother of John the Evangelist and James; IV. Mary Magdalene. These
four women are found in the Gospel. James and Joseph and Judas were
sons of II., the maternal aunt of the Lord. James and John were sons of

---

[15] Förster, who did not know of Haimo's comments, dated the appearance of the Anna legend in its
fully developed form from the late eleventh century. He argued for a Western origin, possibly in
England or Normandy (130).

[16] A 1491 edition of the *Elementarium* in the Bibliothèque Nationale prints 'Aimo' between
'reperiuntur' and 'Iacobus' in the quoted passage, indicating that Haimo was Papias' source
(f. 98v). I have seen the edition only on a microfilm supplied by the University of Illinois. The
microfilm shows no evidence of a title page. I have taken the bibliographical information from
the *NUC*, 440:451, col. 3.

III., another maternal aunt of the Lord. II. Mary, the mother of James the minor and Joseph, wife of Alphaeus, whom John names 'of Cleophas,' either from her father or a tribal relationship or other reason, was the sister of Mary the Lord's mother. III. Mary Salome is named from a husband or a village; some call this same woman 'of Cleophas,' because she had two husbands.)[17]

Papias' final sentence allows for only two husbands of Mary Salome, namely Salome and Cleophas. But then, what is the status of Zebedee, and what has become of Mary Cleophas, distinct from Mary wife of Zebedee in the Anna legend? The testimony of Papias is important because by placing in close proximity the competing explanations of Mary Salome's name, he calls attention to their incompatibility. Papias' unwillingness to favor one explanation over the other suggests that like Haimo he could not decide between them. Others attempted to create a harmonious resolution but met with resistance, if Peter Comestor's careful distancing of himself from their efforts is indicative:

Alii vero videntes mulieres agnominari solere a nominibus virorum, vt Marcia Catonis, dixerunt prioribus viris mortuis, has duas Marias nupsisse Cleophae et Salomae, vel priores viros fuissse binomios, et dictum Zebedaeum Cleopham, Alphaeum Salomam. (*PL*, 198:1564A)

(Others, however, seeing that women used to be surnamed from the names of husbands, such as 'Marcia of Cato,' said that these two Marys, when their first husbands were dead, married Cleophas and Salome, or that their earlier husbands had two names, that Zebedee was also called Cleophas, and Alphaeus was also called Salome.)

A number of thirteenth- and fourteenth-century manuscripts include a Latin version of the Anna legend that Förster dates about 1100 (114). This Latin version, which largely accords with Haimo's, adds that Anna had a sister Emeria, who bore Elizabeth, mother of John the Baptist. It concludes as follows:

Maria, Jacobi minoris mater, et Maria, mater Jacobi maioris et Johannis evangeliste, et Maria Magdalene quesierunt Dominum cum aromatibus in monumento (115)

(Mary mother of James the minor, and Mary mother of James the major and of John the Evangelist [i.e. Mary daughter of Salome], and Mary Magdalene sought the Lord with spices in the tomb.)

Förster prints an Old English translation from a mid-twelfth-century copy in London, British Library, MS Cotton Vespasian D.xiv, ff. 157v–158r (116).[18]

A Mary from a place called Salome or whose father or husband was

---

[17] The Latin, from Oxford, Bodleian Library, MS Bodley 655, f. 286, col. 2, is printed with slightly different punctuation also in Routh 1:16, where it is wrongly attributed to St Papias, the Apostolic Father.

[18] For the date of the Old English copy I have relied on Ker, 271–77, esp. 275 art. 45.

called Salome was thus current in the West well before the thirteenth century, and she was said to be among the women at the tomb. It is natural that the *Ancrene Wisse* author should know of her. Even so, in twelfth-century England not all were comfortable with Mary Salome. In the 1160s two acerbic writers, Maurice, prior of the Augustinian house of Kirkham, Yorkshire, and Herbert of Bosham, Thomas Becket's friend, close adviser, and biographer, object vigorously to the assertion that Salome was the name of a man. Maurice, says M. R. James, 'is fairly obsessed with Salome and with the depravity of those who err on the subject; and he would have been a bold man who ventured in Maurice's presence even to breathe her name' (288–89). As will become clear, it was not 'her' but 'his' name that so exercised Maurice. Maurice's work, surviving in Oxford, Lincoln College, MS Lat. 27 (twelfth century) and Oxford, Bodleian Library, MS Hatton 92 (fifteenth century), consists of two tracts written to Gilbert of Sempringham (d. 1189), a letter to Roger Archibishop of York (1154–81), and some verse correspondence between Maurice and Roger.[19] Beryl Smalley has justly described Herbert as 'a colourful character who enjoyed a scrap,' and one who 'let his tongue and his pen run away with him' (*Becket*, 59, 62).[20] Herbert's views survive in a letter of 1166–67 to Henry the Liberal, count of Champagne (Smalley, 'Commentary', 37 and n. 34), in which Herbert reports with relish his debunking of the story of the thrice-married Anna.[21] Although Maurice and Herbert wrote independently (Smalley, 'Commentary', 38), they address similar issues. Both reject the widespread claim that in *Adversus Helvidium* Jerome endorses the Anna legend (James, 292–93; Herbert, *PL*, 190:1417C).[22] Also, both lament and excuse Peter Lombard's acceptance of the Anna legend, Herbert especially because Peter Lombard had been his teacher (James, 294; Herbert, *PL*, 190:1418B–19B; Peter, *PL*, 192, 101D–102B).

A male Salome could have originated only in the Latin West, from an ambiguity in the Vulgate rendering of Mk 16:1, 'Maria Iacobi et Salome.' It would be easy for someone trained in Medieval Latin but not Hebrew or Greek – that is to say, the typical medieval Christian cleric – to mistake the final 'e' of 'Salome' for a Medieval Latin genitive singular inflection (= Classical Latin '-ae') and to misconstrue the Vulgate to mean 'Mary of James and [Mary] of Salome.' The verses from Roger to Maurice attribute the advent of the male Salome to just this cause:

---

[19] The Lincoln College manuscript contains only short forms of the tracts addressed to Gilbert. MS Hatton is thus the primary source of knowledge about Maurice (James, 288).

[20] Smalley's portrait illustrates Herbert's going out of his way at times to antagonize King Henry II (*Becket*, 62–65).

[21] Most of Herbert's letter has been printed from an acephalous copy in Cambridge, Corpus Christi College MS 123 (*PL*, 190:1415D). A colophon to an extract in London, British Library, MS Royal 6.E.III, f. 50b, identifies Henry as the recipient. The incipit of the extract, 'Et ne verborum pugnas,' corresponds to the passage beginning in *PL*, 190:1417C. Smalley ('Commentary', 37) prints the colophon from Warner and Gilson (1:155, art. 57).

[22] Another example of the appeal to Jerome's authority occurs in an early- or mid-twelfth-century manuscript, Munich, Staatsbibliothek, Clm. 22033, f. 107b, which invokes '*Ieronimus contra Helivdicum* [sic],' i.e. *Adversus Helvidium* (Förster, 113).

Nec bene gramaticam novit . . .
Nomina – qui – tivum Salome fecit genitivum.   (James 296)

(He did not learn grammar well . . .
Who made the nominative 'Salome' a genitive.)

Latin masculine names of the first declension, such as 'Aeneas,' could have provided the necessary models (Förster, 123–26). Some manuscripts of the Anna legend, including the Old English translation in MS Vespasian, indeed name the third husband of Anna 'Salomas' by a back-formation from a presumed genitive Salome (Förster, 116).

One Latin jingle that Maurice quotes illustrates the interpretive latitude the Vulgate rendering of Mk 16:1 permits. After setting out the standard account familiar from the Anna legend (three Marys married to Joseph, Alphaeus, and Zebedee, respectively), the jingle asserts that only Mary Magdalene and Mary of James major, that is, Mary Salome, visited the tomb:

> Stirps generis Salome Jacobus fuit atque Iohannes.
> Est horum genetrix Jacobi Salomeque Maria.
> De nato Jacobi, Salome de patre vocatur;
> Ergo due non tres domini uisere sepulcrum.   (James 291)

(James and John descended from the line of Salome.
Their mother is 'Mary of James' and 'Mary of Salome;'
From her son she is called 'of James,' from her father 'of Salome.'
Therefore two not three women saw the tomb of the Lord.)

With these verses we can compare Peter Comestor's comment on the synoptic narratives of the visit. Peter gives us perhaps yet another Mary Salome, who is the mother of James minor but who may or may not be one of the Mary Cleophases. He begins with a paraphrase combining elements from Mark and Luke, but where the Vulgate says, 'Maria Jacobi et Salome' (Mk 16:1), Peter inserts another 'Maria' before Salome:

> '. . . [V]enit Maria Magdalene, et Maria Jacobi, et Maria Salome ad sepulcrum cum aromatibus, quae paraverant.' Quidam non nisi duas venisse dicunt, quia supra tantum duae dictae sunt considerasse sepulcrum et revertentes parasse aromata. Et dicunt quod additum est hic, et Salome, expositio est alterius Mariae tacitae. Contra quos sufficit opponere usum Ecclesiae, quae tres repraesentat. (*PL*, 198:1635C)

('Mary Magdalene and Mary of James and Mary Salome came to the sepulcher with spices that they had prepared.' Some say that only two women came, because previously only two were said to have seen the tomb and returning were said to have prepared spices. And they say that what has been added here, 'and Salome,' is an explanation of the second Mary [that is, Mary of James], who is implied.[23] Against them it is enough to set the custom of the Church, which shows three.)

---

[23] Peter means, 'implied in the Vulgate, "Maria Jacobi et Salome,"' with which he has tampered by adding an extra 'Maria.'

Peter's insertion of a third 'Maria' amounts to a preemptive strike against the possibility of interpreting the Vulgate to mean that Salome is a second cognomen of Mary of James minor and that Salome and Mary of James are one and the same. Like Maurice, Peter objects to an interpretation of Mark that reduces three women at the tomb to two, although Peter appeals to ecclesiastical custom rather than Hebrew grammar to support his view. Peter's use of 'supra' indicates that motivating the reduction was a desire to reconcile Mk 16:1 with the immediately preceding verse, 'Mary Magdalene and Mary the mother of Joses saw where he was laid' (15:47). Another motive may have been to reconcile Mark's narrative of the visit with Matthew's, which names only 'Mary Magdalene and the other Mary' (28:1). In either case we have here a further example of the old impulse to harmonize.

If Mary Salome is not the daughter or wife of a Salome, there is still the vague but frequent assertion that she is named for a village. Herbert, who deals only with the claims of the Anna legend, does not address this alternative explanation, but Maurice rejects it for the sound reason that no other Salome of antiquity takes her name from a village (James, 289).

We no more than our medieval predecessors can offer a definitive account of Mary Salome. Herbert's letter, however, suggests something further about the origins of the third Mary. He reports his views in the context of a heated exchange at St Denis between a Master William of London and himself (*PL*, 190:1417). The question at issue is whether Salome is the name of a man or a woman. A second William, a monk and former physician, overhears the exchange. He is William Le Mire, later abbot of St Denis (Smalley, 'Commentary', 38–39), and he proposes a resolution to the dispute:

> Cum autem, ut jam dixi, apud Sanctum Dionysium essem et praefatum magistrum Willelmum Londoniensem non quidem procaciter, sed sedulo tamen et instanter super jam saepe dicto nomine Salomae convenirem, inter modestas verborum pugnas quidam alius frater magister Willelmus nomine, quondam officio medicus, . . . supervenit, qui ut altercationis causam advertit, audientia postulata, aiebat se inter Syros aliquanto tempore conversatum, et ibi esse Ecclesiam in honore trium Mariarum dedicatam quam Syri summa venerantur devotione, adjiciens quod sicut juxta populi terrae traditionem acceperat, una sit Maria Magdalena, secunda Maria Jacobi et Joseph mater, tertia mater filiorum Zebedaei, quae et Maria juxta Syros sit appellata, et tunc ad me verbum specialiter dirigens: 'Potuit,' inquit, 'et haec eadem, sicut tu secundum majorum testimonia probabiliter disputas, et Salome appellari.' 'Esto,' dixi, 'in hac parte contentiosum funem non traho,' dummodo constet nomen Salomae a Marco in designatione mulieris poni. (*PL*, 190:1420D–1421A)

> (When also, as I said before, I was at St Denis and I was speaking to the aforesaid Master William of London, not insolently, but carefully and vehemently, concerning the above frequently mentioned name of Salome, during temperate exchanges of words, another brother, Master William by name, formerly a physician, . . . joined us, who as he perceived the

cause of the altercation, after hearing the claims, said that he had for some time lived with the Syrians, and that there was a church there dedicated in honor of the three Marys, whom the Syrians worship with greatest devotion, adding that as he had heard the belief of the people of the land, the one is Mary Magdalene, the second Mary the mother of James and Joseph, the third the mother of the sons of Zebedee, and according to the Syrians she is named Mary, and then directing his words especially to me: 'It could be,' he says, 'credibly that she is one and the same, as you are debating according to the evidence of elders, and that she is named Salome.' 'Let it be,' I said. 'On this side I do not pull the opposing rope,' provided that he agreed that the name of Salome is written by Mark to designate a woman.)

For three reasons Herbert is willing to embrace William Le Mire's conjecture identifying the Syrian third Mary, mother of the sons of Zebedee, with Salome. Herbert respects Origen's surmise that Salome is the name of the mother of the sons of Zebedee (*PL*, 190:1420A–B).[24] He is aware that the Church has long acknowledged the presence of three Marys at the tomb, and he sees that in William's anecdote Salome is a woman:

In hoc, inquam, contentiosus non ero. Siquidem didici Scripturae con-suetudinem eumdem hominem diversis nominibus appellare, quod tamen in feminis multo rarius obtinet. Verumtamen quod mulier illa evangelica, de qua jam multum sermonem serui, non solum Salome sed et Maria dicta sit, probabilem hinc sumo conjecturam: solent siquidem multae Ecclesiae ab antiquo per singulos anni circulos in diluculo resurrectionis Dominicae ad devotionis augmentum, trium Mariarum Dominum in sepulcro operose et devote cum unguentis quaerentium, non irreligiosas ostentare praestigias, et quae sunt hae tres Mariae, verius, ut arbitror, non intimabitur, quam si una dicatur Maria Magdalena, altera Maria Jacobi et Joseph mater, et tertia Maria quae et Salome, mater filiorum Zebedaei. Verum, ut jam diximus, in hac parte contentiosus non ero; duntaxat Salome nomen mulieris fuisse in Marco obtentum fuerit.

                                          (*PL*, 190:1421A–B)

(In this matter, I say, I will not argue. If I have learned that it is the custom of Scripture to call one man by different names, still that very rarely obtains in the case of women. Nevertheless, because that woman of the Gospel, concerning whom I have already devoted much discussion, was called not only Salome but also Mary,[25] I make a likely supposition from this: since many churches from ancient times through every cycle of the year at dawn of Easter Sunday for the enhancement of devotion usually show pious illusions of the three Marys diligently and reverently seeking the lord in the tomb with unguents, and they are these three Marys, it will not be said more truly, as I think, than if one is called Mary Magdalene, the second Mary the mother of James and Joseph, and the third Mary who is also Salome, mother of the sons of Zebedee. Truly, as I

---

[24] Herbert quotes from the Latin version of Origen I have quoted above (*PG*, 13:1796A, 1797C).

[25] Herbert's assertion appears to be an inference from what William Le Mire has told him of Syrian custom and Origen's surmise that Salome is the name of the mother of the sons of Zebedee, or from the entrenched Western tradition that 'Mary Salome' was at the tomb, or both.

have said, I will not take issue on this account, as long as in Mark the name Salome was used of a woman.)

The story of the thrice-married Anna is possibly Carolingian and, as Maurice of Kirkham supposed and Förster persuasively argues, an invention of the Latin West. Mary Salome, however, may spring from much older roots. William Le Mire's allusion to Syrian tradition raises the possibility that the identification of Mary and Salome was continuous in the East from at least Basil's time onward, and that, further, in the East this Mary, as the Codex Sinaiticus hints, was identified with the mother of the sons of Zebedee. It is perhaps no coincidence that the earliest traces of the thrice-married Anna and the other explanations of Mary Salome appear in the West about two and a half centuries before the Crusades, when contact between West and East began to flourish anew. It seems a reasonable proposition that the full story of Mary Salome owes a debt to post-scriptural traditions of the Eastern Church, but for now at least the truth of the proposition cannot be demonstrated, and the nature of the debt cannot be determined.

If for Maurice and Herbert a male Salome is impossible, for most of Western Christendom the fable, as Herbert calls it (*PL*, 190:1417C), of a thrice-married Anna posed no difficulty. The story plausibly fills in gaps in the genealogy of the holy family and demystifies relationships left mysterious in Scripture. It arranges major characters in an immediately intelligible symmetry of threes – three husbands, three daughters, three Marys. Its artistry proved too powerful to be denied. Even so highly regarded a scholar as Peter Lombard could believe it. Also, as Peter Comestor demonstrates, the Anna legend had its uses for combating perverse readings of the Gospel. Once the story of thrice-married Anna had passed into Vincent's *Speculum* and Jacobus' *Legenda Aurea*, its persistence in both popular and scholarly discourse in the West was assured.

Whatever Herbert meant by 'non irreligiosas praestigias,' the 'pious illusions' of the three Marys at Easter services, his comment can serve as a reminder that Mary Salome often appears in medieval drama, the modern study of which has given her continued life. Today her position in the learned world is so secure that standard scholarship often refers to three Marys in plays that specify unnamed women or only one or two Marys.[26] Perhaps this imprecise usage is no more than a shorthand employed by scholars who really know better, but the following statement from Karl Young suggests otherwise: 'In St Mark's account there are three Marys, and

---

[26] A couple of examples will suffice: 'antequam Mulieres et Discipuli ad Sepulchrum venirent,' becomes in Karl Young's paraphrase, 'before the arrival of the Marys and the disciples at the tomb . . .' (1:124). Again, in analyzing four forms of a responsory for Easter Matins, which either omit naming the women or name Mary Magdalene, Mary of James, and Salome, Young says, 'It will be observed that these four versions – of which the first is very much the most common – all recount the same narrative: the journey of the Marys to the tomb at dawn on the first Easter morning . . .' (1:232–33). The most common version is one of those that names Salome. David Bevington likewise refers to three Marys where the primary text does not support the reference (21–29).

one angel seated within the tomb' (1:217). It seems rather that in the specialist's as in the medieval pilgrim Theodorich's mind popular tradition has supplanted the canonical. Young has literally taken fable for Gospel. One consequence of misstating the Gospel narrative is to risk overlooking an evident pattern of development in medieval dramatic representations of the visit to the tomb, namely that the three Marys are more frequent in the later than the earlier plays. A fixture in late cycles, including the Chester, N-Town, and Towneley plays (Lumiansky and Mills, 1:351–52; Spector, 1:359–65; Stevens and Cawley, 1:335–47), Mary Salome is absent from the earliest dramatic pieces. In Young's selections there is little evidence of the three Marys until the thirteenth century, when attestation is ample, and no evidence before the twelfth.

Our chief concern here is with Mary Salome in *Ancrene Wisse*, a work whose origins, like Mary Salome's, remain hidden. Attentive study has repeatedly confirmed that the intellectual milieu of twelfth-century Paris chiefly shaped the thinking of the author of *Ancrene Wisse*. He may well have been aware of the issues that motivated Maurice's and Herbert's attacks on the popular stories of Salome. The nature of their opposition is revealing as to why Mary Salome was acceptable for inclusion in a pious English work. Neither Maurice nor Herbert seriously questions her authenticity. They aim their barbs at those who would transform Salome into a man, the 'Salomites,' as Maurice dubs them. They see the third Mary per se as at worst a harmless product of inferences from Scripture.

For the reception of Mary Salome in England, *Ancrene Wisse* offers important testimony. The author's confident invocation of Mary Salome signifies that by the early decades of the thirteenth century, long before the *Speculum Historiale* and the *Legenda Aurea* appeared, educated opinion in England held her authenticity to be beyond question. More than that, the combined evidence of Maurice of Kirkham, Herbert of Bosham, and *Ancrene Wisse* suggests that before the last quarter of the twelfth century, the learned community not just of England but of Paris as well had accepted, despite nagging questions of her genesis, the historicity of Mary Salome.

Works Cited

Algermissen, Konrad, *et al.*, eds., *Lexikon der Marienkunde, s.v. "Anna."*, vol. 1, cols. 230–56 (Regensburg, 1967)

Bevington, David, ed., *Medieval Drama* (Boston, 1975)

Biblia Sacra, *iuxta Vulgatam Versionem*, ed. Robert Weber, 2 vols. (Stuttgart, 1969)

Bienert, Wolfgang A., 'The Relatives of Jesus', in *Schneemelcher*, 1:470–88.

Brown, Raymond E., *The Death of the Messiah from Gethsemane to the Grave: a Commentary on the Passion Narratives in the Four Gospels*, 2 vols. (New York and London, 1994)

Cullmann, Oscar, ed., 'The Protevangelium of James', in Schneemelcher, 1:421–39

Day, Mabel, ed., *The English Text of the Ancrene Riwle: edited from Cotton Nero A. xiv, on the basis of a transcript by J. A. Herbert*, Early English Text Society o.s. 225 (London, 1952; repr. 1975)

Eusebius, *The Ecclesiastical History*, trans. Kirsopp Lake *et al.*, Loeb Classical Library, 2 vols. (London, 1938–49)

Folda, Jaroslav, *The Art of the Crusaders in the Holy Land: 1098–1187* (Cambridge, 1995)

Förster, Max, 'Die Legende vom Trinubium der hl. Anna', in *Probleme der englischen Sprache und Kultur: Festschrift Johannes Hoops zum 60. Geburtstag überreicht von Freunden und Kollegen*, ed. Wolfgang Keller, Germanische Bibliothek. II Abteilung: Untersuchungen und Texte 20 (Heidelberg, 1925), 105–30

Glorieux, P., *Pour Revaloriser Migne: Tables Rectificatives*, Mélanges de Science Religieuse, 9 Année, Cahier Supplémentaire (Lille, 1952)

Herbert of Bosham, *Herberti de Boseham S. Thomae Cantuariensis clerici a secretis. Opera quae extant omnia*, ed. John A. Giles, Patres Ecclesiae Anglicanae, 2 vols. (Oxford, 1845–46)

Jacobus de Voragine, *The Golden Legend: Readings on the Saints*, trans. William Granger Ryan, 2 vols. (Princeton, NJ, 1993)

James, Montague R., 'The Salamites', *The Journal of Theological Studies* 35 (1934), 287–97

Jerome, *Dogmatic and Polemical Works*, trans. John N. Hritzu, The Fathers of the Church: A New Translation 53 (Washington, D.C., 1965)

Josephus, *Josephus in Nine Volumes, Vol. 9: Jewish Antiquities Books XVIII–XX*, trans. Louis H. Feldman, The Loeb Classical Library (Cambridge, MA, 1965)

Ker, N. R., *Catalogue of Manuscripts Containing Anglo-Saxon* (Oxford, 1957; reissued with supplement 1990)

Kleinschmidt, Beda, *Die Heilige Anna: Ihre Verehrung in Geschichte, Kunst, und Volkstum*, Forschungen zur Volkskunde, Heft 1–3 (Düsseldorf, 1930)

Knox, Ronald, trans., *The Holy Bible, a Translation from the Latin Vulgate in the Light of the Hebrew and Greek Originals* (New York, 1944; repr. 1950)

Lumiansky, R. M., and David Mills, eds., *The Chester Mystery Cycle*, 2 vols., Early English Text Society, s.s. 3, 9 (London, 1974, 1986)

Millett, Bella, *Annotated Bibliographies of Old and Middle English Literature, Vol. 2: Ancrene Wisse, the Katherine Group, and the Wooing Group*, with the assistance of George B. Jack and Yoko Wada (Cambridge, 1996)

Milne, H. J. M., and T. C. Skeat, *The Codex Sinaiticus and the Codex Alexandrinus*, rev. edn (London, 1963)

NUC = National Union Catalog: Pre-1956 Imprints (London, 1968–)

Papias the Lombard, *Elementarium* (Venice, 1491)

PG = Migne, J.-P., ed., *Patrologiae Cursus Completus, Omnium SS, Patrum, Doctorum, Scriptorumque, Ecclesiasticorum; sive Latinorum, sive Graecorum*, Series Graeca, 161 vols. (Paris, 1857–66; repr. Turnhout, Belgium, 196–)

PL = Migne, J.-P., ed., *Patrologiae Cursus Completus*, Series Latina, 221 vols. (Paris, 1844–1902) (In preparing the present essay I have found it most convenient to search in the electronic version of *PL*: Chadwyck-Healey, *Patrologia Latina: The Full Text Database*. I have cut and pasted the Latin directly from the database, though I have consulted the printed volumes.)

Routh, Martin J., ed., *Reliquiae Sacrae, sive auctorum fere iam perditorum secundi tertiique saeculi post Christum natum ad codices mss. recensuit, notisque illustravit, quae supersunt*, 5 vols. (2nd edn 1846–48; repr. Hildesheim and New York, 1974)

Savage, Anne, and Nicholas Watson, trans., *Anchoritic Spirituality: Ancrene Wisse and Associated Works*, with a Preface by Benedicta Ward (New York and Mahwah, NJ, 1991)

Schneemelcher, Wilhelm, ed., *New Testament Apocrypha*, rev. edn trans. R. McL. Wilson, 2 vols. (Louisville, 1991–92)

Shepherd, Geoffrey, ed., *Ancrene Wisse: Parts Six and Seven* (London, 1959; repr. Manchester, 1972)

Smalley, Beryl, 'A Commentary on the *Hebraica* by Herbert of Bosham', *Recherches de Théologie Ancienne et Médiévale* 18 (1951), pp. 29–65

——, *The Becket Conflict and the Schools: a Study of Intellectuals in Politics* (Totowa, 1973)

Spector, Stephen, ed., *The N-Town Play: Cotton MS Vespasian D. 8*, 2 vols., Early English Text Society s.s. 11, 12 (Oxford, 1991)

Stevens, Martin, and A. C. Cawley, eds., *The Towneley Plays*, 2 vols., Early English Text Society, s.s. 13, 14 (Oxford, 1994)

Tatian, *Diatessaron*, in *Tatian: Lateinisch und Altdeutsch*, ed. Eduard Sievers (Paderborn, 1872)

Tischendorf, Constantine, 'The Various Versions of the Bible', in *The Testimony of the Evangelists*, ed. Simon Greenleaf with an Appendix by Constantine Tischendorff [*sic*] (Jersey City, NJ, 1881), 507–35

Tolkien, J. R. R., ed., *The English Text of the Ancrene Riwle: Ancrene Wisse, edited from Corpus Christi College Cambridge 402*, with an Introduction by N. R. Ker, Early English Text Society o.s. 249 (London, 1962)

Vincent of Beauvais, *Speculum Maius*, 4 vols., vol 4, *Speculum Historiale* (Douai, 1624; repr. Graz, 1965)

Warner, George F., and Julius P. Gilson, *Catalogue of Western Manuscripts in the Old Royal and King's Collections*, 4 vols. (London, 1921)

Young, Karl, *The Drama of the Medieval Church*, 2 vols. (Oxford, 1933)

Select Bibliography

This bibliography is a list of basic references selected to help students of Middle English language and literature. For further reading see the individual chapters of this book and *Annotated Bibliographies of Old and Middle English Literature, Vol. 2: Ancrene Wisse, the Katherine Group and the Wooing Group*, edited by Bella Millett with the assistance of George B. Jack and Yoko Wada (Cambridge, 1996).

Editions

TEXTS OF *ANCRENE WISSE*

English text

Baugh, A. C., ed., *The English Text of the Ancrene Riwle, edited from British Museum MS Royal 8 C. I*, EETS o.s. 232 (London, 1956)

Day, Mabel, ed., *The English Text of the Ancrene Riwle, edited from Cotton Nero A. XIV*, EETS o.s. 225 (London, 1952)

Dobson, E. J., ed., *The English Text of the Ancrene Riwle, edited from B. M. Cotton MS. Cleopatra C. vi*, EETS o.s. 267 (London, 1972)

Mack, Frances M., and Arne Zettersten, ed., *The English Text of the Ancrene Riwle, edited from Cotton MS Titus D.XVIII, together with the Lanhydrock Fragment, Bodleian MS Engl. th. c.70*, EETS o.s. 252 (London, 1963)

Morton, James, ed. and trans., *The Ancren Riwle: a Treatise on the Rules and Duties of Monastic Life* (London, 1853)

Tolkien, J. R. R., ed., *The English Text of the Ancrene Riwle, Ancrene Wisse, edited from MS Corpus Christi College Cambridge 402*, EETS o.s. 249 (London, 1962)

Wilson, R. M., ed., *The English Text of the Ancrene Riwle, edited from Gonville and Caius College MS 234/120*, EETS o.s. 229 (London, 1954)

Zettersten, Arne, ed., *The English Text of the Ancrene Riwle, edited from Magdalene College, Cambridge MS 2498*, EETS o.s. 274 (London, 1976)

——, and Bernhard Diensberg, ed., *The English Text of the Ancrene Riwle: the 'Vernon' Text, edited from Oxford, Bodleian Library MS Eng. poet. a. I*, EETS o.s. 310 (London, 2000)

French text

Herbert, J. A., ed., *The French Text of the Ancrene Riwle, edited from British Museum MS Cotton Vitellius F vii*, EETS o.s. 219 (London, 1944)

Trethewey, W. H., ed., *The French Text of the Ancrene Riwle, edited from Trinity College Cambridge MS R.14.7 with variants from Bibliothèque Nationale MS Fr. 6276 and MS Bodley 90*, EETS o.s. 240 (London, 1958)

Latin text

D'Evelyn, Charlotte, ed., *The Latin Text of the Ancrene Riwle, edited from Merton College MS 44 and British Museum MS Cotton Vitellius E vii*, EETS o.s. 216 (London, 1944)

SELECTED EDITIONS

Ackerman, Robert W., and Roger Dahood, ed., *Ancrene Riwle: Introduction and Part I* (Binghamton, NY, 1984)
Hall, Joseph, ed., *Selections from Early Middle English 1130–1250*, 2 vols. (Oxford, 1920), I:54–75 and II:354–407.
Kubouchi, Tadao, *et al.*, ed., *Electronic Parallel Diplomatic Manuscript Texts of Ancrene Wisse, Preface and Parts 1–3: a Printed Trial Version* (Tokyo, 2000)
——, *et al.*, eds., *Electronic Parallel Diplomatic Manuscript Texts of Ancrene Wisse, Part 4: a Printed Trial Version* (Tokyo, 2001)
Millett, Bella, and Jocelyn Wogan-Browne, ed. and trans., *Medieval English Prose for Women* (Oxford, 1990), 110–49 and 157–63
Shepherd, Geoffrey, ed., *Ancrene Wisse. Parts Six and Seven* (London, 1959)
Wada, Yoko, ed. and trans., *'Temptations' from Ancrene Wisse*, I (Osaka, 1994)

FACSIMILE

Doyle, A. I., facs. ed., *The Vernon Manuscript (Bodleian, Eng. poet. a. 1)* (Cambridge, 1987)

Language

Benskin, Michael, and Margaret Laing, 'Translations and *Mischsprachen* in Middle English Manuscripts', in *So Meny People Longages and Tonges: Philological Essays in Scots and Mediaeval English Presented to Angus McIntosh*, ed. Michael Benskin and M. L. Samuels (Edinburgh, 1981), 55–106
Clark, Cecily, ' "Wið scharpe sneateres": Some Aspects of Colloquialism in *Ancrene Wisse*', *Neuphilologische Mitteilungen* 79 (1978), 341–53
Jack, George, 'Morphological Variation in the AB Language and its Implications', in *A Book of* Ancrene Wisse, ed. Yoko Wada (Osaka, 2002), 59–73
Laing, Margaret, and Angus McIntosh, 'The Language of *Ancrene Riwle*, the Katherine Group Texts and *þe Wohunge of ure Lauerd* in BL Cotton Titus D xviii', *Neuphilologische Mitteilungen* 96 (1995), 235–63
Tolkien, J. R. R., '*Ancrene Wisse* and *Hali Meiðhad*', *Essays and Studies* 14 (1929), 104–26
Zettersten, Arne, *Studies in the Dialect and Vocabulary of the 'Ancrene Riwle'* (Lund, 1965)

Textual History

Dobson, E. J., 'The Affiliations of the Manuscripts of *Ancrene Wisse*', in *English and Medieval Studies presented to J. R. R. Tolkien*, ed. N. Davis and C. L. Wrenn (London, 1962), 128–63
——, 'The Date and Composition of *Ancrene Wisse*', *Proceedings of the British Academy* 52 (1966), 181–208
——, *The Origins of Ancrene Wisse* (Oxford, 1976)

Other Critical Studies

Barratt, Alexandra, 'The Five Wits and their Structural Significance in Part II of *Ancrene Wisse*', *Medium Aevum* 56 (1987), 12–24
Dahood, R., '*Ancrene Wisse*, the Katherine Group, and the *Wohunge* Group', in *Middle English Prose: a Critical Guide to Major Authors and Genres*, ed. A. S. G. Edwards (New Brunswick, NJ, 1984), 1–33
——, 'Design in Part I of *Ancrene Riwle*', *Medium Aevum* 56 (1987), 1–11
——, 'The Use of Coloured Initials and Other Division Markers in Early Versions of *Ancrene Riwle*', in *Medieval English Studies presented to George Kane*, ed. E. D. Kennedy, R. Waldron, and J. S. Wittig (Cambridge, 1988), 79–97
Georgianna, Linda, *The Solitary Self: Individuality in Ancrene Wisse* (Cambridge, MA, 1981)
Grayson, Janet, *Structure and Imagery in Ancrene Wisse* (Hanover, NH, 1974)
Innes-Parker, Catherine, 'The Lady and the King: *Ancrene Wisse*'s Parable of the Royal Wooing Re-examined', *English Studies* 75 (1994), 509–22
Lucas, Angela M., *Women in the Middle Ages* (Brighton, 1983)
Millett, Bella, 'The Origins of *Ancrene Wisse*: New Answers, New Questions', *Medium Aevum* 61 (1992), 206–28
——, '*Mouvance* and the Medieval Author: Re-editing *Ancrene Wisse*', in *Late Medieval Religious Texts and their Transmission: Essays in Honour of A. I. Doyle*, ed. A. J. Minnis (Cambridge, 1994), 9–20
Robertson, Elizabeth, *Early English Devotional Prose and the Female Audience* (Knoxville, TN, 1990)
——, 'The Rule of the Body: the Feminine Spirituality of the *Ancrene Wisse*', in *Seeking the Woman in Late Medieval and Renaissance Writings: Essays in Feminist Contextual Criticism*, ed. Sheila Fisher and Janet E. Halley (Knoxville, TN, 1989), 109–34
Salter, Elizabeth, *English and International: Studies in the Literature, Art and Patronage of Medieval England*, ed. Derek Pearsall and Nicolette Zeeman (Cambridge, 1988)
Watson, Nicholas, 'The Methods and Objectives of Thirteenth-Century Anchoritic Devotion', in *The Medieval Mystical Tradition in England. Exeter Symposium 4*, ed. Marion Glasscoe (Cambridge, 1987), 132–53.

Translations (without Middle English text)

Hasenfratz, Robert, ed., *Ancrene Wisse* (Kalamazoo, MI, 2000)
Salu, M. B., trans., *The Ancrene Riwle* (London, 1955)
Savage, Ann, and Nicholas Watson, trans., *Anchoritic Spirituality: Ancrene Wisse and Associated Works* (New York, 1991)
White, Hugh, trans., *Ancrene Wisse. Guide for Anchoresses* (Harmondsworth, 1993)

Anchoresses in the Middle Ages and the Historical Background

Baker, Derek, ed., *Medieval Women* (Oxford, 1978)
Clay, R. M., *The Hermits and Anchorites of England* (London, 1914)
Millett, Bella, 'Women in No Man's Land: English Recluses and the Development of Vernacular Literature in the Twelfth and Thirteenth Centuries', in *Women and Literature in Britain 1150–1500*, ed. Carol M. Meale (Cambridge, 1993), 86–103
Nichols, John A., and Lillian T. Shank, eds., *Distant Echoes: Medieval Religious Women*, I (Kalamazoo, MI, 1984)
Thompson, Sally, *Women Religious: the Founding of English Nunneries after the Norman Conquest* (Oxford, 1991)
Warren, Ann K., *Anchorites and their Patrons in Medieval England* (Berkeley, CA, 1985)

Index of Middle English Words

Index of Manuscripts

General Index